A Publication Sponsored by
the Society for Industrial and Organizational Psychology, Inc.,
A Division of the American Psychological Association

Other books sponsored by the Society include:

Multilevel Theory, Research, and Methods in Organizations
Katherine J. Klein, Steve W. J. Kozlowski, Editors

The Changing Nature of Performance
Daniel R. Ilgen, Elaine D. Pulakos, Editors

New Perspectives on International Industrial/Organizational Psychology
P. Christopher Earley and Miriam Erez, Editors

Individual Differences and Behavior in Organizations
Kevin R. Murphy, Editor

The Changing Nature of Work
Ann Howard, Editor

Team Effectiveness and Decision Making in Organizations
Richard A. Guzzo, Eduardo Salas, and Associates

Personnel Selection in Organizations
Neal Schmitt, Walter C. Borman, and Associates

Work, Families, and Organizations
Sheldon Zedeck, Editor

Organizational Climate and Culture
Benjamin Schneider, Editor

Training and Development in Organizations
Irwin L. Goldstein and Associates

Productivity in Organizations
John P. Campbell, Richard J. Campbell, and Associates

Career Development in Organizations
Douglas T. Hall and Associates

Compensation in Organizations

Current Research and Practice

Sara L. Rynes

Barry Gerhart

Editors

Foreword by Neal Schmitt

JOSSEY-BASS
A Wiley Company
San Francisco

Jossey-Bass books and products are available through most bookstores. To contact Jossey-Bass directly, call (888) 378-2537, fax to (800) 605-2665, or visit our website at www.josseybass.com.

Substantial discounts on bulk quantities of Jossey-Bass books are available to corporations, professional associations, and other organizations. For details and discount information, contact the special sales department at Jossey-Bass.

 Manufactured in the United States of America on Lyons Falls Turin Book. This paper is acid-free and 100 percent totally chlorine-free.

Library of Congress Cataloging-in-Publication Data

Compensation in organizations: current research and practice / Sara L. Rynes, Barry A. Gerhart, editors; foreword by Neal Schmitt.
    p. cm. — (Frontiers of industrial and organizational psychology)
    "A joint publication in the Jossey-Bass business & management series and the Jossey-Bass social and behavioral science series."
    Includes bibliographical references and index.
    ISBN 0-7879-5274-5
    1. Compensation management. I. Rynes, S. (Sara) II. Gerhart, Barry A. III. Series. IV. Jossey-Bass business & management series. V. Jossey-Bass social and behavioral science series.
HF5549.5.C67 C647 2000
658.3'2—dc21   00-021238

FIRST EDITION
HB Printing   10 9 8 7 6 5 4 3 2 1

A joint publication in
The Jossey-Bass
Business & Management Series
and
The Jossey-Bass
Social & Behavioral Sciences Series

Frontiers of Industrial and Organizational Psychology

Contents

Part Three: Conclusion

Foreword

The Society for Industrial and Organizational Psychology (SIOP) established the Frontiers of Industrial and Organizational Psychology Series in 1982 to advance the scientific status of the field. The series was to consist of edited volumes that would address issues of major contemporary significance. Each volume editor was charged with including cutting-edge theory, research, and practice by investigators in industrial and organizational psychology and related disciplines. The objective was to inform members (students, practitioners, and researchers) and other potential readers about these developments and to stimulate additional research and thinking in these areas. It was intended that these volumes be published at such time as developments in a particular area warranted, rather than on a fixed schedule.

Under the capable leadership of three of my editorial predecessors (Ray Katzell, Irwin Goldstein, and Sheldon Zedeck), and beginning with the publication of the volume by Douglas T. Hall in 1986 (*Career Development in Organizations*), a total of twelve previous volumes have been published. My term as editor of the series began in May 1998. The series editorial board has determined the choice of topics and volume editors, though we have openly and actively solicited ideas for volumes from a wide variety of people and continue to welcome such proposals. In planning each volume, there is a considerable exchange between the volume editor and the editorial board. As each volume is developed, the series editor works with the volume editor to coordinate and oversee the activities of the board, the volume editor, the publisher, and the writers.

The success of the series is evidenced by continued strong sales (approximately two thousand copies were sold in the year ending March 1999 and nearly thirty-five thousand in total). In addition, the volumes have continued to receive strong reviews, and individual chapters in them are frequently cited in our research literature.

All royalties from the series go to the Society for Industrial and Organizational Psychology; last year, this amounted to $4,340. This means that the work of the Frontiers board, the volume editors, and the chapter author is done without remuneration. The Society owes them a debt of gratitude for the contribution of their time, effort, and expertise in furthering the discipline both in this financial sense and especially in their contributions to our intellectual vitality.

This volume was proposed and developed while Sheldon Zedeck was editor of the series and owes much to his persistence that a volume on compensation was both needed and possible. With the publication of this volume, *Compensation in Organizations,* edited by Sara L. Rynes and Barry Gerhart, we are continuing our efforts to publish volumes that present new thinking and approaches to our readers. We also hope that the publication of this volume will rekindle interest in this area of our field. Compensation has been relatively neglected by psychologists in recent years, as evidenced by relatively few SIOP programs related to this topic and a lack of articles published on it in our major journals.

However, compensation is not a dead issue for either practitioners or researchers. Much recent work has been conducted in the fields of sociology and economics and is being published in journals not as frequently read by psychologists, such as *Administrative Science Quarterly, Industrial and Labor Relations Review,* and *Academy of Management Journal.* Much of the psychological research has focused on individual affective reactions to pay, while other disciplines have focused on outcomes such as productivity and efficiency. In the first part of this volume, the authors were encouraged to think about compensation in terms of the dependent variables that result from decisions about compensation rather than the decisions themselves. The second part describes new issues that have arisen because of changes in labor market conditions and employment. These changes, which affect how compensation is determined and its influence on employee attitudes and behavior, include increases in temporary and part-time employment, growing inequality of earnings among members of an organization, increased substitution of technology for workers, loosening of job boundaries, globalization, and the transportability of workers across international boundaries.

In Part Three of the book, the editors summarize the most important trends that emerge across the preceding parts and identify promising topics for future research.

Sara Rynes and Barry Gerhart have done an excellent job in selecting topics and authors who were able to describe research and practice in compensation as it relates to these changes. They have also helped the authors consider the implications for theory and practice in compensation. They and the authors deserve our deepest appreciation for taking on the task of writing for our audience and for adapting their thoughts and ideas to fit the integrative framework provided by the editors of the volume. We hope that this volume will return compensation to a central role among the set of human resource activities in which psychologists engage and on which they conduct research.

The production of this volume required the cooperation of a large number of individuals, including the volume editors, chapter authors, and series board, as noted earlier, and also the staff at Jossey-Bass. Cedric Crocker and, more recently, Julianna Gustafson have been very effective in making sure the book received timely and proper attention from the Jossey-Bass production and marketing staff. They worked with us during the planning, development, and final publication of this volume, and we owe them a large debt of gratitude.

January 2000

NEAL SCHMITT
Michigan State University
Series Editor

Preface

Compensation is a fascinating subject that engenders spirited debate and discussion. Consider the following quotes:

> People do work for money—but they work even more for meaning in their lives. In fact, they work to have fun. Companies that ignore this fact are essentially bribing their employees and will pay the price in a lack of loyalty and commitment [Pfeffer, 1998, p. 112].

> Money is the crucial incentive because . . . it is the most instrumental; it can be used to purchase numerous other values. . . . Money is directly or indirectly related to all of man's needs. . . . No other incentive or motivational technique comes even close to money [Locke et al., 1980, pp. 379–381].

> Any incentive or pay-for-performance system tends to make people less enthusiastic about their work and therefore less likely to approach it with a commitment to excellence [Kohn, 1993, pp. 62–63].

> Our analysis of a quarter century of accumulated research provides little evidence that reward reduces intrinsic task interest. . . . Recent research has also shown that reward for a high degree of creative performance can be used to increase generalized creativity. These findings suggest the need to revise conventional views about the detrimental effects of reward [Eisenberger & Cameron, 1996, p. 1162].

> I can't foresee executive pay continuing to grow without something snapping. I do believe significant forces will bring it down and realign it with the rest of the work force [William Patterson, quoted in Lublin, 1999].

> Pay disparities will continue to grow. The scale of what's at stake is enlarging. Business' heightened need for a top-notch decision maker increases the bidding for that spot [Robert Frank, quoted in Lublin, 1999, p. R9].

To me, it's what the market will pay. It's supply and demand [Gerard Roche, chairman of Heidrick & Struggles, on executive compensation, quoted in Stewart, 1998, p. 200].

Economists will tell you that there shouldn't be a major change in pay without a change in supply or demand. Has there been an increase in demand for major-company CEOs? No—they keep merging. A decrease in supply? Hell no. Harvard Business School turns out more than ever, and we have all these women we keep turning down [Graef Crystal, quoted in Stewart, 1998, p. 200].

Employee owners put in extra effort and try unusually hard to satisfy customers because it's money in their pockets. Company performance can be transformed by workers who themselves are personally benefiting from the growth and improved profitability [Jasinowski & Hamrin, 1995, p. 119].

Stock prices are simply too noisy to serve as useful performance measures for lower-level executives or rank-and-file employees [Murphy, 1998, p. 90].

As these examples illustrate, even people who are regarded as "experts" on pay hold widely varying beliefs and opinions about its purposes and consequences. Some of these differences emerge from long-standing sources of disagreement, such as differences in personal values, experiences, constituencies, and goals.

However, other disagreements stem from recent changes in compensation practices, as well as uncertainty regarding the nature of their origins and consequences. Among these changes are the following:

- Dramatic increases in earnings inequality between those at the top versus those at the bottom of the U.S. earnings distribution, as well as between skilled and unskilled workers, public and private employees, and regular and contract employees (Bok, 1993; Crystal, 1991; Frank & Cook, 1995; Galbraith, 1998)
- Rapid expansion of the proportion of employees granted stock or stock options (Gross, 1998; "More Employees," 1999), along with unprecedented growth in the value of some of those options

- Dramatic increases in the number of millionaires under forty years of age (Dillon, 1997; Munk, 1998)
- Rapid growth in the prevalence and size of employee signing bonuses (Munk, 1998; *Show Me,* 1997)
- Increased employee access to salary information (and bargaining power) via the Internet and other forums (Lublin, 1998; *Show Me,* 1997)
- Increased external hiring of people for non-entry-level positions, with consequent pressures on internal salary structures (for example, pay compression or inversion) and resultant organizational adaptations such as broadbanding

The tremendous amount of change in compensation practices—combined with other factors such as increased competition for the best employees, reduced employee loyalty, enhanced employee pay information, and increased variability in pay practices across employers—have made compensation a matter of great interest to organizations and employees. This interest has been reflected in increased coverage of compensation issues in top-tier management journals (for example, *Administrative Science Quarterly* and the *Academy of Management Journal* have held special research forums on compensation), as well as in the popular press (see Kerr, 1997; Kohn, 1992; Pfeffer, 1998).

However, despite the importance, interest, and controversy surrounding compensation, many industrial and organizational psychologists seem to have lost interest in this area. For example, a recent survey of Society of Industrial and Organizational Psychology members revealed that pay and other reward systems ranked twenty-seventh of thirty-seven topics in terms of member interest (Shippmann & Hartmann, 1995). Similarly, May (1996) reported that a call in the *Industrial Psychologist* for information about the impact of the changing nature of work on compensation practices went unanswered. Consistent with these findings, examination of recent SIOP annual programs reveals that very few sessions have been devoted to compensation. Finally, several other volumes in the Frontiers series (for example, *The Changing Nature of Work* and *Levels of Analysis*) have included chapters on specific human resource functions such as selection, training, or performance management but have excluded compensation.

This relative lack of interest in compensation contrasts sharply with the degree of interest shown by corporate boards of directors, vice presidents of human resources, executive search firms, organizational recruiters, business journalists, and those of us who work for a living (see Hardy, 1998; Malone, 1997; Mercer, 1998; Stewart, 1998). Lack of awareness about compensation issues is likely to limit psychologists' contributions to important organizational topics such as strategic human resource management, employee attraction and retention, productivity improvement, knowledge management, and intellectual capital (Stewart, 1997).

In light of these developments, the major objective behind the creation of this volume was to encourage greater understanding of and interest in compensation issues among psychologists and human resource researchers and practitioners. Like May (1996), we believe that psychologists have a variety of skills and knowledge that can contribute significantly to compensation theory, research, and practice. However, in order to do so, we must first be aware of the dramatic changes that have been occurring in compensation practice and research.

Outline of the Book

Compensation in Organizations is divided into three major sections. Part One addresses two basic questions that have inspired extensive streams of compensation research: What are the determinants of compensation, and what are its consequences? In contrast, Part Two focuses on areas of research that have emerged more recently, such as the roles of pay strategy, pay risk, and the changing employment contract in determining pay and pay outcomes. Part Three summarizes the major themes that emerge from the first two parts and offers broad suggestions for enhancing the scope and contribution of future psychological research on pay.

Most of the chapters in Part One emphasize the consequences of compensation (for example, applicant attraction or employee motivation) rather than its antecedents (market forces, supervisory discretion). However, in Chapter One, Sara Rynes and Joyce Bono focus explicitly on what is known—and not known—about how compensation is determined. They focus primarily on recent top-tier psychological research in this area (1986 onward), although research from management and economics is also briefly considered. Suggestions for future research are offered in light of developments in other disciplines, as well as changes in actual compensation practices and the environment in which compensation is determined.

Whereas Chapter One looks at pay as something to be explained (that is, as a dependent variable), Chapters Two through Four examine the *effects* of compensation on employee attitudes and behaviors. In Chapter Two, Alison Barber and Bob Bretz discuss what is known about how compensation affects employee attraction and retention. Given the nature of the literature base, they focus primarily on the effects of pay level, although benefits and pay form are also discussed. Barber and Bretz conclude that considerable work remains to be done in this area and suggest a number of ways in which psychologists can make useful contributions (for example, by examining individual differences in reactions to pay and the processes by which pay information is evaluated by job applicants).

In Chapter Three, Herb Heneman and Tim Judge review the extensive body of psychological research examining pay satisfaction, pay preferences, and perceived pay equity or justice. They note that considerable progress has been made in a number of areas of attitudinal pay research. For example, we now have a better understanding of the dimensions of pay satisfaction and its antecedents; accumulating evidence of the negative consequences of pay dissatisfaction; a growing understanding of the relationships between procedural justice, distributive justice, and pay satisfaction; and accumulating evidence regarding both general pay preferences and sources of individual differences in preferences. At the same time, considerable work remains to be done, particularly in terms of making this research more relevant to organizations.

In Chapter Four, Kay Bartol and Ed Locke summarize and evaluate a wide range of theories and research pertaining to the effects of compensation on employee motivation and performance. Theories reviewed include Deci and Ryan's theories concerning the effects of extrinsic rewards on intrinsic motivation, equity and justice theories, expectancy theory, goal theory, social cognitive theory, and agency, prospect, and tournament theories. Based on this review, the authors distill nine general principles for constructing effective incentive systems (ones likely to promote both productivity and satisfaction to the greatest extent possible).

Part Two of the book examines more recent compensation issues that have emerged from changes in the broader economic and social environments. In Chapter Five, Barry Gerhart reviews the considerable progress that has been made over the past decade toward understanding the relationship between alternative compensation strategies and firm performance. In so doing, he steps back from the micro focus of most psychological research to examine the broader context in which individual pay decisions and employee reactions to them emerge. In particular, he examines findings concerning three basic premises of the compensation strategy literature: that compensation practices differ widely across and within organizations, that managers have considerable discretion in choosing from an array of compensation policies, and that there is benefit to tailoring pay practices to environmental and organizational contingencies.

In Chapter Six, Rob Heneman, Gerry Ledford, and Maria Gresham describe how changes in economic and organizational environments have contributed to a variety of changes in compensation design and delivery. In particular, they describe how changes in technology, business strategy, organizational structure, and job design are prompting shifts from administrative to strategic concerns in compensation policy and from focus on the job as the primary basis for pay to a broader range of pay determinants (such as individual, team, and organizational characteristics and outcomes). Particular emphasis is placed on examining broadbanding, knowledge- or skill-based pay, variable pay, and stock ownership.

In Chapter Seven, Peter Sherer notes that the vast majority of compensation research has been conducted with respect to traditional employment relationships—relationships in which organizations (principals) exercise direct control and authority over employees (agents) who act on their behalf. However, Sherer argues that dramatic increases in alternative work arrangements have created an urgency to examine compensation practices and effects in a broader range of organizational and labor relationships. Sherer uses a variety of occupational labor markets to show that although several different types of pay systems can be used within a given organizational and labor relationship (OLR), some combinations of pay systems and OLRs are more common than others due to legal and institutional factors. Findings from relatively unique occupations (taxi driver, haircutter) are offered to demonstrate commonalities with changes in more common occupations, such as sales or management.

In Chapter Eight, Denise Rousseau and Violet Ho examine how changes in compensation and employment systems have modified the psychological contracts between workers and employers. They argue that because of compensation's centrality and visibility, compensation is likely to be a major factor in how employees interpret and respond to the employment relationship. In addition, they show how several aspects of the psychological contract (for example, characteristics of the status quo contract and whether proposed changes involve core or peripheral contract terms) can help predict likely employee reactions to attempts to change the compensation system. In general, Rousseau and Ho conclude that a variety of changes in the economic environment have made it more difficult for employers to establish relationships that employees are likely to regard as equitable.

In Chapter Nine, Bob Wiseman, Luis Gomez-Mejia, and Mel Fugate encourage psychologists to be more prominently involved in rethinking the role of risk in compensation systems. Building on the history of risk research, they illustrate that considerable variability exists in both conceptualization and measurement of risk. They further show that traditional operationalizations of compensation risk (such as overall variability in compensation) do not correspond well with empirical evidence concerning subjective interpretations of risk, which appear to focus primarily on the prospect of losses. Finally, the authors discuss the importance of reference points in psychological assessments of risk and the associated implications for compensation practice.

In Part Three, we (Sara Rynes and Barry Gerhart) summarize the most important trends, conclusions, and research recommendations to emerge from the preceding discussions. We also point to additional areas requiring study (for example, global compensation) where little information is currently available. Finally, we suggest concepts, methods, and questions that psychologists might adopt from other disciplines in conducting compensation research, and speculate about the contributions that psychologists can make to compensation practice and to other disciplines.

Acknowledgments

As with most books, this one would not have been possible without extensive contributions from many people. First and foremost, we would like to thank the authors of the chapters in this volume. At the outset, we pursued the very best authors we could think of to cover each chapter, and in most cases we were successful in persuading them to say yes. We cannot thank you enough for your hard work and enthusiasm.

In addition, a number of people were helpful at the initial stages of formulating the plan for this book. Among them were Alison Barber, Don Schwab, Bill Hicks, Ken Pearlman, the Frontiers Editorial Board, and Sheldon Zedeck, who was the editor of the Frontiers series when this volume was first proposed. Later on, we received valuable assistance from Neal Schmitt, who served as series editor for this volume, and from Cedric Crocker and Julianna Gustafson at Jossey-Bass.

Last but not least, we thank our families—Paul, Jennifer, and Daniel, and Heather, Christian, and Annie—for the borrowed time, the encouragement, and the fun along the way.

January 2000

SARA L. RYNES
Iowa City, Iowa

BARRY GERHART
Nashville, Tennessee

References

Bok, D. (1993). *The cost of talent: How executives and professionals are paid and how it affects America.* New York: Free Press.

Crystal, G. S. (1991). *In search of excess: The overcompensation of American executives.* New York: Norton.

Dillon, P. (1997, June-July). Money changes everything. *Fast Company,* pp. 79–93.

Eisenberger, R. & Cameron, J. (1996). Detrimental effects of reward: Reality or myth? *American Psychologist, 51,* 1153–1166.

Frank, R. H., & Cook, P. J. (1995). *The winner-take-all society.* New York: Free Press.

Galbraith, J. K. (1998). *Created unequal: The crisis in American pay.* New York: Free Press.

Gross, B. (1998). The new math of ownership. *Harvard Business Review, 76*(6), 68–74.

Hardy, Q. (1998, September 29). Aloft in a career without fetters. *Wall Street Journal,* pp. B1, B4.

Jasinowski, J. & Hamrin, R. (1995). *Making it in America: Proven paths to success from 50 top companies.* New York: Simon & Schuster.

Kerr, S. (1997). *Ultimate rewards: What really motivates people to achieve.* Boston: Harvard Business School Press.

Kohn, A. (1992). *No contest: The case against compensation.* Boston: Houghton Mifflin.

Kohn, A. (1993). Why incentive plans cannot work. *Harvard Business Review, 71*(5), 54–63.

Locke, E. A., Feren, D. B., McCaleb, V. M., Shaw, K. N., & Denny, A. T. (1980). The relative effectiveness of four methods of motivating employee performance. In K. D. Duncan, M. M. Gruneberg, & D. Wallis (Eds.), *Changes in working life* (pp. 363–388). New York: Wiley.

Lublin, J. S. (1998, September 22). Web transforms art of negotiating raises. *Wall Street Journal,* p. B1.

Lublin, J. S. (1999, April 8). Executive pay: Lowering the bar. *Wall Street Journal,* pp. R1–R3.

Malone, M. S. (1997, June-July). Money and the meaning of life. *Fast Company,* pp. 96–102.

May, K. E. (1996). Work in the 21st century: Implications for compensation. *Industrial Psychologist, 34*(2), 73–77.

Mercer, W. M. (1998, April 16). The costs of churning: A Mercer survey on turnover. *Mercer Report,* pp. 4–5.

More employees motivate the rank and file with stock options. (1999, May 18). *Wall Street Journal,* p. A1.

Munk, N. (1998, March 16). The new organization man. *Fortune, 137,* 62–74.

Murphy, K. J. (1998). Executive stock options: An economist's perspective. *American Compensation Association Journal, 7*(1), 88–90.

Pfeffer, J. (1998). Six dangerous myths about pay. *Harvard Business Review, 76*(3), 109–119.

Shippmann, J. S., & Hartmann, S. (1995). SIOP customer survey results II. *Industrial-Organizational Psychologist, 33,* 37–42.

Show me the money. (1997). San Francisco: Wet Feet Press.

Stewart, T. A. (1997). *Intellectual capital.* New York: Doubleday.

Stewart, T. A. (1998, June 8). Can even heroes get paid too much? *Fortune, 137,* 200–201.

The Authors

SARA L. RYNES is the John F. Murray Professor and chair of the Department of Management and Organizations at the Tippie College of Business, University of Iowa. Prior to joining the Iowa faculty, she taught at the University of Minnesota and Cornell University. She holds M.S. and Ph.D. degrees in industrial relations from the University of Wisconsin. Her major research interests are in the areas of compensation, recruitment and selection, job search and choice, diversity, and knowledge transfer between academics and practitioners. Rynes has served on the review boards for the *Journal of Applied Psychology, Personnel Psychology,* the *Academy of Management Journal, Quality Management Journal,* and *Frontiers in Industrial and Organizational Psychology.* She has designed courses and served as a faculty member for both the American Compensation Association and for the College Relations and Recruiting Institute at Cornell. She is a fellow of the American Psychological Association and the Society for Industrial and Organizational Psychology.

BARRY GERHART is the Frances Hampton Currey Professor of Organization Studies and area coordinator at Vanderbilt University's Owen Graduate School of Management. His major fields of interest are human resource management and strategy, compensation and rewards, and employee attitudes. Gerhart received his bachelor's degree in psychology from Bowling Green State University and his Ph.D. degree in industrial relations from the University of Wisconsin–Madison. He serves on the editorial boards of the *Academy of Management Journal, Administrative Science Quarterly, Industrial and Labor Relations Review,* and *Personnel Psychology.* Prior to coming to Vanderbilt University, he chaired the Department of Human Resource Studies at Cornell University and served on the policy board of its Center for Advanced Human Resource Studies. In 1991, he received the Scholarly Achievement Award from the Human Resources Division of the Academy of Management. Gerhart is a coauthor of *Human Resource Management: Gaining a Competitive Advantage,* now in its third edition.

Alison E. Barber is an associate professor of management and assistant dean for undergraduate programs at the Eli Broad Graduate School of Management, Michigan State University. She obtained her Ph.D. degree (1990) in industrial relations from the University of Wisconsin–Madison. She has published research articles on a number of topics associated with recruitment and job search in such journals as the *Journal of Applied Psychology, Personnel Psychology,* and the *Academy of Management Review,* and is the author of *Recruiting Employees: Individual and Organizational Perspectives* (1998). Barber currently serves on the editorial boards of the *Journal of Applied Psychology* and *Personnel Psychology.*

Kathryn M. Bartol is professor of management and organization at the Robert H. Smith School of Business at the University of Maryland. She holds a Ph.D. degree from Michigan State University and is a past president of the Academy of Management. Her research centers on compensation, performance appraisal, and gender issues, with a special interest in information technology. Widely published, Bartol has served on the review boards of the *Journal of Applied Psychology* and the *Academy of Management Review* and is currently on the review board of the *Human Resource Management Review.* Bartol is a fellow of the American Psychological Association, the American Psychological Society, and the Academy of Management and a recipient of the Academy of Management's Sage Scholarship Award.

Joyce E. Bono is a doctoral student at the University of Iowa, studying organizational behavior and personality. She earned her B.A. degree (1990) in liberal arts at Spring Arbor College and her M.S. degree (1995) in administration at the University of Notre Dame. Before entering the Ph.D. program at Iowa, she spent ten years as an executive in both education and health care. She is also a certified community mediator and has served as a volunteer mediator in the small claims court system. Bono's primary research and teaching interests are in the areas of conflict, personality, and leadership. Her work has appeared in *Human Performance* and in conference presentations.

ROBERT D. BRETZ JR. (Ph.D., University of Kansas, 1988) is a professor of management and chair of the Department of Management at Notre Dame University. His research interests include staffing and selection issues such as person-organization fit and career success, the effectiveness of alternative training philosophies, and the link between individual and organizational effectiveness. His articles have appeared in *Personnel Psychology,* the *Journal of Applied Psychology,* the *Journal of Vocational Behavior,* and the *Journal of Management.* Bretz is a fellow of the American Psychological Association and the Society for Industrial and Organizational Psychology and is on the review boards of *Personnel Psychology* and the *Journal of Management.*

MEL FUGATE is a doctoral student majoring in organizational behavior at Arizona State University's College of Business. Fugate earned his bachelor's degree (1990) in engineering and business administration at Michigan State University. His primary research focus is on how employees transition and cope with job changes (mergers, layoffs, promotions, retirement, relocations). He is also interested in the dynamics of teams and has coauthored a chapter in *Advances in Interdisciplinary Studies of Work Teams.*

LUIS R. GOMEZ-MEJIA is a Dean's Council of 100 Distinguished Scholar and a professor at the Arizona State University College of Business. He received his Ph.D. degree (1981) in industrial relations from the University of Minnesota. His research focuses on macro compensation issues, including executive compensation and compensation strategy. He is coeditor of the *Journal of High Technology Management Research* and has published extensively in *Administrative Science Quarterly, Academy of Management Journal, Strategic Management Journal,* and *Journal of Management* and is the coauthor of *Compensation, Organizational Strategy, and Firm Performance* (1992) and *Managing Human Resources* (2nd ed., 1997). He is currently on the board of governors of the Academy of Management and serves as program chair of the Division of Human Resource Management of the Academy of Management.

MARIA T. GRESHAM earned her Ph.D. degree (1999) in labor and human resources at the Max M. Fisher College of Business, Ohio State University. She is currently a consultant with IBM Healthcare

Consultants. Her primary areas of interest are human resource management, strategic human resources, business process reengineering, change management, compensation, and work teams. Her work has appeared in *Human Resource Development Quarterly,* and she has presented her work at the American Psychological Society. She has worked with several public and private sector organizations, including the Central Ohio Transit Authority, Nationwide Insurance, Hewlett-Packard Company, the Caregiver Stress and Health Study, Damon's International Incorporated, and Quantum Corporation.

HERBERT G. HENEMAN III is Dickson-Bascom Professor of Management at the University of Wisconsin–Madison. He also serves as a participating faculty member in the Industrial Relations Research Institute and as a senior research associate at the Wisconsin Center for Education Research. His research is in the areas of staffing, performance appraisal, union membership growth, work motivation, and compensation systems. He is the senior author of four books, a member and former chair of the Human Resources Division of the Academy of Management, and a member of the American Psychological Association, the Society for Industrial and Organizational Psychology, the Industrial Relations Research Association, the American Educational Research Association, the Society for Human Resource Management, the International Personnel Management Association, and the American Compensation Association.

ROBERT L. HENEMAN is director of graduate programs in labor and human resources and an associate professor of management and human resources in the Max M. Fisher College of Business at Ohio State University. He earned his Ph.D. degree (1984) in labor and industrial relations at Michigan State University. He is on the editorial boards of the *Human Resource Management Journal, Human Resource Management Review, Human Resource Planning,* and *Compensation and Benefits Review* and has written two books, *Merit Pay: Linking Pay Increases to Performance Ratings* (1992) and *Staffing Organizations* (1997). He is a member of the certification program faculty of the American Compensation Association (ACA) and has served on its research, education, and academic partnership network advisory boards. His research interests include strategic reward systems and performance management.

VIOLET T. HO is a doctoral student in organizational behavior at the Graduate School of Industrial Administration at Carnegie Mellon University. She received her bachelor's degree (1995) in accounting from Nanyang Technological University in Singapore. Her research interests include the study of multiple referents that people use in evaluating psychological contract breach and the interplay between communication media and transactive memory systems in groups.

TIMOTHY A. JUDGE is the Stanley Howe Professor of Leadership in the Department of Management and Organizations, Tippie College of Business, University of Iowa. He earned his Ph.D. degree from the University of Illinois. Prior to joining the University of Iowa in 1995, Judge was an associate professor in the Department of Human Resource Studies at Cornell University. His research interests are in the areas of personality assessment, staffing, person-organization fit, career success, job attitudes, and leadership. He serves on the editorial review boards of the *Journal of Applied Psychology, Personnel Psychology, Organizational Behavior and Human Decision Processes, Journal of Management, Human Resource Management Review,* and *International Journal of Selection and Assessment* and has held positions on the executive committees of the careers and human resources divisions of the Academy of Management. He is also former program chair of the Society for Industrial and Organizational Psychology's annual conference.

GERALD E. LEDFORD JR. is senior consultant and practice leader for employee effectiveness and rewards at Sibson and Company. Previously, he spent sixteen years at the Center for Effective Organizations, Marshall School of Business, University of Southern California. He earned his Ph.D. degree (1984) in psychology at the University of Michigan. He received the Yoder-Heneman Personnel Research Award (1990) from the Society for Human Resource Management (with Barry Nathan, David Bowen, and Thomas Cummings) and is active in several professional societies, including the Society for Industrial and Organizational Psychology, the American Psychological Association, the Academy of Management, and the American Compensation Association. He is past chair of the Academy of Management's Organizational Development and Change

Division. Ledford has researched, published, and consulted on a wide variety of innovative approaches to organizational effectiveness and employee well-being, including innovative reward systems, employee involvement, organization design, job design, and union-management cooperation.

EDWIN A. LOCKE is Dean's Professor of Leadership and Motivation and a professor of psychology at the Robert H. Smith School of Business, University of Maryland. He earned his Ph.D. degree (1964) in industrial psychology at Cornell University. Locke's main research activities have focused on work motivation through goal setting, the causes of job satisfaction, and leadership. He is the author or editor of six books and more than two hundred articles and chapters. Locke has served on the editorial boards of the *Journal of Applied Psychology* and *Organizational Behavior and Human Decision Processes* and is a fellow of the American Psychological Association, the American Psychological Society, and the Academy of Management. He has received distinguished scientific contribution awards from the Society for Industrial and Organizational Psychology and the Academy of Management's Human Resource Division.

DENISE M. ROUSSEAU is the H. J. Heinz II Professor of Organizational Behavior at Carnegie-Mellon University, jointly in the Heinz School of Public Policy and Management and the Graduate School of Industrial Administration. At CMU, Rousseau is codirector of the Center for the Changing Employment Relationship. She has been a faculty member at Northwestern University, the University of Michigan, and the Naval Postgraduate School (Monterey). Rousseau's research has appeared widely in such publications as the *Journal of Applied Psychology, Academy of Management Review,* and *Administrative Science Quarterly,* and she is incoming editor of the *Journal of Organization Behavior.* She has written several books, including *Psychological Contracts in Organizations,* which received the Academy of Management's Best Book Award in 1996. She is a fellow of the American Psychological Association, the Society for Industrial and Organizational Psychology, and the Academy of Management. She received her Ph.D. degree (1977) in psychology from the University of California, Berkeley.

PETER D. SHERER is associate professor of management at the Charles A. Lundquist College of Business, University of Oregon. He earned his Ph.D. degree (1985) in industrial relations at the University of Wisconsin–Madison. He has taught at the Institute of Labor and Industrial Relations at the University of Illinois, the Helsinki School of Economics, the Wharton School of the University of Pennsylvania, and the Johnson Graduate School of Management at Cornell University. Sherer's main research activities center on understanding variety and change in human resource management practices and how they relate to law, business strategy, and organizational theory. Sherer is currently on the editorial board of the Industrial Relations Research Association and previously served on the editorial board of the *Academy of Management Journal.*

ROBERT M. WISEMAN is an assistant professor of strategic management in the Eli Broad College of Business at Michigan State University. He earned his Ph.D. degree (1992) in strategic management at the University of Minnesota and was an assistant professor at Arizona State University before joining Michigan State. His current research interests include modeling decision behavior under uncertainty and the role of risk in corporate governance and decision making. Wiseman has published in the *Academy of Management Journal, Academy of Management Review, Strategic Management Journal* and *Organization Science.* He is an associate editor of the *Journal of High Technology Management Research* and has won several distinguished reviewer awards from the Academy of Management.

PART 1

Determinants and Consequences of Compensation

CHAPTER 1

Psychological Research on Determinants of Pay

Sara L. Rynes
Joyce E. Bono

> *Market prices are inherently job-related, although the*
> *market may embody social judgments as to the "worth" of*
> *some jobs. Employers are, to that extent, "pricetakers."*
> *They deal with the market as a given, and do not*
> *meaningfully have a "policy" about it.*
> Spaulding v. University of Washington (1984)

> *It is naive . . . to talk of the "competitive wage," the*
> *"equilibrium wage," or the "wage that clears the market."*
> Richard A. Lester (1952)

The majority of the chapters in this book speak primarily to the effects of pay on people's attitudes and behaviors. However, information about people's reactions to pay have little practical importance to employers unless employers have discretion in setting pay and developing pay policies. As indicated elsewhere in this volume (see Chapters Five, Six, and Seven), employers not only have such discretion but have been exercising it in increasingly diverse ways over the past decade. The increasing diversity of pay strategies and practices makes the study of pay determination processes an important and potentially exciting venture.

In this chapter, we summarize the extent to which I/O psychologists have investigated issues related to pay determination over the past decade. In particular, we focus on relevant research that has appeared in the top I/O psychology journals—*Journal of Applied Psychology, Personnel Psychology,* and *Organizational Behavior and Human Decision Processes*—for the period 1986–1998.

We focus on these journals because of their high quality ratings and because of the association between rankings of journal quality and journal citation rates (see Johnson & Podsakoff, 1994; Salancik, 1986). Because the vast majority of academic research builds in small increments on previously published research (Campbell, Daft, & Hulin, 1982; Sackett & Larson, 1990; Webb, 1968), future research is likely to proceed in much the same fashion as past research unless explicit attempts are made to change research priorities. It is therefore helpful to assess the extent to which the current state of the literature serves as an adequate basis for future research.

The remainder of the chapter is divided into three sections: a review of the literature, an evaluation of that literature, and suggestions for future research.

Psychological Research on Determinants of Pay, 1986–1998

Our review uncovered two basic types of studies aimed at discovering pay determinants and/or pay determination processes. One category consists of experimental studies that *directly examine* how managers (or students) use various pieces of information in making compensation decisions. The second category consists of field or laboratory studies that *infer* pay determinants by correlating actual salary distributions with employee, supervisory, or organizational characteristics. The studies we reviewed are summarized in Table 1.1.

Direct Examination of Pay Determination

Most direct examinations of pay determination have been one-of-a-kind studies with respect to the issues investigated. Studies have varied both in terms of dependent variables (pay level, pay increase, job pay, job evaluation points) and independent variables (such as managerial and employee characteristics). However, there has been less variability in methodology, with most studies employing some variant of policy capturing.

For example, Sherer, Schwab, & Heneman (1987) used policy capturing to examine how eleven hospital administrators combined information about (hypothetical) incumbents' current salaries, recent performance, performance consistency over time, length of service, and existence of an external job offer in making pay raise decisions. Results suggested that in general, recent performance was the largest determinant of pay increase decisions. Beyond that, however, administrators exhibited wide individual differences with respect to the weights placed on the other factors, despite the fact that all subjects came from the same hospital. In addition, administrators' direct reports of how they weighted the various factors were substantially at odds with weights inferred via policy capturing.

Using a resource dependence framework (Bartol & Martin, 1988), Bartol and Martin (1989, 1990) conducted a series of in-basket studies to assess the extent to which managers' pay raise decisions are affected by their dependence on subordinates to attain work objectives. Dependence on the subordinate was manipulated in a number of ways, including dependence on the target employee's functional expertise, implicit employee threats of leaving, and employee connections to the company president. They found some support for the notion that managers give larger increases to subordinates on whom they are dependent, but only under certain conditions (such as lack of pay secrecy or subordinate threat of grievance).

Orr, Sackett, and Mercer (1989) used a policy capturing approach to examine whether or not managers consider nonprescribed job behaviors (such as positive attitudes, self-training, and cooperation) in providing SD_y estimates for utility analysis. Seventeen supervisors from a medical supply corporation assigned dollar values to profiles of fifty hypothetical programmers whose performance was experimentally varied along ten prescribed aspects (including creating and running tests, debugging, and adherence to schedules) and three nonprescribed aspects (team cooperation, contribution to morale, and company orientation) of behavior. Based on tests of statistical significance, results suggested that ten of the seventeen managers did consider citizenship behaviors when assessing value. In contrast to Sherer et al. (1987), Orr and colleagues

Table 1.1. Studies on the Determinants of Pay, 1986–1998.

Study	Dependent Variable	Independent Variables	Sample
Experimental Studies of Managerial Pay Decisions			
Bartol & Martin (1989)	Pay raise	Subordinate power, dependency threats, pay secrecy, pay demands	117 managers, 120 managers
Bartol & Martin (1990)	Pay raise	Subordinate power, political connections, job expertise, dependency threats	123 managers
Mount & Ellis (1987)	Job evaluation ratings	Job type, job gender, market pay level	52 professional and scientific employees
Orr, Sackett, & Mercer (1989)	Individual pay level	Prescribed and nonprescribed (citizenship) job behaviors	17 managers
Rynes, Weber, & Milkovich (1989)	Job pay level	Job gender, market rate, job evaluation points, rater gender, current	406 compensation administrators
Sherer, Schwab, & Heneman (1987)	Pay raise	Performance, length of service, current salary, external job	11 supervisors
Singh (1995)	Individual pay level	Relative job inputs of target and comparison worker, pay of comparison worker	17 male students
Singh (1997)	Salary allocation to partners in two-person teams	Individual effort and performance	16 male students
Viswesvaran & Barrick (1992)	Firms to include in salary survey	Firm location, market wage information (source, method, breadth)	35 compensation specialists

Field Studies of Pay Outcomes

Brett & Stroh (1997)	Salary level	Gender, education, work experience	610 managers
Collins, Hatcher, & Ross (1993)	Decision to adopt gainsharing	Union status, perceived organization climate, expected outcomes if implemented	485 upper-level managers from 59 organizations
Dreher & Ash (1990)	Pay level, promotion, pay satisfaction characteristics	Mentoring practices (individual, organizational, and occupational)	320 B.B.A. and M.B.A. graduates
Dreher & Cox (1996)	Total compensation	Mentor relationships, race, gender	1,018 M.B.A. graduates
Gerhart & Rynes (1991)	Starting salary	Pay negotiation, number of other offers, highest other offer, gender	205 M.B.A. graduates
Gist, Stevens, & Bavetta (1991)	Negotiated salary	Learning, goals, self-efficacy, skill maintenance	79 M.B.A. students
Heneman & Cohen (1988)	Salary increase	Supervisor characteristics, employee characteristics	175 manufacturing employees and 61 supervisors
Lyness & Thompson (1997)	Salary level	Demographics, attitudes, performance, career history	107 executives
Markham (1988)	Merit raise	Group and individual performance ratings	71 manufacturing managers and professionals
Stevens, Bavetta, & Gist (1993)	Negotiated salary	Training, goals, self-efficacy, perceived control	60 M.B.A. students

found generally high average correlations ($r = .72$) between directly reported attribute weights and weights inferred via policy capturing, as well as reasonable interrater agreement on weighting for most, though not all, variables.

Giacobbe-Miller, Miller, & Victorov (1998) created a policy capturing bonus allocation task for 120 Russian and 81 American managers. Managers were asked to allocate an $18,000 bonus pool (or 18 million rubles) among eighteen hypothetical employees who were characterized in terms of individual productivity (three levels), relations with coworkers (two levels), and personal financial need (three levels). Their results suggested that both Russian and U.S. managers placed a greater emphasis on individual productivity than the other two factors. Both sets of managers also placed a substantial emphasis on relations with coworkers, although contrary to expectations, this emphasis was stronger for U.S. than for Russian managers. U.S. managers were particularly generous to workers who displayed both high productivity and positive coworker relations, allocating "exceptional" bonuses to this combination ($2,173, versus $1,246 for highly productive employees with poor coworker relations).

In addition, Russian managers, but not U.S. managers, allocated pay at least in part on the basis of need. Finally, managers of both countries allocated a large proportion of the bonuses uniformly among employees. On average, Russian managers gave all employees at least 69.2 percent of what would be predicted by a perfectly egalitarian distribution (1 million rubles), whereas the average U.S. manager gave all employees at least 50.6 percent.

Singh (1995) asked seventeen male college students at an Indian university to assign pay to a hypothetical target worker, based on information about that employee's inputs relative to the inputs and pay of a comparison employee. Results suggested that subjects used nonlinear functions to assign pay, consistent with notions of fair pay ranges (floor and ceiling effects). However, it should be noted that in addition to the potential problems for external validity caused by the small student sample and the hypothetical task, the study was also extremely simplistic in design (for example, employee inputs were described as "very, very low," "moderate," and "very, very high").

In a second series of experimental investigations, Singh (1997) looked at whether student subjects made different dyadic reward allocations when they were given a goal of "fairness" versus a goal of "team harmony." Again, sample sizes were small (sixteen to thirty-two subjects), and manipulated characteristics of hypothetical "team members" were very simplistic (ranging from "extremely poor" to "excellent" performance and effort). The main goal of these studies was to ascertain the functional forms of the models used by decision makers, rather than to draw substantive conclusions about the factors associated with pay allocations.

Given substantial evidence of the importance of occupational segregation to the gender gap in earnings (see, for example, Blau & Ferber, 1998), Rynes, Weber, and Milkovich (1989) used policy capturing to examine whether male versus female domination of a job category affected the way in which 406 compensation administrators assigned job pay rates. Male- and female-dominated job categories were matched on current pay levels, market survey rates, and job evaluation points but differed in terms of job title and brief job description.

Results suggested that current pay and market survey estimates were the most important factors in setting job pay, although job evaluation points also played a role. In contrast, job gender had no detectable effect on pay assignments. It should be noted, however, that each subject assigned pay only to male-dominated or female-dominated job categories, not both. This design was believed necessary because inclusion of the matched pairs in a single survey might have revealed the purpose of the study. However, it probably made job gender a less salient factor in this study than in situations where both male- and female-dominated jobs are evaluated at the same time.

In a related type of investigation, Mount and Ellis (1987) examined whether the job evaluation ratings of fifty-two university professionals and staff members were affected by gender-identified job titles ("nurse aide" versus "orderly," "YMCA director" versus "YWCA director"), holding the actual job description constant. The authors suggested that evaluators slightly favored female-dominated job descriptions ($p < .08$), although the variance explained by job gender was extremely low (1 percent).

Finally, based on evidence that employers have considerable latitude in conducting market pay surveys (Rynes & Milkovich, 1986), Viswesvaran and Barrick (1992) used policy capturing to examine the factors compensation specialists use in deciding which firms to include in initial market surveys and which firms to keep or discard after data have been collected. Survey inclusion was assessed as a function of hypothetical organizational descriptions that varied on industry, location, size, union status, and frequency of hiring.

Results suggested that geographical location was the primary factor in deciding which firms to survey (for secretarial positions) and that closeness of the job match was the primary factor in deciding which data to keep or discard. Similar to Sherer et al. (1987), results also suggested considerable variance in the decision policies of individual administrators that could not be explained by statistical artifacts.

Inferences About Pay Determination

Another group of studies drew indirect inferences about the determinants of pay decisions, based on observed correlations with actual pay outcomes. Although most of these correlations were obtained via field surveys, in two cases they were obtained from experimental negotiation exercises.

For example, Dreher and Ash (1990) examined the effects of a variety of individual difference variables, particularly ones presumed to be associated with gender, on postgraduation salaries of B.B.A. and M.B.A. students from two universities. Results showed that salaries were positively related (in order of effect size) to degree level, male gender, years since graduation, extent of mentoring received, and absence of career interruptions.

Brett and Stroh (1997) examined whether there were gender differences in the pay of 605 male and female managers from twenty Fortune 500 firms and also whether there were differential financial returns to changing employers for men versus women. Raw data showed statistically significant gender differences in both salaries ($66,081 for men versus $51,356 for women) and bonuses ($4,283 versus $2,968). The gender difference remained significant, though smaller, following a regression analysis of total cash compensation that controlled for a variety of human capital and industry characteristics. Specifically, the gap declined to $6,060 ($69,248 for men versus $63,168 for women) after adjusting for differences in control variables.

Next, changes in salary levels were compared by gender for those who had changed companies during the preceding two years. Across genders, leaving one's company was associated with an average increment of $3,324 relative to people who stayed ($4,543 after adjusting for differences in control variables). However, returns to external labor market moves were dramatically different for men and women, with men receiving an average raw return of $8,704 and an adjusted (for differences in human capital) return of $8,292. In contrast, women who switched companies suffered a *loss* of $2,290 (or $671, adjusted for human capital differences) relative to people who stayed.

Lyness and Thompson (1997) compared the career outcomes (including compensation and stock options) of fifty-one female and fifty-six male executives (vice president and above) of a major financial services firm. Like Brett and Stroh (1997), the authors controlled for a wide range of human capital and career history variables. They found no gender differences in base salary or bonuses, but differences in stock options approached significance in the expected direction ($d = -.28$). It should be noted, however, that the (necessarily) small sample sizes in this elite sample reduced the likelihood of finding significant effects.

Dreher and Cox (1996) analyzed the salaries of graduates from nine M.B.A. programs (1969–1989) as a function of graduate characteristics, establishment of mentoring relationships, and mentor characteristics. They found that graduates with white male mentors received an average pay advantage of $16,840 over individuals with other types of mentors and that white males were significantly more likely to have white male mentors than African-Americans, Hispanics, and women were.

Gerhart and Rynes (1991) examined whether men and women are equally likely to negotiate starting salary offers and, if so, whether they are equally successful in obtaining financial returns to their negotiations. They controlled for a variety of variables reflecting human capital characteristics (such as college major and previous work experience) and bargaining power (including number of job offers, highest alternative salary offer, and general labor market conditions).

Results suggested that men and women were not (statistically) significantly different in their tendencies to negotiate, although differences were in the expected direction (15.4 percent of women negotiated, versus 22.9 percent of men). Across genders, negotiation was associated with higher starting salaries of 4.1 percent. However, there was a significant Negotiation × Gender interaction, with bargaining paying off more for men than for women: men received an average 4.3 percent return ($1,973) to their negotiations, while women received only 2.7 percent ($1,231).

As is the case with all such studies, the field survey methodology did not permit examination of whether of these differential returns were attributable to managerial discrimination, less skilled bargaining performances by women, or some combination of the two factors. Fortunately, a subsequent laboratory study by Stevens, Bavetta, and Gist (1993) has suggested at least a partial answer to this question.

Stevens and colleagues used an experimental bargaining simulation to examine gender differences in and potential mediators of bargaining effectiveness. After initial training in negotiation techniques, men performed better than women (they used more tactics and repeated tactics more often) and were awarded higher salaries by trained confederates. Additional analyses showed that gender differences in bargaining effectiveness were mediated by differences in self-set goals but not by differences in tactical knowledge, self-efficacy, or perceived control.

Following the initial negotiation, subjects received additional training in either goal-setting or self-management techniques. In the goal-setting condition, both male and female subjects significantly increased their salaries relative to initial bargaining outcomes, but significant gender differences still remained in the total amounts negotiated. In the self-management condition, both genders again significantly increased their salaries, but women improved their salaries more than men in both absolute and relative (to initial negotiations) terms.

In a related study, Gist, Stevens, and Bavetta (1991) found that negotiated salaries were significantly correlated with self-efficacy and that the effects of initial self-efficacy carried over to a second negotiation performance seven weeks later. However, there was also evidence that the self-efficacy effect operated primarily through differences in self-set goals. The effects of self-efficacy also interacted with training method, in that there were no self-efficacy-related differences in negotiated salary for subjects who received self-management training, while subjects with high self-efficacy negotiated larger salaries than other subjects in the goal-setting training condition.

In sum, the Stevens and colleagues research suggests that men and women may in fact bargain differently and may do so in ways that would be expected to make men more effective in obtaining higher pay outcomes. In addition, their research has provided insight into some of the underlying cognitive mechanisms involved (on the part of the employee, at least), as well as the potential effectiveness of various types of training for improving bargaining outcomes. These are important contributions.

At the same time, it is important to recognize that the pay allocators in this study were confederates who had been trained to allocate pay on the basis of specific negotiator behaviors (for example, use of multiple tactics and tactic repetition). The extent to which such behaviors translate into monetary gains in real negotiations or, equally important, whether these behaviors are interpreted and rewarded in the same way regardless of negotiator gender are important but unanswered questions. In short, we do not know how much particular negotiating behaviors should (or do) pay off in terms of real salary negotiations or whether identical tactics are perceived differently when exhibited by men or by women.

In a study that was not motivated primarily by gender concerns, Heneman and Cohen (1988) examined the salary increases of manufacturing employees as a function of both supervisory and employee characteristics. They found that although 24 percent of the variance in salary increases could be explained as a function of employee characteristics (performance rating, age, and position in salary grade), another 11 percent of the variance appeared to be due to supervisory characteristics (particularly the supervisor's own salary increase). Given the sizable effect of supervisory characteristics, the authors suggested that researchers include supervisory characteristics in future investigations of merit pay research.

Markham (1988) used within- and between-subjects analysis to examine correlations between performance ratings and merit pay increases at three levels of analysis: individuals, work groups, and individuals within work groups. Analyses were conducted on seventy-one managers and professionals from a single organization. Results suggested that the correlation between pay and performance at the group level was considerably larger ($r = .45$) than the pay-performance relationship at the more conventional individual level of analysis ($r = .19$) or at the individual-within-groups level ($r = -.03$).

Such a pay pattern would be typical of an organization with a strong team model, where both performance and pay differ considerably across, but not within, groups. Although this model would not be expected to describe most organizations, Markham (1988) used it as an illustration of how analyzing pay-performance relations only at the individual level of analysis may obscure mediation of pay-performance linkages via group membership.

Finally, Collins, Hatcher, and Ross (1993) attempted to infer the bases of managerial decisions to adopt gainsharing pay systems. They surveyed top management teams from fifty-nine organizations that requested preliminary gainsharing consulting and then waited to see which firms eventually implemented a program. Their objective was to determine whether firms are more likely to adopt gainsharing as a "lead" tactic (to lead changes in organizational culture and strategy) or as a "lag" tactic (to complement existing culture and strategy; see Lawler, 1986).

Results suggested that gainsharing programs were more likely to be implemented in settings where gainsharing principles complemented the existing climate and culture and hence more likely to complement rather than to lead organizational transformation (see Lawler, 1986). However, the results were somewhat ambiguous and partially moderated by union status.

Evaluation

Findings and Contributions

One conclusion that can be drawn on the basis of both direct and indirect studies of pay determination is that factors other than individual productivity generally enter into compensation decisions. For example, Heneman and Cohen (1988) found that supervisors' own salary increases were important determinants of the raises they gave others, whereas Markham's results (1988) suggest that the performance of one's work group as a whole may also influence one's pay. Similarly, Bartol and Martin (1989, 1990) suggest that under certain conditions, pay can be influenced by an individual's political connections, perceived likelihood of leaving, and organizational changes in business strategy.

In addition, policy capturing studies in this area have tended to suggest that there are wide individual differences in pay decision making (for example, Viswesvaran & Barrick, 1992), even among individuals from the same organization (Sherer et al., 1987). This is an important finding, since rater idiosyncrasies increase the probability that pay-setting processes will be seen as arbitrary or unfair by employees. Moreover, decision maker idiosyncrasies may have the effect of increasing employee dependence on supervisors, since they imply that employees must satisfy particularistic tendencies of supervisors, in addition to more general work expectations. To date, however, the underlying sources of differences in decision maker policies have not been investigated.

Recent psychological evidence with respect to pay discrimination suggests mixed conclusions, depending on whether one relies primarily on inferential or direct studies. Specifically, the inferential studies all suggest gender and/or racial variance in pay outcomes, even after controlling for a wide variety of variables (Brett & Stroh, 1997; Dreher & Ash, 1990; Dreher & Cox, 1996; Gerhart & Rynes, 1991; Lyness and Thompson, 1997), whereas the direct studies of decision processes do not (Mount & Ellis, 1987; Rynes et al., 1989).

It should be noted here that a very sizable number of inferential studies have also been conducted in other literatures, most notably in economics, management, and industrial relations. Their findings are generally consistent with the inferential results reported here (Blau & Ferber, 1998). Regardless of disciplinary training or number of control variables, most researchers continue to find race- and sex-associated differences in pay outcomes. Similarly, recent Census Bureau data continue to show race- and gender-based earnings differentials, although the size of those differentials has declined over time (Vobejda, 1998).

However, it must be kept in mind that discrimination in pay-setting procedures can never be conclusively demonstrated via inferential procedures (see Cain, 1986; Milkovich, 1980). Rather, it is always possible that some unmeasured variable, unrelated to discrimination, accounts for the remainder of the earnings gap. Thus, for example, unequal outcomes from salary negotiations or different types of mentoring may reflect unmeasured characteristics of the employees themselves (as might be suggested by Stevens et al., 1993), rather than discrimination in pay setting.

In contrast to findings from the inferential studies, the two studies that directly examined the possibility of discrimination in pay setting (Mount & Ellis, 1987; Rynes et al., 1989) showed little evidence of gender-based discrimination. It should be recognized, however, that each of these studies probably presented rather weak tests of discrimination, though for different reasons.

For example, in the Mount and Ellis study, participants had received twenty hours of job evaluation training and had participated in reevaluation of multiple jobs as part of a comparable worth initiative. Thus participants were clearly sensitized to the role of gender in pay setting and probably determined not to exhibit bias in their evaluations.

The weakness of the test for discrimination in Rynes et al. (1989) was of a different nature. By design, participants in that study were unlikely to be sensitized to gender issues, since each participant received either all-male-dominated or all-female-dominated sets of jobs to be evaluated. Although lack of direct (and potentially obvious) cross-gender comparisons is a desirable feature in studies of possible discrimination, it nevertheless reduces the likelihood of finding gender-related effects.

A second feature of this study that may have reduced the role of gender in subjects' decisions was the provision of three clear quantitative bases for establishing pay (current pay, market survey rate, and job evaluation points). Thus Rynes et al. is probably best interpreted as a closely controlled study showing that under certain conditions (for example, with good quantitative information and no direct comparisons of male- and female-dominated jobs), female-dominated jobs are not penalized relative to male-dominated ones. However, the real world of compensation determination rarely presents such a pristine set of decision conditions.

Of the research reviewed, the series of studies by Bartol and Martin (1988, 1989, 1990) and those by Stevens and colleagues (1993; Gist et al., 1991) seem to provide the most promising models for future psychological research on pay determination processes. First, both sets of studies are firmly grounded in theory—the first set in resource dependence theory and the second in self-efficacy and goal-setting theories. Second, both sets of studies pursue broader research agenda, where different aspects of the problem are investigated in a logical sequence across more than one study. Third, both research programs address questions of substantial practical importance: Bartol and Martin investigate how supervisory dependence on subordinates may influence their pay decisions, while the other researchers investigate not only the determinants of suboptimal pay negotiation outcomes but also possible remedies for them.

Limitations

Limited Cumulation of Knowledge

As indicated earlier, the dominant preoccupation (to the extent that there has been one) of psychological pay determination research has been the attempt to detect bias or discrimination in pay-setting. Although the individual studies in this area have generally been competently performed, as a whole, this body of work is somewhat disappointing.

First, the overall number of these studies has not been large. Second, the conclusions drawn are inconsistent across the two methodological approaches (inference versus direct estimation). Third, the other variables considered (in addition to race or gender) have varied widely across studies, making overall conclusions difficult to summarize. Finally, the underlying causes of the differentials observed in the inferential studies remain undiscovered and might conceivably reflect little more than omitted variable bias.

Another difficulty with psychological pay determination research is that most of it has been atheoretical. One reason may be that no dominant paradigm (or set of competing paradigms) has emerged for studying pay determination in the psychological literature. Convergence around a single paradigm (or two) might prove useful for mapping future research directions and culling unproductive ones (see Pfeffer, 1993; Platt, 1984).

Whatever the cause, the scattered nature of the reviewed research has prevented cumulation of knowledge concerning important pay determinants (such as average effect sizes, confidence intervals, and moderators of important effects). In this regard, psychological research on pay determination has fallen far short of developments in many other areas of I/O psychology (for example, mapping the average validities and boundary conditions associated with major selection devices, multirater performance appraisals, or major personality constructs).

Limits to Generalizability

Other features of this literature potentially limit its generalizability to actual pay decisions. For example, most studies have used either student subjects, subjects from a single organization, or samples where respondent and organizational characteristics are confounded by having only one respondent per organization. This last characteristic makes it impossible to disentangle individual from organizational determinants of pay, with the result that presumed individual differences in pay-related decisions (as in Viswesvaran & Barrick, 1992) may in part represent differences in subjects' organizational policies (see, for example, Weber & Rynes, 1991). In addition, the within-subjects policy capturing studies have had very small sample sizes ($n = 12-36$), further raising the possibility of sampling bias as a source of nongeneralizability.

Finally, and perhaps most important, experimental studies of pay setting may suffer from limited generalizability because making pay decisions about "paper people" is substantially different from making decisions about actual subordinates (for related points in a performance appraisal context, see Latham & Wexley, 1981, and Longenecker, Gioia, & Sims, 1987). Deciding how to allocate resources among paper people removes most (if not all) of the emotional and political elements of decisions making, as well as the visceral awareness of potential long-term consequences of such actions as "punishing" uncooperative employees with low pay. Consequently, laboratory findings in this area may appear considerably more rational or performance-oriented than they actually are in real organizations.

Other Issues

To this point, we have discussed the contributions and limitations of psychological pay determination research largely on its own terms. However, it is also useful to consider how this literature relates to a number of features of the current pay environment. In the remainder of this section, we evaluate this literature in relation to three bases of comparison: changes in actual pay practices over the relevant time period (1986–1998), developments in other disciplines, and concerns of compensation practitioners.

Changes in Practice. There have been at least two major changes in actual compensation practices over the reviewed time period. First, there has been a dramatic increase in the diversity of pay strategies and specific compensation practices used by employers (see Chapters Five, Six, and Seven). Changes include increasing diversity with respect to fixed versus variable compensation, individual versus higher-unit compensation, and pay for the person or pay for skill versus pay for the job.

Despite the clear emergence of these trends in practice, our search uncovered only one I/O study (Collins et al., 1993) that examined the determinants of any of these types of decisions. More generally, top-tier I/O psychology journals have published almost no research over the past decade that seeks to explain changes in "strategic" pay decisions or decisions that lead to alterations of the fundamental compensation "architecture" (see Becker & Gerhart, 1996). Rather, most psychological studies of pay determination processes continue to focus on traditional administrative issues, such as pay for jobs and pay for individuals within jobs. (Studies of the *effects* of strategic pay decisions are discussed elsewhere in this volume, however.)

A second important trend in actual compensation practice has been the dramatic increase in wage inequality between people at the top of organizational hierarchies and those at the bottom (Bok, 1993; Frank & Cook, 1995; Galbraith, 1998). For example, in 1974, the typical CEO of a large American company earned approximately 35 times what an average factory worker earned. By 1990, that figure had increased to 120 times (Crystal, 1991), and by 1998, to 326 (Reingold, Melcher, & McWilliams, 1998). The trend toward increasing inequality appears to be continuing, with executive pay having risen 35 percent in 1997, compared with 2.6 percent for blue-collar and 3.8 percent for white-collar workers (Reingold et al., 1998).

Despite I/O psychology's clear interest in matters of bias and fairness in pay determination (as witnessed by the large number of studies devoted to questions of gender and racial equity reviewed in this chapter, as well as studies devoted to broader questions of equity and fairness reviewed in Chapter Three), we were unable to find a single study that addressed these broader questions of rising inequality. Although this omission may be due to a lack of awareness on the part of psychologists, it seems difficult to escape knowledge of this trend, given the considerable attention devoted to it in the popular press.

Instead, we suspect that the lack of attention to this issue stems from psychology's tendency to examine decisions involving relatively homogeneous units (for example, single organizations or males versus females in the same organization, on the same job, or from the same graduating class). By confining questions to these closely controlled environments, psychologists have missed broader trends in compensation with potentially huge implications for employee motivation, aspiration levels, psychological well-being, and organizational commitment.

The lack of attention to strategic decision making may also reflect the very small number of psychological studies using top executives as subjects or as objects of study. Whereas psychological research in this area has tended to focus on the decisions of students, low-level managers, or compensation administrators, pay determination studies in management and economics journals have increasingly focused on the decisions of top executives and boards of directors (see the 1992 *Administrative Science Quarterly* special research issue or the 1998 *Academy of Management Journal* special research forum). Thus the types of decisions examined are naturally more "strategic" in these literatures.

We see no inherent reason why I/O psychology must continue to focus its interest in compensation decision making only on micro-level decisions (such as starting salaries, job evaluation points, and merit increases). Rather, we believe that psychologists can also apply traditional decision research methods (including policy capturing, process tracing, grounded theory, and ethnography) to more strategic decisions and decision makers.

Developments in Other Disciplines. Compared with I/O psychology, other disciplines (most notably economics and strategic management) have been considerably more interested in questions of pay determination. For example, in the management literature, a review of *Administrative Science Quarterly* and *Academy of Management*

Journal from 1986 through 1996 turned up fifty-five studies where pay was treated as a dependent variable.

In addition to differences in the quantity of research, there have been major differences in theoretical approach between disciplines. In particular, a dominant theoretical approach—agency theory (Jensen & Meckling, 1976)—has emerged for examining pay determination processes and outcomes in management and economics (see also Chapters Four, Five, and Seven). Generally speaking, agency theory focuses on how to design compensation systems to "align the interests" of employees and owners under various conditions, typically through some form of behavioral monitoring or outcome-based reward system (such as stock ownership, profit sharing, or gainsharing).

Economists have also generated a number of theoretical explanations for increasing pay inequality across occupations and organizational levels. These include tournament theory (Lazear & Rosen, 1981), winner-take-all markets (Frank & Cook, 1995), and macroeconomic and public policy explanations (see Galbraith, 1998).

Although a full review of developments in other disciplines is beyond the boundaries of this chapter, we believe it would be helpful for psychologists to become aware of at least some of these theories and the issues they attempt to address. For example, based on an examination of proxy statements, Zajac and Westphal (1995) found that the rationales used by corporate boards to explain (or perhaps justify) executive compensation decisions have been shifting away from human-resource-based explanations toward agency-based ones. One implication is that at least in the executive compensation area, other disciplines appear to be influencing top-level decision making and decision justification where human resource rationales formerly held sway.

A second reason for becoming more aware of developments from other disciplines is that they raise a variety of interesting psychological questions. For example, the most basic premise of agency theory is that the self-interests of principals (owners or shareholder) and agents (executives, managers, and employees) at least partially diverge, such that agents may not always act in the owners' best interests. On the basis of this insight, economists and game theorists have turned their attention to the interrelated roles of competition and cooperation in situations where the parties are partly competitive and partly interdependent (see, for example, Brandenburger & Nalebuff, 1996; Murnighan, 1994). Their investigations have addressed a variety of psychological processes, such as the effects of opening moves, "cheap talk," reciprocation versus retaliation, and cooperative versus competitive language and behaviors.

We view it as a positive development that other disciplines are increasingly interested in the types of issues that psychologists have long considered important. At the same time, however, we wish psychologists themselves were doing more compensation research in these areas.

Practitioner Concerns. To compare psychological pay determination research with issues of concern to compensation practitioners, we reviewed five years' worth (1992–1997) of articles appearing in the *American Compensation Association Journal* and *Compensation and Benefits Review*. This review yielded a total of 207 articles.

Of the 207 articles, nearly half ($n = 98$) pertained to issues related to employee benefits. This presents a clear contrast to I/O research, where benefits have played a distinctly minor role (Barber, Dunham, & Formisano, 1992). Reading between the lines, the dominance of this concern for practitioners arises from the enormous costs and uncertain returns associated with employee benefits.

Most of the remainder of the articles were devoted to recent trends in compensation practices: 25 articles on team-based pay, 23 on linking pay to business strategy or culture, 17 on the changing role of the human resource department in compensation decisions, 16 on pay in a global environment, 16 on skill- or competency-based pay, 11 on broadbanding, 11 on implications of the "end of the job" (Bridges, 1994) for compensation administration, and 6 on employee participation in compensation design. Again, there has been almost no I/O research examining the precipitating factors and decision processes that have led to these changes.

In sum, when the present body of research is evaluated in light of the broader environment, it becomes clear that I/O research has not kept pace with changes in real-world pay systems, with developments in other disciplines, or with the concerns of practitioners. Rather, I/O has been concerned primarily with issues of bias and discrimination in pay setting, harking back to the early days of Title VII and comparable worth. Although these are still worthy issues, psychologists must also move in new directions if they hope to influence future compensation policy and practice. We turn now to suggestions for revitalizing psychological pay determination research.

Suggestions for Future Research

The other chapters in this volume make it abundantly clear that differences in pay practices are associated with differences in attitudinal, behavioral, and performance outcomes at multiple organizational levels. In a world of increasing competition, then, one would expect that executives would design pay practices to be consistent with empirical results concerning pay outcomes. And yet, as with other areas of human resource management (see Johns, 1993; Terpstra & Rozell, 1993), many organizations have not have adopted the types of pay practices that appear to be associated with higher firm performance, such as paying most or all employees at least in part on the basis of firm performance or minimizing differences in rules for pay allocation between executives and other employees (see Pfeffer, 1993; Reichheld, 1996).

The failure of many organizations to follow what would appear to be best practices in compensation raises a number of questions about how pay decisions are actually made. For example, do pay practices diverge from research findings because executives are not aware of existing research or because they do not believe its results? Alternatively, do executives know and believe pay research but feel administratively constrained from implementing its recommendations (see Jacobs, 1991; Johns, 1993; Pfeffer, 1998)? Or does the divergence between research and practice suggest that executives are more intent on serving their own personal interests than on serving the interests of the organizations they manage?

Existing research provides little in the way of answers to these questions. The only way for future research to become more helpful in this regard is to pursue new directions.

One of the most significant changes psychologists could make in pay determination research would be to turn at least some of their attention to pay decisions that are more strategic. These might include decisions about the balance between individual and group rewards; about earnings differentials between the top and bottom of organizations; about the percentage of employees eligible for stock grants, options, or profit sharing; or the number of separate pay systems in an organization.

Moving toward examination of strategic pay decisions will probably require a number of innovations relative to recent I/O pay determination research. For example, although there is nothing to prevent using policy capturing or other experimental designs to examine strategic pay decisions in much the same way as they have been used in the past, we believe that at some point, investigation of strategic decisions must move to the field if it is to be credible. In addition, it must begin to examine the decision processes of individuals who are truly in charge of human resource strategies. This will pose a number of challenges.

One of the biggest challenges will be in gaining access—first to top decision makers and then to their strategic decision processes. One of the most promising avenues for obtaining access (as exemplified by Collins et al., 1993, and O'Reilly, Main, & Crystal, 1988) may be to partner with consulting firms that observe and influence the decision processes of multiple organizations. Alternatively, researchers might create alliances with research consortia such as the Mayflower Group, the Kaufmann Foundation, or the Center for Effective Organizations.

Two particularly promising points for examining strategic pay decisions are during organizational start-ups and at points of strategic change. At both start-up and change points, managers are making nonroutine rather than automated or scripted decisions. As a result, much can be learned about how strategic compensation issues come to the attention of top decision makers (Dutton & Ashford, 1993), how decision makers search for information relevant to a solution (Daft, 1988; Nutt, 1998), and why particular options are accepted or rejected (cost, acceptability to various constituents, and so on).

Another approach would be to study the factors associated with early versus late adopters of strategic innovations in compensation (see Abrahamson, 1991; Gerhart, Trevor, & Graham, 1996; Johns, 1993; Tolbert & Zucker, 1996). Differential adoption patterns may reflect differing characteristics of top executives (such as values or mental models of motivation), industry or firm characteristics (composition of the board of directors, current financial performance, industry dynamism), or some combination of these.

A second important type of contribution psychologists could make would be to illuminate the nature of the decision processes inside the "black box" between environmental conditions and organizational pay practices. Although there have been many cross-sectional empirical investigations suggesting linkages between environmental conditions and compensation strategy (for example, Hitt, Hoskisson, Johnson, & Moesel, 1996), there is nevertheless considerable variance in the strategies adopted by organizations confronting the same general environment (see Miles & Snow, 1984; Reichheld, 1996; Sherer, 1995; Sherer, Rogovsky, & Wright, 1998). To date, however, only a few studies (in any discipline) have come close to examining the mechanisms by which environmental influences are or are not converted into strategic decisions (for partial exceptions, see O'Reilly et al., 1988, or Petty, Singleton, & Connell, 1992). Explicit process investigations of change dynamics may also help illuminate the extent to which efficiency, administrative, or symbolic considerations enter into decisions to pursue compensation innovations (see Abrahamson, 1991; Di Maggio & Powell, 1983; Johns, 1993; Tolbert & Zucker, 1996).

A third area of research well suited to psychological investigation would be to examine managers' mental models of the purposes and effects of compensation for various groups of employees. For example, CEOs almost certainly differ in the extent to which they believe in the efficacy of alternative motivators such as fear, praise and recognition, money, meaningful work, a sense of belonging, or a desire to contribute to customers or society. In addition, they differ in the extent to which they believe in the efficacy of cooperation versus competition or of wide versus narrow pay differentials across organizational levels. There may also be important differences in executives' mental models of how pay works among executives, as opposed to how it works among production workers.

To date, however, there has been little research to ascertain the prevalence, origins, or malleability of various motivational beliefs among executives. However, this type of research could be important, since anecdotal evidence suggests that unique pay strategies often emerge precisely from CEOs' beliefs, values, and vision for the organization (see Olian & Rynes, 1992; Reichheld, 1996). Moreover, recent research suggests that some of the most successful HR strategies may be those that go against the general trends in their industry (see Pfeffer, 1998; Reichheld, 1996; Sherer, 1995). It might therefore prove enlightening to examine the sources of such successful leader insights or inspirations.

A final direction we might suggest would be for investigators to embed pay determination research more explicitly in a social context. For example, descriptions of how executive compensation decisions are actually made have emphasized the "clubby" atmosphere inside socially interlocked boards of directors who as a group have considerable personal stakes in seeing executive compensation rise (Crystal, 1991). Thus, for example, sociologically based management research has demonstrated that an executive's compensation is associated with personal power and social influence (for example, extent of stock ownership in the company, power over board appointees), as well as the executive's demographic similarity to other board members (see O'Reilly et al., 1988; Lambert, Larcker, & Weigelt, 1993). Additional research of this type could fruitfully be pursued by psychologists, considering that questions of power, influence, and peer evaluation fall easily within the domains of social, cognitive, and I/O psychology.

In summary, there are many important issues in pay determination that would benefit from a revitalization of psychological compensation research, as well as from cooperative ventures between psychological researchers and consulting firms, research consortia, and researchers from other disciplines. We hope that a review of the next decade's compensation research will reveal an expansion of psychological interest in the determinants of compensation strategies for individuals, groups, and organizations.

References

Abrahamson, E. (1991). Management fads and fashions: The diffusion and rejection of innovations. *Academy of Management Review, 16,* 586–612.

Barber, A. E., Dunham, R. B., & Formisano, R. A. (1992). The impact of employee benefits on employee satisfaction: A field study. *Personnel Psychology, 45,* 55–75.

Bartol, K. M., & Martin, D. C. (1988). Influences on managerial pay allocations: A dependency perspective. *Personnel Psychology, 41,* 361–378.

Bartol, K. M., & Martin, D. C. (1989). Effects of dependence, dependency threats, and pay secrecy on managerial pay allocation. *Journal of Applied Psychology, 74,* 105–113.

Bartol, K. M., & Martin, D. C. (1990). When politics pays: Factors influencing managerial compensation decisions. *Personnel Psychology, 43,* 599–614.

Becker, B., & Gerhart, B. (1996). The impact of human resource management on organizational performance: Progress and prospects. *Academy of Management Journal, 39,* 779–801.

Blau, F., & Ferber, M. A. (1998). *The economics of women, men, and work.* Upper Saddle River, NJ: Prentice Hall.

Bok, D. C. (1993). *The cost of talent.* New York: Free Press.

Brandenburger, A. M., & Nalebuff, B. J. (1996). *Co-opetition.* New York: Doubleday.

Brett, J. M., & Stroh, L. K. (1997). Jumping ship: Who benefits from an external labor market strategy? *Journal of Applied Psychology, 82,* 331–341.

Bridges, W. (1994, September 19). The end of the job. *Fortune, 130,* 62–74.

Cain, G. G. (1986). The economic analysis of labor market discrimination: A survey. In O. Ashenfelter & R. Layard (Eds.), *Handbook of labor economics.* Amsterdam: Elsevier North-Holland.

Campbell, J. P., Daft, R. L., & Hulin, C. L. (1982). *What to study: Generating and developing research questions.* Thousand Oaks, CA: Sage.

Collins, D., Hatcher, L., & Ross, T. L. (1993). The decision to implement gainsharing: The role of work climate, expected outcomes, and union status. *Personnel Psychology, 46,* 77–104.

Crystal, G. S. (1991). *In search of excess: The overcompensation of American executives.* New York: Norton.

Daft, R. L. (1988). Chief executive scanning, environmental characteristics, and company performance: An empirical study. *Strategic Management Journal, 9,* 123–139.

Di Maggio, P. J., & Powell, W. W. (1983). The iron cage revisited: Institutional isomorphism and collective rationality in organizational fields. *American Sociological Review, 48,* 147–160.

Dreher, G. F., & Ash, R. A. (1990). A comparative study of mentoring among men and women in managerial, professional, and technical positions. *Journal of Applied Psychology, 75,* 539–546.

Dreher, G. F., & Cox, T. H. (1996). Race, gender and opportunity: A study of compensation attainment and the establishment of mentoring relationships. *Journal of Applied Psychology, 81,* 297–308.

Dutton, J. E., & Ashford, S. J. (1993). Selling issues to top management. *Academy of Management Review, 18,* 397–428.

Frank, R. H., & Cook, P. J. (1995). *The winner-take-all society.* New York: Free Press.

Galbraith, J. K. (1998). *Created unequal: The crisis in American pay.* New York: Free Press.

Gerhart, B., & Rynes, S. L. (1991). Determinants and consequences of salary negotiations by male and female MBA graduates. *Journal of Applied Psychology, 76,* 256–262.

Gerhart, B., Trevor, C., & Graham, M. (1996). New directions in employee compensation research. In K. Rowland & G. R. Ferris (Ed.), *Research in personnel and human resources management* (Vol. 14, pp. 143–203). Greenwich, CT: JAI Press.

Giacobbe-Miller, J. K., Miller, D. J., & Victorov, V. I. (1998). A comparison of Russian and U.S. pay allocation decisions, distributive justice judgments, and productivity under different payment conditions. *Personnel Psychology, 51,* 137–163.

Gist, M. E., Stevens, C. K., & Bavetta, A. G. (1991). Effects of self-efficacy and post-training intervention on the acquisition and maintenance of complex interpersonal skills. *Personnel Psychology, 44,* 837–861.

Heneman, R. L., & Cohen, D. J. (1988). Supervisory and employee characteristics as correlates of employee salary increases. *Personnel Psychology, 41,* 345–359.

Hitt, M. A., Hoskisson, R. E., Johnson, R. A., & Moesel, D. D. (1996). The market for corporate control and firm innovation. *Academy of Management Journal, 39,* 1084–1119.

Jacobs, M. (1991). *Short-term America.* Boston: Harvard Business School Press.

Jensen, M. C., & Meckling, W. H. (1976). Theory of the firm: Managerial behavior, agency costs, and ownership structure. *Journal of Financial Economics, 3,* 305–360.

Johns, G. (1993). Constraints on the adoption of psychologically based personnel practices: Lessons from organizational innovation. *Personnel Psychology, 46,* 569–592.

Johnson, J. L., & Podsakoff, P. M. (1994). Journal influence in the field of management: An analysis using Salancik's index in a dependency network. *Academy of Management Journal, 37,* 1392–1407.

Lambert, R., Larcker, D., & Weigelt, K. (1993). The structure of organizational incentives. *Administrative Science Quarterly, 38,* 438–461.

Latham, G. P., Wexley, K. (1981). *Increasing productivity through performance appraisal.* Reading, MA: Addison-Wesley.

Lawler, E. E., III. (1986). *High-involvement management: Participative strategies for improving organizational performance.* San Francisco: Jossey-Bass.

Lazear, E., & Rosen, S. (1981). Rank order tournaments as optimum labor contracts. *Journal of Political Economy, 89,* 841–864.

Lester, R. A. (1952). A range theory of wage differentials. *Industrial and Labor Relations Review, 5,* 483–500.

Longenecker, C. O., Gioia, D. A., & Sims, H. P., Jr. (1987). Behind the mask: The politics of employee appraisal. *Academy of Management Executive, 1,* 183–194.

Lyness, K. S., & Thompson, D. E. (1997). Above the glass ceiling? A comparison of matched samples of female and male executives. *Journal of Applied Psychology, 82,* 359–375.

Markham, S. E. (1988). Pay-for-performance dilemma revisited: Empirical example of the importance of group effects. *Journal of Applied Psychology, 73,* 172–180.

Miles, R. E., & Snow, C. C. (1984). Designing strategic human resources systems. *Organizational Dynamics, 13,* 36–52.

Milkovich, G. T. (1980). The emerging debate. In E. R. Livernash (Ed.), *Comparable worth: Issues and alternatives* (pp. 23–47). Washington, DC: Equal Employment Advisory Council.

Mount, M. K., & Ellis, R. A. (1987). Investigation of bias in job evaluation ratings of comparable worth study participants. *Personnel Psychology, 40,* 85–96.

Murnighan, J. K. (1994). Game theory and organizational behavior. In B. M. Staw & L. L. Cummings (Eds.), *Research in organizational behavior* (Vol. 16, pp. 83–123). Greenwich, CT: JAI Press.

Nutt, P. C. (1998). Framing strategic decisions. *Organizational Science, 9,* 195–216.

Olian, J. D., & Rynes, S. L. (1992). Making total quality work: Aligning organizational processes, performance measures, and stakeholders. *Human Resource Management, 30,* 303–333.

O'Reilly, C. A., III, Main, B. G., & Crystal, G. S. (1988). CEO compensation as tournament and social comparison: A tale of two theories. *Administrative Science Quarterly, 33,* 257–274.

Orr, J. M., Sackett, P. R., & Mercer, M. (1989). The role of prescribed and nonprescribed behaviors in estimating the dollar value of performance. *Journal of Applied Psychology, 74,* 34–40.

Petty, M. M, Singleton, B., & Connell, D. W. (1992). An experimental evaluation of an organizational incentive plan in the electric utility industry. *Journal of Applied Psychology, 77,* 427–436.

Pfeffer, J. (1993). Barriers to the advance of organizational science: Paradigm development as a dependent variable. *Academy of Management Review, 18,* 599–620.

Pfeffer, J. (1998). *The human equation: Building profits by putting people first.* Boston: Harvard Business School Press.

Platt, R. J. (1984). Strong inference. In T. S. Bateman & G. R. Ferris (Eds.), *Method and analysis in organizational research* (pp. 43–53). Reston, VA: Reston Publishing.

Reichheld, F. F. (1996). *The loyalty effect.* Boston: Harvard Business School Press.

Reingold, J., Melcher, R. A., & McWilliams, G. (1998, April 20). Executive pay: Stock options plus a bull market made a mockery of many attempts to link pay to performance. *Business Week,* pp. 64–70.

Rynes, S. L., & Milkovich, G. T. (1986). Wage surveys: Dispelling some myths about the "market wage." *Personnel Psychology, 39,* 71–90.

Rynes, S. L., Weber, C. L., & Milkovich, G. T. (1989). Effects of market survey rates, job evaluation, and job gender on job pay. *Journal of Applied Psychology, 74,* 114–123.

Sackett, P. R., & Larson, J. R. (1990). Research strategies and tactics in industrial and organizational psychology. In M. D. Dunnette & L. M. Hough (Eds.), *Handbook of industrial and organizational psychology* (2nd ed., Vol. 1, pp. 419–489). Palo Alto, CA: Consulting Psychologists Press.

Salancik, G. R. (1986). An index of subgroup influence in dependency networks. *Administrative Science Quarterly, 31,* 194–211.

Sherer, P. D. (1995). Leveraging human assets in law firms: Human capital structures and organizational capabilities. *Industrial and Labor Relations Review, 48,* 671–689.

Sherer, P. D., Rogovsky, N., & Wright, N. (1998). What drives employment relationships in taxicab organizations? Linking agency to firm capabilities and strategic orientations. *Organization Science, 9,* 34–48.

Sherer, P. D., Schwab, D. P., & Heneman, H. G., III. (1987). Managerial salary-raise decisions: A policy-capturing approach. *Personnel Psychology, 40,* 27–38.

Singh, R. (1995). "Fair" allocations of pay and workload: Tests of a subtractive model with nonlinear judgment function. *Organizational Behavior and Human Decision Processes, 62,* 70–78.

Singh, R. (1997). Group harmony and interpersonal fairness in reward allocation: On the loci of the moderation effect. *Organizational Behavior and Human Decision Processes, 72,* 158–183.

Spaulding v. University of Washington. (1984). 35 FEP Cases 217.

Stevens, C. K., Bavetta, A. G., & Gist, M. E. (1993). Gender differences in the acquisition of salary negotiation skills: The role of goals, self-efficacy, and perceived control. *Journal of Applied Psychology, 78,* 723–735.

Terpstra, D. E., & Rozell, E. J. (1993). The relationship of staffing practices to organizational level measures of performance. *Personnel Psychology, 46,* 27–48.

Tolbert, P. S., & Zucker, L. G. (1996). Institutionalization of institutional theory. In S. Clegg, C. Hardy, & W. Nord (Eds.), *Handbook of organisational studies* (pp. 175–190). London: Sage.

Viswesvaran, C., & Barrick, M. R. (1992). Decision-making effects on compensation surveys: Implications for market wages. *Journal of Applied Psychology, 77,* 588–597.

Vobejda, B. (1998, September 25). Poverty rate fell, incomes rose in 1997, Census finds: Economic gains crossed racial, regional divides. *Washington Post,* pp. A1, A14.

Webb, W. B. (1968). A "couple" of experiments. *American Psychologist, 23,* 428–433.

Weber, C. L., & Rynes, S. L. (1991). Effects of compensation strategy on job pay decisions. *Academy of Management Journal, 34,* 86–109.

Zajac, E. J., & Westphal, J. D. (1995). Accounting for the explanations of CEO compensation: Substance and symbolism. *Administrative Science Quarterly, 40,* 283–308.

CHAPTER 2

Compensation, Attraction, and Retention

Alison E. Barber
Robert D. Bretz Jr.

Employment is typically characterized as an exchange relationship: employees provide organizations with something of value (their labor) and in return receive something of value. Work can offer many valuable outcomes to employees, including the opportunity to use their abilities, to make a contribution to society, and to be part of a social group. One outcome of primary importance to the vast majority of employees is compensation. The independently wealthy may be able to ignore compensation issues in establishing or evaluating an employment exchange, but most of the rest of us have little choice but to attend to the financial aspects of work. Indeed, a significant body of empirical work, reviewed in this chapter, confirms the existence of relationships between compensation and both attraction and retention.

This is not to suggest that compensation is necessarily more important than other work outcomes in influencing decisions to join and remain with organizations. Instead, we argue that pay clearly has *some* importance in the employment exchange and that research should focus on explaining and understanding (in addition to estimating) compensation's role in that exchange. Toward that

Note: The authors wish to thank Margo Runkle of the Mutual Insurance Company of America for her assistance in the preparation of this chapter.

end, we review the role of compensation in employee attraction and retention, placing particular emphasis on how and why compensation influences these outcomes, for which employees, and under what kinds of circumstances.

More specifically, our focus is on the psychological processes by which compensation is related to attraction and retention. We believe that psychology and psychologists can contribute much to our understanding of these issues. The advantages of research along these lines are twofold. First, it can enrich our understanding of individuals at work. Second, it can provide practical insights leading to the design and implementation of compensation policies that are effective in terms of attraction and retention.

Our original plan for this chapter was to treat attraction and retention as separate phenomena and to address each in turn. That approach would have been consistent with existing theory and research. However, as we proceeded, we found it difficult to separate the two constructs. Most popular models of employee turnover suggest that dissatisfaction with some aspect of the job causes withdrawal cognitions that prompt the evaluation of alternatives and may ultimately lead to turnover decisions (Lee & Mitchell, 1994; Mobley, Horner, & Hollingsworth, 1978). In other words, aspects of the current job "push" the employee into other jobs. It is also possible that an entirely different causal linkage operates. Turnover can be motivated by a "pull" process whereby information about alternatives is received and evaluated, leading to dissatisfaction with the current job and ultimately to turnover (Hulin, 1991). In either case, the decision to leave an employer (turnover) is tightly coupled with evaluation of potential new employers (attraction). Not surprisingly, then, we found substantial overlap in the psychological processes underlying attraction and retention. We have focused on those common processes in organizing the material that follows.

Before going forward, it is important to note that compensation is multidimensional, incorporating such aspects as pay structure, pay level, systems for recognizing individual differences in performance, and employee benefits (Gerhart & Milkovich, 1992). To date, most existing literature on compensation and attraction has focused on pay level—the amount of compensation offered— and research on compensation and retention has looked at either pay level or benefits. Somewhat less attention has been paid to pay systems and their impact on attraction and retention, despite exciting new developments in organizational practices (such as increasing use of team pay and at-risk pay). Still less attention has been paid to pay structure (relative pay levels within organizations). Our discussion therefore tends to emphasize pay level and to a lesser extent benefits, although we do incorporate other pay dimensions where possible.

In the material that follows, we first provide an overview of empirical research linking compensation practices to attraction and retention. We then discuss two general areas where we feel additional psychological research can add significantly to our understanding of the nature of these relationships: differences in individual reactions to pay and evaluation of pay information. Finally, we discuss how compensation's role in attraction can subsequently influence employee retention.

Empirical Findings on Compensation, Attraction, and Retention

It has long been argued that compensation plays a primary role in the attraction of new employees. According to Rynes (1987), compensation is particularly important as a recruitment tool because (1) it is a vehicle for satisfying a wide array of human needs, (2) salary offers are expressed in clear and comparable terms, (3) starting salaries have implications for future salary progression, and (4) pay systems "communicate so much about an organization's philosophy, values, and practices" (p. 190).

Over the years, many studies have examined compensation's role in attraction, primarily from the individual's point of view. Early job choice research focused on the relative importance of different job characteristics, including pay, to job applicants. A typical approach, known as direct estimation, was to provide research subjects with lists of job factors (for example, pay, opportunities for advancement, nature of work) and ask them either to rate or to rank the factors with respect to their importance. Such studies (see Jurgensen, 1978; Lacy, Bokemeier, & Shepard, 1983; Posner, 1981) typically found pay to be of moderate importance relative to other characteristics. Policy capturing studies, which assess the importance of job attributes as inferred through statistical analysis, also report that pay has a significant impact on job choice (Feldman & Arnold, 1978; Rynes, Schwab, & Heneman, 1983; Schwoerer & Rosen, 1989; Zedeck, 1977); in some cases, it was found to be the most important factor (see Feldman & Arnold, 1978; Zedeck, 1977). Finally, field studies of job choice decisions frequently conclude that pay is among the attributes significantly related to attraction to jobs (Harris & Fink, 1987; Osborn, 1990; Powell, 1984).

All three of these approaches (direct estimation, policy capturing, and field studies) have been used to address the question of which job attributes or aspects of the recruitment process had the greatest impact on individuals' attraction to organizations. The three approaches tend to differ in the degree to which pay (versus other attributes) contributes to attraction, with pay typically taking on the greatest relative importance in policy capturing studies. Because each approach has its unique limitations (Barber, 1998; Schwab, Rynes, & Aldag, 1987), we cannot provide a definitive answer to those who wish to pit pay against other factors in an attraction contest. What is apparent from these studies is that when viewed from the individual's perspective, pay influences attraction to organizations to some degree.

This conclusion was partially confirmed from the organization's vantage point by Williams and Dreher (1992). In a study of teller applications to 352 U.S. banks, they found that pay level was positively related to applicants' job offer acceptance rates. In addition, they found that banks offering flexible benefits were able to fill jobs more quickly than firms that did not offer benefit flexibility and that the percentage of payroll devoted to benefits was positively related to the number of applicants. Somewhat surprisingly, however, they did not find that pay level was associated with number of applicants (an effect that had previously been documented for public sector organizations; see Krueger, 1988).

In contrast to attraction, there has been relatively little research on compensation and turnover per se, particularly from the individual's point of view. Anecdotal evidence suggests that organizations use compensation (including retention bonuses and innovative benefits) to retain top performers during critical organizational transitions (Poe, 1998) or in the face of significant labor market competition (Ermel & Bohl, 1997). What research evidence exists supports the belief that compensation (pay level in particular) can influence turnover decisions. For example, in a large sample of high-level managers, Bretz, Boudreau, and Judge (1994) found that pay level was inversely related to job search behavior. That is, the more these managers were paid, the less likely they were to search for alternative jobs. More recently, in a large sample of exempt employees, Trevor, Gerhart, and Boudreau (1997) discovered that the expected curvilinear relationship between job performance and voluntary turnover was moderated by salary growth. Specifically, very low and very high performing individuals were significantly less likely to quit, and turnover among high performers with rapid salary growth was particularly low.

A number of studies have examined relationships between compensation and retention at the organizational or establishment level. These studies indicate that higher pay levels are associated with lower turnover rates (see Leonard, 1987; Powell, Montgomery, & Cosgrove, 1994). In addition, they provide evidence that firms offering employee benefits such as pensions and health insurance experience lower turnover (Gustman, Mitchell, & Steinmeier, 1994; Ippolito, 1987; Mitchell, 1982). Although these studies do establish relationships between compensation and retention, they shed little light on the psychological processes underlying those relationships.

In summary, existing evidence suggests that compensation is associated with attraction and retention. However, many questions remain about the nature of that association. In the material that follows, we identify two broad areas of research where we believe psychologists can contribute significantly to our understanding of the processes by which compensation influences these critical outcomes: individual differences in reactions to pay and the evaluation of pay information.

Individual Differences in Reactions to Pay: The Importance of Fit

In their chapter on individual differences in the 1990 *Handbook of Industrial and Organizational Psychology*, Ackerman and Humphries noted the centrality of individual difference research in applied psychology, stating that "a major purpose of industrial psychology is to characterize individuals" (p. 224). These authors point to numerous examples of the role of individual differences in such organizational practices as selection and training. Interestingly, however, they offer no examples related to employee attraction or to compensation. This omission may simply reflect the fact that the topic of individual differences has received only scattered attention in either of these areas. Although a few individual studies exist, neither the most recent I/O handbook chapter on recruitment (Rynes, 1991) nor the chapters on compensation (Gerhart & Milkovich, 1992; Lawler & Jenkins, 1992) devote much attention to this issue. (Gerhart & Milkovich do have a section labeled "individual differences" in their compensation chapter, but their use of the expression is significantly different from its typical use in I/O psychology: They use it to refer to means by which individual pay outcomes are differentiated, rather than as a reference to stable characteristics of the individuals themselves.)

The lack of attention to individual differences in reactions to pay is particularly troubling in light of the burgeoning literature on person-organization fit, which suggests that employees prefer to work for organizations that are compatible with their own preferences, personalities, and values (Kristof, 1996). Schneider's attraction-selection-attrition (ASA) model (Schneider, 1987; Schneider, Goldstein, & Smith, 1995) associates person-organization fit with the two outcome variables examined in this chapter. According to the ASA framework, employees prefer to join organizations that they feel are congruent with their own personal characteristics and will leave organizations that they do not fit. In other words, fit can be associated with turnover either through a "pull" mechanism (attraction to another organization offering a greater degree of fit) or a "push" mechanism (desire to leave an organization offering insufficient fit).

Given pay's importance in its own right, as well as its potential use as a signal or symbol of organizational culture and values (Kerr & Slocum, 1987), it seems likely that applicants and incumbents will consider compensation when assessing their fit with an organization. To the extent that individuals differ in preferences, values, and personalities, their reactions to compensation practices should also differ. We therefore believe there is much to be gained by studying compensation's role in attraction and retention from a fit perspective.

One of the difficulties involved in conducting such research is determining which individual differences to study. Rather than prematurely eliminating individual differences that might prove interesting or useful, in the following discussion we address a wide variety of individual differences: demographic differences, ability differences, personality differences, and value differences. We also note that most existing research on pay and fit has focused on attraction rather than on factors that might push an incumbent from an existing job. We return to the notion of "push" factors at the conclusion of this section.

Demographic Characteristics

A number of studies have addressed demographic differences in the importance attached to compensation (versus other attributes) in job choice. To our knowledge, these issues have not been addressed with respect to turnover. In this section, we focus on two demographic characteristics that have been studied repeatedly with respect to organizational attraction: gender and age or experience.

Gender, Pay, and Attraction

There are several reasons one might expect to find gender differences in reactions to compensation (Barber & Daly, 1996). First, men and women have traditionally held different roles in society, with men bearing greater responsibility for financial support of the family unit and women bearing greater responsibility for its emotional support. These social roles may spill over into preferences for work attributes. Second, women may assign importance to rewards in accordance with their expectations of receiving those rewards: a history of pay discrimination against women could result in the devaluation of monetary rewards among women.

Contrary to this reasoning, however, job choice research has typically failed to find gender differences in the relative importance of pay (although differences in the importance of other attributes are not uncommon). For example, Jurgensen (1978) found that men and women gave pay essentially the same rank within a set of ten attributes: For men, pay on average ranked 5.6 out of 10; for women, 6.0 out of 10. Similarly, Lacy et al. (1983) found no significant differences in pay preference by gender. Zedeck (1977) clustered subjects to identify broad groupings that responded differently to attributes and was able to identify subgroups for whom pay was particularly important. However, gender was not a factor on which these subgroups differed. More recently, Turban, Eyring, and Campion (1993), using a technique similar to Jurgensen's, failed to find gender differences in the importance of pay. In contrast, however, Bretz and Judge (1994) identified a cluster of job seekers who were strongly influenced by salary levels and found that individuals in this cluster (called the "pay level dominant" group) were primarily male.

Perhaps a more interesting and potentially more fruitful area of research would focus not on gender differences in the *importance* of compensation but on gender differences in pay *expectations* and in behaviors associated with those expectations (Major & Konar, 1984). It has been argued that women's pay expectations are lower than men's, even within occupations, either because women base their expectations on the (lower) salaries that women typically receive or because women have less accurate salary information than men do (Gerhart & Rynes, 1991). In support of this argument, Stevens, Bavetta, and Gist (1993) found that female M.B.A. students had lower self-set salary goals than male M.B.A. students. Tromski and Subich (1990) also found that women set significantly lower salary standards (minimum acceptable pay levels) than similarly educated men did and that women were more willing than men to accept jobs offering below-average wages.

These different expectations could have lasting implications and indeed might explain at least part of the persistent gender wage gap, if lower expectations lead to different job choice decisions (as Tromski and Subich's study suggests) or to different salary negotiation behaviors. Gerhart and Rynes (1991) provided evidence indicating that men and women were equally likely to negotiate for higher starting salaries but that men received a greater payoff to their negotiations (and therefore higher starting salaries) than women received. This implies either that women and men negotiate differently or that women and men receive different payoffs for engaging in the same negotiation behavior. Stevens et al. (1993) helped clarify this issue, finding that men negotiated higher salaries than women, that men and women engaged in different negotiation behaviors, and that certain types of training can help equalize outcomes. These studies indicate interesting and important gender differences, not in the importance of pay but in pay expectations and behaviors related to those expectations, and suggest the value of additional research along those lines.

Age or Experience, Pay, and Attraction

The second demographic factor examined repeatedly in early job choice research involves age and job experience, two distinct characteristics that are closely related. In contrast to gender, there is consistent empirical support for the relationship between age or experience and the importance of pay in job choice. For example, Jurgensen (1978) found consistent decreases in the importance of monetary compensation as a function of age: pay was ranked 4.5 (out of 10) in importance for men under twenty years of age but ranked 8.4 by men over age fifty-five. Similarly, pay ranked 6.1 in importance for women under twenty and 7.3 for women over fifty-five. Lacy et al. (1983) found a minor age effect, though in a direction consistent with Jurgensen's findings: older respondents placed less importance on income. Zedeck (1977) found that clusters containing relatively young and inexperienced subjects placed greater importance on pay than clusters composed of older, more experienced subjects, a finding corroborated by Bretz and Judge (1994). Finally, Feldman and Arnold (1978) found that experience was inversely associated with importance of pay.

Although the nature of this relationship is fairly clear, the reasons for the relationship are not clear, as these early studies neither proposed nor tested explanations for the effect. One possible explanation can be drawn from needs-based theories of motivation: because age and experience are typically associated with higher earnings, monetary needs may become less salient with age because they are already being met. Other explanations might be drawn from the social psychological literature on life cycle development and aging: as one ages, one may place greater value on nonfinancial outcomes, decreasing the relative importance of pay. In any event, findings that the importance of compensation in attraction declines over time suggests a need for extreme caution in attempting to generalize from existing research, which often relies on college student subjects. Research involving experienced employees who must balance the attraction of new jobs against the advantages of an existing job would do much to improve our understanding of pay's role in attraction and retention.

The Role of Ability

Bretz, Ash, and Dreher (1989) recommend that attraction researchers focus on individual differences associated with important organizational outcomes. Therefore, examination of relationships between applicant or employee ability (or more broadly, knowledge, skills, and abilities, or KSAs) and reactions to compensation practices would seem to be an important area of study. Yet we know virtually nothing about how applicants or incumbents with different KSAs respond to compensation. Much of what we do know must be inferred from research on variation in pay preferences across occupations or across education levels, which suggests that individuals with more education and in higher-status occupations tend to evaluate pay as less important when compared to those with less education and lower-status jobs (see Jurgensen, 1978). Interestingly, despite the prominent role accorded to cognitive ability (g) in selection research, it is almost never mentioned in the attraction and compensation literatures. The only study we could find along these lines was conducted by Tannen (1987), who documented that an increase in educational benefits was associated with higher Armed Forces Qualification Test scores among U.S. Army recruits.

Of course, organizations are interested in KSAs largely because of their relationship to employee performance. Three studies suggest linkages between employee performance, compensation, and turnover. First, Pfeffer and Davis-Blake (1992) provided evidence that may suggest different reactions to compensation as a function of performance. Using a sample of university administrators, they found that relationships between salary dispersion (variation in salaries within an organization) and turnover varied as a function of individual location within the salary range. For individuals with relatively high salaries, greater dispersion was associated with lower turnover. For individuals with relatively low salaries, greater dispersion was associated with higher turnover. To the extent that individual salary levels were a function of past performance in this sample, these results suggest that better performers prefer greater salary dispersion and may leave organizations that do not offer sufficient dispersion.

A second study addressing compensation, performance, and turnover was conducted by Harrison, Virick, and William (1996). This study built on the meta-analytic finding by Williams and Livingstone (1994) that associations between performance and turnover were significantly stronger when rewards were based on performance. Using a sample of 225 field service representatives, Harrison et al. found that the negative performance-turnover relationship was strongest when maximally contingent rewards (pay based solely on commissions) were employed.

Finally, Trevor, Gerhart, and Boudreau (1997) found a curvilinear relationship between performance and turnover in a large sample of exempt employees within a single firm. They also found that salary growth moderated this relationship, such that individuals whose high performance was rewarded were less likely to leave the organization than those whose high performance was not rewarded.

None of these studies was framed as an examination of person-organization fit, and their results may simply indicate rational self-interest on the part of high performers. However, it is also likely that individuals with the capacity to be high performers will perceive greater fit in organizations that reward performance. Research focusing directly on the mechanisms underlying performance and its association with pay preferences is needed and would have significant theoretical and practical implications.

The Role of Personality

In recent years, we have seen increasing empirical support for personality as a predictor of successful performance in organizations (Mount & Barrick, 1995). Again, given the value of focusing on individual differences that matter to organizations, it seems appropriate to learn how different compensation packages might facilitate or hinder the attraction or retention of individuals with specific personality traits. There is some research along these lines, primarily focusing on attraction.

Bretz et al. (1989), in one of the first studies explicitly using the notion of fit in examining compensation and attraction, proposed that organizational choice would be driven by a search for congruence between individual internal need states and aspects of the organization's reward system. Bretz et al. expected that individuals high in need for achievement (nAch) would prefer organizations with individual reward systems and that those with high need for affiliation (nAff) would prefer organizations with group-oriented reward systems. In fact, no main effects for either nAch or nAff were observed, although there was a marginally significant interaction between the two. In addition the authors found that as a group, employees who chose the individually oriented system were higher in nAch than those who chose the other system. In short, then, this study provided provisional support for connections between personality and pay preferences.

Bretz and Judge (1994) also examined relationships between personality and pay systems in a study of the role of human resource systems (promotion systems, family-friendly policies, systems supporting organizational justice, and, most relevant to this chapter, reward systems) in influencing job applicant decisions. Overall, subjects in this study preferred the individual-oriented reward system; however, this preference was stronger among those who preferred working on their own than among those who preferred a more team-oriented environment.

Cable and Judge (1994) provided the most comprehensive study available to date on compensation, attraction, and personality. One novel contribution of this study is its consideration of multiple pay dimensions—it examined not only reactions to pay level and pay contingencies (whether rewards were based on individual or group performance) but also whether pay was based on individual skills or on the requirements of the job, how much variability (risk) was associated with pay, and whether flexible (cafeteria-style) benefits were offered. Overall, subjects preferred high pay levels, individually oriented pay systems, fixed (rather than variable) pay, job-based pay, and flexible benefits. However, Cable and Judge also demonstrated that these preferences were moderated by individual differences: more materialistic job seekers placed greater emphasis on pay level than the less materialistic ones, individualists were attracted more strongly to individually oriented reward systems than collectivists were, individuals with high self-efficacy were more attracted to individually oriented reward systems than individuals low in self-efficacy, and risk-averse individuals were more likely to prefer jobs with fixed (noncontingent) pay than less risk-averse individuals.

These studies indicate that individual personality characteristics do interact with pay policies in influencing attraction to organizations and therefore suggest that additional work along these lines will be fruitful. There is also a need to examine personality traits and reactions to pay from a "push" perspective. An important next step would be to prioritize which personality characteristics (and which dimensions of pay) should be studied. One approach would be to focus on the "Big Five" personality characteristics (Mount & Barrick, 1995). The existence of this parsimonious structure of personality traits has facilitated the accumulation of knowledge of personality effects in selection and could do the same for research on attraction and compensation. Furthermore, the selection literature could be used to identify the personality traits most highly associated with outcomes important to the organization (for example, conscientiousness).

The Role of Values

To a great extent, the person-organization fit literature has focused not on personality but on values. Chatman (1989, 1991) has argued that values are a central element defining organizational culture, as well as a fundamental and enduring individual characteristic. Empirical research on person-organization fit supports the importance of values congruence (Kristof, 1996). Therefore, individual differences with respect to values might be significant factors in the relationship between pay and attraction. However, to date this issue has not been extensively studied.

This lack of research is particularly puzzling given that compensation is often viewed as an expression of organizational values (see Kerr & Slocum, 1987; Rynes, 1987). Again, part of the problem may be the identification of specific values to study. Meaningful hypotheses regarding how values might moderate reactions to pay will require a focus on specific values, but existing value-based fit research tends to deal with value profiles, shedding light on the role of values as a whole but saying little about the role specific values play. Initially, then, researchers might start by considering a wide array of values and identifying those most closely linked conceptually to compensation issues (such as fairness) or those most likely to be of interest to hiring organizations (such as achievement or collaboration).

Because of its conceptual proximity to compensation, one construct that should not be overlooked is the meaning of money. There is a growing body of literature (for example, Furnham, 1996; Mahoney, 1991; Tang, 1992, 1993; Thierry, 1992; Yamauchi & Templar, 1982) focusing on the values individuals attach to money, where and how those values are learned, and how those values influence reactions to money in general and to compensation in particular. As Wernimont & Fitzpatrick (1982) wrote, "It seems clearly self-evident that money does 'mean different things to different people'" (p. 218). For example, for some, money may be associated with consumption opportunities; for others, with security; for others, with power; for others, with status or achievement; for others, with anxiety.

For the purpose of studying pay and attraction or retention, it may be advantageous to simplify the dimensionality of this construct. Several authors (including Krefting, 1980, and Thierry, 1992) have argued that the meanings attached to monetary compensation are a subset of the meanings associated with money in general. Krefting and Mahoney (1977) successfully used a two-dimensional operationalization (recognition orientation versus consumption orientation) to explain individual reactions to pay raises.

It seems likely that the meanings attached to money would also be influential in understanding individuals' reactions to pay policies in an attraction or retention context and that it could therefore be used to help organizations predict the attraction and retention consequences of existing or alternative pay practices. As one example, group-based pay plans such as gainsharing or profit sharing may be attractive to those who value compensation for its monetary or consumption value but less attractive to those who view compensation as recognition of personal achievement. Employers would need to be aware that the use of such pay plans might alter the values orientation of their workforce through self-selection and either accept that outcome or find alternative ways of providing recognition to offset the impact of the group pay plans.

Summary: Attraction, Retention, and Fit

Research on compensation's role in the formulation of perceptions of fit, and its subsequent role in job choice or turnover decisions, is in its infancy but shows promise. Much of the existing research has been conducted in the context of organizational attraction and therefore sheds little light on the "push" aspect of turnover. An important implication of existing research is that compensation policies can influence characteristics of a firm's labor force, a factor that should be taken into account in compensation design.

We believe that pay's role in fit can be critical from the "push" point of view as well, although there is currently little research to support our assertion. In particular, we suspect that major changes in compensation administration (such as implementation of pay-for-performance plans and shifts from individual-based to group-based rewards) may cause individuals to reassess their fit with an organization and ultimately to quit. Such changes may represent the sort of shock that, according to image theory (Beach, 1990; Lee & Mitchell, 1994), prompts individuals to reevaluate their situation and, under certain circumstances, to quit their jobs. Gerhart, Trevor, and Graham (1996) noted the general scarcity of research on the implementation of new pay programs. Research into new programs' impact on fit perceptions, and therefore on retention, would represent an important contribution to an underresearched area.

The Evaluation of Pay Information

A second general area where we believe psychologists can make substantial contributions to our understanding of compensation's role in attraction and retention involves the evaluation of pay information. At least two promising areas for future research fall under this heading: reactions to the amount of pay information provided and use of standards to evaluate pay information.

Reactions to the Amount of Pay Information Provided

Prescriptive writings on the design of recruitment materials (such as advertisements and brochures) suggest that reward systems should be described very early on (see, for example, Redman & Matthews, 1992). This argument is supported by surveys of job applicants who state that they prefer job advertisements that mention salary (Laabs, 1991; Redman & Matthews, 1992). In fact, a Price Waterhouse study of managers seeking jobs (mentioned by Redman & Matthews, 1992) stated that 91 percent of respondents felt that salary information should be included in advertisements, 67 percent used salary information to decide whether to read the remainder of the ad, and 64 percent said the absence of salary information would make them less likely to apply for the job. These reports suggest that the amount of pay information provided to applicants can influence their attraction to the organization.

Such conclusions are consistent with psychological research on uncertainty avoidance in decision making (Curley, Yates, & Abrams, 1986; Stevenson, Busemeyer, & Naylor, 1990). For instance, such research has shown that subjects avoid uncertain alternatives to a degree that violates subjective expected utility theory (in other words, they prefer certain alternatives even when the expected value of the uncertain alternative exceeds that of the certain alternative; Stevenson et al., 1990). This finding, known as Ellsberg's paradox, could result from a tendency to underestimate the probabilities of uncertain events—in other words, decision makers may underestimate the expected value of an uncertain alternative. Alternatively, job seekers may presume that organizations withhold unfavorable information—in other words, that low-paying organizations are less likely to provide pay information than high-paying organizations.

Several studies have examined applicant reactions to ambiguous or uncertain pay information. Rynes and Miller (1983) conducted an experimental (policy capturing) study of recruiter and job attribute influences on the likelihood of pursuing jobs. Although the study was not specifically designed to test reactions to compensation ambiguity, the specificity of pay information was manipulated. In one condition, the recruiter offered information about starting salaries in dollar terms (indicating that the average starting salary was $15,000); in the other condition, pay was described in more general terms ("definitely competitive"). Information specificity on other attributes was also manipulated so that the two conditions varied in terms of overall informativeness rather than informativeness with respect to pay alone. Rynes and Miller found a positive association between the amount of information provided and attraction to the job. They speculated that the lack of specificity in the one condition may have been viewed negatively because it was either "an attempt to evade discussion of unattractive job characteristics" or "an indication of low recruiter interest in the applicant as a future employee" (p. 153).

Barber and Roehling (1993), in a verbal protocol study of reactions to job postings, also pursued the theme of information adequacy. As part of this issue, pay information varied across four postings: salary information was presented either in specific dollar terms or in more general terms (described as "competitive"). In addition, the amount of information provided on benefits, equal employment opportunity (EEO) policy, and number of openings was also varied. Barber and Roehling's results suggested that subjects did attend to information inadequacy in general and with respect to pay in particular. They also found that the posting containing the smallest amount of information was considered least attractive.

One advantage of the verbal protocol approach is that it provided insight into *why* information inadequacy was a concern. Barber and Roehling (1993) found little evidence that applicants believed the salary described only as "competitive" was actually low. Instead, they found that participants viewed the failure to provide specific information in the job posting as an indicator of "sloppy" recruitment and a sign that the company was not much interested in meeting applicants' information needs.

Whereas Rynes and Miller (1983) and Barber and Roehling (1993) took somewhat exploratory or indirect approaches to examining the role of pay information, Yuce and Highhouse (1998) explicitly tested the role of pay ambiguity on applicant reactions to job advertisements. In a study grounded in the uncertainty avoidance literature discussed earlier, Yuce and Highhouse had subjects respond to a number of simulated advertisements for video rental clerk positions, some of which provided actual starting salary information ($5.65 per hour) and others stating only that pay would be "competitive." Surprisingly, these authors found no evidence of a significant pay ambiguity main effect on attraction to the different jobs. Furthermore, when asked to choose one of the jobs, roughly half the subjects chose a job with ambiguous pay information. However, there was an interaction between pay ambiguity and information set size: pay ambiguity had the predicted (negative) effect when the total amount of information provided in the ad was relatively low but no effect when the total amount of information provided was high. This suggests that it may be possible to compensate for ambiguous pay information by providing more information about other characteristics.

Thus it appears that the amount of pay information provided in recruitment materials can influence applicant attraction. However, questions remain regarding the reasons for this effect and the circumstances under which it is most likely to be found. Research into these questions can draw from a vast literature on decision making and could both be enriched by this literature and also enrich it. In addition, such studies would have practical applications, as it is fairly easy for organizations to manipulate the amount of information they provide about compensation in their recruitment materials.

Job incumbents have access to more pay information than job applicants do. They know their own salary and have personal experience with other pay elements such as bonuses or benefits. They may also have learned about their own standing in the organization's pay hierarchy, either through official channels or through the internal "grapevine." Therefore, we anticipate that information adequacy per se will have less impact on decisions to quit a familiar organization than on decisions to join a new one. Although the fact that job incumbents have more information may result in dissatisfaction (if the information is unfavorable) and ultimately turnover, such reactions would be based on the content of the pay information obtained rather than on its availability per se. However, we note that organizations practicing extreme degrees of pay secrecy may arouse negative reactions among current employees that parallel the reactions of job applicants described here.

Identifying Standards Used to Evaluate Pay Information

An important element of the processing of pay information is its evaluation. Evaluation requires some sort of standard against which a job offer or one's current pay can be compared. Understanding what standards are used, and under what circumstances, can add significantly to our understanding of the role of pay in attraction and retention.

Virtually all psychological perspectives on turnover involve comparisons between actual conditions and some referent condition. For example, equity theory (Adams, 1964) suggests that employees who feel underpaid in comparison to referent others will be dissatisfied. Empirical research has confirmed that those who perceive themselves to be underpaid are more likely to form turnover intentions (Finn & Lee, 1972) and to quit their jobs (Dittrich & Carrell, 1976).

Unfortunately, equity theory does not clearly specify how referents are chosen. Many different classes of referents have been proposed: other people, one's own historical standards, and implicit or explicit contractual expectations (Goodman, 1974, 1977). Particularly relevant to job search scenarios, Blau (1964) suggested known or perceived alternative jobs as an additional referent. Referent cognitions theory (Aquino, Griffeth, Allen, & Hom, 1997) adds a different perspective, suggesting that individuals compare their present circumstances against their perceptions of what might have been or what possibly could be. Given the central role that these comparisons are expected to play in decisions to join and remain with organizations, there is surprisingly little research into the nature of the comparisons actually made in the context of such decisions.

Minimum Standards for Pay

Labor economists have long argued that job search decisions are made by comparing the wage offered to the so-called reservation wage, the lowest wage that the applicant is willing to accept. The logic of the reservation wage suggests that at least within some range, pay level plays a noncompensatory role in attraction: all offers falling below the minimum wage will be rejected, regardless of other characteristics. This perspective has been explored in the attraction literature, with several studies finding evidence of noncompensatory uses of pay level in job choice (Osborn, 1990; Rynes et al., 1983) and verifying that applicants do establish minimum standards for pay (Osborn, 1990; Tromski & Subich, 1990).

An interesting question raised by these findings involves how applicants establish their minimum standards. As noted earlier, there is evidence that women tend to set lower standards than men (Stevens et al., 1993; Tromski & Subich, 1990), but to our knowledge, little attention has been paid to other characteristics, either dispositional or situational, that might influence self-set standards.

In addition, we know little about how these minimum standards might come into play once an individual has joined an organization. For instance, we do not know whether job incumbents continue to monitor their pay against such standards or whether the standards are adjusted over time. Recognition that one's pay has fallen below a minimum standard could certainly result in dissatisfaction, job search, and turnover. Therefore, research focusing on minimum standards for retention is in order.

Other Standards of Comparison

Even if pay is evaluated against a minimum standard, criteria are still needed for evaluating compensation that exceeds the standard. In other words, it is unlikely that minimum standards are the only standards used. Additional criteria might include any of the referents previously described. Current thinking is that there is no single referent that is consistently employed; rather, individuals are expected to make multiple comparisons (Scholl, Cooper, & McKenna, 1987). We must therefore ask *when* specific comparisons are made in addition to *whether* they are made.

One interesting study on this topic was a laboratory study (Bazerman, Schroth, Shah, Diekman, & Tenbrunsel, 1994) in which graduating students evaluated either one or several hypothetical job offers. These researchers found that individuals evaluating a single offer were more likely to use social information (such as knowledge of the offers received by others) in interpreting the worth of the offer than individuals who evaluated multiple offers. Those who evaluated multiple offers were more likely to do so by comparing the (hypothetical) offers they had personally received.

Scholl et al. (1987) studied the degree to which specific pay referents were associated with intentions to remain with an organization. They found that occupational referents, self-equity, and pay adequacy were significantly related to intention to remain: individuals who felt that others in their field were better paid, those who perceived that their pay was less than they should be earning, and those who felt that their salaries did not meet their needs were more likely to consider alternative job opportunities. These authors also found that different outcome variables (pay satisfaction, extra-role behaviors) were associated with different sets of pay referents.

One issue that has not been examined is whether choice of pay referent varies as a function of labor market context. For example, social comparisons may be more likely in markets where information regarding others' pay is plentiful (for example, among public sector employees, chief executive officers of private firms, or union-ized employees); self-referents may be more likely when informa-tion about the earnings of others is more difficult to obtain.

We encourage additional psychological research into the fac-tors influencing individual evaluation of wage or salary levels. Ex-isting research suggests that there may be interesting differences between individuals and between situations in terms of how a given offer might be evaluated. Understanding these differences would have substantial practical impact, as organizations cannot predict employee reactions to pay practices without knowledge of the stan-dards against which those practices will be evaluated.

Pay, Attraction, and Post-Hire Outcomes

We have been discussing attraction and retention simultaneously, reasoning that attraction to one organization is closely related (both conceptually and temporally) to the intention to leave an-other. Here we address a different relationship between attraction and retention: the possibility that events that occur as applicants are recruited by an organization influence their later intentions to remain with organizations. Specifically, we discuss how compensa-tion issues at organizational entry might affect employee tenure.

There is evidence that certain aspects of the recruitment process (such as realism of the information provided; Wanous, 1992) can have lasting impact on applicants even after they join the organiza-tion. To date, however, there has been almost no research into how compensation's role in attraction might extend into post-hire con-sequences. This section raises two possibilities: that the extent to which individuals rely on pay in choosing jobs is related to their post-hire attitudes toward the jobs and that the nature of pay negotiations during the job choice period can influence longer-term attitudes (in particular, perceptions of the psychological contract).

Impact of Extrinsic Job Choice Factors on Longer-Term Job Outcomes

O'Reilly and Caldwell (1980) made an interesting and distinctive contribution to the job choice literature by focusing on the cir-cumstances under which job choice is made. They argued that job choice decisions made under conditions of reduced volition (as under financial or geographical constraints) would result in reduced commitment to the job chosen and ultimately to lower job satisfaction than decisions made in the absence of such external constraints. In addition, they drew from the literature on intrinsic and extrinsic rewards (including Deci, 1972; see Kanfer, 1990, for a review) to suggest that jobs chosen for extrinsic reasons (such as higher pay) will ultimately result in lower commitment and satisfaction than jobs chosen for intrinsic reasons.

O'Reilly and Caldwell (1980) studied M.B.A. students who were seeking jobs, employing a longitudinal design to assess the relative importance of extrinsic factors (including financial pressures and salary offered) and intrinsic characteristics in actual job choice decisions. A follow-up survey six months later assessed commitment to and satisfaction with the new jobs. Generally, the authors' expectations were supported: decisions made under external constraints (including financial constraints) were associated with lower levels of satisfaction and commitment later on. However, these authors did not find the anticipated negative relationship between the importance of salary in job choice and post-hire outcomes. In fact, individuals who placed greater importance on salary in choosing a job also reported significantly higher commitment and satisfaction post-hire than those who placed lesser importance on pay. O'Reilly and Caldwell speculated that these individuals may have seen pay as an indicator of competence—in other words, pay may have both intrinsic and extrinsic value (an interpretation consistent with the meaning-of-money literature discussed earlier, as well as with more recent writings on the intrinsic versus extrinsic debate, such as Kanfer, 1990, or Brief & Aldag, 1989).

Impact of the Pay Negotiation Process on Longer-Term Outcomes

In a recent review of the recruitment literature, Barber (1998) argues that research has not paid adequate attention to the ways in which applicant-employer interactions that occur immediately prior to job choice might influence job choice decisions. Salary negotiations are an important aspect of these interactions. Evidence suggests that negotiation does influence salary outcomes (Gerhart &

Rynes, 1991). What remains unknown is whether the negotiation experience also influences post-hire outcomes. To a great extent, the employment relationship is one of exchange, and pay is certainly one of the key elements in that exchange. The manner and style in which the terms of the initial exchange are established could be seen by the applicant as indicative of the nature of the employee-employer relationship in general.

More specifically, there may be connections between initial salary negotiations and the psychological contracts established by applicants who become new hires. A psychological contract has been defined as an individual's beliefs regarding the nature of the reciprocal exchange relationship between that individual and the employer, and these beliefs are expected to be influenced by the individual's interactions with the employer (Rousseau, 1989). Therefore, a firm that engages in hard bargaining (win-lose negotiation) in establishing the exchange relationship may trigger a transactional (short-term and monetizable) contract, whereas more integrative bargaining (win-win negotiation) might trigger more relational long-term contract including nonmonetizable exchanges such as loyalty. The nature of the psychological contract formed is interesting from the standpoint of understanding human behavior in organizations, but research into the establishment of such contracts will also have practical value, as research indicates different types of contracts are associated with different employee attitudes and behaviors (Rousseau, 1990).

Conclusion

This chapter identified numerous open questions about relationships between compensation and employee attraction and retention. Our focus has been on the *nature* of compensation's influence on employee decisions to join or stay with an organization rather than on the *existence* of that influence. We have noted that what little process-oriented research exists on this topic is more fragmented than programmatic and suggest that there is a great need for additional research focusing on the psychological processes that underlie compensation's influence on employment exchange decisions.

We cannot claim to have provided an exhaustive discussion of the many ways in which the psychological perspective can enhance our understanding of compensation's role in attraction and retention. Given constraints on the length of this chapter, we drew from existing literature to suggest several avenues of research that we believe would make significant contributions. More important than the specific recommendations, however, is the recognition that we still have much to learn about how, why, and when compensation influences attraction and retention.

References

Ackerman, P. L., & Humphries, L. G. (1990). Individual differences theory in industrial and organizational psychology. In M. D. Dunnette & L. M. Hough (Eds.), *Handbook of industrial and organizational psychology* (2nd ed., Vol. 1, pp. 223–282). Palo Alto, CA: Consulting Psychologists Press.

Adams, J. S. (1964). Toward an understanding of inequity. *Journal of Abnormal and Social Psychology, 67,* 422–436.

Aquino, K., Griffeth, R. W., Allen, D. G., & Hom, P. W. (1997). Integrating justice constructs into the turnover process: A test of a referent cognitions model. *Academy of Management Journal, 40,* 1208–1227.

Barber, A. E. (1998). *Recruiting employees: Individual and organizational perspectives.* Thousand Oaks, CA: Sage.

Barber, A. E., & Daly, C. L. (1996). Compensation and diversity: New pay for a new workforce? In E. E. Kossek & S. A. Lobel (Eds.), *Managing diversity: Human resource strategies for transforming the workplace* (pp. 194–216). Cambridge, MA: Blackwell.

Barber, A. E., & Roehling, M. V. (1993). Job postings and the decision to interview: A verbal protocol analysis. *Journal of Applied Psychology, 78,* 845–856.

Bazerman, M. H., Schroth, H. A., Shah, P. P., Diekman, K. A., & Tenbrunsel, A. E. (1994). The inconsistent role of comparison others and procedural justice in reactions to hypothetical job descriptions: Implications for job choice decisions. *Organizational Behavior and Human Decision Processes, 60,* 326–352.

Beach, L. R. (1990). *Image theory: Decision making in personal and organizational contexts.* Chester, England: Wiley.

Blau, P. M. (1964). *Exchange and power in social life.* New York: Wiley.

Bretz, R. D., Jr., Ash, R. A., & Dreher, G. F. (1989). Do people make the place? An examination of the attraction-selection-attrition hypothesis. *Personnel Psychology, 42,* 561–581.

Bretz, R. D., Jr., Boudreau, J. W., & Judge, T. A. (1994). Job search behavior of employed managers. *Personnel Psychology, 47,* 275–301.

Bretz, R. D., Jr., & Judge, T. A. (1994). The role of human resource systems in job applicant decision processes. *Journal of Management, 20,* 531–551.

Brief, A. P., & Aldag, R. A. (1989). The economic functions of work. In K. M. Rowland & G. R. Ferris (Eds.), *Research in personnel and human resources management* (Vol. 7, pp. 1–23). Greenwich, CT: JAI Press.

Cable, D. M., & Judge, T. A. (1994). Pay preferences and job search decisions: A person-organization fit perspective. *Personnel Psychology, 47,* 317–348.

Chatman, J. A. (1989). Improving interactional organizational research: A model of person-organization fit. *Academy of Management Review, 14,* 333–349.

Chatman, J. A. (1991). Matching people and organizations: Selection and socialization in public accounting firms. *Administrative Science Quarterly, 36,* 459–484.

Curley, S. P., Yates, J. F., & Abrams, R. A. (1986). Psychological sources of ambiguity avoidance. *Organizational Behavior and Human Decision Processes, 38,* 230–256.

Deci, E. L. (1972). Effects of contingent and noncontingent rewards and controls on intrinsic motivation. *Organizational Behavior and Human Performance, 22,* 113–120.

Dittrich, J. E., & Carrell, M. R. (1976). Dimensions of organizational fairness as predictors of job satisfaction, absence, and turnover. *Academy of Management Proceedings,* 79–83.

Ermel, L., & Bohl, D. (1997). Responding to a tight labor market: Using incentives to attract and retain talented workers. *Compensation and Benefits Review, 29*(6), 25–29.

Feldman, D. C., & Arnold, H. J. (1978). Position choice: Comparing the importance of organizational and job factors. *Journal of Applied Psychology, 63,* 706–710.

Finn, R. H., & Lee, S. M. (1972). Salary equity: Its determination, analysis, and correlates. *Journal of Applied Psychology, 56,* 283–292.

Furnham, A. (1996). Attitudinal correlates and demographic predictors of monetary beliefs and behaviors. *Journal of Organizational Behavior, 17,* 375–388.

Gerhart, B., & Milkovich, G. T. (1992). Employee compensation: Research and practice. In M. D. Dunnette & L. M. Hough (Eds.), *Handbook of industrial and organizational psychology* (2nd ed., Vol. 3, pp. 481–570). Palo Alto, CA: Consulting Psychologists Press.

Gerhart, B., & Rynes, S. L. (1991). Determinants and consequences of salary negotiations by male and female M.B.A. graduates. *Journal of Applied Psychology, 76,* 256–262.

Gerhart, B., Trevor, C. O., & Graham, M. E. (1996). New directions in compensation research: Synergies, risk, and survival. In K. M. Rowland & G. R. Ferris (Eds.), *Research in personnel and human resources management* (Vol. 14, pp. 143–203). Greenwich, CT: JAI Press.

Goodman, P. S. (1974). An examination of referents used in the evaluation of pay. *Organizational Behavior and Human Performance, 12,* 170–195.

Goodman, P. S. (1977). Social comparison processes in organizations. In B. M. Staw & G. Salancik (Eds.), *New directions in organizational behavior* (pp. 97–132). Chicago: St. Clair.

Gustman, A. L., Mitchell, O. S., & Steinmeier, T. L. (1994). The role of pensions in the labor market: A survey of the literature. *Industrial and Labor Relations Review, 47,* 417–438.

Harris, M. M., & Fink, L. S. (1987). A field study of applicant reactions to employment opportunities: Does the recruiter make a difference? *Personnel Psychology, 40,* 765–783.

Harrison, D. A., Virick, M., & William, S. (1996). Working without a net: Time, performance, and turnover under maximally contingent rewards. *Journal of Applied Psychology, 81,* 331–345.

Hulin, C. L. (1991). Adaptation, persistence, and commitment in organizations. In M. D. Dunnette & L. M. Hough (Eds.), *Handbook of industrial and organizational psychology* (2nd ed., Vol. 2, pp. 445–505). Palo Alto, CA: Consulting Psychologists Press.

Ippolito, R. A. (1987). Why federal workers don't quit. *Journal of Human Resources, 22,* 281–293.

Jurgensen, C. E. (1978). Job preferences (What makes a job good or bad?). *Journal of Applied Psychology, 63,* 267–276.

Kanfer, R. (1990). Motivation theory and industrial and organizational psychology. In M. D. Dunnette & L. M. Hough (Eds.), *Handbook of industrial and organizational psychology* (2nd ed., Vol. 1, pp. 75–170). Palo Alto, CA: Consulting Psychologists Press.

Kerr, J., & Slocum, J. W. (1987). Managing corporate culture through reward systems. *Academy of Management Executive, 1,* 99–108.

Krefting, L. A. (1980). Differences in orientations toward pay increases. *Industrial Relations, 19,* 81–87.

Krefting, L. A., & Mahoney, T. A. (1977). Determining the size of a meaningful pay increase. *Industrial Relations, 16,* 83–93.

Kristof, A. L. (1996). Person-organization fit: An integrative review of its conceptualizations, measurement, and implications. *Personnel Psychology, 49,* 1–50.

Krueger, A. B. (1988). The determinants of queues for federal jobs. *Industrial and Labor Relations Review, 41,* 567–581.

Laabs, J. J. (1991). Nurses get critical about recruitment ads. *Personnel Journal, 70*(7), 63–69.

Lacy, W. B., Bokemeier, J. L., & Shepard, J. M. (1983). Job attribute preferences and work commitment of men and women in the United States. *Personnel Psychology, 36,* 315–329.

Lawler, E. E., III, & Jenkins, D. J. (1992). Strategic reward systems. In M. D. Dunnette & L. M. Hough (Eds.), *Handbook of industrial and organizational psychology* (2nd ed., Vol. 3, pp. 1009–1055). Palo Alto, CA: Consulting Psychologists Press.

Lee, T. W., & Mitchell, T. R. (1994). An alternative approach to the unfolding model of voluntary employee turnover. *Academy of Management Review, 19,* 51–89.

Leonard, J. S. (1987). Carrots and sticks: Pay, supervision, and turnover. *Journal of Labor Economics, 5,* S136–S152.

Mahoney, T. A. (1991). The symbolic meaning of pay contingencies. *Human Resource Management Review, 1,* 179–192.

Major, B., & Konar, E. (1984). An investigation of sex differences in pay expectations and their possible causes. *Academy of Management Journal, 27,* 777–792.

Mitchell, O. S. (1982). Fringe benefits and labor mobility. *Journal of Human Resources, 17,* 286–298.

Mobley, W. H., Horner, S. O., & Hollingsworth, A. T. (1978). An evaluation of precursors of hospital employee turnover. *Journal of Applied Psychology, 63,* 408–414.

Mount, M. K., & Barrick, M. R. (1995). The Big Five personality dimensions: Implications for research and practice in human resources management. In G. R. Ferris (Ed.), *Research in personnel and human resources management* (Vol. 13, pp. 153–200). Greenwich, CT: JAI Press.

O'Reilly, C. A., III, & Caldwell, D. F. (1980). Job choice: The impact of intrinsic and extrinsic factors on subsequent satisfaction and commitment. *Journal of Applied Psychology, 65,* 559–565.

Osborn, D. P. (1990). A reexamination of the organizational choice process. *Journal of Vocational Behavior, 36,* 45–60.

Pfeffer, J., & Davis-Blake, A. (1992). Salary dispersion, location in the salary distribution, and turnover among college administrators. *Industrial and Labor Relations Review, 45,* 753–763.

Poe, A. C. (1998, March). Retention bonuses prove effective for companies in transition. *HRMagazine,* pp. 53–59.

Posner, B. Z. (1981). Comparing recruiter, student, and faculty perceptions of important applicant and job characteristics. *Personnel Psychology, 34,* 329–339.

Powell, G. N. (1984). Effects of job attributes and recruiting practices on applicant decisions: A comparison. *Personnel Psychology, 37,* 721–732.

Powell, I., Montgomery, M., & Cosgrove, J. (1994). Compensation structure and establishment quit and fire rates. *Industrial Relations, 33,* 229–248.

Redman, T., & Matthews, B. P. (1992). Advertising for effective managerial recruitment. *Journal of General Management, 18,* 29–44.

Rousseau, D. M. (1989). Psychological and implied contracts in organizations. *Employee Responsibilities and Rights Journal, 2,* 121–139.

Rousseau, D. M. (1990). New hire perceptions of their own and their employer's obligations: A study of psychological contracts. *Journal of Organizational Behavior, 11,* 389–400.

Rynes, S. L. (1987). Compensation strategies for recruiting. *Topics in Total Compensation, 2,* 185–196.

Rynes, S. L. (1991). Recruitment, job choice, and post-hire consequences. In M. D. Dunnette & L. M. Hough (Eds.), *Handbook of industrial and organizational psychology* (2nd ed., Vol. 2, pp. 399–444). Palo Alto, CA: Consulting Psychologists Press.

Rynes, S. L., & Miller, H. E. (1983). Recruiter and job influences on candidates for employment. *Journal of Applied Psychology, 68,* 146–154.

Rynes, S. L., Schwab, D. P., & Heneman, H. G., III. (1983). The role of pay and market pay variability in job application decisions. *Organizational Behavior and Human Performance, 31,* 353–364.

Schneider, B. (1987). The people make the place. *Personnel Psychology, 40,* 437–454.

Schneider, B., Goldstein, H. W., & Smith, D. B. (1995). The ASA framework: An update. *Personnel Psychology, 48,* 748–773.

Scholl, R. W., Cooper, E. A., & McKenna, J. F. (1987). Referent selection in determining equity perceptions: Differential effects on behavioral and attitudinal outcomes. *Personnel Psychology, 40,* 113–124.

Schwab, D. P., Rynes, S. L., & Aldag, R. A. (1987). Theories and research on job search and choice. In K. M. Rowland & G. R. Ferris (Eds.), *Research in personnel and human resources management* (Vol. 5, pp. 129–166). Greenwich, CT: JAI Press.

Schwoerer, C., & Rosen, B. (1989). Effects of employment-at-will policies and compensation policies on corporate image and job pursuit intentions. *Journal of Applied Psychology, 74,* 653–656.

Stevens, C. K., Bavetta, A. G., & Gist, M. E. (1993). Gender differences in the acquisition of salary negotiation skills: The role of goals, self-efficacy, and perceived control. *Journal of Applied Psychology, 78,* 723–735.

Stevenson, M. K., Busemeyer, J. R., & Naylor, J. C. (1990). Judgment and decision-making theory. In M. D. Dunnette & L. M. Hough (Eds.), *Handbook of industrial and organizational psychology* (2nd ed., Vol. 1, pp. 283–374). Palo Alto, CA: Consulting Psychologists Press.

Tang, T. L. (1992). The meaning of money revisited. *Journal of Organizational Behavior, 13,* 197–202.

Tang, T. L. (1993). The meaning of money: Extension and exploration of the money ethic scale in a sample of university students in Taiwan. *Journal of Organizational Behavior, 14,* 93–99.

Tannen, M. B. (1987). Is the Army college fund meeting its objectives? *Industrial and Labor Relations Review, 41,* 50–62.

Thierry, H. (1992). Payment: Which meanings are rewarding? *American Behavioral Scientist, 35,* 694–707.

Trevor, C. O., Gerhart, B., & Boudreau, J. W. (1997). Voluntary turnover and job performance: Curvilinearity and the moderating influences of salary growth and promotions. *Journal of Applied Psychology, 82,* 44–61.

Tromski, J. E., & Subich, L. M. (1990). College students' perceptions of the acceptability of below-average salary offers. *Journal of Vocational Behavior, 37,* 196–208.

Turban, D. B., Eyring, A. R., & Campion, J. E. (1993). Job attributes: Preferences compared with reasons given for accepting and rejecting job offers. *Journal of Occupational and Organizational Psychology, 66,* 71–81.

Wanous, J. P. (1992). *Organizational entry: Recruitment, selection, orientation, and socialization of newcomers* (2nd ed.). Reading, MA: Addison-Wesley.

Wernimont, P. F., & Fitzpatrick, S. (1982). The meaning of money. *Journal of Applied Psychology, 56,* 218–226.

Williams, C. R., & Livingstone, L. P. (1994). Another look at the relationship between performance and voluntary turnover. *Academy of Management Journal, 37,* 269–298.

Williams, M. L., & Dreher, G. F. (1992). Compensation system attributes and applicant pool characteristics. *Academy of Management Journal, 35,* 571–595.

Yamauchi, K. T., & Templar, D. I. (1982). The development of a money attitude scale. *Journal of Personality Assessment, 46,* 522–528.

Yuce, P., & Highhouse, S. (1998). Effects of attribute set size and pay ambiguity on reactions to "Help Wanted" advertisements. *Journal of Organizational Behavior, 19,* 337–352.

Zedeck, S. (1977). An information processing model and approach to the study of motivation. *Organizational Behavior and Human Performance, 18,* 47–77.

CHAPTER 3

Compensation Attitudes

Herbert G. Heneman III
Timothy A. Judge

This chapter deals with matters pertaining to compensation attitudes, which we consider to include employees' affective reactions to both amounts of pay received and administration of pay delivery systems. We contend that such affective reactions also have potentially important implications about how employees choose to behave. We focus on three attitudinal issues: pay satisfaction, pay justice, and pay preferences. In each of these areas, we briefly review the theoretical underpinnings and then turn our attention to research. We summarize individual studies and draw their findings together to suggest key new knowledges that have emerged from research from roughly the mid-1980s to the present. For each of these three areas, we also suggest numerous directions for future research, emphasizing a need to refocus our research and to make it more organizationally relevant. We are worried about bridging what we see as a research-practice gap and have framed our research suggestions in ways that will, we hope, shrink that gap.

Pay Satisfaction

In this section, we first review the two general models of pay satisfaction, along with modifications to them that have served as the conceptual foundations for most pay satisfaction research. We then review research conducted on pay satisfaction since Heneman's 1985 review. The research is reviewed in four major areas: measurements of pay satisfaction, pay comparisons, antecedents of pay satisfaction, and pay satisfaction influences on outcomes. Our emphasis is in summarizing the methodology and major results of the research, along with providing observations and generalizations about findings that have emerged from it. The sheer complexity of most studies required us to be brief in our summaries; the reader is urged to consult the original sources for greater detail. Suggestions for further research conclude our discussion of pay satisfaction.

Models of Pay Satisfaction

The two most widely known and used models of pay satisfaction are the equity model (Adams, 1965) and a close derivative, the discrepancy model (Lawler, 1971, 1981). In the equity model, pay satisfaction depends on the comparison of the person's outcome-input ratio to the outcome-input ratio of a comparison other. The greater the similarity of the ratios, the greater the person's pay satisfaction. The discrepancy model suggests that pay satisfaction depends on the degree of discrepancy between individuals' perceptions of the amounts of pay that they should receive and what they actually do receive. In turn, "should receive" perceptions are due to perceived personal job inputs, perceived inputs and outcomes of referent others, and perceived job characteristics. The "does receive" perceptions are a function of perceptions about the perceived pay of referent others and the amount of pay actually received. The equity model (and by extension the discrepancy model) also suggests that pay dissatisfaction creates a dissonance that the person seeks to reduce. Dissonance reduction may occur through changing perceptions of one's own outcomes or inputs, changing perceptions of the comparison other's outcomes or inputs, changing the comparison other (or others), or undertaking changes in actual behavior that will restore equity (such as lowering effort or leaving the job for a more equitable situation).

Heneman (1985), based on Heneman and Schwab (1979), suggested two modifications to the equity and discrepancy models. The first modification was to suggest that the term *pay* was too nebulous because of the multiple ways that pay is actually administered by the organization and received by the individual. Heneman (1985) suggested that *pay* should be replaced by reference to four dimensions of pay: pay level (pay for the job), pay structure (pay for job relative to pay for other jobs), pay system (pay raises), and pay form (benefits). Individuals may thus experience different feelings of pay satisfaction for each dimension, based on separate "should receive" and "does receive" perceptions for each. The second modification was the addition of "pay policies and administration" as a determinant of pay satisfaction. This addition was based on the premise that people react not only to the amount of pay they should and do receive but also to how that pay is administered and delivered to them by the organization.

Two other modifications to models of pay satisfaction should be noted. First, Miceli and Lane (1991) differentiated and created separate models for pay amounts (pay level, benefits) and pay system (pay range, pay hierarchy, benefits). The two "amount" models were based on the discrepancy between the perceived amount that the person should receive and does receive, with numerous antecedents to each component proposed. The three system models used a discrepancy between the manner in which the system should operate and is perceived to operate. Antecedents to the "should operate" component emphasized factors such as employee preferences, system flexibility, system procedures, and communication. Second, concepts of distributive and procedural justice were proposed by Greenberg (1987, 1990; Folger & Greenberg, 1985), and these concepts have direct relevance to pay satisfaction. These concepts are discussed later in this chapter.

Measurement of Pay Satisfaction

Prior to 1985, pay satisfaction measurement was characterized by two disparate research streams: ad hoc measurement and standardized measurement (Heneman, 1985). Ad hoc measures were specially constructed for use in a substantive study, and little or nothing was known of their construct validity. Although these measures were tailor-made to the research question and settings and were convenient for researchers, lack of common item content and unknown construct validity worked against the building of an accumulated empirical knowledge base. In contrast, standardization of measures provided a scale of set items with demonstrated construct validity that, when used across research settings, facilitated the comparison and accumulation of results. The Minnesota Satisfaction Questionnaire

(MSQ) and the Job Descriptive Index (JDI) pay satisfaction scales were the most widely known and used standardized measures in pay satisfaction research. Heneman and Schwab (1985) argued that the MSQ and the JDI were primarily measures of pay level satisfaction. They speculated that to capture compensation satisfaction more fully, a multidimensional measure of pay satisfaction might be needed.

Publication of initial research on the development and construct validation of the Pay Satisfaction Questionnaire (PSQ) (Heneman & Schwab, 1985) provided new insights into the nature of pay satisfaction and its measurement. Based on the modified discrepancy model (Heneman, 1985; Heneman & Schwab, 1979), it was hypothesized that employees experience differential satisfaction with pay level, pay structure, pay raises, and pay form (benefits) and that employees also independently experience satisfaction with the organization's pay policies and pay administration. In short, it was hypothesized that pay satisfaction was multidimensional and that the generic term *pay satisfaction* may be something of a misnomer.

To investigate this hypothesis, twenty questionnaire items (four per dimension) were constructed and administered to sample of white-collar employees from multiple organizations. Confirmatory factor analysis results supported the hypothesized five dimensions, in that each item had its highest loading on its a priori dimension. A few of the items also had high cross-loadings, however, creating a bit of ambiguity in the factor structure. Deletion and reconfiguration of items lead to a "modified" PSQ that contained eighteen items assigned to four pay satisfaction dimensions: pay level (four items), benefits (four items), pay raises (four items), and structure and administration (six items).

The factor structure results were replicated on a nationwide random sample of nurses. Additional analyses on both the white-collar and nurse samples revealed that intercorrelations among scale scores for the dimensions were positive but not excessive and that the pay satisfaction scales from the MSQ and the JDI correlated primarily with the PSQ pay level scale. Based on these results, it was concluded that (1) the overall results provided strong support for the hypothesis that pay satisfaction is a multidimensional construct, (2) the pay level and benefits scales were particularly distinct empirically, (3) the pay raise scale showed a somewhat more equivocal factor structure and correlations with the other scales,

(4) the pay structure and pay administration items inexplicably formed a single factor, and (5) the MSQ and JDI pay satisfaction scales were most appropriately thought of and used as measures of pay level satisfaction only (Heneman & Schwab, 1985).

The initial research on the PSQ lead to an outpouring of subsequent research on its psychometric characteristics, particularly its factor structure and scale intercorrelations (Ash, Dreher, & Bretz, 1987; Brown & Huber, 1992; Carraher, 1991; Carraher & Buckley, 1996; Heneman, Greenberger, & Strasser, 1988; Judge, 1993; Judge & Welbourne, 1994; Mulvey, Miceli, & Near, 1992; Orpen & Bonnici, 1987; Scarpello, Huber, & Vandenberg, 1988). Emerging from these studies was a fairly robust set of findings about the psychometric properties of the PSQ and, more generally, a broadened understanding of the nature of pay satisfaction.

The first finding was that pay satisfaction was definitely multidimensional. Results from all studies pointed to the multidimensional empirical character of the PSQ and thus pay satisfaction. Hence the expression "pay satisfaction" is truly a misnomer in that employees respond differentially to the different ways that organizations administer and deliver compensation to them. It would be useful to replace the single expression "pay satisfaction" with a designation to the type of pay satisfaction being referenced, such as "pay level satisfaction."

A second finding was that when confirmatory factor analysis was used, allowing for correlated pay factors, the resultant factor structure revealed that pay level, benefits, and pay raise items had high loadings on their hypothesized dimensions and low cross-loadings on the other dimensions. More equivocal results were obtained when using exploratory factor analysis and specifying uncorrelated factors. The latter procedures are inappropriate for testing the hypothesized dimensionality of the PSQ, however, since exploratory factor analysis is driven by the data themselves rather than by the hypothesized factor structure, and the assumption that the factors are uncorrelated is often unwarranted (Judge, 1993).

A third finding was that the structure and administration items yielded somewhat inconsistent patterns of factor loadings. These items simply did not always "hang together" empirically, raising obvious questions about what they were actually measuring. Unfortunately, none of the studies has experimented with rewritten or new items so as better to tap the original structure and administration constructs or to refine the meaning of these constructs, as recommended by Heneman & Schwab (1985). Hence the structure and administration results provided are in need of further investigation.

Fourth, differential prediction evidence further buttressed the case for distinctiveness of the dimensions. Judge (1993), for example, hypothesized that each of several predictors would be significantly related to a only single dimension of pay satisfaction. Examples of these predictors include pay raise history, salary grade, age, and manager influence over pay. It was found that each predictor was significantly correlated with its hypothesized dimension and that each predictor had its highest correlation with its hypothesized dimension. In addition, Heneman, Greenberger, and Strasser (1988) found that among several predictors, a pay-for-performance perception variable had its largest significant beta weight with pay raise satisfaction and small insignificant beta weights with benefits satisfaction and structure and administration satisfaction.

Fifth, some data were offered as indicating that the factor structure, or number of factors, of the PSQ varies according to organizational and individual characteristics. For example, Scarpello, Huber, and Vandenberg (1988) found different patterns of factor loadings for the raise and the structure and administration items (but not level and benefits items) across job classifications. In addition to true factor structure differences, however, the results could also have reflected a confounding of individual characteristics with job classification and the use of exploratory (as opposed to confirmatory) factor analysis. Carraher and Buckley (1996) investigated whether respondents' cognitive complexity levels were associated with different factor structures for the PSQ. Although goodness-of-fit indices for a four-factor solution varied among cognitive complexity subgroups, the similarity of the factor loadings in practical terms across cognitive complexity levels was very high. In short, based on limited data, it did not appear that the factor structure of the PSQ is likely to vary much as a function of organizational and individual characteristics.

Sixth, although the factors underlying the items of the PSQ were quite distinct (especially level, benefits, and raises), factor scores on the dimensions were intercorrelated to some degree. This was to be expected, however, since the dimensions are administratively related to one another. For example, the dollar value of one's benefits is at least in part a function of one's actual level of pay. Also, pay raises are usually based on, and built into, one's base pay. These linkages between actual components of pay create naturally occurring links between satisfaction with the components, thus accounting for the obtained intercorrelations among the PSQ's dimensions.

Pay Comparisons

All models of pay satisfaction accord pay comparisons a prominent role as a process people use and as a determinant of their pay satisfaction. Studies investigating the pay comparison–pay satisfaction relationship are summarized in Table 3.1.

Inspection of the table reveals that the studies have used a mixture of types of employees and, with one exception, have used cross-sectional designs in which questionnaires were the common method of measurement for both pay comparison and pay satisfaction variables. Pay comparisons were operationalized in various ways, typically requiring the respondent to provide ratings of self and comparison others' pay and inputs. Most of the focus was on pay level or benefits. All studies controlled for actual pay, along with other factors, when assessing the pay comparison–pay satisfaction relationship.

Results of the pay comparison studies, with the exception of Berkowitz, Fraser, Treasure, & Cochran (1987), were straightforward and consistent. Specifically, it was found that the less the discrepancy in pay and inputs between self and comparison others, the greater the pay satisfaction. This held for both internal (including self) and external comparisons. Thus the data clearly support a basic tenet of pay satisfaction models. The veracity of this conclusion, however, must be tempered by the cross-sectional and common measurement method features of the studies.

Antecedents of Pay Satisfaction

There are two basic issues of concern regarding the antecedents of pay satisfaction. First, how does peoples' actual pay influence their pay satisfaction? Second, how do the numerous other hypothesized determinants of pay satisfaction affect pay satisfaction beyond the effects of actual pay itself?

Table 3.1. Pay Comparisons and Pay Satisfaction.

Study	Sample	Design	Pay Comparisons	Pay Satisfaction	Significant Results
Williams (1995)	122 employees from 13 libraries	C	Rating scale (much less to much more) of my benefits versus benefits received by others doing my job in other libraries, others with similar education and responsibility, and others of my age	PSQ benefits	After controlling for numerous personal and perceptual variables, pay comparison rating was positively related to benefits satisfaction.
Judge (1993)	176 managers, 265 professional and technical employees, 63 sales employees, and 126 nonexempt employees in a strategic business unit	C	Single-item rating (much lower to much higher) of my pay relative to others performing similar work in other organizations	PSQ benefits, raise, structure and administration	After controlling for actual pay and numerous perceptual variables, pay comparison related positively most strongly to pay level satisfaction but also related to benefits, raise, and structure and administration satisfaction.
Brown & Huber (1992)	101 managerial and operating-level bank employees	L	Ratings of amount of self-reward and effort, divided to form self-reward-to-effort ratio; ratings of amount of other within-company reward and effort, divided to form other-reward-to-effort ratio	Pay outcome and process modified from PSQ level and structure and administration	After controlling for pay and numerous perceptual variables, both before and after introduction of an incentive system, self-reward-to-effort ratio was positively related to both pay outcome and pay process satisfaction.

Study	Sample		Measure	Criterion	Findings
Micelli, Jung, Near, & Greenberger (1991)	1,029 middle managers and 912 executives in 22 agencies of the U.S. federal government	C	Single-item rating (much less to much more) of my pay compared to nongovernment workers doing similar job	Reactions to salary (reason to leave versus reason to stay)	After controlling for whether merit pay increase was received and numerous perceptual variables, comparisons were positively related to reactions to salary for both managers and executives.
Rice, Phillips, & McFarlin (1990)	169 mental health professionals	C	Specifying salary deserved for my job in the company (deserved salary), salary of person I most compare myself with at work (other's salary), average salary of others doing comparable job in the region (average salary), minimum acceptable salary for person holding job comparable to yours (minimum salary)	Pay level	After controlling for actual pay and demographics, all four comparisons predicted pay level satisfaction: lower standards of comparisons are associated with higher pay satisfaction; combined impact is greater than any single standard; also some interactions among comparison standards.
Sweeney, McFarlin, & Interrieden (1990)	550 working adults nationwide; 642 working adults nationwide; 633 working adults nationwide; 651 employees of a bank	C	Social comparison ratings of fairness (not fair to fair) or similarity of pay (larger to smaller) of external and internal comparison others	Pay level	After controlling for pay and numerous perceptual variables, social comparisons were positively related to pay satisfaction in all four samples.

Table 3.1. Pay Comparisons and Pay Satisfaction, Cont'd.

Study	Sample	Design	Pay Comparisons	Pay Satisfaction	Significant Results
Berkowitz, Fraser, Treasure, & Cochran (1987)	248 employees in organizations throughout a county	C	Social comparison frequency, using series of both internal and external referent others	Pay level	After controlling for pay and numerous other demographic and perceptual variables, no significant effect obtained.
Oldham, Kulick, Stepina, & Ambrose (1986)	265 employees of 20 data processing departments in a state government	C	Whether or not employee used no comparison referent or each of four referents: self-inside, self-outside, other-inside, other-outside	Pay level and benefits (description, not necessarily satisfaction)	After controlling for job (pay) level and other job characteristics, long-tenure employees used other-inside referents and short-tenure employees used self-outside comparisons when evaluating their pay.

Note: C = cross-sectional; L = longitudinal; PSQ = Pay Satisfaction Questionnaire (Heneman & Schwab, 1985).

Pay Itself

Models of pay satisfaction all suggest that the amount of pay itself should have a direct impact on pay satisfaction. A summary of previous research on this relationship concluded that "the consistency of the pay level–pay satisfaction relationship is probably the most robust (though hardly surprising) finding regarding the causes of pay satisfaction" (Heneman, 1985, p. 131). Subsequent research on the relationship has examined it within the context of using pay as a control variable when investigating other antecedents' (or outcomes') relationships with pay satisfaction. In those studies (see Tables 3.1, 3.2, and 3.3), the zero-order correlation between pay and pay satisfaction is typically reported for descriptive purposes, and the previously noted robustness of the pay–pay satisfaction empirical relationship is apparent. It should be noted, however, that the simple pay level–pay satisfaction correlation is quite weak—typically, $r = .15$—just as the pay satisfaction models imply would be the case. It should also be noted that the relationship has been tested as a linear one, although one study found that pay level satisfaction was better explained by treating pay level in quadratic rather than linear terms (Heneman, Porter, Greenberger, & Strasser, 1997).

Pay Program Characteristics and Perceptions

Heneman (1985) found few studies investigating how pay satisfaction is influenced by perceptions of pay programs or actual characteristics of pay programs. Since then, numerous such studies have been conducted. They included (1) cross-sectional studies in which questionnaire-measured perceptions of pay program characteristics and pay satisfaction were correlated, (2) cross-sectional studies correlating actual program characteristics with pay satisfaction, and (3) longitudinal studies in which actual or perceived pay program changes were related to pay satisfaction.

Summaries of the studies are contained in Table 3.2. Several characteristics of the studies should be noted. They involved occupationally diverse groups in both private and public sectors. More than half of the studies were longitudinal, as opposed to cross-sectional. The studies investigated a wide variety of programs, including pay systems (pay-for-performance, merit, incentive, bonus, employee stock ownership), pay structures (two-tier wage systems), and benefits (cost, coverage, choice). Also, multiple measures of pay satisfaction were used, mostly assessing satisfaction with pay amount and pay process fairness.

Table 3.2. Influence of Pay Program Characteristics and Perceptions on Pay Satisfaction.

Study	Sample	Design	Pay Program Characteristics or Perceptions	Pay Satisfaction	Significant Results
Williams (1995)	122 employees from 13 libraries	L	Benefits coverage regarding life insurance, time off, retirement, and medical insurance	PSQ	Benefits administration and benefit comparisons (perceived inputs and outcomes of referent others) were positively related to benefits satisfaction. Employee cost of medical insurance premium was negatively related to benefits satisfaction.
Judge (1993)	176 managers, 265 professional and technical employees, 63 sales employees, and 126 non-exempt employees in a strategic business unit	C	Pay-for-performance perceptions and pay attitudes under a variable-time merit pay program	PSQ raise, benefits, structure and administration	Pay-for-performance perceptions, pay attitudes, and actual pay level and raise history were all related to the dimension of pay satisfaction they were hypothesized to predict.
Barber, Dunham, & Formisano (1992)	110 white-collar employees of a professional management company	L	Introduction of flexible benefits plan	Benefits	A preplan-postplan comparison showed a significant (more than one standard deviation) increase in benefits satisfaction.
Brown & Huber (1992)	101 managerial and operating-level bank employees	L	Introduction of an earnings-at-risk bonus and incentive system	Pay process, pay outcome	After introduction of an earnings-at-risk pay program, employee base pay dropped 6.72 percent and incentive pay dropped 27.65 percent. Mean pay process and pay

					outcome satisfaction both dropped significantly from their preprogram levels. Regression analysis showed that postprogram pay outcome satisfaction was due to percentage change in incentive pay, perceived reward-to-effort ratio, preferred base pay, and understanding of pay system. Postprogram pay process satisfaction was due to preferred effort-to-reward ratio and understanding of pay system.
Petty, Singleton, & Connell (1992)	L	618 blue-collar and 587 white-collar employees in experimental and control divisions of an electric utility	Introduction of an organizational incentive pay plan, with performance teams	Fairness of pay plan, continue under pay plan	Employees in the experimental group felt that the plan was fair and that they earned their incentive pay. Problems occurred with free riders and some teams being ineligible for team incentives. Most employees favored continuing to work under the plan.
Micelli, Jung, Near, & Greenberger (1991)	C	1,029 middle managers and 912 executives in 22 agencies of the U.S. federal government	Perceptions of merit pay and bonus programs in the U.S. federal government	Reactions to salary, pay system fairness, pay system fairness and success (executives only)	Receipt of merit pay increases and performance awards and bonuses, endorsement of merit pay concept, and perceptions of effort-reward consonance were significantly related to salary reactions. External comparisons were more closely related to salary reactions, while internal (self) comparisons were more closely related to pay system fairness. Procedural justice items showed mixed pattern of significant relationships with pay system fairness (and success).

Table 3.2. Influence of Pay Program Characteristics and Perceptions on Pay Satisfaction, Cont'd.

Study	Sample	Design	Pay Program Characteristics or Perceptions	Pay Satisfaction	Significant Results
Cappelli & Sherer (1990)	423 craft employees (mechanics, pilots, ground crew, clerical) and 156 flight attendants for an airline	L	Two different two-tier wage plans for the two employee groups	Pay level, future pay	Controlling for numerous variables, low-tier craft workers had significantly greater pay level and future pay satisfaction than high-tier craft workers. There were no significant differences between the two flight attendant tiers in pay level or future pay satisfaction.
Dreher, Ash, & Bretz (1988)	2,925 uniformed highway patrol officers in eight state agencies	C	Standardized composite indices of level of benefit coverage across seven benefits and of benefit cost to employees across two cost measures	PSQ level, benefits	After controlling for several demographics, coverage had significant positive correlation with benefits satisfaction and significant negative correlation with pay level satisfaction. Cost to employees had significant negative correlation with benefits satisfaction and no correlation with pay level satisfaction. Accuracy of coverage and cost knowledge moderates these relationships somewhat, especially for coverage and benefits satisfaction.

Heneman, Greenberger, & Strasser (1988)	104 white-collar, hospital employees	C	Pay-for-performance perceptions under a merit pay plan	PSQ level, raise, benefits, structure and administration	Pay-for-performance perceptions explained significantly more variance in pay raise and pay level satisfaction than explained by a set of control variables alone.
Klein (1987)	2,804 employees (random samples) in 37 ESOP companies	C	Characteristics of ESOPs and employees' attitudes about their ESOP	ESOP	Employee ESOP satisfaction is significantly related to management commitment to the concept of employee ownership, managements' amount of financial contribution to the plan, and the extensiveness of communication about the ESOP.
Martin & Peterson (1987)	1,935 retail store employees in 27 stores	L	Wage tier (high, low), employment status (full-time, part-time), and store age (new, old)	Pay equity	Pay equity was significantly lower for low-wage-tier employees and employees in old stores. Part-timers felt significantly greater pay equity than full-timers except in new-store and high-tier conditions.

Note: C = cross-sectional; ESOP = employee stock ownership plan; L = longitudinal; PSQ = Pay Satisfaction Questionnaire (Heneman & Schwab, 1985).

In a general examination of the results in Table 3.2, it is striking to observe the vast number of significant findings showing that (1) actual pay program characteristics and changes in them consistently influenced pay satisfaction and (2) perceptions of pay program characteristics were consistently correlated with pay satisfaction. Thus both actual and perceived pay program characteristics truly do influence pay satisfaction, a conclusion that could not be drawn previously (at the time of Heneman, 1985).

As expected, employees were sensitive to the "is received" component of pay satisfaction, including increases or decreases in incentive pay, employee-paid cost of benefits and benefit reductions, and reductions in base pay. An anomaly was the finding that airline craft workers in the low wage tier had greater satisfaction with their pay level and their future pay than those in the high wage tier (Cappelli & Sherer, 1990). This unexpected difference was likely due to differences in employees' expectations and comparison others between the high and low wage tiers, again reinforcing the importance of not equating amount of pay received with pay satisfaction.

It is important to note that actual and perceived characteristics of the pay program (beyond just pay received or costs incurred) were consistently related to pay satisfaction, particularly as pertains to pay systems. A consistent emerging theme was that communication with employees about the nature of the program, or of program changes, enhanced pay satisfaction. Such communication likely increases employees' knowledge and understanding of the program and their subsequent evaluation of its fairness.

Pay Satisfaction Influences on Outcomes

The equity model suggests that feelings of inequity (dissatisfaction) create a dissonance in the employee that triggers actions to reduce it. These actions may be cognitive or behavioral. Cognitively, employees may change their perceptions of outcomes (including pay) and inputs, both for oneself and for comparison others, in order to create greater equality in outcome-input ratios. Behaviorally, employees may seek to change their actual pay (or other outcomes) and inputs, take forward-looking steps that they hope will lead to subsequent inequity reduction, or withdraw from the situation and seek a more equitable one. Heneman (1985) found few studies that had investigated these potential inequity reduction impacts.

Since then, several such studies have been conducted; they are summarized in Table 3.3. The diversity of samples and outcomes are noteworthy, as is the prevalence of longitudinal designs. Pay dissatisfaction has been operationalized as measured pay dissatisfaction, inferred pay dissatisfaction based on organizational conditions or experimental manipulations, and anticipated pay dissatisfaction. In most instances, actual pay was used as a control variable, so that the dissatisfaction-outcome linkages were net of actual pay influences. Inspection of the results in Table 3.3 shows that pay dissatisfaction consistently influenced both cognitive and behavioral changes. These included input changes (performance, commitment, trust), outcome changes (salary negotiation, theft), steps toward change (job interview sign-up, job search, pro-union voting), and withdrawal (turnover intentions, turnover, job transfer, lateness). Thus it is abundantly clear that employees revert to a number of cognitive and behavioral ways of reducing their pay dissatisfaction. From an organizational perspective, these actions involve undesirable consequences and outcomes.

Directions for Future Pay Satisfaction Research

In some senses, substantial strides have been made in pay satisfaction research over the past fifteen years. The basic equity and discrepancy models have turned out to serve us well. Modifications to these models, particularly the identification of multiple pay satisfaction dimensions and of pay process factors, have sharpened and refined our conceptual views of pay satisfaction. In addition, research has demonstrated or affirmed that (1) there are distinct dimensions of pay satisfaction for pay level, pay raises, and benefits; (2) pay itself is a weak, though consistent, predictor of pay satisfaction; (3) employees make external and internal pay comparisons that influence their pay satisfaction; (4) pay administration and process factors, particularly those enhancing employee knowledge and understanding of pay practices, contribute importantly to pay satisfaction; and (5) pay dissatisfaction has numerous undesirable consequences.

In another sense, however, we have fallen way behind. Organizations' pay practices have changed dramatically and forcefully, and our research has simply ignored or glossed over the changes. Examples include growing pay inequalities within the organization,

Table 3.3. Influences of Pay Satisfaction on Outcomes.

Study	Sample	Design	Pay Satisfaction	Outcomes	Significant Results
Heneman & Milanowski (1998)	1,150 schoolteachers in 130 schools of a district with a school-based performance award (bonus) program	L	PSQ pay level; inferred from whether teacher worked in bonus or nonbonus school	Turnover (leave school district), job transfer (change schools in district)	After controlling for school and teacher characteristics, actual pay predicted school turnover but not school transfers. Pay level satisfaction was positively related to school turnover, but not transfers. Teachers in nonbonus schools were more likely to transfer schools but not leave the district. Turnover intentions were positively related to both school turnover and school transfers.
Koslowsky, Sagie, Krausz, & Singer (1997)	30 samples for a meta-analysis of variables related to employee lateness	C	Ad hoc measures of overall pay satisfaction	Lateness	The uncorrected and corrected correlations between pay satisfaction and lateness were –.17 and –.22, respectively. There was no evidence of the presence of moderators.
Barber & Roehling (1993)	49 undergraduate students actively seeking employment	L	Anticipated satisfaction with salary and benefits, manipulated by job postings that differed in pay and benefits being offered for the jobs, along with other attributes	Signing up for job interview	Using verbal protocol analysis, it was found that after job location, salary and benefits were the attributes paid most attention and most influential in determining whether to sign up for a job interview.

Study	Sample	Type	Measure	Outcome	Findings
Davy & Shipper (1993)	757 employees throughout the United States who had participated in union certification elections	L	Ad hoc measures of overall pay satisfaction	Pro-union vote	The lower the pay satisfaction, the more likely that employees voted for the union, even after controlling for other facets of job satisfaction.
Lane (1993)	212 employees of a service organization	C	PSQ benefits combined with ad hoc items	Organizational commitment, trust in management, turnover intention, stress	After controlling for pay, age and tenure, benefits satisfaction was related to organizational commitment, trust in management, turnover intention, and stress.
Greenberg (1993)	102 undergraduate students taking part in a laboratory experiment	L	Manipulation of pay equity, crossed with manipulations of the validity of information about pay received and the sensitivity of the experimenter to the subjects' pay received	Theft	Equitably paid subjects took from a pool the amount of money ($5.00) they were told they would be paid; inequitably paid subjects took a greater amount ($3.84) from the pool than they were told they would be paid ($3.00), a form of theft. Amount of pay taken interacted with validity and sensitivity, with the smallest excess taken in the high-sensitivity and high-validity condition.
Hindman & Smith (1993)	270 employees in a federal arsenal	L	Ad hoc measure of overall pay satisfaction for employees (some were members of the existing union) who were voting in a challenge union election	Intention to vote pro-union	Intent to vote for the union was significantly related to pay dissatisfaction in a univariate test, but not in a multivariate test.

Table 3.3. Influences of Pay Satisfaction on Outcomes, Cont'd.

Study	Sample	Design	Pay Satisfaction	Outcomes	Significant Results
Bretz & Thomas (1992)	116 baseball salary arbitration cases settled by an arbitrator	L	Inferred by whether the player won (equity, satisfaction) or lost (inequity, dissatisfaction) the arbitration case	Performance, job (team) transfer, turnover	Players who lost their arbitration case were more likely to decrease their playing performance; winners with a large salary demand-offer differential showed a greater performance decrease than winners with a small demand-offer differential. Losers were more likely to move to other teams and to leave baseball.
Gerhart & Rynes (1991)	205 M.B.A. students from a highly ranked business school looking for jobs	L	Inferred by the level of initially salary offered for the job ultimately taken and by the amount of difference between initial salary offer and highest alternative offer	Propensity to negotiate starting salary	Propensity to negotiate over starting salary was higher for those with lower offers and higher differences between initial offer and highest alternative offers. There were no gender differences in propensity to negotiate. Those who negotiated received higher starting salaries, through men fared better than women (4.3 versus 2.7 percent increase).

Study	Sample	Design	Measures	Outcome	Results
Miceli, Jung, Near, & Greenberger (1991)	1,029 middle managers and 912 executives in 22 agencies of the U.S. federal government	C	Ad hoc measures of reactions to salary pay system fairness, pay system fairness and success (executives only)	Job search, intent to retire	Generally, reactions to salary and to pay system fairness were positively related to lack of recent job search, intent to stay until retirement, and intent not to retire as soon as eligible.
Greenberg (1990)	Employees in plants A ($n = 55$), B ($n = 30$), and C ($n = 58$) of a manufacturing company	L	Inferred from 15 percent pay cut for employees in plants A and B but not C; ad hoc pay level satisfaction also measured	Theft	Employee theft was similar in all plants before pay cut, then increased during the time the pay cut was announced in plants A and B. Theft was greater in the plant (A) receiving an inadequate explanation for the pay cut than in the plant (B) receiving an adequate explanation. There was no change in theft in the control plant (C). Employees who received an inadequate explanation for the pay cut expressed lower pay satisfaction, while those who received an adequate explanation did not.

Note: C = cross-sectional; L = longitudinal; PSQ = Pay Satisfaction Questionnaire (Heneman & Schwab, 1985).

pay disruption through job loss, expanding overtime, pay structure modifications such as broadbanding and organizational delayering, shifting of benefit costs to employees, reduction and elimination of benefit coverage, pay concessions, starting pay reductions, variable-pay innovations and modifications (team-based pay, earnings at risk, bonuses, employee stock ownership), knowledge- and skill-based pay, and top-level executive performance pay. When viewed against this backdrop, our pay satisfaction research seems meager, misguided, and myopic.

Furthermore, there appears to be little interest in behavioral pay research generally, let alone pay satisfaction specifically. A recent survey of SIOP members and participants in SIOP preprogram workshops found that "reward systems and compensation" was rated twenty-seventh out of thirty-seven areas of interest, and there was little difference among academic, nonprofit, consulting, or business respondents (Shippmann & Hartmann, 1995). Inspection of the 1998 SIOP and Academy of Management's Human Resources and Organizational Behavior divisions' programs reveals only a handful of papers devoted to pay topics, with only a few dealing with pay satisfaction.

The paucity of pay research and interest in it does not bode well for the future. Unless we begin to conduct more research—research that is viewed as useful by organizations—we will remain on the sidelines. This seems like a squandering of our considerable research competency and our ability to generate organizationally useful knowledge about what is arguably the most important and readily manipulable organizational reward of all. The suggestions for future research that follow will, we hope, not only chart new directions but also stimulate more interest in pay research that will be useful to organizations.

Methodological Expansion

We are struck by researchers' use of surveys to gather both independent and dependent variables (often within a single instrument for cross-sectional studies). Such usage lends itself to the benefits of standardization of measurement, ease and efficiency of data collection, and model testing through increasingly sophisticated statistical procedures. The price of survey reliance may have been to overlook the complexity and richness of pay satisfaction, to miss out on studying pay situations that do not lend themselves to survey usage, and to foster an infatuation with pay satisfaction measurement. We recommend moving toward greater usage of qualitative measurement procedures (such as interviews and participant observation) and intensive case studies, being mindful of the rich payoffs that have come from these approaches in early pay research (see Slichter, Healy, & Livernash, 1960; Whyte, 1955). We think they will be particularly useful in initial forays into the study of the many pay practice changes, noted in this chapter, that we have ignored. We must enter the field, rather than merely survey it, if we are fully to understand and appreciate its content and changes. An added benefit is that such research may be more "real" and understandable for practitioners.

Pay Satisfaction Dimensions

Empirical research has shown that employee pay satisfaction exists along at least the relatively separate dimensions of pay level, benefits, and raises. Are there others? This is an important question, particularly given the many changes in pay practices that we have noted. We need to begin conceptualizing if and how employees might perceive other pay amounts, such as variable pay payouts, pay reductions, and overtime.

Pay Satisfaction Measurement

We call for a moratorium on research examining the factor structure and scale intercorrelations of the Pay Satisfaction Questionnaire. The PSQ was developed to test hypotheses about the nature and domain of pay satisfaction (Heneman & Schwab, 1985), not to be a definitive research or survey instrument. Instead we recommend that researchers begin to develop items that attempt to tap the expanded domain of pay satisfaction called for in our discussion and then put those items to confirmatory tests. Out of this will emerge a clearer and agreed-on domain of pay satisfaction, along with some potentially useful instruments that either supplement or replace the PSQ. Many of the studies reviewed here experimented in a sense with new pay satisfaction items through the use of ad hoc measures. While not discouraging such a practice, we would hope that this would be done at least in part with more careful attention being paid to the pay satisfaction domain.

The only exception to this recommended moratorium is research on the cross-cultural dimensionality of pay satisfaction. Since almost all of the studies on pay satisfaction dimensionality have been conducted on American samples, it would be useful for future research to determine whether the structure of pay satisfaction that appears to be so robust in the United States generalizes to other cultures.

Pay Comparisons

It is clear that employees make comparisons and that such comparisons influence their pay satisfaction. We must now move beyond additional replication of these findings. We suggest that researchers investigate (1) whether comparison others chosen differ across the pay satisfaction dimensions (there are some data to support this, summarized in Table 3.1), (2) if use of pay comparisons has any implications for pay satisfaction consequences, and (3) whether and how comparison others may be changed, such as through communication and persuasion attempts.

Antecedents of Pay Satisfaction

We are puzzled by the apparent weak empirical link between objective pay and pay satisfaction. To piece this puzzle together, we recommend further research on the pay level–pay satisfaction linkage where there is large variability in pay level among employees. We speculate that one of the reasons for the weak pay level–pay satisfaction linkage may simply be a reflection of small differences in pay level among employees studied. We also speculate that the linkage may be attenuated by differences among employees in their comparison others. Furthermore, we must move beyond examining only static pay level–pay satisfaction linkages and begin examining how growth in pay level is related to pay satisfaction. The link between pay growth and pay satisfaction may also have behavioral implications, as Trevor, Gerhart, and Boudreau (1997) found with respect to salary growth and turnover.

Beyond pay level, the list of potentially important antecedents of pay satisfaction, particularly if there is a separate set for each pay satisfaction dimension (Miceli & Lane, 1991), is almost endless. We see little value in creating more such lists, unless accompanied by qualitative data from employees about what factors they focus on when evaluating their level of pay satisfaction. We should also use evaluations of pay program changes (see Table 3.2) as naturally occurring situations in which program-induced changes in pay satisfaction are assessed. Since organizations are constantly changing pay programs, simple before-and-after pay satisfaction comparisons (ideally with controls, though realistically unlikely) could be routinely incorporated into the change effort to help us build an accumulated knowledge base of how employees respond to changes in their compensation and how it is delivered to them.

Pay Satisfaction Influences on Outcomes

Research has unequivocally shown that pay dissatisfaction can have important and undesirable impacts on numerous employee outcomes. We need to make further exploration and identification of these pay dissatisfaction–outcome linkages a high priority for future research. Results will help attach practical significance to the study of pay satisfaction, be helpful to organizations in strategically changing their compensation delivery systems, and trigger a resurgence of interest in conducting pay satisfaction research.

To move this research forward, we suggest beginning with the construction of pay dissatisfaction–outcome models for each of the dimensions of pay satisfaction, based on the reasonable assumption that, for example, dissatisfaction with one's pay level may lead to actions different from those caused by dissatisfaction with one's pay raise. Since the equity and discrepancy models are relatively silent on exactly what actions employees are likely to take to reduce feelings of pay dissatisfaction, the newly constructed models would help guide hypothesis formulation and testing in the field.

As these models are being constructed, they need to be more behaviorally specific in terms of likely employee reactions to pay dissatisfaction. An excellent example of the direction we have in mind is provided by Roznowski and Hulin (1992). Their model of job dissatisfaction (though not specifically pay dissatisfaction) postulates that job dissatisfaction may influence four categories of consequences: attempts to increase job outcomes, psychological job withdrawal, behavioral job withdrawal or avoidance, and specific change behavior. Within each category are examples of specific intentions and behaviors that may result from job dissatisfaction. This model could be used as a starting point for construction of the recommended pay dissatisfaction models. Dissatisfaction with pay level, for example, might be hypothesized to cause a person to seek overtime pay (increase job outcomes), reduce inputs such as effort and on-task work time (psychological job withdrawal), increase absences and lateness (behavioral job withdrawal or avoidance), and seek an upgraded job classification (specific change behaviors). Construction of these models would be greatly aided by qualitative research in which employees are asked to describe how they have handled or would likely handle various pay dissatisfaction situations. Undoubtedly, a wide range of specific examples of intention and behavior change would emerge from their responses. Model testing could then proceed by examining employee responses to dissatisfying pay situations in actual field settings, using both survey instruments and qualitative procedures to capture the changes induced in employees.

We should note that, consistent with most pay satisfaction research, we have been considering the implications of pay satisfaction for various outcomes at the individual level of analysis. It would be worthwhile for future research also to consider pay satisfaction–outcome linkages at the organizational level of analysis, as two studies have done with respect to job (not pay) attitudes (Ostroff, 1992; Ryan, Schmit, & Johnson, 1996). Of course, such attempts should be preceded by careful model construction, as called for earlier.

Organization Practices

How concerned are organizations with pay satisfaction, and do they base pay decisions and programs on knowledge of employee pay satisfaction and its impacts on employee outcomes? A recent national survey of employees' satisfaction with pay level, benefits, raises, and other rewards concluded that "although employees are concerned about their pay, they are more concerned about how they are paid. . . . Simply throwing more money at people will not necessarily increase satisfaction with pay. People want to know that the 'system' for administering pay is effective, fair, and inclusive" (Le Blanc & Mulvey, 1998, p. 6). Are these findings and conclusions likely to be treated seriously by organizations and lead them to reevaluate their pay practices? Some recent data from 206 companies indicated that they believed turnover was strongly influenced by dissatisfaction over compensation, that they were using several tools to measure reasons for turnover (exit interviews, employee surveys, employee focus groups, and postemployment interviews), and that 48 percent had changed their compensation programs in the past year, and another 15 percent planned to do so, in order to reduce turnover (Mercer, 1998). Findings such as these suggest some activity by organizations in trying to learn about and change pay satisfaction through alteration of their pay practices. This study prompts us to recommend that we dig deeper to learn about actual organization pay practices and the influence of pay satisfaction on them. Research must more systematically identify how and why organizations come to be concerned about pay satisfaction, how they collect data or otherwise make inferences about pay satisfaction, how they fashion pay policy and program changes in response to pay satisfaction inputs, and how often they actually evaluate the impact of such changes on pay satisfaction.

Organizational Justice

A few years ago, one of us conducted a survey of 230 university employees. One of the questions on the survey asked employees what salary they thought they should be paid. When this figure was compared to the employees' actual salaries, perhaps not surprisingly, only two employees (less than 1 percent) thought they were overpaid. More surprising was the fact that less than 15 percent of employees felt they were paid what they deserved. Eighty-four percent of employees felt they were underpaid, by an average of 19 percent.

Distributive and Procedural Justice

Assuming that these results are an accurate description of the way most employees feel about their pay—and we think they are—they point to an interesting fact about pay satisfaction: The vast majority of employees feel they are unfairly compensated by their employers. How can one explain this little discussed (but implicitly understood) reality, and what are its consequences? This is where the literature on organizational justice enters the picture.

As alluded to earlier, research on organizational justice indicates that employees may make two judgments about the fairness of their treatment by their employers: distributive justice and procedural justice. Distributive justice is said to concern the degree to which employees perceive their pay as fair ("Is my salary fair?" "Did I receive the raise I deserve?" "Are my benefits equitably distributed?"). Procedural justice is said to concern the perceived fairness of the means or methods used to determine the amount of pay (Folger & Konovsky, 1989). Although there is reason to expect that procedural and distributive justice are related (Sweeney & McFarlin, 1993), with respect to pay, distributive justice concerns *what* one is paid while procedural justice concerns *how* one is paid. As writers in the area of organizational justice have noted, historically researchers have been much more concerned with distributive than with procedural justice.

Fairness, whether considered in terms of distributive or procedural justice, is central to pay satisfaction. As will be reviewed shortly, employees' attitudes are more affected by the perceived fairness of how their pay is determined than the actual level of pay itself. For example, Alexander and Ruderman (1987) found that federal government employees' concerns about how they were paid was a more important predictor of overall job satisfaction that what they actually received in pay. Similarly, Berkowitz and colleagues (1987) found that perceptions of inequity negatively predicted pay satisfaction. These studies suggest that researchers have been remiss in ignoring the effect of procedural justice on pay satisfaction.

Justice Perceptions and Pay Satisfaction

Despite the potentially important role of procedural justice, a number of studies have shown that perceptions of distributive justice are more strongly correlated with pay satisfaction than perceptions of procedural justice are. Folger and Konovsky (1989) found that controlling for procedural justice perceptions, distributive justice perceptions explained twice as much incremental variance in pay raise satisfaction (18.7 percent) as procedural justice perceptions controlling for distributive justice perceptions (8.6 percent) did. McFarlin and Sweeney (1992), in a study of 675 midwestern bank employees, found that distributive justice perceptions correlated .63 with pay level satisfaction, whereas procedural justice perceptions correlated .51 with pay level satisfaction. Similarly, the same researchers' study of 188 engineers working in an electric utility company (Sweeney & McFarlin, 1993) determined that distributive justice perceptions were more strongly correlated with overall pay satisfaction ($r = .44$) than procedural justice perceptions ($r = .24$) were. Finally, Scarpello and Jones (1996), in a study of 612 county government salaried employees, found that perceptions of outcome fairness strongly predicted pay satisfaction ($\beta = .80$), whereas perceptions of procedural fairness did not ($\beta = .08$). Thus although procedural justice and distributive justice are important to pay satisfaction, distributive justice perceptions are relatively more important.

Practical Implications of Justice Perceptions

When one considers the behavioral consequences of organizational justice, both procedural and distributive justice appear to be relevant. Greenberg (1990) found that in several manufacturing plants experiencing a temporary 15 percent pay cut, the workers felt underpaid and theft rates were as much as 250 percent higher than normal. Greenberg found that theft increased in all the plants experiencing a pay cut, but theft was much higher in the plants where little explanation was given for the pay cut (low procedural justice). Another study by Greenberg (1993) found that when students were faced with distributive injustice in a laboratory experiment (given less pay than they were promised) and were given the opportunity to steal, many students did steal. However, procedural justice substantially moderated this relationship—when the students were given a valid explanation for the underpayment and when the experimenter displayed interpersonal sensitivity (expressed regret about the situation), the amount of stealing virtually disappeared. So even if distributive justice is a more important predictor of pay satisfaction, both procedural and distributive justice appear to be critical factors in predicting behavioral responses to pay dissatisfaction.

These results have clear implications for employers. In many situations, an employer cannot avoid treating some employees adversely with respect to their pay. However, the negative consequences of these actions are substantially (though not totally) mitigated by the ability of the employer to provide a procedurally just explanation for the actions. How can employers explain negative compensation decisions? Leventhal (1980) has identified several components of fair reward allocation procedures. Extrapolating from Leventhal's research, pay policies that are distributively fair should be free from bias, based on accurate information, consistent across persons and over time, correctable (open to appeals), and representative of employee concerns. The implication of these components to compensation practices is direct. When confronted with pay decisions likely to be seen as unfair to employees, employers should attempt where possible to adhere to these pay policies. If they do, adverse consequences to distributive injustices may be substantially mitigated.

Directions for Future Compensation Justice Research

Research is needed in several areas regarding organizational justice and pay satisfaction. The most compelling areas for future research are reviewed here.

Clarifying Constructs and Their Relationships

In considering the role of justice in pay satisfaction research, there appears to be something of a paradox in the literature. On the one hand, research consistently suggests that procedural justice perceptions have a more important influence than distributive justice perceptions on overall ratings of fairness. In fact, Greenberg (1987) showed that procedural fairness had a relatively strong effect on distributive justice perceptions, whereas distributive fairness had relatively little effect on procedural justice perceptions. On the other hand, distributive justice perceptions consistently correlate more highly with pay satisfaction than procedural justice perceptions do (Folger & Konovsky, 1989; McFarlin & Sweeney, 1992; Scarpello & Jones, 1996; Sweeney & McFarlin, 1993). What might explain this apparent incongruity? One potential explanation is that whereas distributive justice is influenced by procedural justice (and not vice versa) and procedural justice is a more important influence on overall justice perceptions than distributive justice, distributive justice is the more proximal influence on pay satisfaction. The resulting model could be depicted as follows:

PROCEDURAL JUSTICE → DISTRIBUTIVE JUSTICE →
PAY SATISFACTION

If this model is an accurate depiction of reality, it does not mean that procedural justice is irrelevant to pay satisfaction. Rather, it would indicate that most of the influence of procedural justice on pay satisfaction is mediated through its direct effect on distributive justice. Since procedural justice has a strong influence on distributive justice, this means that procedural justice cannot be ignored, even though its influence on pay satisfaction is comparatively weaker.

Another important aspect of the relationship between organizational justice and pay satisfaction relates to construct correspondence (Hulin, 1991). Since organizational justice is a more general construct than procedural and distributive justice, and overall pay satisfaction has four specific facets, perhaps the procedural and distributive justice facets should be linked to different facets of pay satisfaction. For example, it seems plausible that distributive justice would correlate more highly with the facets pertaining to the amount of compensation received (pay level satisfaction, raise satisfaction, and benefits satisfaction), while procedural justice would correlate more highly with satisfaction with the way in which pay is administered (structure and administration satisfaction). Under this hypothesis, distributive justice would be more strongly related to three of the four facets of pay satisfaction, which would be consistent with the higher correlations between distributive (versus procedural) justice and overall pay satisfaction.

As an alternative to the model just described, positing an indirect effect of procedural justice and a direct effect of distributive justice on pay satisfaction, we might imagine another possible view of these constructs. Because pay satisfaction refers to satisfaction with the amount of pay received in the form of level, raises, benefits, and structure (Heneman & Schwab, 1985), the focus is on the actual amount received and how it compares to referent others. For all practical purposes, then, it could be argued that pay satisfaction is identical to distributive justice. Procedural justice, alternatively, refers to the processes and procedures used by organizations to deliver pay amounts to jobs and to individuals. This is similar to Heneman's "pay policies and administration" modification to the pay satisfaction model (1985) and the Miceli and Lane (1991) "system" models. Thus rather than distributive justice and pay satisfaction being distinct constructs that are causally related, it is possible they are indistinct constructs. To clarify some of this construct confusion, future research is needed.

Determinants of Fairness Perceptions

Although fairness perceptions appear to be strongly related to pay satisfaction, this does not address the question of how employees come to feel that their pay is unfair to begin with. To be sure, it is easy to design experiments where unequal treatment in manipulated. However, in actual organizational contexts, the situation would appear to be much more complex. Research on equity theory reveals that employees do feel unfairly treated when they receive lower-than-expected outcomes. However, when employees are over-rewarded, the dissatisfaction or guilt predicted by the theory does not materialize. In fact, Miceli, Jung, Near, and Greenberger (1991) found that perceived overreward led to more positive reactions to pay than perceived equitable reward or underreward did. Thus more research is needed on the factors that cause employees to feel unfairly compensated, whether these factors appear "objectively" unfair, and if not, what personal and contextual circumstances influence the interpretation of fairness. Because equity is multi-dimensional construct (Tremblay, Saint-Onge, & Toulouse, 1997), it would also be useful to consider the relative importance of various conceptions of equity in judgments of pay satisfaction.

Methodological Issues

Research linking justice perceptions to pay satisfaction has suffered from several methodological limitations. Nearly all of the data in these studies have been collected from the same survey at the same point in time, raising questions about the degree to which common method variance may underlie the associations. Furthermore, the presumed causal ordering among the variables is open to question. It has been assumed that justice leads to pay satisfaction, but given the methodological designs, the opposite causality seems equally likely. Dissatisfied employees may simply attribute their dissatisfaction to unfair circumstances. More sophisticated research designs would be capable of answering these questions.

Determining Which Justice Perceptions Are Most Important

The relative importance of procedural and distributive justice in pay satisfaction research needs further clarification. Distributive justice predicts pay satisfaction better than procedural justice, yet procedural justice appears critical in predicting how employees will restore equity in response to distributive injustice. Thus it is possible that the relative importance of procedural and distributive justice may be different in predicting pay satisfaction (and pay dissatisfaction) versus the responses to pay dissatisfaction. Future research and theoretical development are needed here as well.

Centrality of Equity Theory–Based Models

Finally, by both historical (discrepancy models) and contemporary (justice theory) standards, fairness is a central construct (perhaps even the central construct) in pay satisfaction research. On the one hand, this focus seems warranted. It is difficult to imagine an employee who believes he or she is unfairly paid reporting a high degree of pay satisfaction. Both research on equity models and practical experience suggest that perceptions of unfairness and dissatisfaction with respect to pay often go together.

On the other hand, there is something unsatisfying about this focus. One of the fundamental problems with equity theory is that what is deemed fair by one person is often not regarded as fair by another. Equity theory attempts to deal with differing conceptions of equity via the choice of referents—who is chosen as a referent other will explain why two people with the same outcome-input ratio will feel differentially satisfied. Unfortunately, equity theory—and hence discrepancy and justice models—do not help us understand why people choose the referents they do (Ash & Bretz, 1988). Yet this choice is fundamental to perceptions of fairness and, by implication, pay satisfaction. Choosing the most successful individual in one's field as one's pay referent, as opposed to the least successful person in one's organization, will "tell the tale" of one's pay satisfaction. Thus perceptions of fairness are an integral part (whether a cause or an attribution) of pay satisfaction, and referent choice is an integral part of perceptions of fairness. Yet until we understand more clearly why people choose to focus on particular referents to the exclusion of others, the value of discrepancy and justice models in explaining pay satisfaction will be limited.

Pay Preferences: What Do Employees and Applicants Want?

As informative as the literature on the relationship between pay program characteristics and pay satisfaction has been (see Table 3.2), it does not present a complete picture of what employees want with respect to their pay. It is one thing to relate current pay system characteristics, or changes in them, to pay satisfaction. It is quite another to ask employees to state their preferences for pay or benefit systems or for the types of pay they would find satisfying. Surprisingly little research has addressed this issue. The closest approximation is research on pay preferences among employees and job applicants, which we will review.

Unfortunately, only a handful of studies have investigated applicant and employee pay preferences. Turban and Keon (1993) found that hypothetical job applicants (college students) expressed a relatively strong preference for merit-based (as opposed to tenure-based) reward systems. This effect was particularly strong for students who scored high on need for achievement. Bretz and Judge (1994) found that job applicants preferred individual-based incentive systems. These two studies suggest that applicants prefer individual merit pay to team-based or tenure-based reward systems.

Not only do applicants prefer individual merit pay to other forms of pay delivery systems, but they also prefer that their pay be fixed. A national survey completed a decade ago revealed that 63 percent of employees surveyed preferred a fixed wage or salary (Bureau of National Affairs, 1988). Consistent with these findings, Cable and Judge (1994) found that individuals, when evaluating hypothetical as well as actual jobs, expressed preferences for individual versus group-based pay, fixed versus contingent pay, and flexible versus rigid benefits. Cable and Judge also found that personality characteristics moderated these preferences. For example, individualistic job applicants expressed stronger preferences for individual-based pay, risk-averse applicants more strongly preferred fixed pay, and individuals with an internal locus of control were more likely to prefer flexible benefits.

Thus when looking for jobs, college-educated individuals appear to prefer jobs where pay is based on individual (rather than group or organizational) performance (rather than seniority), where the pay based is stable (not at risk), and where employees have some control over the choice of their benefits. Do these studies of job-seeking college students generalize to a wide range of employees? A recent study of a nationally representative sample of workers suggests that they do. As the authors of this study commented, "U.S. workers today want rewards to be focused on the individual—not the team, group, or company—and they want increased pay to be fixed, that is, delivered to their base pay rather than in the form of one-time payments such as bonuses or incentives" (Le Blanc & Mulvey, 1998, p. 5).

Directions for Future Pay Preferences Research

Research on pay preferences has provided a modest degree of insight into the pay system characteristics that tend to satisfy (and dissatisfy) individuals. There are a number of areas requiring further research.

Combinations of Pay System Characteristics

How do pay system characteristics combine one with the other? For example, though employees may prefer fixed (stable base) pay, would they be more amenable to variable pay if it is based on individual performance? Are group-based pay plans more acceptable to employees if such plans include a clear link between group performance and pay? Very few studies have considered possible combinations among pay system characteristics. However, given that few of these characteristics operate in isolation, more work in this area is needed.

Trade-Offs in Achieving Optimal Pay Mix

Similarly, research is needed into trade-offs between pay system strategies and characteristics. For example, many organizations cannot afford to continue a policy of merit pay, at least at the same level of increases as employees have been accustomed to. Thus to control compensation costs, organizations are often forced to choose among several alternatives, such as reducing the raise pool, delivering pay in the form of bonuses rather than rolling the increase into base pay, or devising a variable pay scheme. Evidence suggests that employees do not like any of these options. Yet some options, for a particular organization, are probably more tenable than others. More research is needed into trade-offs—if an organization must lower its compensation expenditures, which option or options will lead to the least dissatisfaction?

Relative Importance of Pay

When people are asked about their pay, they seem to downgrade the importance of pay relative to other job attributes. As was noted earlier, the relationship between pay level and pay (and overall job) satisfaction is relatively weak. Furthermore, when asked to rank various job attributes, pay level typically falls far down the list (see Jurgensen, 1978). Although some of these findings are quite dated and the issue of the importance of pay to employees has been dormant for quite a long time, we think the topic is ripe for reexamination. It is clear from the data reviewed in this chapter that pay is in fact important to people. It influences their pay satisfaction (albeit not strongly), and more important, it influences numerous behaviors. So will employees in today's work environments continue to tell us that pay is an unimportant work outcome to them, and if so, why? From an organizational perspective, strategic choices about pay delivery are based on implicit premises about how important pay is to employees and how much they are likely to respond to it. Is an organization better off investing a given amount of money in a pay raise or in providing better working conditions and more challenging jobs? Or how much of an increase should an organization provide in order to compensate employees for increased travel and weekend work? Answers to these questions are inextricably bound to the relative importance of pay to individuals; framed this way, learning more about the relative importance of pay to people is an imperative if we are ultimately to learn how to use pay more effectively.

Individual Differences

Although a small literature has accumulated on individual differences in pay preferences, room for future work remains. For example, surprisingly little research has examined the role of job performance in pay preferences. High-performing employees are the core of any business. Yet we know little about what they prefer in terms of pay and pay systems. It is possible that high performers' preferences are generally aligned with average or below-average performers; it is just as possible that their preferences diverge. Also, although the "Big Five" personality characteristics are currently very popular in personnel selection, little is known about how these characteristics influence pay preferences. For example, are neurotic employees likely to react more negatively to pay at risk? Are agreeable or extroverted individuals more attracted to group-based pay plans? Future research is needed on these and other individual differences.

Applicant Attraction Strategies

Organizations are constantly adjusting their pay and benefits systems. Many of these adjustments are made in an attempt to align pay practices more closely with applicant pay preferences. One example is the increased use of signing bonuses. Another example is the proliferation of work-family benefits. To what extent do these applicant-driven inducements lead to more favorable organizational outcomes—higher job offer acceptance rates, greater pay satisfaction, and more favorable retention? Though it is frequently believed that such links in fact exist, they have yet to be fully demonstrated empirically.

Considering the other side of this issue, what about organizations that make changes in their compensation plans that are unpopular with job applicants? For example, it was noted earlier that individuals do not like team-based pay, yet this is a direction in which many organizations have moved. Is this leading to decreases in employee job offer acceptance rates, decreased pay satisfaction, and higher turnover? Are certain types of employees more positively responsive to team-based pay? Again, the links need to be investigated.

Finally, beyond their direct preferences for certain types of pay systems, little is known about the inferences applicants make about a company based on its pay level and pay system. Do applicants believe that an organization that places some of their pay at risk has an entrepreneurial culture? Are these inferences warranted, and how do they affect applicants?

International Comparisons

Almost all of the research that has been conducted on pay preferences has studied U.S. workers. Given that values differ widely across cultures, it seems unlikely that the pay system characteristics that satisfy American workers will be the same as those in another culture. The United States is the most individualistic nation in the world (Hofstede, 1980). Thus the preference of American workers for individual-based pay plans is not surprising. However, workers in collectivistic cultures (especially in Asia and South America) may actually dislike individual-based pay plans. Furthermore, even the relative importance and satisfaction potential of pay may differ across cultures. Finally, given the growth in expatriate assignments, another issue worthy of further study is the pay satisfaction of expatriates and host-country nationals.

Because most expatriates are amply rewarded as inducements for their assignments, one wonders whether local employees in the host country feel unfairly compensated relative to the expatriates. The pay satisfaction of local nationals relative to expatriates has been little studied. Future research in all of these areas is needed.

Conclusion

This chapter has focused on pay attitude research since Heneman's 1985 review. We are impressed by the progress we have made on several fronts. We have successfully begun mapping out a multidimensional pay satisfaction domain that has helped us understand that employees truly do respond differentially to various aspects of their compensation environment as it is administered by organizations. Further, pay satisfaction is not simply or primarily a matter of how much pay is received; rather, it involves pay comparison processes that greatly complicate the prediction of how satisfied people are with their pay. We have also learned that pay satisfaction has a direct and important impact on several employee outcomes of concern to the organization. This issue of justice or fairness in pay has also entered into research on pay attitudes, with justice being conceived of in distributive and procedural terms. Though these constructs await greater clarification, distributive justice appears analogous to satisfaction with amount of pay received, and procedural justice is a matter of pay processes and how fairly they are administered. Finally, the long-simmering question of how important pay is to employees has resurfaced. This is a fundamental issue that underlies virtually all compensation strategies and activities of organizations, and hence its reappearance is welcomed.

The pay attitude research we reviewed has clearly shown that pay attitudes are important to study and that an escalation of pay attitude research is warranted. We also hope that through better model building and more varied methodologies, the quality and organizational relevance of that research will improve. We especially urge that concerns of organizational usefulness remain foremost in researchers' minds so that our research becomes more visible and serves as a better foundation for compensation strategies and programs of the future.

References

Adams, J. S. (1965). Inequity in social exchange. In L. Berkowitz (Ed.), *Advances in experimental social psychology* (Vol. 2, pp. 267–299). Orlando, FL: Academic Press.

Alexander, S., & Ruderman, M. (1987). The role of procedural and distributive justice in organizational behavior. *Social Justice Research, 1,* 177–198.

Ash, R. A., & Bretz, R. D., Jr. (1988, April). *A multifocus equity theory model of compensation satisfaction.* Paper presented at the annual meeting of the Society for Industrial and Organizational Psychology, Dallas, TX.

Ash, R. A., Dreher, G. F., & Bretz, R. D., Jr. (1987, April). *Dimensionality and stability of the pay satisfaction questionnaire.* Paper presented at the annual meeting of the Society for Industrial and Organizational Psychology, Atlanta.

Barber, A. E., Dunham, R. B., & Formisano, R. A. (1992). The impact of flexible benefits on employee satisfaction: A field study. *Personnel Psychology, 45,* 55–75.

Barber, A. E., & Roehling, M. V. (1993). Job postings and the decision to interview: A verbal protocol analysis. *Journal of Applied Psychology, 78,* 845–856.

Berkowitz, L., Fraser, C., Treasure, F. P., & Cochran, S. (1987). Pay, equity, job gratifications, and comparisons in pay satisfaction. *Journal of Applied Psychology, 72,* 544–551.

Bretz, R. D., Jr., & Judge, T. A. (1994). The role of human resource systems in job applicant decision processes. *Journal of Management, 20,* 531–551.

Bretz, R. D., Jr., & Thomas, S. L. (1992). Perceived equity, motivation, and final-offer arbitration in major league baseball. *Journal of Applied Psychology, 77,* 280–287.

Brown, K. A., & Huber, V. L. (1992). Lowering floors and raising ceilings: A longitudinal assessment of the effects of an earnings-at-risk plan on pay satisfaction. *Personnel Psychology, 45,* 279–311.

Bureau of National Affairs. (1988). Changing pay practices: New developments in employee compensation. *Labor Relations Week, 2,* 575–588.

Cable, D. M., & Judge, T. A. (1994). Pay preferences and job search decisions: A person-organization fit perspective. *Personnel Psychology, 47,* 317–348.

Cappelli, P., & Sherer, P. D. (1990). Assessing worker attitudes under a two-tier wage plan. *Industrial and Labor Relations Review, 43,* 225–244.

Carraher, S. M. (1991). On the dimensionality of the pay satisfaction questionnaire. *Psychological Reports, 69,* 887–890.

Carraher, S. M., & Buckley, M. R. (1996). Cognitive complexity and the perceived dimensionality of pay satisfaction. *Journal of Applied Psychology, 81,* 102–109.

Davy, J. A., & Shipper, F. (1993). Voter behavior in union certification elections: A longitudinal study. *Academy of Management Journal, 36,* 187–199.

Dreher, G. F., Ash, R. A., & Bretz, R. D., Jr. (1988). Benefit coverage and employee cost: Critical factors in explaining compensation satisfaction. *Personnel Psychology, 41,* 237–254.

Folger, R., & Greenberg, J. (1985). Procedural justice: An interpretive analysis of personnel systems. In K. M. Rowland & G. R. Ferris (Eds.), *Research in personnel and human resources management* (Vol. 3, pp. 141–184). Greenwich, CT: JAI Press.

Folger, R., & Konovsky, M. A. (1989). Effects of procedural and distributive justice on reactions to pay raise decisions. *Academy of Management Journal, 32,* 115–130.

Gerhart, B., & Rynes, S. L. (1991). Determinants and consequences of salary negotiations by male and female M.B.A. graduates. *Journal of Applied Psychology, 76,* 256–262.

Greenberg, J. (1987). Reactions to procedural injustice in payment distributions: Do the means justify the ends? *Journal of Applied Psychology, 72,* 55–61.

Greenberg, J. (1990). Employee theft as a reaction to underpayment inequity: The hidden cost of pay cuts. *Journal of Applied Psychology, 75,* 561–568.

Greenberg, J. (1993). Stealing in the name of justice: Informational and interpersonal moderators of theft reactions to underpayment inequity. *Organizational Behavior and Human Decision Processes, 54,* 81–103.

Heneman, H. G., III. (1985). Pay satisfaction. In K. M. Rowland & G. R. Ferris (Eds.), *Research in personnel and human resources management* (Vol. 3, pp. 115–140). Greenwich, CT: JAI Press.

Heneman, H. G., III, & Milanowski, A. (1998, March). *Employees' withdrawal responses to their individual base pay and group incentive pay systems.* Paper presented at the meeting of the Southern Management Association, New Orleans.

Heneman, H. G., III, & Schwab, D. P. (1979). Work and rewards theory. In D. Yoder & H. G. Heneman Jr. (Eds.), *ASPA handbook of personnel and industrial relations* (pp. 6–1–6–22). Washington, DC: Bureau of National Affairs.

Heneman, H. G., III, & Schwab, D. P. (1985). Pay satisfaction: Its multidimensional nature and measurement. *International Journal of Psychology, 20,* 129–142.

Heneman, R. L., Greenberger, D. B., & Strasser, S. (1988). The relationship between pay-for-performance perceptions and pay satisfaction. *Personnel Psychology, 41,* 745–759.

Heneman, R. L., Porter, G., Greenberger, D. B., & Strasser, S. (1997). Modeling the relationship between pay level and pay satisfaction. *Journal of Business and Psychology, 12,* 147–158.

Hindman, H. D., & Smith, C. G. (1993). Correlates of union membership and joining intentions in a unit of federal employees. *Journal of Labor Research, 14,* 439–454.

Hofstede, G. (1980). *Culture's consequences.* Thousand Oaks, CA: Sage.

Hulin, C. L. (1991). Adaptation, persistence, and commitment in organizations. In M. D. Dunnette & L. M. Hough (Eds.), *Handbook of industrial and organizational psychology* (2nd ed., Vol. 2, pp. 445–505). Palo Alto, CA: Consulting Psychologists Press.

Judge, T. A. (1993). Validity of the dimensions of the pay satisfaction questionnaire: Evidence of differential prediction. *Personnel Psychology, 46,* 331–355.

Judge, T. A., & Welbourne, T. M. (1994). A confirmatory investigation of the dimensionality of the pay satisfaction questionnaire. *Journal of Applied Psychology, 79,* 461–466.

Jurgensen, C. E. (1978). Job preferences (What makes a job good or bad?). *Journal of Applied Psychology, 50,* 479–487.

Klein, K. J. (1987). Employee stock ownership and employee attitudes: A test of three models. *Journal of Applied Psychology, 72,* 319–332.

Koslowsky, M., Sagie, A., Krausz, M., & Singer, A. D. (1997). Correlates of employee lateness: Some theoretical considerations. *Journal of Applied Psychology, 82,* 79–88.

Lane, M. C. (1993, January). *The effect of employee benefit satisfaction on organizational consequences.* Paper presented at the annual meeting of the Industrial Relations Research Association, Anaheim, CA.

Lawler, E. E., III. (1971). *Pay and organizational effectiveness.* New York: McGraw-Hill.

Lawler, E. E., III. (1981). *Pay and organizational development.* Reading, MA: Addison-Wesley.

Le Blanc, P. V., & Mulvey, P. W. (1998). How American workers see the rewards of work. *Compensation and Benefits Review, 30,* 1–6.

Leventhal, G. S. (1980). What should be done with equity theory? In K. J. Gergen, M. S. Greenberg, & R. H. Willis (Eds.), *Social exchange: Advances in theory and research* (pp. 27–55). New York: Plenum.

Martin, J. E., & Peterson, M. M. (1987). Two-tier wage structures: Implications for equity theory. *Academy of Management Journal, 30,* 297–315.

McFarlin, D. B., & Sweeney, P. D. (1992). Distributive and procedural justice as predictors of satisfaction with personal and organizational outcomes. *Academy of Management Journal, 35,* 626–637.

Mercer, W. M. (1998, April 16). The costs of churning: A Mercer survey on turnover. *Mercer Report,* pp. 4–5.

Miceli, M. P., & Lane, M. C. (1991). Antecedents of pay satisfaction: A review and extension. In K. M. Rowland & G. R. Ferris (Eds.), *Research in personnel and human resources management* (Vol. 9, pp. 235–309). Greenwich, CT: JAI Press.

Miceli, M. P., Jung, I., Near, J. P., & Greenberger, D. B. (1991). Predictors and outcomes of reactions to pay-for-performance plans. *Journal of Applied Psychology, 76,* 508–521.

Mulvey, P. W., Miceli, M. P., & Near, J. P. (1992). The pay satisfaction questionnaire: A confirmatory factor analysis. *Journal of Social Psychology, 132,* 139–141.

Oldham, G. R., Kulik, C. T., Stepina, L. P., & Ambrose, M. L. (1986). Relations between situational factors and the comparative referents used by employees. *Academy of Management Journal, 29,* 599–608.

Orpen, C., & Bonnici, J. (1987). A factor analytic investigation of the pay satisfaction questionnaire. *Journal of Social Psychology, 127,* 391–392.

Ostroff, C. (1992). The relationship between satisfaction, attitudes, and performance: An organizational-level analysis. *Journal of Applied Psychology, 77,* 963–974.

Petty, M. M., Singleton, B., & Connell, D. W. (1992). An experimental evaluation of an organizational incentive plan in the electric utility industry. *Journal of Applied Psychology, 77,* 427–436.

Rice, R. W., Phillips, S. M., & McFarlin, D. B. (1990). Multiple discrepancies and pay satisfaction. *Journal of Applied Psychology, 75,* 386–393.

Roznowski, M., & Hulin, C. L. (1992). The scientific merit of valid measures of general constructs with special reference to job satisfaction and job withdrawal. In C. J. Cranny, P. C. Smith, & E. F. Stone (Eds.), *Job satisfaction* (pp. 123–164). San Francisco: New Lexington Press.

Ryan, A. M., Schmit, M. S., & Johnson, R. (1996). Attitudes and effectiveness: Examining relations at an organizational level. *Personnel Psychology, 49,* 853–882.

Scarpello, V., & Jones, F. F. (1996). Why justice matters in compensation decision making. *Journal of Organizational Behavior, 17,* 285–299.

Scarpello, V., Huber, V. L., & Vandenberg, R. J. (1988). Compensation satisfaction: Its measurement and dimensionality. *Journal of Applied Psychology, 73,* 163–171.

Shippmann, J. S., & Hartmann, S. (1995). SIOP customer survey results: II. *Industrial-Organizational Psychologist, 33*(2), 37–42.

Slichter, S. H., Healy, J. J., & Livernash, E. R. (1960). *The impact of collective bargaining on management.* Washington, DC: Brookings Institution.

Sweeney, P. D., & McFarlin, D. B. (1993). Workers' evaluations of the "ends" and the "means": An examination of four models of distributive and procedural justice. *Organizational Behavior and Human Decision Processes, 55,* 23–40.

Sweeney, P. D., McFarlin, D. B., & Interrieden, E. J. (1990). Using relative deprivation theory to explain satisfaction with income and pay level: A multistudy examination. *Academy of Management Journal, 33,* 423–436.

Tremblay, M., Saint-Onge, S., & Toulouse, J. (1997). Determinants of salary referents relevance: A field study of managers. *Journal of Business and Psychology, 11,* 463–484.

Trevor, C. O., Gerhart, B., & Boudreau, J. W. (1997). Voluntary turnover and job performance: Curvilinearity and the moderating influences of salary growth and promotion. *Journal of Applied Psychology, 82,* 44–61.

Turban, D. B., & Keon, T. L. (1993). Organizational attractiveness: An interactionist perspective. *Journal of Applied Psychology, 78,* 184–193.

Williams, M. L. (1995). Determinants of employee benefit level satisfaction: Tests of a model. *Journal of Management, 21,* 1097–1128.

Whyte, W. F. (1955). *Money and motivation.* New York: HarperCollins.

CHAPTER 4

Incentives and Motivation

Kathryn M. Bartol
Edwin A. Locke

The problem of how to motivate people to work by means of monetary incentives has been a primary concern of owners and managers since the beginning of the industrial revolution. The fact that the problem has never been fully solved is a reflection of its complexity.

One major challenge in using incentives to motivate is the dynamic nature of organizations and competitive environments. A plan that yields competitive advantage today can be copied by others tomorrow. An above-market wage in one year may be below-market the next. What works for one type of product, technology, or market might not work for another. It has taken generations of trial and error to explore various options and begin to identify the advantages and disadvantages of each. Meanwhile, new approaches continue to emerge.

A second major challenge in understanding the effectiveness of monetary incentives is the existence of differing views regarding the nature of fairness or justice. People disagree as to what they consider just, and these views also change over time.

Nevertheless, because pay systems are an essential part of every profit-making enterprise and most nonprofit organizations, understanding what makes such systems effective is critical. Our understanding has increased as studies of incentive systems and incentive theories have multiplied over the past fifty years.

In this chapter, we summarize the major theories that are relevant to the design of pay and incentive systems, identify the principles that can be induced from such theories, and offer suggestions for future research.

Incentives and Motivation Theory

Deci and Ryan Theory

Deci and Ryan (1985) argue that extrinsic rewards undermine intrinsic motivation by undermining the needs for autonomy and self-determination. They conducted experiments in which, typically, one group of subjects was rewarded for performing a task and then was allowed to continue to perform the task, at will, after the incentive was withdrawn. Subjects in this condition spent less "free" time on the task than those who had not been rewarded in the first place.

Although the early experiments seemed to support Deci and Ryan's predictions, later research revealed that there were numerous contingencies that affected the outcome of these intrinsic motivation studies. The most recent and complete meta-analysis of intrinsic motivation studies was conducted by Eisenberger and Cameron (1996). They found that free time spent on the task was reduced only when the reward was tangible (material), expected, and independent of performance. When tangible rewards were dependent on performance, there was no detrimental effect of reward. When rewards were verbal (for example, recognition), intrinsic motivation was enhanced. They also found that reported task interest and satisfaction were not undermined in any condition. Attitudes were enhanced when the reward was verbal and when the tangible reward was dependent on performance quality.

It is worth asking which of these two dependent variables is more theoretically relevant and valid. Deci and Ryan (1985) prefer the performance criterion (free time spent on the task), even though they have used satisfaction as the variable of interest (Deci, Connell, & Ryan, 1989). Bandura (1986) and Eisenberger and Cameron (1996) have noted that there are certain risks in the use of free time spent on the task in that people may continue or stop working on a task for many different reasons. For example, the withdrawal of a reward, due to the contrast effect, may be experienced as punishing. Furthermore, positive attitudes do not necessarily improve performance. Thus measuring both types of outcomes seems advisable.

The central problems associated with Deci and Ryan's theory, however, are more theoretical than experimental.

Control

Deci and Ryan (1985) claim that incentives undermine self-determination when and because they are "controlling." However, to the authors' knowledge, they have never validated the claim that loss of control is the mediating factor using an action measure as the dependent variable. It is paradoxical, in relation to the theory, that hourly (non-performance-based) pay undermines intrinsic motivation whereas incentive pay, which allegedly "forces" one to perform in order to get the money, does not (Eisenberger & Cameron, 1996).

Although obvious, it is important to stress that monetary incentives consist only of inanimate matter—or more precisely, potential inanimate matter. They cannot control anything unless the individual values them and chooses to pursue them. It is puzzling that the need for autonomy and self-determination, which Deci and Ryan consider to be the core of human motivation, can be, according to them, overwhelmed so readily, not only by money but by virtually every social situation people encounter daily (including goals, standards, deadlines, pressure, conflict, negative feedback, obligations, external appraisals, surveillance, anxiety, and ego involvement). Such a fragile need would be of dubious importance in the grand scheme of human life.

Self-Efficacy

Deci and Ryan acknowledge that rewards can have an informational aspect in addition to a controlling aspect. Information that implies competency (for example, pay given for high performance), they argue, can enhance intrinsic motivation, although they never make clear how one knows when the controlling or the informational aspect is most salient or how the two opposing forces combine.

It is also clear that the concept of self-efficacy (task-specific confidence) should play a critical role in their theory, but it is not acknowledged explicitly. Self-efficacy is a key concept in Bandura's social cognitive theory (1986, 1997); he has documented the critical role played by self-efficacy in human motivation and action. Bandura (1997) has shown that if individuals do not think they can perform at the level required to get a reward, the reward will be ineffective. In some cases, efficacy may need to be enhanced (through various procedures such as training, role modeling, and persuasion) before an incentive system can work. By building efficacy, managers can not only make people more confident of being able to earn rewards but can also make employees resilient in the face of negative feedback, failures, and external pressures. When employees develop enough efficacy to attain higher performance and thereby receive higher rewards, self-efficacy and therefore motivation should be enhanced further.

The Concept of Intrinsic Motivation

There is great confusion about what intrinsic motivation actually is. Implicitly, it is used to refer to two things: enjoyment of the task activity itself and enjoyment of confronting and overcoming challenges and attaining a standard of excellence. The proper name for the second type of motivation is *achievement motivation* as McClelland (1961) originally conceived it. It is a mistake to treat the two types as synonymous. Enjoyment of an activity is different from being explicitly goal-oriented. In the case of true intrinsic motivation, the pleasure comes from the action itself (for example, taking a walk). In the case of achievement motivation, the pleasure comes from performing well in relation to a standard.

Research by Amabile (1993), who, like Deci and Ryan, defines intrinsic motivation as involving both task enjoyment and challenge, found that when she tried to develop trait measures of the various Deci and Ryan concepts, the "intrinsic" items clustered into two scales, which she labeled "enjoyment" and "challenge," thus validating further the distinction made here. Interestingly, the extrinsic items also clustered into two factors: "recognition" and "compensation." (This last is consonant with Eisenberger and Cameron's finding that verbal recognition and money rewards had somewhat different effects.) Amabile suggests that some types of extrinsic incentives enhanced motivation (reward for creative ideas, clear goals, feedback), whereas other types (win-lose competition, negative feedback, constraints) undermined it.

Ideally, one could presume that the highest level of performance and satisfaction would result when intrinsic, achievement, and extrinsic motivation (of the right type) were all high, as when one got paid and recognized for something that was fun and involved high standards of excellence, especially if one had a high sense of efficacy for the task in question. However, this "summative" model (see also Gerhart & Milkovich, 1992) implies a very different view of motivation than that of Deci and Ryan.

Generalizability

It is not clear that the Deci and Ryan theory can be generalized to ordinary work settings. Studies of intrinsic motivation are generally conducted in laboratory settings in which rewards are given to the experimental group and then withdrawn. This contradicts an essential feature of real organizational settings in which the actions of interest are those that occur when the incentives are in operation. Except in volunteer organizations, people are not expected to work for free. Thus what people do during the time they are not being paid is of no central importance.

However, it might be of interest to organizations to see what causes people who are on salary to work exceptionally long hours. We would predict that such dedication would be affected by leadership and norms (if everyone comes in on Saturday, you had better too if you want to get ahead), ambition, project deadlines, and future potential rewards such as promotion (partnership) and stock options, among other factors. Observe that this list includes factors that Deci would call controlling, although we would argue that they all involve choice (Binswanger, 1991).

Creativity

Much has been made of Deci and Ryan–type studies that have claimed that creativity is undermined when people are offered monetary incentives. (These studies have typically been done using children as subjects). However, Eisenberger and Selbst (1994) and Eisenberger, Armeli, and Pretz (1998) found that tangible rewards can be effective if they are made contingent on creative thinking over a period of time. Large rewards were most effective if they were not made salient—by keeping them out of sight. This is an interesting finding, because it more closely replicates real organizational settings where tangible rewards do not pile up in front of you as you earn them. Shalley (1991) and Amabile (1993) find that the keys to promoting creativity are to set goals for it, to give people autonomy as to the means, and then to reward the result.

Equity and Justice Theories

Distributive justice theory (Adams, 1965) is concerned with the issue of fairness in the allocation of rewards. Adams argued that people compare the ratio of their inputs (such as performance) and outputs (such as rewards) to those of others and take action to restore equity if the ratios are not equal. Early laboratory studies allowed subjects to restore equity by adjusting their input-output ratios (for example, raising quantity of productivity without regard to quality to correct piece-rate underpayment; increasing quality and lowering quantity of productivity to eliminate overpayment).

It is not clear whether these laboratory studies have abstracted out the essential features of typical equity situations in work settings (Locke, 1986). For example, very few people admit to being overpaid. Thus the relationship between perceived inequity and subsequent performance in real work settings remains to be determined. One field study (Summers & Hendrix, 1991) found that perceived inequity affected pay and job satisfaction but not performance. Another field study (Scholl, Cooper, & McKenna, 1987) found that self-reports of pay equity were associated with self-reports of extra-role actions.

Theoretically, one would not expect any fixed relationship between inequity and performance. The first reaction to pay inequity is dissatisfaction. We know from the job satisfaction literature that there are many actions people take in response to perceived dissatisfaction in addition to or instead of modifying their work performance (see, for example, Fisher & Locke, 1992). These include protesting to a higher authority (such as one's boss), taking aggressive action (such as filing a lawsuit), taking revenge (such as stealing or sabotage; see Greenberg, 1990a), defying authority (as by ignoring regulations) or reducing cooperation, withdrawing from the job (through absenteeism or lateness), quitting the job or the organization (see Bretz & Thomas, 1992; Summers & Hendrix, 1991), taking no overt action (tolerating the injustice), and cognitively adjusting one's comparison or fairness standards.

No developed theory predicts which of the various action or nonaction options an individual will choose in a given case. Obvious factors that would need to be considered would be the individual's moral values, sensitivity to inequity (Miles, Hatfield, & Huseman, 1989), personality factors such as conscientiousness and self-esteem, self-efficacy with respect to the ability to carry out various actions, and expectations of reward or punishment.

The issue of cognitive adjustment brings up further complications for equity theory. The theory does not specify what inputs and outputs people will choose as relevant, and it does not specify how people choose the people to whom they will compare themselves. Scholl et al. (1987) identified numerous possible comparison groups, including people on the same job, people in the same company, people in the same occupation, people with the same education, and people of the same age. They found that pay satisfaction was most affected by comparisons to people in the same occupation and by direct estimates of how much they were over-or underpaid (for example, "I earn about 30 percent less than I should be earning"). These latter discrepancies were correlated with all of the equity estimates based on the various comparison groups. This implies that people use multiple reference groups to decide how much they should be paid.

Organizations can, in some instances, manage the external comparison process by giving employees data regarding the organization's pay scale in relation to those of relevant occupational groups or similar local companies. However, this could backfire if the organization uses biased data or makes misleading comparisons or if the data reveal that its pay scales are below average. Furthermore, continually updating the information could be expensive. It is doubtful if organizations can effectively manage internal comparison processes. Pay secrecy could limit objective comparisons but not subjective guesswork.

Procedural justice theory focuses on the processes by which pay and reward decisions are made rather than the outcome itself (Greenberg, 1987, 1993). Perceptions of procedural justice are based on such factors as having fair criteria and applying them fairly and on such things as lack of bias, accuracy, consistency, trust, and feedback.

Brockner and Wiesenfeld (1996) performed a meta-analysis on studies of distributive and procedural justice and found that they affect satisfaction interactively. The greatest degree of dissatisfaction results when there is a combination of low distributive and low procedural justice. The other three combinations produce an equal degree of satisfaction. If there is high perceived distributive justice, people are not concerned with the procedure. Most interesting is the finding that a combination of low distributive justice and high procedural justice produces as much satisfaction as high distributive justice. In short, people can accept an unfair result if it was the result of a fair procedure.

Aside from the Brockner and Wiesenfeld (1996) findings, the wild card in all justice theories is determining what, exactly, is just. Here is where conflict inevitably occurs because people have different views as to what constitutes fair pay or a fair procedure. Such disputes can range all the way from basic values to details of application. For example, pure Marxists will consider all pay schemes unfair that do not distribute all profits to the workers. Extreme egalitarians will resent all pay differentials—or at least large differentials, whereas strongly pro-capitalist individuals will consider them fully just. Those who favor seniority over merit will resent younger workers getting more than they do, whereas pro-merit advocates will support ignoring seniority. Subjectivists may dispute all outcomes or procedures that do not favor them at the expense of others and in selecting comparison others will choose people who make them look underpaid and ignore those who make them look overpaid. In contrast, people who strive to be objective will look at all relevant evidence. Individuals who suspect sex or racial biases everywhere will tend to assume faulty procedures if white males' salaries are higher than those of other groups, whereas persons who assume no such bias will not automatically fault existing procedures. Such individual differences pose an enormous challenge for designers of pay systems.

Our point is not that "everything is subjective," as the postmodernists claim; we do believe that there are objective principles of justice (which must be derived from moral philosophy), but in today's culture, philosophies are as varied as snowflakes. This guarantees conflict whenever the issue of justice arises.

Expectancy Theory

Expectancy theory (Vroom, 1964; see also Porter & Lawler, 1968) holds that people make choices based on (1) their *expectancy* that their efforts will lead to a certain level of performance, (2) their belief that their performance will lead to valued outcomes (*instrumentality*), and (3) the degree of value they place on those outcomes (*valence*). Thus incentive systems should be most effective when people believe that they can do what it takes to earn money and when they value money as a reward.

Here it is important to note that for most people the value of pay is not just a matter of buying necessities; it has important symbolic value. Fox, Scott, and Donohue (1993), for example, found that the best valence predictor of performance under an incentive system was a measure that focused on pay as an enhancer of the self-concept. Valence measures centered around the social benefits of pay or its value in paying bills were not associated with performance.

In a very general way, one can say that the expectancy model is true, especially if the predictions are made regarding the choices individuals make from a range of alternatives rather than between people based on a given alternative (Van Eerde & Thierry, 1996). People often do consider these components when making choices. However, when it gets to specifics, many complications arise. They all center around the fact that no particular method of taking account of the three expectancy theory components is built into the human psyche. For example, people may act intuitively (based on their subconscious) rather than consciously calculate the pros and cons of alternative courses of action. When they do calculate, they may combine the components in many different ways and even ignore components, they may consider one value or many, they may consider material as well as nonmaterial outcomes (such as morality or pride), they may focus on the long term or the short term, and they may maximize or satisfice or neither.

All this makes it very difficult to know just what to measure and how to combine the measures when attempting to predict specific actions. Expectancy theory seems to work best when conditions are highly structured so that the alternative courses of action and consequences are clearly laid out (for example, see Riedel, Nebeker, & Cooper, 1988). This reduces individual variability in the types of calculations made.

Incentive schemes that are clearly structured are readily applicable to analysis in terms of expectancy theory concepts. For example, incentive plans cannot work if people believe that they cannot perform well enough to earn the rewards. Nor can they succeed if people believe that even if they perform well, they will not get what they deserve. Note that belief in the instrumentality of one's actions is really the same thing (in this context) as belief in distributive justice: "I'll actually get what I earn." Procedural justice may be involved as well: "I'll actually get what they promised me." Finally, incentive systems cannot work if people do not sufficiently value the money—either because there is not enough of it or because the cost of obtaining it is too great with respect to time or effort or other values forgone or because earning it may lead to negative actions or consequences (such as dishonesty or layoffs).

Group and companywide incentives can be especially problematic from the point of view of instrumentality because one's individual efforts may have a very minimal effect on the size of the bonus pool. This can be compensated for to an extent by the belief that coordination and cooperation will pay off (Lawler, 1971). Furthermore, group or company members can exert pressure on other members to do their fair share such that if all members do their jobs, the group as a whole can succeed.

Some theorists have argued that predictions of performance based on expectancy theory conflict with those based on equity theory. For example, Harder (1991) argued that baseball free agents let their batting averages drop during their option year for equity reasons (they had not been treated fairly) but kept up their home run ratio for expectancy theory reasons—because the latter was more likely to be subsequently rewarded (based on what happened to players in the past) than the former. However, we find the theoretical distinction here unconvincing; both fit the expectancy theory model in that the players put less emphasis on actions that they thought were going to be less generously rewarded. As noted, noninstrumentality is a type of injustice: a high batting average does not pay, so we see no grounds for conflicting predictions.

A key factor that must be considered in this and other examples is time perspective. Player actions that were not rewarded in year one by one team may be rewarded in later years by another team. Recall that a common outcome of inequity is dissatisfaction leading to turnover. The premise behind such turnover is that what has not been rewarded in the past will be rewarded in the future—by another organization. We can hypothesize that individuals who focus only on past injustice will be more likely to show a performance decline—perhaps on the implicit premise that good performance will never be rewarded—than those who focus on the future. If there is a perceived future chance for reward, keeping up one's performance and skill level, even in the face of temporary injustice, is the most advantageous procedure.

In sum, there is no inherent contradiction between equity theory and expectancy theory; in fact, they are fully integratable. What is critical in either case is how the individual frames the situation, including the time frame. Individuals can respond to past injustice by lowered performance, but they can also respond to it by calculating what actions they might take to get justly rewarded in the future.

Goal Theory and Social Cognitive Theory

We treat these two theories together because they have several common elements and can be readily integrated (Bandura, 1986, 1997; Locke & Latham, 1990). Both theories view goals and self-efficacy as immediate causes of human action, and both agree that self-efficacy influences personal goals as well as commitment.

As noted earlier, social cognitive theory argues that incentives do not motivate action unless the individual believes that the actions required to get the incentive can be taken. Self-efficacy is similar in meaning to expectancy in expectancy theory except that it is wider in scope. In expectancy theory, expectancy traditionally refers to effort-performance expectancy, whereas self-efficacy refers to the conviction that one can attain a certain performance result using whatever resources one can mobilize (effort, tenacity, integration of skills, problem-solving ability, creativity, stress management, and so on). In expectancy theory, if the E (expectancy) component is 0, the product term goes to 0. In social cognitive theory, self-efficacy mediates incentive effects. In both cases, if there is no expectancy, there is no effect of incentives. Thus the two propositions amount to the same thing conceptually.

With respect to incentives, then, the core theoretical issue pertains to their relationship to goals, efficacy, and commitment and the relationship of all of these to performance. Wright (1989) found that bonus pay led to higher goal commitment than hourly pay. In a subsequent study, Wright (1992) found that both piece rate and bonus pay led to higher goal commitment than hourly pay. Riedel et al. (1988) also found that incentives affected commitment. In contrast, Lee, Locke, and Phan (1997) did not find any effect of payment type on commitment.

Commitment becomes most critical when people are trying for difficult goals (Locke & Latham, 1990), although the variance accounted for by this variable may be limited (Donovan & Radosevich, 1998), since gaining commitment to easy and moderate goals in laboratory settings is often quite routine. Lee et al. (1997) found that commitment was significantly related to performance among subjects who were assigned difficult goals.

The evidence for mediation of pay effects by goals is inconsistent. In some cases, incentives improve performance even when personal goals and commitment are controlled (Latham, Mitchell, & Dossett, 1978; Pritchard & Curtis, 1973), suggesting no mediation effect. In other cases, partial mediation of incentive effects has been found for goals and commitment (Riedel et al., 1988). In contrast, Lee et al. (1997) found that personal goals and self-efficacy, but not commitment, completely mediated the effects of incentives on performance. Some of the issues may be methodological; for example, Lee and colleagues' study was the only one to include a goal measure, a self-efficacy measure, and a validated measure of commitment. Wright (1989, 1992) encountered certain methodological problems (noted in Lee et al., 1997) that precluded a full test of mediation, but he did find that commitment mediated an incentive-goal interaction in the 1992 study.

Lee et al. (1997) suggested that in some cases, commitment might serve as a (partial) proxy for goals and self-efficacy. For subjects assigned difficult goals, goal commitment was significantly correlated with both self-set goals and self-efficacy, as well as performance. However, the correlations with performance were much higher for the latter measures. This is why they mediated the incentive effect and commitment did not. This result suggests that if one has measured both self-set goals and efficacy, measuring commitment might be superfluous. The self-set goal measure has the advantage of revealing not only if the person is trying for the assigned goal but also, if not, what he or she will try for instead.

If goals and self-efficacy are the key mediators of incentives, it remains to identify what types of incentive systems will work best. The most intriguing finding in the goal and incentive literature is that by Mowen, Middlemist, and Luther (1981). They found an interaction between goal difficulty and incentive system, such that people with hard goals performed better under a piece-rate system that paid for performance, whereas people with medium goals did better under a bonus system that paid only for goal success. Hard-goal subjects under a bonus system did poorly, presumably because they did not think they could attain the goals needed to get the bonus.

Lee et al. (1997) replicated the interaction between assigned goal difficulty and incentive systems and found, as noted earlier, that it was fully mediated by self-set goals and self-efficacy. The difficult goal subjects, most of whom failed on the first of two trials and who were under a bonus system, subsequently lowered their self-set goals and their self-efficacy relative to the medium-goal subjects, and this caused their lower performance. In contrast, the self-set goals, efficacy, and performance of piece-rate (and hourly-rate) subjects with difficult goals remained high relative to those of the medium-goal subjects.

The interesting aspect of these findings is that an all-or-none bonus system seems to exacerbate the effect of failure. The hard goals did not discourage subjects who got their hourly pay anyway or who got paid for performance rather than goal success. Possibly bonus subjects framed the task situation differently than those in other conditions.

This poses a dilemma for the designers of incentive systems. The central problem is how to get people to take the risk of trying for a very hard goal (assuming one can know how hard a goal is in advance—a problematic issue in itself). Management-by-objectives (MBO) systems became very unpopular because, as one CEO put it, "It was a system whereby smart managers tried to convince their bosses that their easy goals were hard." Such a premium was put on goal success under MBO that managers were loath to undertake challenges that could lead to failure and the subsequent ruination of their careers. MBO, to the extent that it is practiced in this manner, is totally at odds with the major findings of goal theory (Locke, 1997; Locke & Latham, 1990).

We believe that there are three possibilities for incentive systems that will foster the setting of high goals:

1. *Use all-or-none bonuses with difficult goals.* The bonus method did not work very well in our previously cited laboratory study, but some hard-nosed CEOs use it. They seem to get around the failure issue by hiring only very capable people and firing those who cannot get the job done (this method is used at General Electric). If the bonuses are substantial, such people can be highly motivated, especially people at the managerial level. A benefit of setting goals that almost seem to be impossible, based on past experience, is that it encourages people to approach tasks in entirely new ways since that is their only hope of reaching the goals.

In a laboratory study, Knight, Durham, and Locke (1998) found that all-or-none bonuses motivated teams to undertake riskier task strategies than teams not offered bonuses. In this case, the teams did not get discouraged because the riskier strategies paid off, although it is obvious that risk taking does not always pay. Knight et al. found that the highest performance was attained by teams that had difficult goals and were offered bonuses for goal attainment. These teams, in addition to taking greater risks, implemented their tactics better than teams offered no bonuses.

Care must be taken in real organizational settings that agents do not take foolish risks or engage in dishonest practices in order to reach their goals. Leaders who insist on "success at all costs" usually find that the results are very costly. When leaders set "stretch" goals that map out seemingly impossible targets that require significant alterations in organizational processes for attainment, they need to be prepared to help facilitate change through such mechanisms as opening information access and shortcutting approval requirements (Thompson, Hochwarter, & Mathys, 1997).

To avoid the risks of setting goals that are too hard to attain, CEOs could set moderate goals instead (for example, goals based on average previous achievement or the 50th percentile). This is very likely to produce some subsequent performance improvement (barring economic downturns or strategic error), but the degree of improvement would be more modest than in the case of hard goals.

2. *Pay for degrees of goal success.* Difficult goals can be assigned, but people can be rewarded for degrees of success in relation to the goal. For example, there could be a proportional pay increment for every performance increment above a certain minimally acceptable goal level with the full bonus reserved for those who fully attain the assigned goal. Or there could be discrete categories—for example, five goal-performance levels, starting from a minimum, with the bonus increased at each level. Under such a system, a manager who tried for a 20 percent sales increase and achieved only 10 percent could still be rewarded. Attaining only 50 percent of a very difficult goal may still be much more valuable to the company than attaining 100 percent of a much easier goal, such as 5 percent. To our knowledge, no experimental studies of such a payment system have been reported.

3. *Use self-set goals to motivate performance, and determine rewards after the fact.* Let people set their own goals in order to motivate

them to produce, but pay bonuses not on performance in relation to their goals but in relation to the value they have created for the company. This requires a post hoc judgment call on the part of the CEO or top executive and, without some prior agreement regarding the criteria to be used, could lead to considerable misunderstanding. It certainly conflicts with the tenets of expectancy theory but might be useful in cases where the CEO does not know how to specify what should be accomplished or how to reward performance in advance. For example, setting what the CEO thought to be hard goals that turned out to be very easy could demotivate additional performance improvement. A modified version of this procedure could involve the CEO's setting a minimal, though not unchallenging, goal level for all units and letting the executives or managers decide how far they wanted to go beyond this level. Pay would be for accomplishment, regardless of goal level.

The wild card in any goal-incentive system is, of course, what do you set goals for? This is a crucial question and one that can be very hard to answer. For the CEO of a publicly traded company, it is not so hard. The ultimate goal is to create stockholder value. But after that, things get more complicated. The immediate precursors of profit and growth, which drive stock value, are revenues (sales) and costs. Most successful companies attack on both fronts. They take continual actions to increase the first and decrease the second. But how is this done? The key is to make a causal chain that identifies those actions and results. This requires a thorough knowledge of the business, the competition, the firm's strengths and weaknesses, and the business strategies that will win in the long run. A major error in any of these judgments can lead to disaster.

A related issue is time perspective, especially the need to integrate the short term with the long term. Markets and technologies are changing so fast today that leaders have to be prepared to change some goals rapidly when needed, even as they stick tenaciously to others. This means that incentives have to change also.

Agency Theory

Agency theory (Eisenhardt, 1989; Jensen & Meckling, 1976; Jensen & Murphy, 1990) addresses the common agency relationship in which a principal delegates work to an agent who is supposed to perform the work. The theory is typically applied to the relationship between stockholder-owners (principals) and managers (agents), but it is also applicable to relationships between managers (principals) and employees (agents).

The theory focuses on solving two major problems associated with agency situations. First, the agency problem occurs when the goals of the principal and agent are in conflict and it is difficult or costly for the principal to monitor the actual behavior of the agent. Under such conditions, agents may operate in ways that serve their own short-term interests rather than those of principals (for example, shirking on duties). Second, the risk problem presents itself due to differing attitudes toward risk held by the principal and agent. Generally, agents are assumed to be more risk-averse than principals because agents have difficulty diversifying their employment, while principals can typically more easily diversify their investments.

Given these potential problems, agency theory attempts to specify the most efficient contract in a particular situation that will help more closely align the interests of agents with those of principals. Two types of contract possibilities are behavior-oriented and outcome-oriented. According to the theory, when it is possible to monitor the behavior of the agent at low cost, a behavior-oriented contract is the most efficient, with compensation provided as salary. When such monitoring is not possible at low cost, principals must either expend more funds to develop better information systems or set up an outcome-oriented contract.

Outcome-oriented contracts, however, represent a transfer of risk to agents. This is because actually achieving outcomes typically involves more uncertainly than engaging in behaviors. Therefore, agents are unwilling to accept such contracts without compensation premiums (such as bonuses, stock options, and commissions) that are commensurate with the degree of added risk. Thus in thinking about contract possibilities, principals must weigh the costs of measuring behaviors against the costs of measuring outcomes, which also involve risk transfers to agents.

Agency theory has been shown to have some explanatory power in predicting the types of compensation systems in operation (see Eisenhardt, 1988; Milkovich, Gerhart, & Hannon, 1991). As Eisenhardt (1989) has pointed out, agency theory can be extended in a number of ways by varying assumptions regarding such aspects as the degree of risk aversion of agents or the degree of goal conflict between principals and agents. One important factor is task programmability, which deals with the extent to which the relevant behaviors leading to desired outcomes are known and can be specified in advance. She speculates that the less programmable the task, the greater the likelihood that outcome-based contracts will be used.

Given that high-level executive positions are likely to be characterized by low task programmability, agency theory suggests that outcome-based contracts will usually be most appropriate for executives. In a laboratory study, Tosi, Katz, and Gomez-Mejia (1997) found that incentives were more effective than monitoring for ensuring that agents act in the interests of owners. However, they did find that a combination of high incentives and high monitoring was useful in reducing a long-term tendency to escalate (make higher investments in previously poor choices). As the researchers point out, further conceptual work in agency theory regarding the extent to and circumstances under which behavior-oriented and outcome-oriented controls complement or substitute for one another would be helpful. They also note the difficulty of studying these issues at executive levels using archival data (such as the proportion of outside board members) as proxies for monitoring because such proxies do not provide sufficient information regarding whether monitoring has actually occurred. Although agency theory provides a useful starting point for thinking about appropriate methods of compensation, it needs to be supplemented with other perspectives (Eisenhardt, 1989; Gomez-Mejia & Wiseman, 1997).

Prospect Theory

Prospect theory (Kahneman & Tversky, 1979) has recently been cited in discussions of compensation plans (see Gomez-Mejia & Wiseman, 1997). The theoretical framework has the potential to be particularly useful in predicting likely reactions to at-risk pay plans and also links conceptually to risk issues in agency theory.

Briefly, prospect theory proposes that individuals handle risk situations differently when a situation is characterized in terms of a possible gain than when it is presented in terms of a possible loss. When a positive frame is used, the benefits inherent in the situation are highlighted. When a negative frame is presented, the potential risks of loss inherent in the situation are emphasized. Effects related to the way an issue is framed have been observed in various situations, including negotiations (Neale, Huber, & Northcraft, 1987), survivors' reactions to job layoffs (Brockner, Wiesenfeld, & Martin, 1995), and punishment (Dunegan, 1996).

According to prospect theory, the differential responses to the two frames are caused by a human tendency to be risk-averse in situations involving the possibility of gain and risk-seeking in situations involving the threat of loss. Because avoiding a loss is more strongly valued than achieving a gain, individuals are strongly motivated to avoid a loss, even to the point of accepting a risky choice. However, individuals are less likely to take a risk in order to achieve a gain (Bazerman, 1984). Applying prospect theory to compensation issues suggests that the way in which the possibilities of gains and losses are framed may affect reactions to potential rewards.

The idea of involving employees in the risks inherent in running major corporations by placing pay at risk has recently gained popularity (Macey & Sabounghi, 1996). For example, a customized pay-for-performance plan called "achievement sharing" was put in place by the Du Pont Corporation's Fibers Division in 1988. Under this plan, an individual employee's pay was based on the performance of the division as a whole. Furthermore, although the new plan offered Fibers Division employees the possibility of earning a bonus above the base rate of pay, it also involved risk in the form of a loss of some base pay if the assigned goals were not met. The program was reported extensively in the business press, and descriptions clearly pointed out that there was a risk of losing some base pay under the plan (McNutt, 1990). The program covered about twenty thousand employees.

The new Fibers Division pay program was a success in its first full year; employees received $109 for each $100 that had been at risk, up to 2 percent of pay (McNutt, 1990). In the second year, the at-risk amount went up to 4 percent, and employees were to have the maximum amount of 6 percent at risk during the third year. However, the program was terminated in its second year due to widespread employee discontent. The reason for the discontent was apparently that the Fibers Division had lost money in the second year of the plan, and workers faced a certain loss of 2 percent and a possible loss of 4 percent of their pay (Koenig, 1990).

A field study (Brown & Huber, 1992) examined a somewhat similar pay-at-risk compensation system that was installed in a large U.S. bank. Again, despite careful planning and an extensive communication program, the plan was terminated shortly after implementation due to significant employee dissatisfaction. Even those who made the same or more pay under the new plan registered lower satisfaction with both pay processes and pay outcomes. The bank reinstituted base pay pegged to the market and provided variable pay as an add-on in the form of bonuses for reaching performance goals.

Prospect theory offers a possible explanation for these pay system failures. The employees likely devalued the loss of their expected pay more strongly than they valued the possible gain of bonus pay. Moreover, there was a particularly strong negative reaction when a loss was imminent. Prospect theory is compatible with agency theory in the sense that both address issues of risk aversion, but prospect theory emphasizes the special case of loss aversion (Gomez-Mejia & Wiseman, 1997).

Before leaving this discussion of prospect theory, we note some differences in the use of the term *at-risk* that sometimes cause confusion in the compensation literature (see also Chapter Nine in this volume). In this chapter, we are using *at-risk* narrowly to describe pay plans that explicitly discount base pay by some amount (for example, 5 percent) and then offer variable pay that provides employees the potential not only to meet but also to exceed their base pay earnings (Schuster & Zingheim, 1992). Variable pay is performance-related compensation that does not permanently increase base pay and must be re-earned to be received again. Examples of variable pay are bonuses that do not become part of base, commissions, piece-rate systems, gainsharing, and stock options. Some compensation professionals use the term *at risk* to describe all variable pay because, since it is performance dependent, there is a possibility that it will not be earned or received (Macey & Sabounghi, 1996).

Tournament Theory

Tournament theory (Lazear, 1998; Lazear & Rosen, 1981) argues that movement up hierarchies in organizations can be viewed as sets of contests in which workers vie with one another for promotions to the next level so as to receive increased rewards. According to the theory, upward movement depends primarily on relative performance among potentially eligible promotion candidates because most organizations promote mainly from within. Therefore, when the salary differential at the next level is sizable, employees will be willing to compete with one another for the promotion. This competition in turn leads employees to expend greater amounts of effort and leads to higher levels of productivity than would be the case if the salary spread between levels were narrow. Tournament theory argues that such compensation systems are useful in situations in which monitoring is too costly or is not reliable.

Lazear (1998) theorizes that the larger the wage spread between levels, the greater the potential payoff from a promotion and therefore the greater the effort that employees will put forth. The theory assumes that employees will have sufficient self-efficacy and a sufficiently high valence for money to be motivated to pursue the next higher level. Some support for tournament theory has been found in studies of golf tournaments (Ehrenberg & Bognanno, 1990) and auto racing (Becker & Huselid, 1992). One acknowledged disadvantage of tournament compensation systems is that they can encourage excessive competition because employees are evaluated relative to one another. Therefore, Lazear (1998) suggests that tournament systems not be used in situations in which cooperation is important. In that case, he recommends that employees can be paid on the basis of absolute performance so that there is no incentive to be uncooperative.

Integration of Theoretical Perspectives

Let us now attempt to integrate the best elements of the various theoretical perspectives. Ideally, a compensation system will promote both productivity and satisfaction. Given that it is unlikely that any pay plan will ever satisfy all employees, the emphasis is on the satisfaction of higher performers. It is lower performers who are often dissatisfied with pay-for-performance systems (Zenger, 1992). The various perspectives suggest that an effective incentive system should meet the following criteria:

- The pay philosophy is clearly specified and communicated to organizational members. (This principle is implicit in expectancy theory but is focused at a more general level.)
- The plan is implemented in a fair and objective manner. This would include an appeal process for members who believe they have been treated unjustly.
- The plan encourages members to pursue challenging goals.
- Members have high self-efficacy, as a result of selection, experience, training, and empowering leadership practices.
- Bonuses, monetary payments, and other rewards (such as recognition) are made contingent on high performance (including progress toward a difficult or stretch goal).
- The money increment (or other reward) for high performance is enough to be highly valued.
- Money must be considered in relation to other rewards. Although it was not stressed in most theories (but is implicit in expectancy theory), money is not the only reward people get from work. Frequently people will trade off some money in return for other values. These include work interest and challenge, opportunities for growth, outstanding leadership (including recognition), fringe benefits, job security, stimulating colleagues, and convenient location.
- Goals and incentives direct members to achieve outcomes (including group, unit, and company outcomes) that are important, organizationally relevant, and in line with the interests of principals.
- The focus is on upside potential and does not risk losses to base pay or pay that has already been awarded or promised.

These principles reflect, in our view, the major implications and findings of the valid parts of the theories we have discussed. The application of such principles involves many difficulties and does not guarantee that everyone will be satisfied. However, the application of these principles should greatly increase the chances of achieving a highly motivated and satisfied workforce.

Note that we have not mentioned points of contention among the various theories because, by and large, they are complementary rather than competing. The various theories deal with different aspects of monetary incentives. However, as we shall see, the extant theories do not begin to encompass all the complex issues involved in constructing effective pay systems. Even on their own terms, the theories, although providing helpful guidelines, are quite general. Implementing equity, for example, is a lot harder than just specifying a few general principles.

One might even offer the radical hypothesis that the manner in which an incentive plan is implemented is at least as important as the basic structure of the plan itself (see Greenberg, 1990b). For example, a well-implemented individual incentive plan might work better than a poorly implemented group plan even under conditions of high task interdependence (for example, individuals could be rewarded for cooperating).

Research Issues

Because of the general nature of existing theories and the many implementation issues yet to be resolved in linking compensation to enhanced performance, there is a great need for further research. In this next section, we point to some of the major areas in need of additional theory development and empirical inquiry.

Is the most effective compensation system contingent on an organization's strategy, or are there "best" compensation practices? Conceptual arguments and empirical data suggest there are reasons to expect that appropriately matching business strategies and compensation systems may have positive impacts on organizational productivity. For example, Gomez-Mejia and Balkin (1992) have attempted to match pay systems to defender and prospector strategies (Miles & Snow, 1984). They argue that pay systems that are predetermined and standardized (for example, base salary, minimal variable pay, emphasis on internal equity) are more suited to a defender strategy, whereas pay systems that are flexible and adaptive (for instance, substantial incentives in addition to base salary, sensitivity to external market) are more compatible with a prospector strategy (see also Gomez-Mejia, 1992). Montemayor (1996) also found evidence for a contingency approach in that high-performing firms had pay systems that were a good fit with their respective strategies, while poor-performing firms did not.

Instead of focusing exclusively on the compensation system–strategy link, some other researchers have included pay with other human resource practices in investigating links with strategy. The rationale is that any one human resource practice in isolation, such as a compensation system, is unlikely to have the desired effects. For example, Youndt, Snell, Dean, and Lepak (1996) tested two different types of human resource systems, administrative and capital-enhancing. Each type comprised practices related to staffing, training, performance appraisal, and compensation. For example, among other things, the administrative human resource system included compensation based on hourly pay, individual incentives, and internal equity. In contrast, the capital-enhancing system included compensation based on salary, skill-based pay, group incentives, and external equity. The researchers found some support for a contingency approach—that is, that properly aligning systems of human resource practices with appropriate strategies was positively related to performance.

Conversely, Gerhart, Trevor, and Graham (1996) suggest that the results of several studies attempting to forge a link between strategy and human resource practices fit an alternative model associated with the adoption of "best practices" almost as well. For example, Huselid (1995) found that high-performance work practices were positively related to organizational performance regardless of strategy. One dimension of his measure of high-performing work practices included some characteristics of the compensation system—namely, the proportion of the workforce with access to organizational incentive plans, profit-sharing plans, or gainsharing plans. But other practices (such as proportion of the workforce who are administered attitude surveys on a regular basis) were added to the dimension as well.

In an extensive review, Gerhart et al. (1996) have noted that there appear to be disagreements regarding the characteristics of pay systems that are included in the various conceptualizations of human resource systems (for example, Arthur, 1994; Huselid,

1995). Thus there is a need for further conceptual work in linking compensation plans not only to strategy but also to appropriate configurations of human resource practice systems.

Overall, it is probably unrealistic to expect the very global characterizations of pay plans (such as percentage of variable pay or hourly pay versus salary) typically used in studies of compensation-strategy linkages to uncover very strong strategic connections. This is particularly true when pay plan characteristics are imbedded in configurations of human resource practices. To make further meaningful progress, it will now be necessary to develop more complex models to depict different pay systems (for instance, salary, piece-rate system, team-based pay) and also find ways to take into account the fact that different pay systems can exist in the same organization.

How can the appropriate level of aggregation for pay incentives be determined? Whereas historically much of the emphasis on incentives has been aimed at the individual level, interest in offering incentives at the group and organizational levels is on the rise (Bartol & Hagmann, 1992). One potential value often mentioned is that such systems have the potential to foster cooperation among organizational members. In a recent *Harvard Business Review* article, Pfeffer (1998) strongly argued against individual incentive pay, maintaining that "the more aggregated the unit used to measure performance, the more reliably performance can be assessed" (p. 117). He recommended providing large amounts of collective rewards based on organizational or subunit performance, citing Herbert Simon as recognizing that people in organizations are interdependent.

Unfortunately, many more questions exist regarding level of aggregation issues than Pfeffer portrayed. For one thing, serious questions (as in expectancy theory) exist regarding the motivational consequences of basing pay on the performance of large organizational units. Such circumstances can make it difficult for individuals to see how their own performance can make a difference, undermining the perceived effort-performance connection (Lawler & Jenkins, 1992; Locke, Feren, McCaleb, Shaw, & Denny, 1980). For another, free riding may be a potential problem with rewarding at the group level, particularly when large groups are involved (Gerhart, Minkoff, & Olsen, 1995).

Furthermore, evidence supporting the effectiveness of some pay systems for use at plant, division, and organizational levels is not particularly strong. Although gainsharing seems to be a successful approach, this conclusion must be tempered by the fact that most available studies are case studies and/or are based on data collected after the programs had already been implemented (Welbourne & Gomez-Mejia, 1988). The limited evidence supporting a possible positive influence of profit-sharing must also be viewed with caution because the supporting underlying studies tend to be fairly weak (Florkowski, 1987; Weitzman & Kruse, 1990). There is a major need for more rigorous longitudinal studies in these areas.

Although interdependence may well be an important factor in considering aggregation issues, the degree of task interdependence varies considerably across situations (Montemayor, 1994). In investigating interdependence issues, Wageman (1995) found that service teams at Xerox did best when both their tasks and outcomes were either purely group-oriented or purely individual-oriented. Hybrid groups, whose tasks and outcomes were a mix of individual and group factors, performed poorly, demonstrated low-quality interaction processes, and experienced low group member satisfaction. Wageman suggested that providing group-level rewards undermined the hybrid team members' sense of individual responsibility without substituting sufficient motivation to develop an interdependent process. The study has some limitations, including the possibility that the hybrid task interdependence was not a good match with the task. It also used a short time frame (four months) within which the reward system effects were evaluated. It can take a considerable period of time before the cumulative effects of incentive systems are apparent (Wagner, Rubin, & Callahan, 1988). Wageman's research does help illustrate the complexity of the issues that must be investigated further. Studies are particularly needed to evaluate the prospects for basing pay on both individual and group factors, since jobs with individual and group tasks are common in organizations.

What is the best way to combine pay and goals? We addressed this question earlier. The problem is how to use incentives to get people to accept the risk of failure that high goals entail. We suggested three possibilities: all-or-none incentives with able people only, a graded series of goal levels with progressively higher bonuses given to the attainment of higher goals, and self-set goals with bonuses, decided after-the-fact, to be based on performance, not goal success. There has been no research comparing such systems with each other or with more conventional systems (such as merit pay with annual salary adjustment).

Should pay systems directly reward development of strategic knowledge and skills? A number of organizations are experimenting with competency-based pay. This approach compensates individuals for the breadth and depth of relevant knowledge, skills, and other performance-relevant characteristics they possess, rather than for the particular job they hold at a given point in time (Lawler, 1994). Interest in the competency approach is on the rise because organizations are seeking ways to encourage employee development of capabilities in areas of strategic importance. An important question is how paying for competencies will translate to better performance.

Although competencies are personal characteristics that "enable performance" (Ledford, 1995), there is a difference between being able to perform and doing so. Bandura (1997) posits that goal systems should foster the development of competencies that enable people to perform more effectively so that they can experience pride in their work and enhanced self-efficacy. Is it feasible to develop compensation systems that reward both competency development and performance? Or is there a danger that individuals will focus on developing their competencies at the expense of doing certain aspects of the job (particularly those that are more mundane)?

A related issue is identifying the right competencies for incorporation in the pay system. The resource-based strategic model of the firm argues that capabilities of strategic value must be rare, be difficult to imitate, and add value in the sense of helping the organization capitalize on opportunities or nullify threats (Barney, 1991). At the same time, human capital theory (Becker, 1975) suggests that organizations should allocate resources to training that is specific to the needs of the organization and is not readily transferable to other organizations. Otherwise, individuals may use the training they have obtained to negotiate better-paying positions in competing organizations. How can compensation systems help balance these competency development, performance, and retention needs?

What are the trade-offs in basing pay on behaviors and processes rather than outcomes? The issue of whether to base pay on behaviors and processes or on outcomes has been a recurring one. Lee (1985; see also Ouchi, 1977) proposes that the use of behaviors and processes is the appropriate means to evaluate work when the transformation process (means-ends) is well understood but reliable and valid output measures are not readily available. Evaluation of outcomes is a better approach when reliable and valid output measures are available, but the transformation is not well understood. Either can be used when both the transformation process is well understood and good measures are available. When neither condition exists, careful selection and extensive training are necessary.

Agency theory is generally compatible with the process versus outcomes trade-off, calling for salary when behavioral monitoring or control is possible and the use of incentives when outcomes must be used. Few studies have actually assessed whether basing pay on behaviors versus outcomes under the conditions outlined actually leads to higher productivity. In one related study of retail salespeople, Banker, Lee, Potter, and Srinivasan (1996) found that sales gains from implementing outcome-based controls were lower when a high level of behavioral control already existed. At this point, we also don't know very much about the implications of mixing behavioral and outcome control for the same job (Tosi et al., 1997). The same is true for various blendings of salary and incentives (Moorthy, 1993).

A danger of using incentives to reward behaviors is that people may engage in the behaviors (for example, visit all customers at least once each month) but may not show any interest in the outcomes of these behaviors (say, sales). Unless behaviors are tied directly to outcomes, people may get rewarded simply for being compliant and performing rituals.

How do different degrees of variable pay and associated risk affect performance? Variable pay has been gaining in popularity as a compensation approach because it allows organizations greater flexibility and control over labor costs. The approach, though, essentially shifts risk to employees—the amount depending on the proportion of compensation that is fixed versus variable. As noted by agency theory, individuals tend to be risk-averse. Prospect theory further suggests that individuals are particularly sensitive about perceived losses and may take imprudent actions to avoid them.

Although use of variable pay is increasing in organizations, we have insufficient knowledge regarding its impact on performance. Gerhart and Milkovich (1990) found some support for the notion that proportion of variable pay is associated with higher organizational performance, but many questions remain. For example, do people work harder when their pay is variable or when it is fixed? What are the effects of framing pay in terms of risk (potential losses) versus gains (potential to increase pay)? Given that individuals tend to be risk-averse, how much variable pay is too much, and what are the governing conditions? Do individuals take imprudent risks with business decisions when compensation risk is high? How much of a premium do people expect when outcomes are somewhat uncertain (Shelley & Omer, 1996)?

Agency theory provides some clues but is far from sufficiently prescriptive (Eisenhardt, 1989). Given the difficulties chronicled by Brown and Huber (1992) when a large bank attempted to install variable pay in bank branches and by Petty, Singleton, and Connell (1992) in a union environment, how can variable pay be successfully introduced in contexts in which pay has been fixed? Bandura (1997) suggests that individuals perceive greater risk when they have low self-efficacy. Perhaps strong self-efficacy may be particularly important with variable pay.

Many of these same issues also apply at the CEO level. For example, drawing on prospect theory, Gomez-Mejia and Wiseman (1997) hypothesize that the use of market-based measures (such as stock price) versus accounting measures (such as profits) raises the level of uncertainty executives face (because market-based measures are less controllable). Thus market-based measures may promote more productive risk taking, whereas accounting measures may be more likely to promote accounting and related maneuvers.

A related issue here is whether CEOs should be required to own actual stock (as opposed to or in addition to stock options) in the company, even if they prefer not to. This way, like their principals (other stockholders), they would face the risk of personal loss if company performance lagged, as well additional possibilities of gains if good company performance positively influenced stock prices. Of course, requiring additional stock ownership may cause CEOs to demand more compensation to make up for the additional risk and may increase the risk level (for better or for worse) of the decisions they make. Evidence also suggests that individuals vary in their risk propensity (Bromiley & Curley, 1992), an issue that can have major strategic implications for organizations.

Can pay systems be designed that provide managers with some alloca-tion flexibility for strategic and operational reasons without undermining pay-for-performance perceptions? Managers sometimes face situations in which it is particularly important to retain certain employees for strategic or operational reasons. Bartol and Martin (1988, 1989, 1990) have shown that when there are threats to retention under these types of circumstances, managers are prone to award larger raises than might be warranted from a strict pay-for-performance point of view. Similar questions arise regarding whether to make counteroffers when strategically important and difficult-to-replace individuals receive external job offers (Williamson, 1975). Often making such counteroffers has the potential to disrupt internal or individual equity in the immediate work unit and even beyond. Such phenomena are likely to occur more frequently as organizations give greater consideration to building strategic human resources and deciding what capabilities provide competitive advantage (Barney, 1991; Lepak & Snell, 1999). What are the implications of such strategic departures from pay-for-performance norms? Are there ways to handle these situations without seriously damaging pay-for-performance perceptions?

How do people trade off money with other job values? Pfeffer (1998) recently implied that academics and others have falsely taught busi-nesspeople that employees are motivated only by money. However, we have never met anyone who literally believed or taught this, al-though people do differ on how important they believe money is compared to other factors.

Money, of course, is a core incentive because, as a medium of ex-change, people use it to buy the things that they need to live suc-cessfully, safely, securely, and happily. Recent research shows that people who are not poor actually outlive people who are poor. Money may not guarantee happiness, but it helps. Most fundamentally, money gives people more control over their lives.

It does not follow from this, however, that everyone tries to maximize earnings. There is no evidence that people are born with built-in value hierarchies (despite Maslow's claim)—they acquire them through knowledge and experience. People differ enor-mously in what they want, and these wants change over time. In the job realm, people routinely trade off some earnings for other values. Consider this: Professor A has tenure at the associate level at a second-tier business school near a major city where he gets above average pay and has friendly, intellectually stimulating colleagues. He is offered a chaired professorship yielding a 30 percent raise at a third- or fourth-tier school plus promotion to full professor. The colleagues are less stimulating and less collegial, and the school is in a small town. What should Professor A do?

We have known many professors who faced choices similar to this one. Some have stayed where they were; others have left. The values involved here are pay, title, colleagues, institutional prestige, and location. This list of job values is far from exhaustive. For example, job challenge, leadership, recognition, benefits, and time demands are critical issues for many people. Expectancy theory research has documented that people choose jobs by looking at the degree to which the jobs are instrumental in providing them with what they want (Vroom, 1966).

But what has not been studied sufficiently is how people view and make trade-offs between money and other values. Those who value money very highly in relation to other values will presumably be more willing to give those other values up in return for more money, whereas those who value money less highly in relation to other values should not respond so readily to offers of more money if it means giving up other things they want (Lawler, 1971).

It would be interesting to plot trade-off functions: "How much additional money would it take to convince you to work in a small town?" (for those who preferred a city) or "How much money would you forgo to have a challenging job of type X?" Such functions would be an indirect way of measuring value importance. For example, it would be intriguing to see how often people would claim that there are things they would refuse to trade away for any amount of money.

In a related study using a policy capturing approach, Rynes, Schwab, and Heneman (1983) found that the majority of subjects seemed to evaluate employment opportunities in relation to a reservation wage standard. A reservation wage is an amount below which an individual will not accept a job offer, regardless of the attractiveness of the other attributes (Milkovich & Newman, 1996). The Rynes et al. findings further showed that variability of pay in the market influenced the importance that participants placed on pay in the sense that when there was low variability in pay (which presumably ruled out distributive justice as an issue), participants attributed greater importance to other job attributes. Personality traits also appear to be factors in how pay levels are evaluated (Cable & Judge, 1994).

If more could be learned about how individuals evaluate pay relative to other job attributes, it could help organizations structure their incentive and other related reward systems in ways that would be more effective. It could also help organizations that cannot afford to pay top salaries compete with those that do, by offering compensating values (perhaps while also meeting reservation wage standards).

Can intrinsic, achievement, and extrinsic motivation be complementary? Pay and other rewards are facts of life—at least for people working in organizations. Copious evidence indicates that compensation systems in organizations of any appreciable size involve external, internal, and individual equity issues that are not easily balanced or ignored (see Gerhart & Milkovich, 1992; Lawler & Jenkins, 1992; Milkovich & Newman, 1996). The presence of such issues unfortunately makes it virtually impossible to follow simplistic prescriptions to downplay the importance of pay in the interest of fostering intrinsic motivation. Another reason why it is difficult simply to deemphasize pay is evidence that noncontingent pay (given independently of performance) can actually be detrimental to intrinsic motivation (Eisenberger & Cameron, 1996).

Factors such as goal setting and self-efficacy are important elements in compensation systems and tend to be linked not only to extrinsic motivation but to intrinsic and achievement motivation as well (Bandura, 1997; Locke & Latham, 1990). For these reasons alone, linkages to productivity are complex. Given that pay is not going to disappear from organizations anytime soon, research related to intrinsic, achievement, and extrinsic motivation needs to focus on seeking ways that the three types of motivation can work effectively in tandem (Bartol, 1992).

How do people choose reference groups when they make comparative justice estimates? Can companies manage the process by openly using certain reference groups? Although equity theory suggests that we make comparisons regarding our own inputs and outcomes against those of significant others, specifying just who these referent others are has proved illusive (Kulik & Ambrose, 1992). Kulik and Ambrose argue that individuals are most likely to use themselves as the primary or default referent. In support of this view, Bartol and Martin (1998) found evidence that individuals tend to make comparisons between their current pay and previous wages earned—a type of self-equity assessment. Availability of information and referent attractiveness appear to be major factors influencing the selection of referents (Goodman, 1974; Levine & Moreland, 1987).

Although other forms of equity or distributive justice comparisons have been identified—individual, internal, and external—there has been insufficient research regarding the relative importance individuals attach to them (Gerhart & Milkovich, 1992). Because it is difficult to design pay systems that optimize all three, it would be helpful to know their relative impact on productivity and affective responses.

Another important question is the extent to which organizations can influence referent choice. Given that availability of information appears to be a major choice factor, possibilities for influence are likely. For example, would it be useful for an organization to cite competitive pay information as a benchmark (perhaps the average pay raises provided nationally based on information from a credible source, such as the American Compensation Association, or industry averages)? Would this backfire in years when the organization's pay raise averages are lower, or would it be a good vehicle to convey information regarding organizational performance and standing?

How much of the impact of incentive systems is informational—letting people know what is important? Locke, Alavi, and Wagner (1997) propose that a useful perspective for assessing the impact of participation is to recast it as a process of knowledge transfer and information exchange. It would be interesting to apply this same logic to explore the ways in which incentive rewards convey information. For example, by seeing how rewards are distributed, employees can discover what the real or operating company philosophy is: Are people rewarded or promoted on the basis of politics or performance, quantity or quality, honesty or dishonesty, leadership ability or seniority? Seeing how the reward system operates can be beneficial if the company has integrity and harmful (and a cause of cynicism) if it does not. Unfortunately, as Lawler and Jenkins (1992) point out, it is common for organizations to keep secret even basic aspects of pay systems, such as average salary increase and salary range—thus greatly reducing the informational value of compensation. Of course, going to the other extreme and making pay completely open by revealing the specific pay of all individuals is likely imprudent because it could lead some individuals to focus obsessively and microscopically on distributive justice issues.

Another interesting dimension is the fact that reward system characteristics influence the nature and timing of the information they provide. For example, pay incentive plans specify in advance the desired performance outcomes, whereas merit pay plans tend to reveal after the fact which behaviors and/or outcomes are valued.

How are pay allocation decisions best communicated to individuals? In a classic article based on some studies they had done, Meyer, Kay, and French (1965) argued that traditional performance appraisal approaches encompass two objectives that are essentially in conflict. Specifically, they posited that it is difficult in the same discussion session to justify salary action and also effectively motivate individuals to improve work performance. Instead, Meyer et al. recommended holding multiple work planning and review sessions throughout the year. Salary action discussions would then be held separately.

In a partial test of the Meyer et al. (1965) approach, Prince and Lawler (1986) did not find any evidence of a negative impact associated with including salary in the annual review discussion, and they uncovered some indications of positive results for lower performers. One of the serious limitations of the study, however, was the fairly low level of agreement between managers and employees regarding whether salary was ever discussed. Further research is needed.

A major rationale for separating the pay discussion from the performance appraisal discussion is that it is difficult for individuals to be candid about their development needs when pay issues are at stake. Perhaps a better reason for separation is a procedural justice one. It is difficult to have a meaningful two-way discussion of an individual's performance when the pay has been determined a priori. Given the likelihood that most managers need to discuss pay allocations with at least their immediate superior before making them, they would not be empowered to make a change in the pay if other appraisal data surfaced during the discussion. Thus in a single-discussion scenario, the idea of a two-way problem-solving appraisal discussion would be thwarted by the fact that pay has already been determined.

Conversely, a double discussion (one on appraisal and development and a separate one on pay) may make it more difficult to establish the performance-outcome connection called for by expectancy theory. This latter issue is made more complex by the fact that some organizations make comparisons among individuals at the same level across work units before making salary allocations (Mohrman, Resnick-West, & Lawler, 1989).

Little is known about how this process is handled and its impact on performance and on perceptions of distributive and procedural justice. Also, research related to interactional justice, which refers to the fairness of the interpersonal treatment received during the carrying out of a procedure (Bies & Moag, 1986), suggests that managerial behaviors during allocation discussions may also influence subordinates' perceptions of fairness (Moye, Masterson, & Bartol, 1997). Considerably more research is needed to clarify the complex mechanisms involved in the interface between performance appraisal and salary actions.

What is the relative importance of pay and internal standards in motivating productivity? Of course, people want to be paid fairly for their accomplishments, but for many this is a long-term expectation. On a day-to-day basis, however, do people really think in terms of "How much money will this make me?" or are they motivated by other considerations, such as conscientiousness, goals, personal ambitions, desire not to let the boss down, pleasure in achievement, and competition? Perhaps pay is more important in getting people to stay at or leave organizations (due to equity considerations) than it is in getting them to work hard on specific jobs or tasks. In other words, people who are dissatisfied with their pay, rather than merely goofing off, will more likely instead look for a better job. This does not make pay systems unimportant, because inequitable systems can lead to the loss of valuable employees. But it implies that at least for some jobs and people, pay would not need to be a primary consideration in motivating day-to-day performance. Obviously, there are job differences (for example, non-programmed versus programmed) and individual differences (ambitious professionals versus others) here.

How much of the impact of performance-contingent pay plans on productivity is due to effects on retention—who stays and who leaves? Based on a meta-analysis of fifty-five studies, Williams and Livingstone

(1994) concluded that reward contingencies moderate the relationship between individual performance and voluntary turnover. Specifically, the results suggest that making rewards contingent on good performance encourages better performers to stay and poorer performers to leave. Research by Zenger (1992) indicates that the dynamics may be even more complex than the meta-analytic results suggest. Zenger found that when organizations reward at the extremes (that is, when they provide high rewards mainly for high performers, penalize only very low performers, and give the rest average rewards), high performers tend to stay and lower performers tend to leave. However, he also found that focusing on the extremes causes above-average performers to leave and marginally average performers to stay. Similarly, Harrison, Virick, and William (1996) found that a maximally contingent reward system (in this case, 100 percent commission) encouraged low performers to leave but also led to turnover among individuals who experienced a significant performance decrement during a particular pay period despite their good overall performance to date. The situation improved when individuals were provided advances based on average past performance, a system that smoothed the large pay fluctuations somewhat and provided a more encouraging frame. Thus there is evidence that the structure of performance-reward contingencies can affect the productive capacity of organizations through effects on retention. Few studies have addressed this issue or the mechanisms involved.

Should pay system change precede, occur simultaneously with, or follow other organizational changes—or does it depend on circumstances? And what are the most effective ways to implement changes in compensation systems? Lawler (1990) argues that it is impossible to design compensation systems that will add value without first establishing strategic objectives in such areas as the performance the organization wants to motivate, the types of individuals it wishes to attract and retain, and the type of structure that will be in place. This logic indicates that pay systems should not be the first thing to change, but it does not deny the usefulness of implementing pay system changes simultaneously with other changes or soon after. Kerr (1995) has pointed out the "folly of rewarding A while hoping for B."

This does not mean that changing pay systems is easy. Evidence from institutional theory (Zucker, 1987; Eisenhardt, 1988) suggests that managers tend to base compensation systems on industry norms, company traditions, visible management fads, and similar factors. Thereafter, systems are likely to become entrenched and are difficult to alter even when organizational circumstances change.

Despite numerous articles in the popular and professional press, little is known about success and failure rates in implementing changes in compensation systems (Gerhart et al., 1996). Clearly, some compensation systems are failures and are abandoned—sometimes more because of the conflicts they create than their inability to enhance performance (see Petty et al., 1992).

Lawler (1990) suggests that the best compensation design approach is the use of task forces, which allow organization member participation. His reasoning is that this approach provides better information for design decisions, fosters understanding of the decisions, and builds commitment and acceptance. He estimates, though, that this approach to system design takes three to six months—a fairly lengthy time frame. We need studies that evaluate the effectiveness of various alternatives to the design process. Such studies also need to assess the trade-offs associated with a speedier top-down process versus a slower bottom-up approach and identify other alternatives to make compensation systems more amenable to change.

Of course, these fifteen questions do not encompass all of the remaining issues related to compensation and productivity. But further research and theory contributions related to these questions will add immeasurably to our understanding of the complex issues surrounding linkages between incentives and motivation.

References

Adams, J. S. (1965). Inequity in social exchange. In L. Berkowitz (Ed.), *Advances in experimental social psychology.* (Vol. 2, pp. 267–300). Orlando, FL: Academic Press.

Amabile, T. M. (1993). Motivational synergy: Toward new conceptualizations of intrinsic and extrinsic motivation in the workplace. *Human Resource Management Review, 3,* 185–201.

Arthur, J. B. (1994). Effects of human resource systems on manufacturing performance and turnover. *Academy of Management Journal, 37,* 670–687.

Bandura, A. (1986). *Social foundations of thought and action: A social cognitive view.* Upper Saddle River, NJ: Prentice Hall.

Bandura, A. (1997). *Self-efficacy: The exercise of control.* New York: Freeman.

Banker, R. D., Lee, S., Potter, G., & Srinivasan, D. (1996). Contextual analysis of performance impacts of outcome-based incentive compensation. *Academy of Management Journal, 39,* 920–948.

Barney, J. (1991). Firm resources and sustained competitive advantage. *Journal of Management, 17,* 99–120.

Bartol, K. M. (1992). Rewarding continuity and innovation: Strategies for effective pay systems. In S. Srivasta & R. E. Fry (Eds.), *Executive and organizational continuity: Managing the paradoxes of stability and change* (pp. 284–306). San Francisco: Jossey-Bass.

Bartol, K. M., & Hagmann, L. L. (1992). Team-based pay plans: A key to effective teamwork. *Compensation and Benefits Review, 25*(6), 24–29.

Bartol, K. M., & Martin, D. C. (1988). Influences on managerial pay allocations: A dependency perspective. *Personnel Psychology, 41,* 361–378.

Bartol, K. M., & Martin, D. C. (1989). Effects of dependence, dependency threats, and pay secrecy on managerial pay allocations. *Journal of Applied Psychology, 74,* 105–113.

Bartol, K. M., & Martin, D. C. (1990). When politics pays: Factors influencing managerial compensation decisions. *Personnel Psychology, 43,* 599–614.

Bartol, K. M., & Martin, D. C. (1998). Applicant referent information at hiring interview and subsequent turnover among part-time workers. *Journal of Vocational Behavior, 53,* 334–352.

Bazerman, M. H. (1984). The relevance of Kahneman & Tversky's concept of framing to organizational behavior. *Journal of Management, 10,* 333–343.

Becker, B. E., & Huselid, M. A. (1992). The incentive effects of tournament compensation systems. *Administrative Science Quarterly, 37,* 336–350.

Becker, G. S. (1975). *Human capital.* Chicago: University of Chicago Press.

Bies, R. J., & Moag, J. S. (1986). Interactional justice: Communication criteria of fairness. *Research on Negotiation in Organizations, 1,* 43–55.

Binswanger, H. (1991). Volition as cognitive self-regulation. *Organizational Behavior and Human Decision Processes, 50,* 154–178.

Bretz, R. D., Jr., & Thomas, S. L. (1992). Perceived equity, motivation, and final-offer arbitration in major league baseball. *Journal of Applied Psychology, 77,* 280–287.

Brockner, J., & Wiesenfeld, B. M. (1996). An integrative framework for explaining reactions to decisions: Interactive effects of outcomes and procedures. *Psychological Bulletin, 120,* 189–208.

Brockner, J., Wiesenfeld, B. M., & Martin, C. L. (1995). Decision frame, procedural justice, and survivors' reactions to job layoffs. *Organizational Behavior and Human Decision Processes, 63,* 59–68.

Bromiley, P., & Curley, S. P. (1992). Individual differences in risk taking. In J. F. Yates (Ed.), *Risk-taking behavior* (pp. 87–132). New York: Wiley.

Brown, K. A., & Huber, V. L. (1992). Lowering floors and raising ceilings: A longitudinal assessment of the effects of an earnings-at-risk plan on pay satisfaction. *Personnel Psychology, 45,* 279–311.

Cable, D. M., & Judge, T. A. (1994). Pay preferences and job search decisions: A person-organization fit perspective. *Personnel Psychology, 47,* 317–348.

Deci, E. L., Connell, J. P., & Ryan, R. M. (1989). Self-determination in a work organization. *Journal of Applied Psychology, 74,* 580–590.

Deci, E. L., & Ryan, R. M. (1985). *Intrinsic motivation and self-determination in human behavior.* New York: Plenum.

Donovan, J., & Radosevich, D. (1998). The moderating role of goal commitment on the goal difficulty-performance relationship: A meta-analytic review and critical reanalysis. *Journal of Applied Psychology, 83,* 308–315.

Dunegan, K. J. (1996). Fines, frames, and images: Examining formulation effects on punishment decisions. *Organizational Behavior and Human Decision Processes, 68,* 58–67.

Ehrenberg, R. G., & Bognanno, M. L. (1990). The incentive effects of tournaments revisited: Evidence from the European PGA tour. *Industrial and Labor Relations Review, 43,* 74-S–88-S.

Eisenberger, R., Armeli, S., & Pretz, J. (1998). Can the promise of reward increase creativity? *Journal of Personality and Social Psychology, 74,* 704–714.

Eisenberger, R., & Cameron, J. (1996). Detrimental effects of reward: Reality or myth? *American Psychologist, 51,* 1153–1166.

Eisenberger, R., & Selbst, M. (1994). Does reward increase or decrease creativity? *Journal of Personality and Social Psychology, 66,* 1116–1127.

Eisenhardt, K. M. (1988). Agency- and institutional-theory explanations: The case of retail sales compensation. *Academy of Management Journal, 31,* 488–511.

Eisenhardt, K. M. (1989). Agency theory: An assessment and review. *Academy of Management Review, 14,* 57–74.

Fisher, C. D., & Locke, E. A. (1992). The new look in job satisfaction research and theory. In C. J. Cranny, P. C. Smith, & E. F. Stone (Eds.), *Job satisfaction* (pp. 165–194). San Francisco: New Lexington Press.

Florkowski, G. W. (1987). The organizational impact of profit sharing. *Academy of Management Review, 12,* 622–636.

Fox, J. B., Scott, K. D., & Donohue, J. M. (1993). An investigation into pay valence and performance in a pay-for-performance field setting. *Journal of Organizational Behavior, 14,* 687–693.

Gerhart, B., & Milkovich, G. T. (1990). Organizational differences in managerial compensation and financial performance. *Academy of Management Journal, 33,* 663–691.

Gerhart, B., & Milkovich, G. T. (1992). Employee compensation: Research and practice. In M. D. Dunnette & L. M. Hough (Eds.), *Handbook of industrial and organizational psychology* (2nd ed., Vol. 3, pp. 481–570). Palo Alto, CA: Consulting Psychologists Press.

Gerhart, G., Minkoff, H. B., & Olsen, R. N. (1995). Employee compensation: Theory, practice, and evidence. In G. R. Ferris, S. D. Rosen, & D. T. Barnum (Eds.), *Handbook of human resource management* (pp. 528–547). Oxford: Blackwell.

Gerhart, G., Trevor, C. O., & Graham, M. E. (1996). New directions in compensation research: Synergies, risk, and survival. *Research in Personnel and Human Resources Management, 14,* 143–203.

Gomez-Mejia, L. R. (1992). Structure and process of diversification, compensation strategy, and firm performance. *Strategic Management Journal, 13,* 381–397.

Gomez-Mejia, L. R., & Balkin, D. B. (1992). *Compensation, organizational strategy, and firm performance.* Cincinnati, OH: South-Western.

Gomez-Mejia, L. R., & Wiseman, R. M. (1997). Reframing executive compensation: An assessment and outlook. *Journal of Management, 23,* 291–374.

Goodman, P. S. (1974). An examination of referents used in the evaluation of pay. *Organizational Behavior and Human Performance, 12,* 170–195.

Greenberg, J. (1987). Reactions to procedural injustice in payment distribution: Do the means justify the ends? *Journal of Applied Psychology, 72,* 55–61.

Greenberg, J. (1990a). Employee theft as a reaction to underpayment inequity: The hidden cost of pay cuts. *Journal of Applied Psychology, 75,* 561–568.

Greenberg, J. (1990b). Organizational justice: Yesterday, today, and tomorrow. *Journal of Management, 16,* 399–432.

Greenberg, J. (1993). The social side of fairness: Interpersonal and informational classes of organizational justice. In R. Cropanzano (Ed.), *Justice in the workplace: Approaching fairness in human resource management* (pp. 79–103). Mahwah, NJ: Erlbaum.

Harder, J. (1991). Equity theory versus expectancy theory: The case of major league baseball free agents. *Journal of Applied Psychology, 76,* 458–464.

Harrison, D. A., Virick, M., & William, S. (1996). Working without a net: Time, performance, and turnover under maximally contingency rewards. *Journal of Applied Psychology, 81,* 331–345.

Huselid, M. (1995). The impact of human resource management practices in turnover, productivity, and corporate financial performance. *Academy of Management Journal, 38,* 635–672.

Jensen, M., & Meckling, M. (1976). Theory of the firm: Managerial behavior, agency costs, and ownership structure. *Journal of Financial Economics, 3,* 305–360.

Jensen, M., & Murphy, K. (1990). Performance pay and top-management incentives. *Journal of Political Economy, 98,* 225–264.

Kahneman, D., & Tversky, A. (1979). Prospect theory: An analysis of decisions under risk. *Econometrica, 47,* 262–291.

Kerr, S. (1995). On the folly of rewarding A while hoping for B. *Academy of Management Executive, 9*(2), 7–14.

Knight, D., Durham, C. C., & Locke, E. A. (1998). *The relationship of team goals, efficacy, and incentives to riskiness of chosen strategies, tactics, and performance.* Unpublished manuscript, R. H. Smith School of Business, University of Maryland at College Park.

Koenig, R. (1990, October 25). Du Pont plan linking pay to fibers profit unravels. *Wall Street Journal,* pp. B1, B4.

Kulik, C. T., & Ambrose, M. L. (1992). Personal and situational determinants of referent choice. *Academy of Management Review, 17,* 212–237.

Latham, G. P., Mitchell, T. R., & Dossett, D. L. (1978). Importance of participative goal setting and anticipated rewards on goal difficulty and job performance. *Journal of Applied Psychology, 63,* 163–171.

Lawler, E. E., III. (1971). *Pay and organizational effectiveness.* New York: McGraw Hill.

Lawler, E. E., III. (1990). *Strategic pay: Aligning organizational strategies and pay systems.* San Francisco: Jossey-Bass.

Lawler, E. E., III. (1994). From job-based to competency-based organizations. *Journal of Organizational Behavior, 15,* 3–15.

Lawler, E. E., III, & Jenkins, G. D., Jr. (1992). Strategic reward systems. In M. D. Dunnette & L. M. Hough (Eds.), *Handbook of industrial and organizational psychology* (2nd ed., Vol. 3, pp. 1009–1055). Palo Alto, CA: Consulting Psychologists Press.

Lazear, E. P. (1998). *Personnel economics for managers.* New York: Wiley.

Lazear, E. P., & Rosen, S. (1981). Rank-order tournaments as optimum labor contracts. *Journal of Political Economy, 89,* 841–864.

Ledford, G. E., Jr. (1995). Paying for the skills, knowledge, and competencies of knowledge workers. *Compensation and Benefits Review, 28*(4), 55–62.

Lee, C. (1985). Increasing performance appraisal effectiveness: Matching task types, appraisal process, and rater training. *Academy of Management Review, 10,* 322–331.

Lee, T. W., Locke, E. A., & Phan, S. H. (1997). Explaining the assigned goal-incentive interaction: The role of self-efficacy and personal goals. *Journal of Management, 23,* 541–559.

Lepak, D. P., & Snell, S. A. (1999). The human resource architecture: Toward a theory of human capital allocation and development. *Academy of Management Review, 24,* 31–48.

Levine, J. M., & Moreland, R. L. (1987). Social comparison and outcome evaluation in group contexts. In J. C. Masters & W. P. Smith (Eds.), *Social comparison, justice, and relative deprivation: Theoretical, empirical, and policy perspectives* (pp. 105–127). Mahwah, NJ: Erlbaum.

Locke, E. A. (1986). *Generalizing from laboratory to field settings*. San Francisco: New Lexington Press.

Locke, E. A. (1997). The motivation to work: What we know. In *Advances in motivation and achievement* (Vol. 10, pp. 375–412). Greenwich, CT: JAI Press.

Locke, E. A., Alavi, M., & Wagner, J. A., III. (1997). Participation in decision making: An information exchange perspective. In G. R. Ferris (Ed.), *Research in personnel and human resources management* (Vol. 15, pp. 293–331). Greenwich, CT: JAI Press.

Locke, E. A., Feren, D. B., McCaleb, V. M., Shaw, K. N., & Denny, A. T. (1980). The relative effectiveness of four methods of motivating employee performance. In K. D. Duncan, M. M. Gruneberg, & D. Wallis (Eds.), *Changes in working life* (pp. 363–388). London: Wiley.

Locke, E. A., & Latham, G. P. (1990). *A theory of goal setting and task performance*. Upper Saddle River, NJ: Prentice Hall.

Macey, S. J., & Sabounghi, J. M. (1996). A roundtable discussion on defining, designing, and evaluating pay at risk programs. *ACA Journal, 5*(4), 8–19.

McClelland, D. C. (1961). *The achieving society*. New York: Van Nostrand Reinhold.

McNutt, R. P. (1990). Sharing across the board: Du Pont's achievement sharing program. *Compensation and Benefits Review, 22*(4), 17–24.

Meyer, H. H., Kay, E., & French, J. R. P., Jr. (1965). Split roles in performance appraisal. *Harvard Business Review, 43*(1), 123–129.

Miles, E. W., Hatfield, J. D., & Huseman, R. C. (1989). The equity sensitivity construct: Potential implications for worker performance. *Journal of Management, 15*, 581–588.

Miles, R. E., & Snow, C. C. (1984). Designing strategic human resources systems. *Organizational Dynamics, 13*(1), 36–52.

Milkovich, G. T., Gerhart, B., & Hannon, J. (1991). The effects of research and development intensity on managerial compensation in large organizations. *Journal of High Technology Management Research, 2*, 133–150.

Milkovich, G. T., & Newman, J. M. (1996). *Compensation* (5th ed.). Burr Ridge, IL: Irwin.

Mohrman, A. M., Jr., Resnick-West, S. M., & Lawler, E. E., III. (1989). *Designing performance appraisal systems: Aligning appraisals and organizational realities*. San Francisco: Jossey-Bass.

Montemayor, E. F. (1994). A model for aligning teamwork and pay. *ACA Journal, 3*(2), 18–25.

Montemayor, E. F. (1996). Congruence between pay policy and competitive strategy in high-performing firms. *Journal of Management, 22*, 889–908.

Moorthy, K. S. (1993). Theoretical modeling in marketing. *Journal of Marketing, 57,* 92–106.

Mowen, J. C., Middlemist, R. D., & Luther, D. (1981). Joint effects of assigned goal level and incentive structure on task performance: A laboratory study. *Journal of Applied Psychology, 66,* 598–603.

Moye, N. A., Masterson, S. S., & Bartol, K. M. (1997, August). *Differentiating antecedents and consequences of procedural and interactional justice: Empirical evidence in support of separate constructs.* Paper presented at the annual meeting of the Academy of Management, Boston.

Neale, M. A., Huber, V. L., & Northcraft, G. B. (1987). The framing of negotiations: Contextual vs. task frames. *Organizational Behavior and Human Decision Processes, 39,* 228–241.

Ouchi, W. (1977). The relationship between organizational structure and organizational control. *Administrative Science Quarterly, 22,* 95–113.

Petty, M. M., Singleton, B., & Connell, D. W. (1992). An experimental evaluation of an organizational incentive plan in the electric utility industry. *Journal of Applied Psychology, 77,* 427–436.

Pfeffer, J. (1998). Six dangerous myths about pay. *Harvard Business Review, 76*(3), 108–119.

Porter, L. W., & Lawler, E. E., III. (1968). *Managerial attitudes and performance.* Burr Ridge, IL: Irwin.

Prince, J. B., & Lawler, E. E., III. (1986). Does salary discussion hurt the developmental performance appraisal? *Organizational Behavior and Human Decision Processes, 37,* 357–375.

Pritchard, R. D., & Curtis, M. I. (1973). The influence of goal setting and financial incentives on task performance. *Organizational Behavior and Human Performance, 10,* 175–183.

Riedel, J. A., Nebeker, D. M., & Cooper, B. L. (1988). The influence of monetary incentives on goal choice, goal commitment, and task performance. *Organizational Behavior and Human Decision Processes, 42,* 155–180.

Rynes, S. L., Schwab, D. P., & Heneman, H. G., III. (1983). The role of pay and market pay variability in job application decisions. *Organizational Behavior and Human Performance, 31,* 353–364.

Scholl, R. W., Cooper, E. A., & McKenna, J. F. (1987). Referent selection in determining equity perceptions: Differential effects on behavioral and attitudinal outcomes. *Personnel Psychology, 40,* 113–124.

Schuster, J. R., & Zingheim, P. K. (1992). *The new pay: Linking employee and organizational performance.* San Francisco: New Lexington Press.

Shalley, C. E. (1991). Effects of productivity goals, creativity goals, and personal discretion on individual creativity. *Journal of Applied Psychology, 76,* 179–185.

Shelley, M. K., & Omer, T. C. (1996). Intertemporal framing issues in management compensation. *Organizational Behavior and Human Decision Processes, 66,* 42–58.

Summers, T. P., & Hendrix, W. H. (1991). Modeling the role of pay equity perceptions: A field study. *Journal of Occupational Psychology, 64,* 145–157.

Thompson, K. R., Hochwarter, W. A., & Mathys, N. J. (1997). Stretch targets: What makes them effective? *Academy of Management Executive, 11,* 48–60.

Tosi, H. L, Katz, J. P., & Gomez-Mejia, L. R. (1997). Disaggregating the agency contract: The effects of monitoring, incentive alignment, and term in office on agent decision making. *Academy of Management Journal, 40,* 584–602.

Van Eerde, W., & Thierry, H. (1996). Vroom's expectancy models and work-related criteria: A meta-analysis. *Journal of Applied Psychology, 81,* 575–586.

Vroom, V. (1964). *Work and motivation.* New York: Wiley.

Vroom, V. (1966). Organizational choice: A study of pre- and postdecision processes. *Organizational Behavior and Human Performance, 1,* 212–225.

Wageman, R. (1995). Interdependence and group effectiveness. *Administrative Science Quarterly, 40,* 145–180.

Wagner, J. A., III, Rubin, P., & Callahan, T. J. (1988). Incentive payment and nonmanagerial productivity: An interrupted time series analysis of magnitude and trend. *Organizational Behavior and Human Decision Processes, 42,* 47–74.

Weitzman, M. L., & Kruse, D. L. (1990). Profit sharing and productivity. In A. S. Blinder (Ed.), *Paying for productivity: A look at the evidence* (pp. 95–141). Washington, DC: Brookings Institution.

Welbourne, T. M., & Gomez-Mejia, L. R. (1988). Gainsharing revisited. *Compensation and Benefits Review, 20*(4), 19–28.

Williams, C. R., & Livingstone, L. P. (1994). Another look at the relationship between performance and voluntary turnover. *Academy of Management Journal, 37,* 269–298.

Williamson, O. (1975). *Markets and hierarchies.* New York: Free Press.

Wright, P. M. (1989). Test of the mediating role of goals in the incentive-performance relationship. *Journal of Applied Psychology, 74,* 699–705.

Wright, P. M. (1992). An examination of the relationships among monetary incentives, goal level, goal commitment, and performance. *Journal of Management, 18,* 677–693.

Youndt, M. A., Snell, S. A., Dean, J. W., Jr., & Lepak, D. P. (1996). Human resource management, manufacturing strategy, and firm performance. *Academy of Management Journal, 39,* 836–866.

Zenger, T. R. (1992). Why do employers only reward extreme performance? Examining the relationships among performance, pay, and turnover. *Administrative Science Quarterly, 37,* 198–219.

Zucker, L. G. (1987). Institutional theories of organizations. *Annual Review of Sociology, 13,* 443–464.

Emerging Compensation Issues

CHAPTER 5

Compensation Strategy and Organizational Performance

Barry Gerhart

Strategy has been defined as "the determination of the basic long-term goals and objectives of an enterprise, and the adoption of courses of action and the allocation of resources necessary for carrying out these goals" (Chandler, 1962, p. 13). Of course, goals in organizations are seldom equally shared and valued by all members. Instead, interests vary among owners, top management, and employee groups. In each case, inducements must be offered in exchange for continued participation in the organization. In the case of top management and employees, compensation is a key inducement offered in exchange for active behavioral contributions toward a set of common goals (March & Simon, 1958).

How are these goals chosen and achieved? In Fama and Jensen's model (1983; see Barney, 1997), top management initiates action plans (strategy formulation), which must be ratified by the board of directors. Following ratification, it is up to top management to execute these plans (strategy implementation). Finally, according to the model, the board of directors measures (or monitors) the performance of management in strategy formulation and execution and compensates management accordingly. (See Barkema & Gomez-Mejia, 1998, for recent evidence on this aspect of the model.) Compensation strategy is likely to provide a key mechanism by which the board, on behalf of owners, can influence each step of the strategy process.

Similar processes roll down the rest of the organization hierarchy. For example, in a multidivisional organization, division general managers formulate and implement division-level strategies and are monitored by senior management. The translation of goals from one level to the next and their implementation, monitoring, and resulting compensation constitute critical elements of governance and control in the organization.

In addition to its importance in influencing the goals and behaviors of current organization members, compensation has at least two other important influences (Gerhart & Milkovich, 1992). First, it plays a major role in the attraction and retention of organization members (Rynes, 1987; see also Chapter Two of this book). Thus it shapes the composition of the organization in terms of its human capital and competencies. Second, compensation decisions have a major influence on costs. Blinder (1990) states that, on average, labor accounts for at least 70 percent of total costs. Taken together, the influence of compensation strategy on goals and behaviors, workforce composition, and costs suggests that it is a major determinant of success in strategy formulation and implementation and, by implication, business success.

Despite the importance of compensation strategy, the first major review of the compensation strategy literature appeared only about a decade ago, suggesting that research might not have kept up with the importance of the topic. In his 1988 review, George Milkovich described the strategic perspective on compensation as having three basic tenets. First, compensation policies and practices differ widely between organizations and between employee groups within organizations. Second, and closely related, these differences indicate that managers have the discretion to choose from an array of compensation policies. In other words, compensation policy is not solely determined by environmental constraints such as industry, size, technology, and type of employee. Third, "making compensation policies and practices contingent on organizational and environmental conditions has some desired effects on employee behaviors and the performance of organizations" (p. 264). Milkovich referred to this as the "most fundamental" of the tenets.

Milkovich also assessed the evidence available for evaluating each of the three tenets at that point in time. He noted that evidence regarding the first tenet, differences between organizations, was mostly "anecdotal" and "sporadic" and that such differences were seen by some as "random noise with little relevance" (p. 264). The second tenet, managerial discretion, also did not seem to have been systematically studied. Rather, much of the research available at that time focused on the ability of corporate and business unit strategy to predict compensation strategy. The third and most fundamental tenet, which dealt with performance consequences, was described as "probably the biggest leap of faith" (p. 264) with little in the way of "solid footings" (p. 283).

The purpose of this chapter is to review the work that has been done since Milkovich's review, to assess progress regarding the issues he raised, and to suggest directions for future researchers. Much research has been conducted on these issues since Milkovich's review. For example, there is solid evidence that organizations differ in their pay strategies and that these differences reflect managerial discretion. There is also solid evidence that compensation decisions affect business performance. However, research on the specific question of how the fit between pay and strategy influences business performance remains relatively underdeveloped, despite some interesting and supportive studies on fit between organizational strategy and pay strategy.

I organize my discussion in the following manner. First, I briefly review evidence on between-firm differences in compensation strategies and the roles of market forces and managerial discretion in explaining such differences. My discussion of other determinants of pay strategy is limited, except insofar as it relevant to understanding the consequences of different pay strategies, which is my main interest. Also, previous reviews (Gerhart & Milkovich, 1992; Gomez-Mejia & Balkin, 1992; Milkovich, 1988) have looked at the literature on determinants in some detail.

Second, I review evidence on the consequences of pay strategies. In their 1992 book, Gomez-Mejia and Balkin argued that "the ultimate dependent variable when making strategic pay choices is organizational performance." Yet they note that "because compensation has traditionally been a micro field of study buried within personnel management as a functional area, the connection between pay strategies and firm performance has been a neglected subject" (p. 130). Therefore, my focus is on performance measured at either the firm or strategic business unit level of analysis. I also limit my review to studies using either multiple firms or business units as the units of analysis.

Third, I examine the measurement of key constructs, including business performance, business strategy, and compensation strategy, because construct validity issues can have an important impact on the conclusions reached in substantive research (Cook & Campbell, 1979; Schwab, 1980). Finally, I suggest a set of issues that I believe future research should address.

Do Firms Differ?

In the neoclassical economics model, workers choose jobs that maximize their utility, meaning that they consider not only income but also nonpecuniary factors—job security, safety, work environment, and other factors that matter to them. Jobs that have less desirable nonpecuniary characteristics should command positive compensating wage differentials, while jobs with more favorable characteristics should carry lower rates of pay. This hedonic theory of wages holds that levels of pay should not differ across firms, once differences in nonpecuniary factors are controlled, and that any differences that are observed should be transitory. Otherwise, higher-wage firms would be flooded with applicants, which would drive pay rates lower within this group of firms, whereas the shortage of workers at other firms would drive pay rates higher there. Thus competitive market forces lead to equalization of pay rates across firms. In contrast, during the 1940s and 1950s, work by "post-institutional" (Segal, 1986) economists suggested that organizations in the same industry often had different and enduring pay levels for the same occupations (Dunlop, 1957; Lester, 1946; Reynolds, 1946) because of factors such as historical precedent, equity beliefs, and ability to pay. For example, an employer might need to raise wages to increase employment in the face of a tight labor market. Even though the labor market might eventually loosen, the employer might choose to maintain its higher pay rates because reductions to what had become the norm to employees would risk causing employee relations problems.

By the late 1950s and early 1960s, there was another shift, this time to a focus on supply-side factors as determinants of pay at the level of the individual employee. Most notable was the development of the human capital framework, which viewed education and work experience as investments that improved one's marginal product and earned a rate of return sufficient to provide an incentive for such investments (Becker, 1975; Schultz, 1963). Demand-side differences in pay level across employers due to different pay-level policies came to be deemphasized or even ignored.

However, by the 1980s, there was something of a resurrection of interest in demand-side differences, especially organization differences in pay, as a focus of study in sociology (Baron & Bielby, 1980), economics (Akerlof, 1984; Yellen, 1984), and management (Eisenhardt, 1988; Milkovich, 1988). Empirical studies of pay level that documented important and stable differences between employers again began to appear (Gerhart & Milkovich, 1990; Groshen, 1988, 1991; see Leonard, 1988, for an exception). In addition, policy capturing work also demonstrated that when faced with the same pay decision scenario, compensation professionals chose different pay strategies based in part on differences in pay strategies at their companies (Weber & Rynes, 1991).

In addition to pay level, Gerhart and Milkovich (1990) looked at differences in how organizations paid managers by measuring the ratio of annual bonus payments to base pay and the percentage of managers eligible for long-term incentives. They used data on roughly sixteen thousand managers from the top six levels at roughly two hundred organizations and followed them over a period of up to five years. Controlling for differences in human capital, job level, and organization characteristics, they found, consistent with Groshen (1988), that there were significant and stable employer differences in base pay over the five-year period. However, they found even larger stable employer differences in annual bonus and long-term incentive plans. They inferred that although organizations had some discretion regarding *how much* they paid, they had even more regarding *how* they paid.

Their explanation for the difference in discretion was that labor market pressures (paying enough to attract and retain employees of acceptable quality) set a floor for pay level, while product market pressures (keeping labor costs low enough to maintain product price competitiveness) set a ceiling. But the same amount of pay could be delivered in a variety of ways. More than thirty years earlier, Haire, Ghiselli, and Gordon (1967) had made the same point: organizations may have more discretion in terms of how they pay (versus how much) because delivery systems "can be varied by a company without increasing the total salary expense" (p. 10).

Two points regarding the role of discretion are necessary. First, agency theory suggests that employees are risk-averse and that a compensating pay differential is necessary for employees to accept risk sharing. Thus how organizations pay likely does have cost consequences, even if they are not as readily observable. This risk premium (and the risk aversion of employees) means that the discretion in pay delivery is perhaps not quite as great as suggested by Gerhart and Milkovich and Haire and colleagues.

Second, although researchers have often interpreted organizational differences in pay practices to mean that managers have significant discretion in setting pay strategy, more direct (as opposed to inferential) measures of discretion have also been used (Hambrick & Finkelstein, 1987). The psychometric properties of this discretion measure appear promising, particularly where care is taken to use multiple and expert raters (Hambrick & Abrahamson, 1995). Magnan and Saint-Onge (1997) found that a firm-level measure of discretion in banks was positively associated with the strength of the pay-for-performance link. Thus we may find that managerial strategic intentions (for example, as to link pay to performance) are more likely to be translated into action where sufficient discretion exists. Consequently, direct measures of discretion should probably be used to a greater extent in the pay strategy literature.

In summary, the importance of organization differences in compensation practices has returned as a central focus of compensation research. In addition, progress has been made in developing a scale to measure discretion at the organization level. Thus the field has shifted since the Milkovich (1988) review, a time at which there was still some question about whether organizational differences in compensation were really strategic. Finally, as the later examination of empirical research implies, the organizational differences in pay strategy that are most important have to do with how pay is delivered.

Consequences: Do Strategic Differences Matter?

Human Resource Strategies

It is useful to begin the discussion of pay consequences within the broader framework of the literature on human resources and business performance. Becker and Gerhart (1996) have noted an increasing effort by researchers to identify the relationships between human resource practices and business performance. Studies at both the firm level (for example, Delery & Doty, 1996; Huselid, 1995) and the facility level (Ichniowski, Shaw, & Prennushi, 1997; MacDuffie, 1995) have reported such relationships. Typically, the conceptual basis for such relationships is that certain human resource practices have a positive impact on either competencies or motivation, which in turn influences business performance.

Furthermore, Hansen and Wernerfelt (1989) compared the predictive power of economic and organizational models of firm performance and found that human resource factors explained more variance in business performance than more traditional economic determinants did. Using five-year average return on assets as the dependent variable, they found that the economic model, which included industry profitability, relative market share, and size, accounted for 14 percent of the variance in firm performance. The organizational model, which measured two aspects of organizational climate—average employee perceptions of emphasis on human resources and emphasis on goal accomplishment—explained an additional 32 percent of the variance in firm performance. These findings suggest, first, that firms similarly positioned within their respective industries can have very different organizational climates and, second, that such differences in climate may be important in explaining firm performance differences.

Although Hansen and Wernerfelt (1989) strongly suggest the importance of looking beyond the industry level to understand firm performance, two limiting features of their study should be noted. First, there were no controls for industry membership per se—only for industry profitability and market share within an industry. Thus the study does not permit us to make statements regarding the importance of organizational climate in explaining performance within industries where firms face similar product market conditions. Second, there is no description in the study regarding the timing of measurement of the variables. It is therefore impossible to determine whether firm performance was measured subsequent to organizational climate. Without such information, it is difficult to establish the time precedence necessary for causal inference.

A key question in the literature on human resources and firm performance is whether there is a set of core best practices or whether effectiveness depends on the alignment between HR practices and the organization's strategy (Becker & Gerhart, 1996). Although the latter notion of vertical fit has intuitive appeal, at this point in time, researchers have not marshaled convincing evidence of the importance of vertical fit. Rather, much of the evidence is more consistent with a best practices approach (Becker & Gerhart, 1996; Delery & Doty, 1996; Gerhart, Trevor, & Graham, 1996; Huselid, 1995; Pfeffer, 1994, 1998). This finding implies either that fit does not matter or else that there are a variety of statistical, conceptual, and design challenges that have not yet been successfully overcome in testing for fit (Gerhart et al., 1996). In any case, a key task of the present review is to examine fit evidence in the pay strategy literature.

However, prior to that, I describe a second and third type of fit that are conceptually important but for which empirical evidence is lacking in the pay strategy literature. The second type of fit is in some sense even more fundamental than vertical fit. This is the question of whether the consequences of pay strategies depend on their alignment or fit with other human resource practices such as employee involvement, staffing, development, and work organization. If the answer is yes, studying pay strategy in isolation could yield incorrect inferences. For example, one possibility is that pay strategy is confounded with other human resource practices such as employee involvement in decisions that influence business performance. If this is so, omitting involvement from the model would bias the estimated pay strategy effect, perhaps upward (Gerhart et al., 1996). An alternative scenario is that there are indeed synergies (as evidenced by statistical interactions, for example) between pay strategies and other HR practices such as involvement. In that case, omitting involvement would miss these nonlinear effects and thus either underestimate or overestimate the impact of pay strategies that are, respectively, horizontally well-aligned or misaligned with other HR practices.

Gerhart et al. (1996) concluded that there was only "weak support" (p. 164) for statistical interactions between compensation policies and other human resource policies in influencing effectiveness measures. Among the empirical studies they reviewed were those by Cooke (1994) on gainsharing and participation, and Kruse (1993) on profit sharing, participation, autonomous work teams, and suggestion systems. They also reviewed broader studies by MacDuffie (1995), Huselid (1995), and Ichniowski et al. (1997)

where pay was not the central focus. The evidence supporting horizontal alignment was again weak.

These findings suggest that pay strategy and other HR effects are typically additive, implying that omitting other HR variables may not be a problem. Nevertheless, this research is in its early stages, and subsequent work may provide stronger support for fit. Thus it would be both well-advised and instructive to include other HR variables in pay strategy research when possible.

A third fit question, the importance of internal alignment between dimensions of pay strategy, also remains unexplored, although different authors have made a variety of implicit assumptions about this issue. For example, Gomez-Mejia and Balkin's measure of pay strategy (1992) combines forty-eight items about different pay policies into seventeen subscales and a single overall scale ranging from algorithmic to experiential. Briefly, algorithmic strategies emphasize "mechanistic, predetermined, standardized, repetitive procedures," whereas the experiential pattern is "flexible and adaptive" (Gomez-Mejia, 1992, p. 382). (I return to this measure later.) The fact that scores on these items are added to form a linear combination implies that the effects of pay policy dimensions are additive and compensatory rather than nonlinear and synergistic. No empirical evidence on the validity of this assumption is available.

That central questions about alignment or fit remain unaddressed is an important gap in the literature, for two reasons. First, if there are statistical interactions, then estimates of main effects are misleading. Second, fit may be especially important in using pay strategy to develop a sustained competitive advantage if one follows the logic of the resource-based view of the firm (Gerhart et al., 1996). The resource-base view of the firm (Barney, 1991) emphasizes that resources contribute to sustained competitive advantage not only by creating value but also by being rare, difficult to imitate, and not having substitutes. If a resource adds value (only), it may help a firm achieve competitive parity but not competitive advantage. Presumably, a firm that follows the same best practices as other firms can only achieve parity. To go beyond that, it would need to develop unique alignments between elements of its pay strategy and between the pay strategy, other HR practices, and the business strategy.

Pay Strategies

Conceptual Framework

Before addressing fit issues, it is useful to describe the general mechanisms by which pay can have main effects on performance. Expectancy theory and agency theory suggest that linking pay to performance can have a positive influence on motivation and alignment of interests, respectively—two closely related concepts. Expectancy theory specifies that motivation to choose a particular course of action from multiple alternatives is a function of (1) the belief that effort will result in the target behavior (expectancy), (2) the belief that the behavior will result in valued outcomes (instrumentality), and (3) the anticipated value from such outcomes (valence).

Pay systems can influence each component. For example, expectancy perceptions can be increased through the use of skill-based and competency-based pay. Instrumentality perceptions can be increased by linking pay to controllable aspects of behavior. Money presumably has a positive valence for everyone.

According to agency theory, an agency relationship is one where one or more principals (such as stockholders) contract with one or more agents (for example, managers) "to perform some service on their behalf which involves delegating some decision making authority to the agent" (Jensen & Meckling, 1976, p. 308). Although agency theory is most often applied to the case where owners are principals and top managers are agents, Jensen and Meckling argue that "agency costs arise in any situation involving cooperative effort . . . by two or more people even though there is no clear cut principal-agent relationship" (p. 309).

Compensation policies play a central role in the contracts (implicit or explicit) just cited by providing an incentive for the agent to act on behalf of the principal. From the principal's point of view, contract enforcement is constrained by information asymmetry, which means that the principal has less information than the agent. This uncertainty opens the door for agents to exploit the situation to their advantage either by straying from the contracted behaviors (moral hazard problem) or misrepresenting their abilities prior to establishment of the contract (adverse selection).

Under a behavior-based contract, the principal seeks to monitor the behaviors of the agent and make judgments regarding their effectiveness. Pay is linked to these evaluations of behaviors (this is merit pay). Under an outcome-based contract, pay is again linked to performance, but this time to outcomes (such as stock returns or profits) instead of behaviors. Outcome-based contracts may be preferred where it is difficult or costly for the principal to monitor and evaluate specific behaviors. Agency theory predicts that a risk premium will be required under an outcome-based contract to compensate the agent for increased risk bearing, which results from the fact that agents have less direct control over outcomes relative to behavior. (For example, regardless of a manager's efforts, a firm's stock price can vary widely as a result of a host of external factors.) Under both types of contracts, linking pay to performance—whether measured as behaviors or outcomes—is recommended as an effective means of influencing effectiveness.

Beyond the hypothesized best practice effect of pay for performance, certain types of pay strategies (or contracts) may work better when aligned with important contingency factors. As noted earlier, although several types of alignment may be relevant, the literature has thus far focused largely on vertical alignment, the fit between pay and organizational strategies. We know, for example, that corporate strategy features such as the degree and type of diversification are associated with different compensation strategies (Pitts, 1976). Specifically, pay is more closely linked to business unit performance in more diversified firms and more strongly linked to corporate performance in firms that are either less diversified or where business units are in closely related product areas or require greater coordination.

Agency theory is helpful in understanding the link between diversification and pay strategy. As firms diversify into unrelated product markets, corporate directors have less expertise regarding such product markets, thus reducing their ability to monitor the behaviors of business unit managers. An alternative contracting arrangement is to link business unit managers' pay more strongly to formula-driven, outcome-based plans that depend on business unit performance.

Another element of corporate strategy is whether the firm is in the start-up or growth phase, as opposed to a more mature or maintenance stage of business (Ellig, 1981). At the growth stage, firms may need to conserve cash for investments in product development and marketing, leaving less money available for cash compensation and benefits. Thus growth firms, especially those in the early stages, may find it more effective to keep fixed costs (such as base pay and benefits) below the market but provide long-term earnings opportunities through such things as stock plans that can lead to total compensation levels well above the market.

At the business unit level, most attention has been devoted to the generic defender and prospector strategies described by Miles and Snow (1978, 1994).[1] The defender strategy tends toward centralized decision making, a limited and stable product line, and an emphasis on cost efficiency through high volume and market penetration. In contrast, prospector organizations are characterized by broad, changing product lines that require decentralized decision making to facilitate innovation, flexibility, and rapid response to changing conditions.

Given the central importance of coordination and efficiency, as well as the fact that defenders typically operate in mature markets, one would predict that above-market base pay and benefits and centralized and consistent pay policies are optimal for defenders. In contrast, the prospector strategy's focus on growth, innovation, and quick response leads to the recommendation that pay have a substantial incentive component and that pay decisions be decentralized to permit fit with different market conditions.

Empirical Literature

Early Studies. At the time of Milkovich's review (1988), only two studies on the performance consequences of compensation strategies and fit (Balkin & Gomez-Mejia, 1987; Gomez-Mejia, 1987) were available, and both were limited by the use of subjective assessments of firm performance as a dependent variable. This caused Milkovich to conclude that "the effects of compensation strategy and the degree of its 'fit' with organization strategy on performance remains unplowed turf. Considering the elusiveness of the notion of the 'degree of fit,' it seems like risky research" (p. 284).[2]

However, four years later, Gomez-Mejia and Balkin (1992) had a more optimistic assessment: "empirical evidence supports the theoretical expectation that compensation strategies can make a significant contribution to firm performance, whether measured perceptually or objectively. The strength of this relationship increases as a function of their integration with other organizational elements" (p. 146).

Gomez-Mejia and Balkin based their conclusion in large part on six studies that were available at the time. Only two of these studies (Balkin & Gomez-Mejia, 1987; Gomez-Mejia, 1992) were available at the time of the Milkovich review. I now turn to an examination of the six early studies, which have formed the basis for subsequent research.

1. Balkin and Gomez-Mejia (1987) surveyed 105 single-product firms located in the Boston area. Approximately one-third were classified as high-technology firms (their research and development expenditures were at least 5 percent of sales); the other two-thirds were not. The focus of the study was scientists and engineers in the research and development units of the surveyed firms. The dependent variable, pay effectiveness, was measured using subjective assessments provided by the top human resource executive responsible for compensation at each firm. Compensation strategy was also measured using subjective assessments from the same respondent at each firm. The key dimension of compensation was the degree to which each firm used an incentive-based strategy. Organization characteristics were size, high technology (yes or no), and life cycle stage (growth, mature).

Balkin and Gomez-Mejia hypothesized and reported empirical support for an incentive-based strategy being most effective for firms that were small, in high technology, or in the growth stage.[3]

2. Balkin and Gomez-Mejia (1990) also examined the influence of compensation strategy on subjective assessments of effectiveness using business unit strategy (in this case, life cycle) as a contingency factor. However, their 1990 study differed in two ways. First, compensation strategy was measured using thirteen subscales rather than a single dimension. Second, corporate strategy (diversification) was added as a contingency variable. I summarize just a few of the key findings here. First, consistent with their 1987 study, the use of an incentive-based pay strategy was seen as more effective in growth firms than in maintenance firms. Second, an incentive-based pay strategy was most effective in single-product firms and least effective in related-product firms. However, this analysis used no control variables and reported no measure of variance explained (R^2, for example). It is therefore difficult to know precisely

how much of a difference the contingency factors made in firm performance.

3. Gomez-Mejia and Balkin (1989) used self-reports of effectiveness provided by 175 research and development employees from 175 firms in the Boston area. They found that the respondents in this sample generally believed that team-based and organization-based (such as stock and profit-sharing) incentive plans were more effective than individual-oriented plans. No fit questions were examined.

4. In contrast to the previous three Balkin and Gomez-Mejia studies, Gomez-Mejia (1992) used an objective measure of firm performance as the dependent variable. Specifically, he used a composite of five-year averages (1982–1986) of earnings per share, return on investment, average return on common stock, and average annual percent change in firm's market value. Based on this composite, each firm was assigned to performance quartiles. As with the earlier Balkin and Gomez-Mejia studies, corporate strategy was measured in terms of extent of diversification. In addition, process of diversification was measured, with steady state referring to internal growth that tends to be related to current businesses and with evolutionary processes referring to growth through acquisition of new businesses. Also, as in the earlier Balkin and Gomez-Mejia work, compensation strategy was measured by an assessment provided by a single respondent at each firm.

A new set of items was used. Forty-one items, covering fifteen subscales, were factor-analyzed and reported to be explained by a single dimension that was used to classify firms as having either algorithmic or experiential pay strategies. (Gomez-Mejia & Balkin, 1992, subsequently modified the measure to have forty-eight items and seventeen subscales.) However, as Table 5.1 indicates, there are many other differences between the two pay strategies, including their emphasis on incentives, risk sharing, and internal versus external equity.

Gomez-Mejia (1992) found that there was no main effect for compensation strategy on firm performance. However, there was support for interactions between compensation strategy and corporate strategy. Experiential strategies were found to be most effective in single-product and evolutionary firms. Contrary to what was hypothesized, an experiential strategy did not add value in conglomerates.

Table 5.1. Strategic Pay Choices.

Algorithmic	Experiential
Basis for pay	
Job	Skills
Membership	Performance
Individual performance	Aggregate performance
Short-term orientation	Long-term orientation
Risk aversion	Risk taking
Corporate performance	Division performance
Internal equity	External equity
Hierarchical	Egalitarian
Qualitative performance measures	Quantitative performance measures
Design Issues	
Above-market salary and benefits	Below-market salary and benefits, above-market salary and incentives
Emphasis on salary and benefits	Emphasis on incentives
Infrequent rewards	Frequent rewards
Emphasis on intrinsic rewards	Emphasis on extrinsic rewards
Administrative Framework	
Centralized	Decentralized
Pay secrecy	Pay openness
Managers make pay decisions	Employees participate in pay decisions
Bureaucratic	Flexible

Source: Adapted from Gomez-Mejia (1992, Table 3–1).

Algorithmic strategies were found to be most effective in dominant-product, related-product, and steady-state firms.

The magnitude of effects was substantial. The interactions just described explained 11 percent of the variance in firm performance, in addition to the 14 percent explained by the control (life cycle, firm size, labor cost ratio, research and development intensity) and strategy variables. Further, mean differences in firm performance were large, depending on the fit of the compensation strategy. For example, a single-product firm using an algorithmic strategy had a mean firm performance quartile of 2.04, versus a mean performance quartile of 3.37 for a single-product firm using an experiential strategy.

Nevertheless, there are again issues that make interpretation difficult. First, and most important, is the fact that the dependent variable, firm performance, was measured over the period 1982–1986, whereas the independent variables, compensation and business or corporate strategy, were measured afterward (in 1988). Thus there is no time precedence, an important requirement for establishing causality. Second, when the corporation is the unit of analysis, to the extent that firms are diversified, it is not clear how either life cycle (see Milkovich, 1988) or compensation strategy can be meaningfully measured.

5. Gomez-Mejia and Balkin (1992) describe additional unpublished results obtained by Gomez-Mejia, apparently using the sample in the study just described. Essentially, the unpublished results indicate that business strategy (in this case, whether a business unit is a defender or prospector) makes a difference in the effectiveness of pay strategy. Consistent with his hypotheses, Gomez-Mejia found that an experiential pattern was more effective for prospectors than for defenders, who performed better when an algorithmic strategy was used.

In summary, although the innovative research by Gomez-Mejia and Balkin has provided an important start for the field, there are many issues that must be addressed before their substantive findings can be interpreted with more confidence. One impediment has been the change in the nature of the compensation strategy measure used in each study. Although this has no doubt been a result of efforts toward continuous improvement in measurement, the changes make it more difficult to cumulate findings. There have also been problems with the performance-dependent variables. In some cases, the performance measure is subjective and the referent is pay effectiveness rather than firm effectiveness. In the one case where effectiveness was measured objectively using the firm as the referent, the timing of the measurement was a problem in that the independent variables were measured after firm performance.

6. In a study described earlier, Gerhart and Milkovich (1990) used return on assets (ROA) as their dependent variable and three dimensions of compensation as independent variables: base pay, bonus-to-base ratio, and long-term incentive eligibility. Archival data on individuals were aggregated to develop firm-level means (adjusted for individual and job characteristics). Thus in contrast to the previous five studies, both compensation and firm performance were measured using objective data.

For each employee, a residual score was obtained for each compensation variable that adjusted for firm differences in employee education, age, tenure, job level, and levels supervised. The residuals were then averaged by firm to generate firm-level compensation strategy scores.

These scores were then used to predict either year-to-year changes in ROA or a multiyear average of ROA (mean = 6.1 percent). Depending on the specification (whether within organizations or within two- and three-digit industries), an increase of 10 percentage points in the bonus-to-base ratio was associated with a 0.5 to 0.9 percentage point increase in ROA (that is, increases of 8 to 15 percent). An increase of 10 percentage points in long-term incentive eligibility was associated with a 0.2 percentage point increase (or 3 percent) in average ROA. Thus, for example, an organization moving from having 20 percent of its managers eligible for long-term incentives to having 80 percent eligible would be expected to increase its return on assets by $6 \times 0.2 = 1.2$ percentage points, a substantial increase.

Like the others, the Gerhart and Milkovich (1990) study suffers from drawbacks. For example, although their controls for individual characteristics were fairly extensive, controls for industry- and firm-level determinants of firm performance were limited to industry categories (a mix of two- and three-digit industry codes). In addition, their study ignored fit questions.

More Recent Studies. Since the early studies, several additional studies published in *Strategic Management Journal, Administrative Science Quarterly,* and the *Academy of Management Journal* have examined the relationship between compensation strategy and firm performance. These more recent studies, along with the six earlier ones, are summarized in Table 5.2. In addition, several other studies not using firm performance as the dependent variable have used strategic decisions, which are believed to intervene between pay decisions and firm performance, as a the dependent variable. These studies are summarized in Table 5.3. I will review recent studies of both types.

Firm Performance. Table 5.2 summarizes fifteen studies linking pay decisions to firm performance, eleven of which were published since the Milkovich and Gomez-Mejia and Balkin reviews. Of these eleven more recent studies, eight either focused exclusively on main effects of pay decisions or included pay decisions as part of a broader group of human resource policies (so that the fit between pay per se and other factors was not directly examined). By far the predominant theoretical base for these studies was agency theory, followed by expectancy theory approaches.

In seven of the eight main-effects studies, it was found that firm performance was higher when some sort of pay-for-performance plan was used. The exception was the study by Seward and Walsh (1996), which found that the market reaction to spinoff companies was not influenced by the degree to which the chief executive officer and directors of the spinoff had their pay linked to performance. Of the seven supportive studies, two used perceptual measures of firm performance, while the other five used growth, profitability, or stock-related measures.

The effect sizes in these studies were at times quite substantial. For example, Delery and Doty (1996) found that banks that were one standard deviation above the mean in use of results-oriented performance appraisals and profit sharing for loan officers had a return on assets that was 23 percent higher (1.32 versus 1.07) and a return on equity that was 23 percent higher (15.81 versus 12.87) than firms at the mean. As another example, Welbourne and Andrews (1996), in a sample of 132 initial public offerings (IPOs), found that IPOs one standard deviation above the mean on both human resource value and organization-based pay for performance had a five-year survival rate of 92 percent versus a five-year survival rate of 34 percent for IPOs one standard deviation below the mean on both dimensions. Two of the studies focused not on pay for performance per se as the independent variable but rather on whether the firm was manager- or owner-controlled. The rule of thumb typically used in the literature is that a firm is owner-controlled if a single investor owns at least 5 percent of the company's stock. Kroll, Wright, Toombs, and Leavell (1997) found that the market reaction to major acquisitions was negative when the acquiring firm was manager-controlled but positive when it was owner-controlled. Tosi and Gomez-Mejia (1994) reported that monitoring of managerial actions (measured using a seventeen-item scale) was more important for achieving strong good performance in manager-controlled firms than in owner-controlled firms. In summary, these two studies support the basic agency theory assumption that owners' and managers' interests are not aligned and that misalignment is associated with lower firm performance.

Only two of the more recent studies built on the path forged by Gomez-Mejia and Balkin in their earlier work (1989, 1992) on the consequences of fit between pay and organization strategies. However, both were supportive of this earlier work. In the first study, Rajagopalan (1996) used data on fifty investor-owned electric utility firms over a five-year period to yield about 235 observations. Because of deregulation, many of the firms adopted new incentive plans for their senior managers.

Rajagopalan (1996) argued that both managerial discretion and incentive alignment problems (agency issues) differ according to business unit strategy. (Note that he used single-product firms.) In prospectors, not only do managers have more discretion, but also managerial behaviors cannot be specified a priori because of the greater uncertainty and focus on new products, markets, and creativity. Therefore, incentives become especially important for promoting risk taking and a long-term orientation. Overall, his hypotheses were supported. Prospectors performed better on both accounting and market return measures when long-term stock plans were used for senior managers. He also found that defenders did better on the accounting return measure when they used annual bonus plans and worse when they used long-term stock plans. Rajagopalan found the main effects of pay strategy to be essentially zero; rather, effects depended on the business unit strategy.

Table 5.2. Performance Outcomes of Pay Strategies.

Dependent Variable	Finding	Theory	Outcome Unit of Analysis	Pay Unit of Analysis	Study
Return on assets Return on equity	Higher with profit sharing	Agency	Firm	Loan officers	Delery & Doty (1996)
Initial price premium of initial public offering; survival probability of initial public offering	Lower and higher, respectively, with greater use of stock options, profit sharing, and gainsharing	Population ecology	Firm	Employee cross section	Welbourne & Andrews (1996)
Perceived organizational performance	Higher with more emphasis on job performance in determining pay	Ability and motivation	Firm	Employee cross section	Delaney & Huselid (1996)
Perceived organizational effectiveness	Higher when outcome-based pay used in high agency cost situations	Agency	Business unit (foreign subsidiaries)	Business unit senior managers	Roth & O'Donnell (1996)
Growth in number of stores	More with greater use of franchising (residual claimant versus salaries manager)	Agency	Firm	Store managers/owners	Shane (1996)
Sales per employee; Tobin's *Q*; return on assets	Higher (except for ROA) to the extent that pay was linked to performance appraisal results, formal appraisal process was in place, and promotion was based on merit	Ability and motivation	Firm	Employee cross section	Huselid (1995)
Profitability; stock performance; self-reported firm performance	Monitoring more strongly related to firm performance in manager-controlled firms	Agency	Firm	Senior managers	Tosi & Gomez-Mejia (1994)
Return on assets	Firms that rely more heavily on annual incentive and long-term incentive plans for managers had higher ROA	Agency expectancy	Firm	Managers within six levels of the board	Gerhart & Milkovich (1990)

Study	Sample	Level	Perspective	Measure	Findings
Kroll, Wright, Toombs, & Leavell (1997)	Senior managers	Firm	Agency	Cumulative abnormal market returns	Market reactions to major acquisitions are negative when acquiring firm is manager-controlled, positive when owner-controlled
Seward & Walsh (1996)	CEO and directors	Firm	Agency	Cumulative abnormal market returns	Market reaction to spinoffs did not depend on whether performance-contingent pay was used for the CEO and directors
Balkin & Gomez-Mejia (1987)	Employee cross section	Firm	Administrative fit	*Perceived* effectiveness of pay	Incentive-based pay perceived as more effective for growth, small, and high-technology firms
Balkin & Gomez-Mejia (1990)	Employee cross section	Firm; business unit	Administrative fit	*Perceived* effectiveness of pay	Incentive-based pay perceived as more effective for moderately diversified (versus single-product) firms and for business units at the growth stage
Gomez-Mejia (1992)	Employee cross section	Firm	Administrative fit	Composite of five-year average of earnings per share, return on investment, return on common stock, and change in market value	Single-product firms performed better with experiential pay, whereas dominant-product, related-product, and steady-state firms performed better with algorithmic pay
Rajagopalan (1996)	Senior managers	Firm	Agency; managerial discretion; fit	Annual return on capital employed; total shareholder return	Main effects of pay plans are basically zero; effects depend on fit with business strategy; prospectors perform better with long-term stock plans; some weaker evidence that defenders perform better with short-term bonus plans
Bloom & Milkovich (1998)	Top and middle-level managers	Firm	Agency fit	Total shareholder return	Annual incentive plans have negative effects on total shareholder return in firms that have high variability in stock performance

The Rajagopalan (1996) study provides some of the most convincing evidence to date on the fit between pay and business strategy. The use of single, narrowly defined industry controls for extraneous influences on firm performance and the use of longitudinal data on changes in pay strategies also strengthen causal inference. Rajagopalan also addresses some interesting external validity issues in his article. For example, he notes that the findings of Beatty and Zajac (1994) regarding the possible negative effects of too much risk in pay were obtained using a sample of initial public offerings where senior managers held 55 percent of equity on average. In his study, by contrast, the average was 1.5 percent, meaning that the drawbacks of too much risk probably had not yet come into play.

In a second study, Bloom and Milkovich (1998) addressed the compensation risk issue directly. They used longitudinal data on a diverse set of approximately seven hundred firms and one hundred fifty thousand top- and middle-level managers in those firms. They also introduced hierarchical linear modeling to the pay strategy literature, which is very useful for analyzing data taken from multiple levels of analysis. Their theoretical focus was on the role of business risk as a key determinant of base pay and bonus pay policies and as a moderator of their influence on firm performance. Greater business risk is expected to create greater employment risk and thus greater risk to future income among managers. Bloom and Milkovich hypothesized that firms with more business risk would be less likely to add income risk to managerial pay by using incentive pay and that business risk would be associated with higher base pay (a compensating risk differential). They expected business risk and incentive pay to be more strongly and negatively related in manager-controlled firms. Finally, Bloom and Milkovich hypothesized that as business risk increased, greater use of incentive pay would result in decreases in firm performance, as measured by total shareholder return.

There was at least some support for each of Bloom and Milkovich's hypotheses. I focus here on the results for the firm performance equation. Controlling for other variables, they found that a firm having firm-specific business risk and incentive pay one standard deviation above the mean had a predicted shareholder return of –0.025, whereas a firm with the same risk but incentive pay one standard deviation below the mean had a predicted total shareholder return of 0.047. (Mean total shareholder return for the entire sample was 0.17.) Thus these results suggest that adding risk to pay through the use of annual bonuses can have substantial and negative effects on shareholder return. Bloom and Milkovich's use of longitudinal data and other features such as the large sample size and well-tested risk measures from the finance literature make their finding regarding the importance of risk as a contingency factor one of the most convincing in the literature.

Together with the Beatty and Zajac (1994) findings, the Bloom and Milkovich (1998) findings suggest that attempting to use outcome-based contracts to align interests and share risks can have troublesome consequences. As noted previously, the very high level of pay risk in the Beatty and Zajac study is a key boundary variable. In the Bloom and Milkovich study, the mean ratio of annual bonus to base pay was 0.20. Although this may appear to be less pay risk, it should be remembered that Bloom and Milkovich looked at several levels of managers (average base pay of $85,000), whereas Beatty and Zajac's sample was composed of CEOs. Thus the amount of risk experienced may not have been terribly different if the lower overall compensation in the Bloom and Milkovich sample made potential variability in income more consequential. In contrast, the sample used by Rajagopalan (1996) had much lower pay at risk.

One caveat in interpreting studies of risk should be noted. Bloom and Milkovich did not include stock plans in their measures of compensation. However, we know from the Black-Scholes approach to pricing stock options, for example, that the value of options increases as risk increases. This is because volatility in the stock price means there is a greater chance that the option can be exercised at a price that is well above the strike price of the option. We also know that companies may reprice options (lower) when the stock price drops significantly or issue more options to take advantage of what is hoped to be a temporary price decline. Thus it is possible that adding risk to compensation by granting stock options may not have the same negative impact as adding risk through annual bonus plans.

Strategic Decisions. An additional twelve studies looked at strategic management decisions as the dependent variable. To my knowledge, none of these studies was reviewed by either Milkovich (1988) or Gomez-Mejia and Balkin (1992). With one exception (Cowherd

& Levine, 1992), all of these studies were grounded in agency theory. Thus the primary focus in all studies is the degree to which managers engage in strategic actions that the authors judge likely to be in the best interests of owners. Generally, this means less risk aversion, less growth through acquisition of unrelated product lines, less managerial entrenchment (Shleifer & Vishny, 1989), and a longer-term investment-oriented approach.

Such studies can be viewed as using dependent variables that are proxies for performance or as examinations of variables that may intervene between compensation strategy and firm performance. In the latter case, such studies offer the possibility of insights into the causal mechanisms by which pay influences performance, thus improving our understanding and confidence regarding the nature of the relationship.

As Table 5.3 indicates, with some exceptions (Buchholtz & Ribbens, 1994; Kosnik, 1992; Sapienza & Gupta, 1994), there was general support for the impact of pay strategies on strategic decisions. In particular, a higher degree of ownership among senior managers and officers was associated with greater spending on research and development (Hill & Snell, 1989), whereas linking pay to short-term accounting measures was associated with less such spending (Hitt, Hoskisson, Johnson, & Moesel, 1996). In addition, stock ownership was also associated with a longer-term approach to human resources (Galbraith & Merrill, 1991; Gerhart & Trevor, 1996). There was also evidence that stock ownership was more likely to encourage internal growth and less likely to encourage external growth through diversification (Hill & Snell, 1989; Hitt et al., 1996; Phan & Hill, 1995), whereas pay linked to short-term profit and cash flow objectives was more likely to encourage diversification through external acquisitions.

Yet as noted earlier, more ownership is not always necessarily better. Consistent with ideas developed earlier by Zajac and Westphal (1994), Wright, Ferris, Sarin, and Awasthi (1996), for example, found that risk taking by senior executives and board members increased as their ownership of company stock increased. However, beyond a certain point, ownership actually reduced risk taking. This finding is important because it suggests that there is an optimal level of risk sharing. Too little or too much can both reduce risk-taking behavior, which would in turn be expected to reduce firm performance if higher-risk, higher-return projects are bypassed.

Indeed, this expectation fits nicely with Bloom and Milkovich's findings. (See Chapter Nine for a more detailed analysis of the role of risk in compensation.)

The lone study not using an agency theory approach was conducted by Cowherd and Levine (1992). These researchers used a distributive justice framework that led them to hypothesize that business units having larger pay differentials between senior managers and other employees would be characterized by greater feelings of injustice or inequity among employees, which would translate into behaviors that would negatively affect customer perceptions of product quality. Their empirical findings supported this hypothesis.

This finding is clearly very relevant for the current controversy regarding the magnitude of executive pay. Although increasing the amount of ownership among senior managers may have positive effects on attraction, retention, and alignment of their interests with those of owners, there may well be an offsetting consequence of such a policy. In addition to the possibility that too much risk will reduce risk taking, discussed previously, there is also the danger that the increased compensation generated by higher ownership levels will have negative consequences for the alignment of nonexecutive employees' interests with those of both top executives and owners.

Summary. On one hand, the empirical evidence strongly supports the importance of pay strategy as a determinant of business performance. When reported, the effect sizes in these studies are often substantial, suggesting that organizations have a clear avenue through which they can influence overall business performance. The same conclusion holds true for the types of strategic actions examined in the research summarized in Table 5.3. These studies provide clear implications for how the strategic focus and direction of organizations can be influenced. They indicate that there has been a great deal of progress regarding the consequences of pay strategy since Milkovich's 1988 review.

On the other hand, there are a number of key questions for which the answers are less clear. First, there is essentially no research that specifies and tests a complete causal model that includes not only pay strategy and business performance but also the hypothesized intervening motivational, attitudinal, and behavioral variables through which causation is believed to operate (see Gerhart & Milkovich, 1992). Even looking at multiple studies, it is not yet possible to develop estimates for the intervening structural paths.

Table 5.3. Strategic Decisions Outcomes of Pay Strategies.

Dependent Variable	Finding	Theory	Outcome Unit of Analysis	Pay Unit of Analysis	Study
Employment variability	Less with long-term incentives for top and middle managers	Agency	Firm	Managers within six levels of the board	Gerhart & Trevor (1996)
External innovation (acquiring new markets or products by acquisition of companies); internal innovation (R&D spending, new products)	Use of financial controls (outcome-based evaluation using measures like ROA, cash flow) associated with greater external innovation and less internal innovation	Agency	Firm	Business unit managers	Hitt, Hoskisson, Johnson, & Moesel (1996)
Risk taking (higher standard deviation in analysts' forecasts of earnings per share)	Higher when senior executives and board members held greater ownership stakes up to 7.5 percent ownership; thereafter, increased holdings associated with less risk taking	Agency	Firm	Senior executives and directors	Wright, Ferris, Sarin, & Awasthi (1996)
Efficiency; growth; diversification; decentralization	More emphasis on efficiency, less on growth, less diversification, and more decentralization where management's stock holdings are larger percentage of debt plus equity	Agency	Firm	Senior managers	Phan & Hill (1995)
Negativity in president's letter to investors	No relationship with share ownership by corporate officers; less negativity where greater ownership by outside directors	Agency	Firm	Senior managers and directors	Abrahamson & Park (1994)
Amount of CEO interaction with venture capitalists	No relationship with CEO ownership stake	Agency	Firm	CEO	Sapienza & Gupta (1994)

Takeover resistance	Unrelated to existence of golden parachute; contrary to prediction, size of golden parachute positively related to takeover resistance	Agency	Firm	CEO	Buchholz & Ribbens (1994)
Poison pill adoption	Less likely where inside directors own larger percentage of shares	Agency	Firm	Directors	Mallette & Fowler (1992)
Resistance to greenmail	Resistance to company stock repurchases to resist a takeover attempt higher when senior management equity holdings are higher; no main effect of board member equity holdings; resistance is higher when management holdings are low and board member holdings are high	Agency	Firm	Directors and senior managers	Kosnik (1990)
Value added per employee; unrelated diversification; R&D investment	Management equity holdings are positively related to R&D investment and value added per employee and negatively related to unrelated diversification	Agency	Firm	Senior managers	Hill & Snell (1989)
Customer perceptions of product quality	Customer perceptions were more favorable when pay differentials between top management levels and both hourly and lower-level exempt employees were smaller	Distributive justice, equity theory	Business unit	Employee cross section	Cowherd & Levine (1992)
Investment in employee training; investment in R&D, new products	Long-term incentives were associated with more of each	Agency	Business unit	Business unit manager	Galbraith & Merrill (1991)

Second, although there is some evidence to support the vertical fit hypothesis, it is also true that a portion of this research is open to alternative interpretations because of methodological concerns such as simultaneity, omitted variables, and as discussed next, measurement issues. In addition, empirical evidence on other types of fit, such as that between pay strategy components and between pay strategy and other HR practices, is virtually nonexistent.

Measurement of Key Concepts

Cook and Campbell (1979) describe construct validity as the ability to generalize from results obtained using fallible measures to make inferences regarding relationships between constructs. Thus any observed relationship between measures depends not only on the relationship between the constructs but also on the way the constructs are measured. Therefore, it is important to examine the central constructs in the pay strategy literature and how they have been measured in order to make more accurate inferences regarding causal relationships.

Business Performance

Both literature on organizations (such as Goodman & Pennings, 1977) and on strategy (such as Barney, 1997) recommend defining and measuring performance in terms of multiple dimensions. Results-oriented criteria include both accounting profits (for example, return on assets) and economic returns (for instance, total shareholder return). The capital asset pricing model (CAPM) suggests that securities markets efficiently price the value of an investment in a firm by estimating the net present value of cash flows, adjusted for the amount of risk the security would add to a market portfolio. Such estimates make use of all available information. Thus any changes in information (such as earnings reports, new product announcements, or changes in compensation arrangements) are recognized immediately by the market in pricing securities. Consequently, total shareholder return is often regarded as the preferred means of measuring firm performance.

The CAPM's efficient market hypothesis has three forms (Milgrom & Roberts, 1992). The weak form says that current prices, but not past prices, predict future stock prices. The semistrong form says that public information influences future stock prices. The strong form hypothesizes that both public and nonpublic information influence stock prices.

Despite its conceptual appeal, evidence on the validity of the CAPM model is seen as less than compelling by some observers, even for the weak form (Milgrom & Roberts, 1992; Barney, 1997). For example, research has found strong, negative correlations between stock prices over periods of three to five years, which is inconsistent with the weak version (Milgrom & Roberts, 1992). In addition, even if markets efficiently incorporate new information into prices, it sometimes appears that markets either incorrectly evaluate information or must work with information that later turns out to be erroneous.

As an example, consider the market's recent history in pricing Sunbeam's stock. In July 1996, Sunbeam's stock price had fallen to about $15 per share. Then a new CEO, "Chainsaw" Al Dunlap, was hired. He cut headcount by one-half, and the stock price jumped. By early 1998, the price had risen to about $50 per share. However, shortly thereafter, analysts began to question the accuracy of accounting reports on profits. Before long, Al Dunlap was dismissed, and the Securities and Exchange Commission launched an investigation of possible accounting improprieties. By July 1998, the stock price had fallen below $10 a share (at a time when the broader market was at an all-time high). It seems unlikely that Sunbeam's "true" performance fluctuated to this degree. Rather, in this case, stock price appears to have been an unreliable indicator of performance.

Thus while shareholder return is a key measure of firm performance, it too has its limitations. Regarding Sunbeam, it would be difficult to make a case for the validity of either accounting-based or market-based measures. So what can researchers do to overcome such problems?

One response is to use the sort of logic underlying the balanced scorecard approach (Kaplan & Norton, 1996), which calls for balancing multiple indicators of effectiveness. In its simplest form, the balanced scorecard calls for indicators that reflect shareholder, customer, and employee outcomes (Gubman, 1998). For each of the three areas, multiple measures can be used. With this approach, one can determine whether findings are sensitive to the type of performance measure, as well as examine intervening variables (Becker & Gerhart, 1996).

Another suggestion is to use multiple years of data whenever possible. Doing so has many potential advantages. First, time precedence can be established, which is necessary for showing causality. Second, change models can be used, which can better control for stable omitted variables. Third, averaging over time can increase the reliability of measures by helping minimize the influence of short-term fluctuations of the sort described earlier. Of course, whether to average over time also depends on the conceptual model and the time frame during which pay strategy effects are expected. Presumably, however, the long-term viability of organizations (or their component businesses) is what matters most.

Business Strategy

As noted earlier, research on vertical alignment of pay strategy is closely linked to the broader organizational strategy field. Corporate strategy is the choice of what businesses the firm will be in. This in turn drives degree of diversification and direction (growth, stability, retrenchment). And growth and diversification can be achieved either through internal growth and product development or through external acquisition (Daft, 1991).

Also, within strategic business units, business strategy entails choosing how to compete in those particular product markets. Until recently, there have been three especially influential business strategy frameworks. First, Michael Porter has identified three types of business unit strategies: differentiation, cost leadership, and focus. Second, the Miles and Snow typology classifies firms as prospectors, defenders, analyzers, or reactors. Finally, a directional strategy (growth, stability, retrenchment) can also be followed at the business-unit level.

Chadwick and Cappelli (1999) have argued that generic strategies (such as cost leadership or differentiation) may be too general to be useful in analyzing the specific circumstances of a particular firm. Earlier, in the pay strategy literature, Milkovich (1988) noted that corporate strategy frameworks of a directional nature were of limited use because part of a corporation could be in a growth phase while other parts could be in a retrenchment phase. In addition, organizations increasingly find that they must combine elements of different generic strategies. For example, Victor and Boynton (1998) describe how firms are increasingly combining the previously separate strategies of mass production and customization into what they call "mass customization" to compete effectively.

It is also not difficult to find examples of successful companies that "violate" the prescribed fit between organization and pay strategy. For example, Lincoln Electric would appear to be a single-line-of-business company that follows the expected cost leader (or defender) business strategy. Yet key aspects of its pay strategy (such as focus on extrinsic rewards and heavy use of variable pay, including a substantial portion linked to organization performance) are part of the experiential pay strategy. Similarly, Sears has reversed its previous foray into diversification to refocus on its retail business. Like Lincoln Electric, it would appear to be a single-line-of-business company following a defender (or cost leader) business strategy. However, it too has shifted its pay strategy to greater use of variable pay, with an emphasis on company and store performance as criteria. Thus it may be that previous strategic frameworks are too generic to represent adequately the competitive challenges that particular firms face

Pay Strategy

In their review, Gerhart and Milkovich (1992) identified five dimensions of pay found in the previous literature: level, structure, basis, benefits, and administration.[4] Milkovich and Newman (1996) use a similar framework. Level is often used to describe how much employees are paid in all forms. Structure refers to differentials based on job level, job content, skills used, business units, and so forth. For example, two structures may differ in the number of pay levels, the rate of pay growth as one moves up the levels, and the relative value placed on work performed by people with different skills and working in different parts of the organization. Basis pertains to whether pay is based on seniority, performance ratings, productivity, customer satisfaction, profits, stock performance, and so forth. Benefits refers to the amount of compensation allocated to noncash or deferred cash programs such as health insurance and retirement plans. Finally, administration refers to policies such as communication of pay policies and the degree of participation employees and managers have in designing pay policies.

A significant development was creation of the experiential versus algorithmic compensation strategy scale by Balkin and Gomez-Mejia (Balkin & Gomez-Mejia, 1990; Gomez-Mejia, 1992; Gomez-Mejia & Balkin, 1992, esp. Tables 3-1 and 3-2). The scale (see Table 5.1) consists of forty-one items and seventeen subscales. Gomez-Mejia (1992) performed a principal component analysis of the scales using a sample of 243 respondents. He found that one component explained approximately 60 percent of the variance in the multiple scales (eigenvalue = 9.76).

The ability to use just one scale to capture key pay strategy differences between organizations is a big advantage in terms of parsimony, especially when contingency factors are introduced and cross-product terms are constructed to test statistical interactions. The trade-off is that this approach does not recognize the possibility that certain aspects of compensation strategy may be more important than others in influencing firm performance either alone or in concert with contingency factors. The decision by Balkin and Gomez-Mejia to use subscales (rather than items) as the input to the principal component analysis may help explain why a single component was able to capture most of the variance—this approach is analogous to using a second-order factor analysis.

As the field advances, it may be useful to revisit this measurement approach and determine whether certain dimensions of pay strategy are more or less strategic than others. In addition, it would be useful to know whether the subscales combine in a compensatory or noncompensatory model. For example, can a firm with a very low score on performance emphasis still create an experiential pay strategy (and its performance consequences) by having very high scores on egalitarianism, decentralization, and participation? Or does a firm with high scores on all such dimensions experience synergy such that the effects are multiplicative rather than additive?

Another measurement issue that is relevant for any subjective assessment of organization or unit properties is reliability. As a rule, researchers measuring such properties report internal consistency estimates of reliability, which estimate error due to item sampling. However, there is strong evidence that error due to the sampling of raters is a more serious concern (Gerhart, 1999; Gerhart, Wright, McMahan, & Snell, 1998). In fact, there is good reason to believe that when both items and raters are recognized as sources of measurement error, the reliability of single-rater self-reports may be less than .20. Yet most strategy research, including that on pay, continues to rely on a single rater to measure organization- and unit-level properties.

The consequences of this approach depend on the situation. In the bivariate case, low reliability (random measurement error) of pay strategy ratings will, *ceteris paribus,* lead to a downward bias in estimating the main and interactive effects of pay strategy. In contrast, if there is systematic measurement error, the observed pay strategy–business performance relationship could be biased upward.

Summary

Each of the constructs examined—firm performance, organizational strategy, and pay strategy—warrants further attention in future work. In each case, measurement decisions can and do have an impact on the substantive conclusions drawn from pay strategy research. The problem that is perhaps most troublesome and common to each area, yet most straightforward to remedy, is measurement error (at least of the random type). There is abundant evidence that single raters do not provide reliable assessments of organization-level properties (Gerhart et al., 1998). The severity of the unreliability problem can be expected to introduce considerable bias in effect size estimates. Furthermore, these problems are typically exacerbated when cross-product terms are used to test for statistical interactions between these variables.

A second issue that needs to be addressed is the dimensionality of compensation strategies. Is a single dimension truly adequate for representing the array of decisions that organizations make regarding how they pay their diverse populations of employees? Are there interactions between dimensions of compensation strategy? Which dimensions are most important? Finally, researchers need to consider whether generic typologies of organization strategies are sufficiently rich to capture the diversity of conditions individual organizations face.

Future Research Directions

I have examined the literature regarding the consequences of pay strategies for business-unit and firm-level performance and choice of strategic actions. The empirical evidence is consistent in its support for the key role of pay strategies in influencing performance and managerial decisions. This is consistent with Gomez-Mejia review of the literature (1992) and represents a good deal of progress since the Milkovich review (1988). In addition, some evidence suggests that choosing the appropriate fit between pay strategy and organizational strategy can contribute to still better levels of business performance. However, the progress on this front has been slower. Furthermore, other types of fit have not received sufficient attention in pay strategy research.

Based on my review, I suggest that pay strategy researchers include the following issues on their future research agendas:

Fit

Using pay strategies that are common across organizations does not, by definition, permit a firm to gain a competitive advantage. However, for many firms, a first step will be to gain competitive parity by changing pay strategies to be consistent with what better-managed firms are doing. However, the road to competitive advantage would seem to depend on successfully achieving vertical, horizontal, and internal alignment of pay strategy, because alignment can both add value and be difficult to imitate.

Despite the presumed importance of alignment or fit, the pay strategy literature has thus far systematically addressed only some aspects of vertical fit (fit with organizational strategy). Alignment among dimensions of pay strategy (internal) and alignment between pay strategy and other aspects of human resource strategy (horizontal) have received virtually no attention. This situation needs to be rectified.

Causality

Ideally, we would like to be able to interpret observed relationships between pay strategy and performance as causal. However, most of the research falls short with respect to two essential criteria for causality: time precedence and the ruling out of alternative causes. Time precedence can be established by using longitudinal data. However, ruling out alternative explanations for the relationship between pay strategies and firm performance requires attention to intervening and control variables. Testing for intervening variables, such as attitudes and behaviors, is necessary for us to place more confidence in statements about the causal effects of pay strategy. Therefore, we need answers to such questions as these: Do different pay strategies create different profiles of attitudes and behaviors within firms? Different cultures? Different perceptions of risk or pay-for-performance links? In turn, do these different attitudes, behaviors, cultures, and perceptions create different levels of efficiency, quality, customer experience, innovation, and speed to market?

These questions are particularly well suited to the abilities and interests of psychologists. Some very interesting work has appeared in the past decade looking at the relationship between attitudes and effectiveness at the organization level (Ostroff, 1992) and at the facility level (Ryan, Schmit, & Johnson, 1996; Schneider, White, & Paul, 1998). More such work is needed, particularly at the business-unit or firm level, using financial measures of effectiveness. The one organization-level study (Ostroff) used a sample of schools. Thus the relationship between attitudes and financial performance at the firm level remains unknown. More generally, efforts to explain how pay strategies influence any of the key intervening variables (such as culture) and how the intervening variables in turn influence business performance would be valuable.

Culture

Culture is an especially interesting variable because case studies suggest that it is import in creating value on a sustained basis and that it is difficult to imitate (Barney, 1986; Collins & Porras, 1994). Yet as noted, there has been no systematic examination of either the importance of pay strategies in creating and sustaining different cultures or which pay strategies best fit different types of cultures.

Globalization

In 1970, roughly 25 percent of annual world economic output was traded internationally. According to the Hudson Institute's Workforce 2020 report, that figure is expected to reach 50 percent this year and 67 percent by 2020. With only a few exceptions (such as Roth & O'Donnell, 1996), the compensation strategy literature does not yet seem to have come to terms with this fact. Both geographical and cultural distance would appear to be contingencies that will only increase in importance when designing pay strategies.

A second aspect of globalization has to do with whether people in different countries react similarly to particular pay strategies. Milkovich and Bloom (1998) suggest that national cultural differences are probably less important than often believed. This question deserves further attention.

The Role of Top Management

Most studies continue to measure pay strategy in terms of how CEOs or a few top managers are paid. To be sure, top managers are in a position to have a great impact on firm performance. But it is also true that top managers cannot execute strategies successfully without an appropriate pay strategy in place for the people who actually design, produce, and sell the firm's goods and services. Therefore, there is a need to measure pay strategies that are used for the broader population of employees and to link these to firm performance differences.

Of course, related research has been done at the individual and group levels of analysis on individual incentives, gainsharing, and so forth; it is reviewed in other chapters in this volume. However, the findings of this research at the individual and group level have not been explicitly integrated with research conducted at the business-unit and firm level. In addition, the individual and group-level work tends not to attend to questions of internal, horizontal, and vertical alignment.

There is also a body of research on the relationship between profit sharing and firm performance (for example, Kruse, 1993; Weitzman & Kruse, 1990), but this research is quite narrow in the sense that profit sharing is the only aspect of pay strategy examined. It, too, also tends to focus on main effects of pay rather than fit issues.

Stock Market Performance

Finally, substantial fluctuations in stock market levels worldwide remind us that total annual shareholder return may not necessarily be in double digits forever. During recent years, when returns have been at this level, companies have moved toward much greater emphasis on stock plans, both by shifting greater shares of compensation for top managers into such plans and by extending coverage of stock plans to employees not previously included. It is possible that the effectiveness of this strategy is different in an era of rising stock prices than in an era of stagnant or falling prices. For example, the practice of repricing stock options held by managers or employees is something we often see when a company's stock price falls to the point where there is concern about resulting incentive problems. Research on the consequences of repricing options (or not) would be interesting.

Conclusion

As I noted at the beginning of this chapter, compensation strategy is believed to play a central role in the successful formulation and execution of a business strategy. The evidence reviewed here supports this general proposition and provides some insights into the likely consequences of different compensation strategies. However, my review also suggests that the study of compensation strategy is relatively new and that many opportunities remain for researchers to make important contributions to knowledge and practice.

Notes
1. Another major business unit strategy classification classifies companies as following a cost leadership, differentiation, or focus strategy (Porter, 1985). The cost leadership and differentiation strategies are similar to the defender and prospector strategies, respectively.
2. Although the April 1998 issue of the *Academy of Management Journal*, edited by Barkema and Gomez-Mejia, contained a "special research forum" on managerial compensation and firm performance, none of the articles in the forum examined consequences of pay decisions. The original call for papers for the forum stated that the purpose was to

improve understanding of both the determinants of managerial compensation and how internal and external forces interact to affect firm performance. One assumes that the latter fell by the wayside because no acceptable papers on the topic were submitted for consideration by the special issue editors. If so, Milkovich's concerns about such research being risky would appear to have continued relevance.

3. In some cases, Balkin and Gomez-Mejia did not control for main effects when cross-product terms were entered into the regressions. In such cases, the coefficients on the cross-product terms estimate not the interaction but rather the combined main effects and interactions. Thus caution is necessary in interpreting these results.

4. Actually, Gerhart and Milkovich identified level, structure, individual differences, benefits, and administration. However, I will use the term *basis* rather than *individual differences*.

References

Abrahamson, E., & Park, C. (1994). Concealment of negative organizational outcomes: An agency theory perspective. *Academy of Management Journal, 37,* 1302–1334.

Akerlof, G. A. (1984). Gift exchange and efficiency-wage theory: Four views. *American Economic Review, 74,* 79–83.

Balkin, D. B., & Gomez-Mejia, L. R. (1987). Toward a contingency theory of compensation strategy. *Strategic Management Journal, 8,* 169–182.

Balkin, D. B., & Gomez-Mejia, L. R. (1990). Matching compensation and organizational strategies. *Strategic Management Journal, 11,* 153–169.

Barkema, H. G., & Gomez-Mejia, L. R. (1998). Managerial compensation and firm performance: A general research framework. *Academy of Management Journal, 41,* 135–145.

Barney, J. B. (1986). Organizational culture: Can it be a source of sustained competitive advantage? *Academy of Management Review, 11,* 656–665.

Barney, J. B. (1991). Firm resources and sustained competitive advantage. *Journal of Management, 17,* 99–120.

Barney, J. B. (1997). *Gaining and sustaining competitive advantage.* Reading, MA: Addison-Wesley.

Baron, J. N., & Bielby, W. T. (1980). Bringing the firms back in: Stratification, segmentation, and the organization of work. *American Sociological Review, 5,* 737–765.

Beatty, R., & Zajac, E. J. (1994). Managerial incentives, monitoring, and risk bearing: A study of executive compensation, ownership, and board structure in initial public offerings. *Administrative Science Quarterly, 39,* 313–335.

Becker, B., & Gerhart, B. (1996). The impact of human resource management on organizational performance: Progress and prospects. *Academy of Management Journal, 39,* 779–801.

Becker, G. (1975). *Human capital: A theoretical and empirical analysis, with special reference to education* (2nd ed.). Chicago: University of Chicago Press.

Blinder, A. S. (Ed.). (1990). *Paying for productivity.* Washington, DC: Brookings Institution.

Bloom, M., & Milkovich, G. T. (1998). Relationships among risk, incentive pay, and organizational performance. *Academy of Management Journal, 41,* 283–297.

Buchholtz, A. K., & Ribbens, B. A. (1994). Role of chief executive officers in takeover resistance: Effects of CEO incentives and individual characteristics. *Academy of Management Journal, 37,* 554–579.

Chadwick, C., & Cappelli, P. (1999). Alternative to generic strategy typologies in strategic human resource management. *Research in Personnel and Human Resources Management* (Suppl. 4), 1–29.

Chandler, A. D., Jr. (1962). *Strategy and structure.* Cambridge, MA: MIT Press.

Collins, J. C., & Porras, J. I. (1994). *Built to last: Successful habits of visionary companies.* New York: Harper Business.

Cook, T. D., & Campbell, D. T. (1979). *Quasi-Experimentation.* Skokie, IL: Rand McNally.

Cooke, W. N. (1994). Employee participation programs, group-based incentives, and company performance: A union-nonunion comparison. *Industrial and Labor Relations Review, 47,* 594–609.

Cowherd, D. M., & Levine, D. I. (1992). Product quality and pay equity between lower-level employees and top management: An investigation of distributive justice theory. *Administrative Science Quarterly, 37,* 302–320.

Daft, R. L. (1991). *Management.* Orlando, FL: Dryden Press.

Delaney, J. T., & Huselid, M. A. (1996). The impact of human resource management practices on perceptions of organizational performance. *Academy of Management Journal, 39,* 949–969.

Delery, J. E., & Doty, H. D. (1996). Modes of theorizing in strategic human resource management: Tests of universalistic, contingency, and configurational performance predictions. *Academy of Management Journal, 39,* 802–835.

Dunlop, J. T. (1957). The task of contemporary wage theory. In G. W. Taylor & F. C. Pierson (Eds.), *New concepts in wage determination* (pp. 117–139). New York: McGraw-Hill.

Eisenhardt, K. M. (1988). Agency- and institutional-theory explanations: The case of retail sales compensation. *Academy of Management Journal, 31,* 488–511.

Ellig, B. R. (1981). Compensation elements: Market phase determines the mix. *Compensation Review, 13*(3), 30–38.

Fama, E. F., & Jensen, M. C. (1983). Separation of ownership and control. *Journal of Law and Economics, 26,* 301–325.

Galbraith, C. S., & Merrill, G. B. (1991). The effect of compensation program and structure of SBU competitive strategy: A study of technology-intensive firms. *Strategic Management Journal, 12,* 353–370.

Gerhart, B. (1999). Human resource management and firm performance: Measurement issues and their effect on causal and policy inferences. *Research in Personnel and Human Resources Management* (Suppl. 4), 31–51.

Gerhart, B., & Milkovich, G. T. (1990). Organizational differences in managerial compensation and financial performance. *Academy of Management Journal, 33,* 663–691.

Gerhart, B., & Milkovich, G. T. (1992). Employee compensation: Research and practice. In M. D. Dunnette & L. M. Hough (Eds.), *Handbook of industrial and organizational psychology* (2nd ed., Vol. 3, pp. 481–570). Palo Alto, CA: Consulting Psychologists Press.

Gerhart, B., & Trevor, C. (1996). Employment stability under different managerial compensation systems. *Academy of Management Journal, 39,* 1692–1712.

Gerhart, B., Trevor, C., & Graham, M. (1996). New directions in employee compensation research." In G. R. Ferris (Ed.), *Research in personnel and human resources management* (Vol. 14, pp. 143–203). Greenwich, CT: JAI Press.

Gerhart, B., Wright, P., McMahan, G., & Snell, S. (1988, August). *Measurement error in research on human resource decisions and firm performance: How much error is there, and how does it influence effect size estimates?* Paper presented at the 58th annual meeting of the Academy of Management, San Diego, CA.

Gomez-Mejia, L. R. (1987). *The relationship between organizational strategy, pay strategy, and compensation effectiveness: An exploratory study.* Working paper, University of Colorado.

Gomez-Mejia, L. R. (1992). Structure and process of diversification, compensation strategy, and firm performance. *Strategic Management Journal, 13,* 381–397.

Gomez-Mejia, L. R., & Balkin, D. B. (1989). Effectiveness of individual and aggregate compensation strategies. *Industrial Relations, 28,* 431–445.

Gomez-Mejia, L. R., & Balkin, D. B. (1992). *Compensation, organizational strategy, and firm performance.* Cincinnati, OH: South-Western.

Goodman, P., & Pennings, J. (Eds.). (1977). *New perspectives on organizational effectiveness.* San Francisco: Jossey-Bass.

Groshen, E. L. (1988). Why do wages vary among employers? *Economic Review, 24,* 19–38.

Groshen, E. L. (1991). Sources of intra-industry wage dispersion: How much do employers matter? *Quarterly Journal of Economics, 106,* 869–885.

Gubman, E. L. (1998). *The talent solution.* New York: McGraw-Hill.

Haire, M., Ghiselli, E. E., & Gordon, M. E. (1967). A psychological study of pay [Monograph]. *Journal of Applied Psychology, 51,* 1–24.

Hambrick, D. C., & Abrahamson, E. (1995). Assessing managerial discretion across industries: A multimethod approach. *Academy of Management Journal, 38,* 1427–1441.

Hambrick, D. C., & Finkelstein, S. (1987). Managerial discretion: A bridge between polar views on organizations. In L. L. Cummings & B. M. Staw (Eds.), *Research in organizational behavior* (Vol. 9, pp. 369–406). Greenwich, CT: JAI Press.

Hansen, G. S., & Wernerfelt, B. (1989). Determinants of firm performance: The relative importance of economic and organizational factors. *Strategic Management Journal, 10,* 399–411.

Hill, C. W. L., & Snell, S. A. (1989). Effects of ownership structure and control on corporate productivity. *Academy of Management Journal, 32,* 25–46.

Hitt, M. A., Hoskisson, R. E., Johnson, R. A., & Moesel, D. D. (1996). The market for corporate control and firm innovation. *Academy of Management Journal, 39,* 1084–1119.

Huselid, M. A. (1995). The impact of human resource management practices on turnover, productivity, and corporate financial performance. *Academy of Management Journal, 38,* 635–672.

Ichniowski, C., Shaw, K., & Prennushi, G. (1997). The effects of human resource management practices on productivity: A study of steel finishing lines. *American Economic Review, 87,* 291–313.

Jensen, M. C., & Meckling, W. H. (1976). Theory of the firm: Managerial behavior, agency costs, and ownership structure. *Journal of Financial Economics, 3,* 305–360.

Kaplan, R. S., & Norton, D. P. (1996). Using the balanced scorecard as a strategic management system. *Harvard Business Review, 74*(1), 75–85.

Kosnik, R. D. (1990). Effects of board demography and directors' incentives on corporate greenmail decisions. *Academy of Management Journal, 33,* 129–150.

Kroll, M., Wright, P., Toombs, L., & Leavell, H. (1997). Form of control: A critical determinant of acquisition performance and CEO rewards. *Strategic Management Journal, 18,* 85–96.

Kruse, D. L. (1993). *Profit sharing: Does it make a difference?* Kalamazoo, MI: Upjohn Institute for Employment Research.

Leonard, J. S. (1988). Wage structure and dynamics in the electronics industry. *Industrial Relations, 28,* 251–275.

Lester, R. A. (1946). Wage diversity and its theoretical implications. *Review of Economics and Statistics, 28,* 152–159.

MacDuffie, J. P. (1995). Human resource bundles and manufacturing performance: Organizational logic and flexible production systems in the world auto industry. *Industrial and Labor Relations Review, 48,* 197–221.

Magnan, M. L., & Saint-Onge, S. (1997). Bank performance and executive compensation: A managerial discretion perspective. *Strategic Management Journal, 18,* 573–581.

Mallette, P., & Fowler, K. J. (1992). Effects of board composition and stock ownership on the adoption of "poison pills." *Academy of Management Journal, 35,* 1010–1035.

March, J. G., & Simon, H. A. (1958). *Organizations.* New York: Wiley.

Miles, R. E., & Snow, C. C. (1978). *Organizational strategy, structure, and process.* New York: McGraw-Hill.

Miles, R. E., & Snow, C. C. (1994). *Fit, failure, and the hall of fame: How companies succeed or fail.* New York: Free Press.

Milgrom, P., & Roberts, J. (1992). *Economics, organization, and management.* Upper Saddle River, NJ: Prentice Hall.

Milkovich, G. T. (1988). A strategic perspective on compensation management. *Research in Personnel and Human Resources Management, 6,* 263–288.

Milkovich, G. T., & Bloom, M. (1998). Rethinking international compensation. *Compensation and Benefits Review, 30,* 15–23.

Milkovich, G. T., & Newman, J. M. (1996). *Compensation.* Burr Ridge, IL: Irwin.

Ostroff, C. (1992). The relationship between satisfaction, attitudes, and performance: An organizational level analysis. *Journal of Applied Psychology, 77,* 963–974.

Pfeffer, J. (1994). *Competitive advantage through people.* Boston: Harvard Business School Press.

Pfeffer, J. (1998). *The human equation.* Boston: Harvard Business School Press.

Phan, P. H., & Hill, C. W. (1995). Organizational restructuring and economic performance in leveraged buyouts: An ex post study. *Academy of Management Journal, 38,* 704–739.

Pitts, R. A. (1976). Diversification strategies and organizational policies of large diversified firms. *Journal of Economics and Business, 8,* 181–188.

Porter, M. (1985). *Competitive advantage.* New York: Free Press.

Rajagopalan, N. (1996). Strategic orientations, incentive plan adoptions, and firm performance: Evidence from electric utility firms. *Strategic Management Journal, 18,* 761–785.

Reynolds, L. G. (1946). Wage differences in local labor markets. *American Economic Review, 32,* 366–375.

Roth, K., & O'Donnell, S. (1996). Foreign subsidiary compensation strategy: An agency theory perspective. *Academy of Management Journal, 39,* 678–703.

Ryan, A. M., Schmit, M. J., & Johnson, R. (1996). Attitudes and effectiveness: Examining relations at an organizational level. *Personnel Psychology, 49,* 853–882.

Rynes, S. L. (1987). Compensation strategies for recruiting. *Topics in Total Compensation, 2,* 185–196.

Sapienza, H. J., & Gupta, A. K. (1994). Impact of agency risks and task uncertainty on venture capitalist–chief executive officer interaction. *Academy of Management Journal, 37,* 1618–1632.

Schneider, B., White, S. S., & Paul, M. (1998). Linking service climate and customer perceptions of service quality: Test of a causal model. *Journal of Applied Psychology, 83,* 150–163.

Schultz, T. (1963). *The economic value of education.* New York: Columbia University Press.

Schwab, D. P. (1980). Construct validity in organizational behavior. *Research in Organizational Behavior, 2,* 3–43.

Segal, M. (1986). Post-institutionalism in labor economics: The forties and fifties revisited. *Industrial and Labor Relations Review, 39,* 388–403.

Seward, J. K., & Walsh, J. P. (1996). The governance and control of voluntary corporate spin-offs. *Strategic Management Journal, 17,* 25–39.

Shane, S. (1996). Hybrid organizational arrangements and their implications for firm growth and survival: A study of new franchisors. *Academy of Management Journal, 39,* 216.

Shleifer, A., & Vishny, R. W. (1989). Management entrenchment: The case of manager-specific investments. *Journal of Financial Economics, 25,* 123–139.

Tosi, H. L., & Gomez-Mejia, L. R. (1994). CEO compensation and firm performance. *Academy of Management Journal, 37,* 1002–1016.

Victor, B., & Boynton, A. (1998). *Built here.* Boston: Harvard Business School Press.

Weber, C. L., & Rynes, S. L. (1991). Effects of compensation strategy on job pay decisions. *Academy of Management Journal, 34,* 86–109.

Weitzman, M. L., & Kruse, D. L. (1990). Profit sharing and productivity. In A. S. Binder (Ed.), *Paying for productivity* (pp. 95–141). Washington. DC: Brookings Institution.

Welbourne, T. M., & Andrews, A. (1996). Predicting the performance of initial public offerings: Should human resource management be in the equation? *Academy of Management Journal, 39,* 891–919.

194 Compensation in Organizations

Wright, P., Ferris, S. P., Sarin, A., & Awasthi, V. (1996). Impact of corporate insider, blockholder, and institutional equity ownership on firm risk taking. *Academy of Management Journal, 39,* 441–563.

Yellen, J. L. (1984). Efficiency wage models of unemployment. *American Economic Review, 74,* 200–205.

Zajac, E. J., & Westphal, J. D. (1994). The costs and benefits of managerial incentives and monitoring in large U.S. corporations: When is more not better? *Strategic Management Journal, 15,* 121–142.

CHAPTER 6

The Changing Nature of Work and Its Effects on Compensation Design and Delivery

Robert L. Heneman
Gerald E. Ledford Jr.
Maria T. Gresham

In 1966, Opsahl and Dunnette issued a challenge to the industrial and organizational (I/O) psychology research community:

> Strangely, in spite of the large amounts of money spent and the obvious relevance of behavioral theory for industrial compensation practices, there is probably less solid research in this area than in any other field related to worker performance. We know amazingly little about how money interacts with other factors or how it acts individually to affect job behavior. Although the relevant literature is voluminous, much more has been written about the subject than is actually known. Speculation, accompanied by compensation fads and fashions, abounds; research studies designed to answer fundamental questions about the role of human motivation are all too rare. (p. 94)

Considerable research in I/O psychology, as well as in sociology, industrial relations, business strategy, and labor economics, has advanced our understanding of many compensation issues during the past three decades. Yet compensation topics continue to be under-represented in I/O psychology relative to the importance of compensation to individuals and organizations. The challenge to conduct more and better research is still as relevant today as it was more than thirty years ago.

Research needs have shifted, however, due to dramatic changes in compensation practices during the past decade (Ledford, Lawler, & Mohrman, 1995). These changes are in part a response to fundamental changes in the nature and design of work in contemporary organizations. This chapter reviews many such changes, including the decreasing use of job descriptions and job analysis as a basis for organization design, the delayering of the organizational hierarchy, the increasing use of team-based structures, and changes in technology. In response to these forces and others, many elements of employee compensation design are changing significantly. Base pay design is shifting from job-based pay to person-based approaches that reward skill, knowledge, and competency. Pay for performance is increasingly based on collective (team, unit, and corporate) rather than individual performance. Spending on employee benefits is being challenged, and cafeteria-style benefits plans are now a widespread method of cost control. The overall compensation budget is being reallocated, with the ratio of variable performance-based pay to base pay increasing. Documentation of these trends can be found in ongoing surveys by the Conference Board, the American Compensation Association, and the Center for Effective Organizations (Heneman & Gresham, 1998). These changing compensation practices are part of a profile that has many names. It been called strategic pay (Lawler, 1990), the new pay (Schuster & Zingheim, 1992), alternative rewards (McAdams & Hawk, 1994), and innovative pay systems (Wilson, 1995).

These new approaches to compensation are in need of research that helps us understand why and where they are adopted, their effectiveness, and the key design variables that explain success and failure. As in 1966, the practice of compensation has far outrun the research literature. Practitioners are not waiting for research results. There is tremendous practitioner interest, excitement, and confusion about compensation issues, and practitioners are relying on whatever information they find available. For example, at least nine trade books about new forms of compensation were published between 1990 and 1996 (Heneman & Gresham, 1998).

This chapter attempts, first, to summarize what we know about the changing nature of work and how it is affecting compensation. Second, we will outline the innovations taking place in the field of compensation and contrast those changes with traditional compensation practices. We will consider such new forms of pay as broadbanding, pay for skills and competencies, pay for team and organizational performance (variable pay), and employee ownership. Third, we will review the limited available research on the effects of these new pay systems on individual and organizational effectiveness outcomes. Finally, we will offer a framework to guide future research.

Changes in the Nature of Work

Changes in the nature of work are having, and will continue to have, profound effects on the management of human resources in organizations (Cappelli et al., 1997; Howard, 1995). We will review the major changes that are likely to affect compensation strategy and practice in organizations. Such changes are a response to changing business strategies that demand more flexible, nimble organizational forms and work. In turn, these create the need for new forms of compensation. Our focus here is on five areas in which fundamental changes in the nature of work are taking place: employment relationships, technology, business strategy, organizational structure, and job design.

Changes in the Employment Relationship

The nature of the employment relationship appears to be changing in fundamental ways (Crandall & Wallace, 1997). The new employment relationship implies a change in the commitments of the parties to one another at both the institutional and psychological levels. Both have a bearing on the compensation system and will be discussed in turn.

From an institutional perspective, Tsui, Pearce, Porter, and Tripoli (1997) define four types of employment relationships:

quasi-spot contracts, mutual investment contracts, underinvestment contracts, and overinvestment contracts. Although these researchers directed little attention to compensation issues, these four exchange philosophies would appear to have compensation implications. For example, a quasi-spot contract is one where the employer offers short-term economic rewards for very specific employee contributions. Traditional short-term performance incentives such as piecerate and sales commissions would seem appropriate to this type of relationship. A mutual investment contract is one where there are broad, unspecified, and open employer inducements and employee contributions. Forms of compensation that may be appropriate here include skill-based pay as an investment in human capital, stock as an incentive for long-term participation, and benefits (such as dependent care or concierge services) to allow the employee to make a high commitment to work. An underinvestment contract is one where the employee has broad and open-ended obligations to the employer while the employer provides short-term monetary rewards. An example of this type of pay system may be a sales force organized by teams, with broad and open-ended roles for team members, where pay is provided on the basis of individual commissions. Overinvestment is characterized by the employee's performing very specific job functions while the employer provides open-ended and broad-range rewards. Providing part-time, seasonal, or temporary employees with a profit-sharing check is an example of this.

The highest level of performance in the Tsui et al. (1997) study was associated with mutual investment, and underinvestment consistently produced the worst results. Perceptions of commitment, trust, and fairness were highest for overinvestment and mutual investment. Although compensation was not investigated, the results suggest that long-term incentives such as stock ownership and pay plans that invest in human capital (for example, skill-based pay) may be helpful to organizations that want to transition from quasi-spot contracts to mutual investment contracts.

At the psychological level, employees form perceptions about the employment relationship offered by the employer. In particular, they respond to the employer's collection of reward practices. The employee's understanding of these practices is referred to as a psychological contract and has two notable aspects (Rousseau, 1997) that can be related to compensation practices.

First, individuals use schemata when evaluating rewards, such that different forms of compensation may not be evaluated independent from one another. Traditionally, as evidenced in the pay satisfaction literature, pay system components (such as level, raises, structure, administration, and benefits; see Heneman & Schwab, 1985) are not considered by researchers relative to one another. Employees may apply more complicated schemata when they look at the relationship of compensation components to one another and the relationship of compensation to rewards other than compensation (such as training).

Second, psychological contracts are dynamic. Thus changes in the nature of the institutional contract are likely to spell changes in the psychological contracts as well. For example, compensation systems may need to be modified to match the duration of the employment contract more appropriately (von Hippel, Mangum, Greenberger, Heneman, & Skoglind, 1997).

For example, organizations using temporary employees may not include them in a competency-based pay system because the investment they make in knowledge, skill, and development may be lost to a rival organization when the employees leave. But not all temporary employees are alike (von Hippel et al., 1997). Some employees are voluntary temporaries, meaning that they desire to remain temporary, while others are involuntary temporaries, meaning that they view temporary work as a vehicle to full-time job placement. Organizations may be more likely to provide competency pay to involuntary than to involuntary temporaries because the latter are more likely to remain with the organization. Moreover, survey data indicate that pay is a more important motivator for voluntary than for involuntary temporaries (von Hippel et al., 1997).

Changes in Technology

New technology has made it easier for organizations to monitor employee performance in terms of both content and process. Regarding content, improved information systems have made it possible to monitor vast amounts of data at the individual, team, and organizational levels. Not only has the amount of data increased, but so has their quality. Heightened focus on financial performance has resulted in new financial modeling techniques, such as economic value added, being used and applied to compensation systems. Similarly, heightened focus on the operational aspects of the organization through programs such as Total Quality Management (TQM) has resulted in an increased sensitivity by managers to improved operational indicators of success and the linking of these indicators to compensation through gainsharing and goal-sharing plans. Although the data are better, they are not perfect. For example, the customer service construct has not been fully explicated (Cardy & Dobbins, 1994).

Regarding process, electronic technology (telephone, video, computer) has made it possible to monitor employees in remote locations and to monitor a large number of employees at the same time. This capability is increasingly important as organizations expand into world markets and as spans of control grow due to a flattening of managerial hierarchies. However, electronic performance monitoring is not without its problems. For example, research reviewed by Hedge and Borman (1995) suggests that electronic performance monitoring may sensitize employees to overemphasize monitored activities while underemphasizing nonmonitored aspects.

Interestingly, economic theories such as efficiency wage theory and agency theory suggest that the new forms of performance-based compensation may produce less, rather than more, need for electronic performance monitoring (Conlon & Parks, 1990). Performance-based pay may decrease monitoring for three reasons. First, performance-based pay is usually granted in addition to base pay. As total pay increases, there is more of an incentive for employees to monitor their own performance. As total compensation rises with performance and eventually exceeds the market average, employees will not be able to replace this level of total compensation in the market. As a result, there is an incentive to do well to retain one's position. Second, as will be discussed later in the chapter, performance-based pay plans are increasingly team-based. As a result, there is incentive for employees to monitor one another because payment may be dependent on the performance of the entire team. Third, some of the new performance-based pay provides equity (in the form of stock) for employees. Hence it is in employees' best interest to act like owners in order to build the value of their equity holdings.

Changes in Business Strategy

The strategic compensation literature suggests that a major, if not the major, goal of a compensation system is to improve organizational performance. This goal is believed to be attained through the alignment of compensation components with one another and with other HR practices, as well as with organizational goals and context (Lawler & Jenkins, 1992). This perspective is in contrast to the traditional approach to compensation systems, which views the objectives of compensation systems in terms of attraction, retention, and motivation (Patten, 1977). These traditional objectives are to be achieved by influencing the expenditure, direction, and sustainability of employee effort rather than by aligning compensation systems with organizational goals. Both in practice and in research, traditional compensation systems have been focused on the performance of the individual. In contrast, strategic compensation systems focus on the performance of the entire organization.

Recent reviews have placed heavy emphasis on the importance of business strategy to compensation system design and implementation (Gomez-Mejia & Balkin, 1992; Lawler & Jenkins, 1992). The major point made in this body of literature is that components of the compensation system must be in alignment with organizational goals in order for compensation systems to lead to improved organizational performance (Heneman & Gresham, 1998; Lawler, 1990).

An example of this new strategic focus as it relates to compensation comes from Montemayor (1996). He found that components of the pay system (compensation philosophy, external competitiveness, mix of incentive to base pay, merit pay increases, and pay administration) varied by business strategy (cost leadership, differentiation, innovation) in a sample of 280 multi-industry organizations. Alignment between business strategy and compensation system components was associated with enhanced organizational effectiveness (using perceptual measures of organizational effectiveness). Other empirical work of this type has been conducted by Gomez-Mejia and Balkin (1992).

As noted by Wright and Snell (1998), a strategic focus also implies an alignment between components of the compensation system. For example, Heneman (in press) shows how merit pay has been used in conjunction with other reward systems in organizations, such as profit sharing and competency-based pay. This added dimension of human resource strategy is often overlooked in the compensation literature.

Another dimension of business strategy as it relates to compensation is the larger context in which business strategy is embedded (Hambrick & Snow, 1989). For example, Snell and Dean (1994) found in a sample of manufacturers pursuing an "integrated manufacturing" strategy that the relationship between work processes used (advanced manufacturing technology, TQM, and just-in-time inventory) was not related to the use of compensation system components (individual incentives, group incentives, hourly pay, salary, seniority, skill-based pay). Relationships among these manufacturing processes and pay system components were obtained when organizational context variables (size, performance, unionization, plant location) were entered as moderators of this relationship.

Changes in Organizational Structures

New organizational structures are being formed to coordinate and integrate the work of employees. Presumably, there should be a link between structure and the compensation system because structure in part determines the type of work people perform, which in turn partly determines compensation. Unfortunately, very little empirical work has taken place in this area, with one noticeable exception: the extent to which individual, group, or individual-plus-group rewards should be used in a team-based organizational structure (see Crown & Rosse, 1995; Wageman, 1995). Although this issue is important, it ignores the fact that there are different types of teams with different potential compensation implications. It also ignores the fact that there are new organizational structures other than teams that are also likely to have implications for organizations. Shaw and Schneier (1995) summarize three typologies of teams and suggested pay systems for each (Lawler & Cohen, 1992; Montemayor, 1994; Saunier & Hawk, 1994). Gross (1995) also provides a typology of teams and appropriate rewards. For example, spot bonuses might be more appropriate for a team of limited duration such as a task force, whereas skill-based pay might be more appropriate for an ongoing team such as a self-directed work team.

Along with differences between teams, changes have been occurring in organizational structures other than teams. Newly emerging organizational structures include virtual organizations, networks, and cellular forms. According to Crandall and Wallace (1997), a virtual organization is one where people from multiple corporate entities work together at a common site. Virtual organizations arise as a result of a variety of factors (for example, former competitors forming alliances to control the market; new mergers of technology, markets, and opportunities; or vertical and horizontal integration) and develop in three stages: (1) telecommuting; (2) front-line model, where sales and service functions are located in the field close to the customer; and (3) cyberlink model, where organizations manage work collaboratively with customers and teams from both producers and suppliers.

Although further construct explication is required, the virtual organization does point to the need to reexamine basic compensation concepts. For example, how is equity established when multiple organizations with multiple compensation systems work on a common project? How is the effectiveness of the compensation system to be assessed when multiple organizations house differing compensation objectives?

Miles, Snow, Mathews, Miles, and Coleman (1997) differentiate between five types of organizational structures: functional, divisional, matrix, network, and cellular. Again, compensation systems may need to vary by type of structure. For example, functional and divisional structures were begun in an era (1850–1950) of product and service standardization and specialization. Traditional job evaluation methods helped promote standardization across specialized jobs. Matrix, network, and cellular organizations emerged in an era (1950–2000) when the market began to demand customized products and services. In matrix and network structures, jobs are highly interdependent. As a result, traditional job evaluation systems may not be appropriate. Instead, the team rather than the job becomes the unit of analysis, and the compensation system may need to be team-based. Currently, we are in an era of innovation that requires network structures and cellular organizations. Under these structures, work is formed into cells (such as self-directed work teams) that interact inside and outside the organization. The cell must continually transform itself to survive in the organization as innovations create new requirements of people. With the cellular structure, the focus is on the creation of new knowledge and skills. As a result, the units of analysis become the person and the team, rather than the job. Person-based pay programs (such as skill-based pay) and team-based pay would seem to be a natural fit here.

Changes in Job Design

Fundamental changes are taking place in the nature of jobs (Cappelli et al., 1997). These changes fall into several categories: number of jobs, types of jobs, and relationships between jobs. In terms of the number of jobs, several trends stand out. First, reductions in force are no longer concentrated solely in manufacturing, but have spread to the service sector as well (bank tellers, for example). Second, management positions are being eliminated, with some organizations replacing supervisors and mid-level managers with self-directed work teams. Both in theory (see Ilgen & Hollenbeck, 1991) and in practice (see Bridges, 1995; O'Neal, 1995), organizations are beginning to shift the unit of analysis from jobs to people. Instead of describing work in terms of elements, tasks, and duties, work is beginning to be defined in terms of roles and competencies. Roles refer to expected patterns of behavior for people (Naylor, Pritchard, & Ilgen, 1980); competencies refer to knowledge, skills, abilities, and other attributes of people related to effective job performance (Heneman & Ledford, 1998).

Controversy surrounds the distinction between jobs versus people as the unit of analysis for compensation decisions (Cohen & Heneman, 1994). One element of the controversy concerns the extent to which person-based systems are actually used in practice. A recent survey shows that although organizations have begun to build role- and competency-based systems for selection and development purposes, there are very few actual applications of such systems with respect to compensation (American Compensation Association, 1996). A second aspect of controversy is that the distinction between jobs and people is cloudy at a conceptual level. For example, traditional job evaluation systems, like competencies, also measure skill and effort. In addition, Cohen and Heneman (1994) found that human resource professionals use both person- and job-based attributes in compensation decision making. These considerations suggest that the distinction between person- and job-based systems may be an oversimplification. Interestingly, I/O psychologists such as Ilgen and Hollenbeck (1991) seem to be moving away from job-based to role- and competency-based explanations. At the same time, economists are beginning to move away from the person (in human capital theory) to look at the job (see Lazear, 1992).

The net result of the controversy seems to be that organizations must delicately balance the mix of job and person requirements in compensation systems. The relative balance is likely to be a function of the strategy, structure, processes, and people in organizations (Finegold, Lawler, & Ledford, 1998). Industrial and organizational psychologists should be quite helpful in this area, with expertise in both job analysis and the measurement of individual differences. In terms of relationships between jobs, traditional organizations featured clearly defined upward mobility paths for employees with promotional pay increases. However, career moves now take many avenues other than upward mobility, which sometimes results in career paths that look more like lattices than ladders (Heneman, Heneman, & Judge, 1997). Not only has the concept of promotions begun to change, but so have the rewards associated with promotions. In traditional organizations, promotions result in a new job title and a new rate of pay before demonstrating actual competence at the new job. In contrast, organizations with enriched jobs and broadbanded job classifications may not offer a new job title or provide pay increases until after the competencies on the new job have been certified as being mastered. Clearly, the message between these two systems is different, but the behavioral and attitudinal reactions to these differences have yet to be studied.

As a result of changes in business strategy, organizational structure, employment relationships, technology, and jobs, employers have begun to experiment with new types of compensation systems. Before examining the new types of compensation systems, a review of the differences in conceptual foundations between traditional and new pay systems will be presented.

Conceptual Foundations of New Pay Systems

Traditional compensation models rely on an administrative framework, wherein compensation is viewed from the perspective of the HR department (Heneman & Schwab, 1979). More recently, however, a shift has been taking place, wherein pay is increasingly viewed from a strategic perspective (Gomez-Mejia & Balkin, 1992; Lawler & Jenkins, 1992). That is, the focus has shifted away from the HR department to a focus on the business strategy of the entire organization. Differences between the administrative focus and strategic focus are shown in Table 6.1.

Traditional pay systems provide pay for the job (Milkovich & Newman, 1996). The amount paid to each job is based on an assessment of its internal and external worth. Internal worth is established through the use of job evaluation systems, while external worth is established using market surveys. A pay structure is established to set boundaries on pay, based on the results of the job evaluation and market survey. Movement takes place within the pay structure based on time spent by the individual in the job category, or by "merit."

For organizations to focus employee efforts on business results, pay systems have begun to emphasize providing pay for the mastery of knowledge and skills and for the accomplishment of individual

Table 6.1. Pay System Focus: Administrative Versus Strategic.

Administrative Focus	Strategic Focus
Job	Person
Individual	Team
Time	Output
Lag system	Lead system
Top-down	Bottom-up
Centralized	Decentralized
Static	Dynamic
Internal equity	External equity
Fixed	Variable

and team goals. Pay is provided for skill and knowledge mastery to ensure that the workforce is lean, flexible, and adaptable to change (Kanfer & Heggestad, 1997). Work is organized around teams, and individual pay is supplemented with team pay to break down barriers between functional areas that may interfere with customer responsiveness. Pay is provided for output, rather than time on the job and job tasks and duties. Output may be assessed by the certification or mastery of skill and knowledge blocks, by the demonstration of behaviors critical to organizational success, or by actual output of teams and individuals (Heneman & von Hippel, 1996). That is, inputs, throughputs, and outputs are measured and rewarded. These measures closely reflect the strategy of the organization.

Measurements may be formed in response to business strategies, or business strategies may be formed as a result of compensation measurements. The former approach is referred to as a lag system, and the latter as a lead system (Lawler, 1981). One survey by the American Compensation Association (1996) of over six hundred new pay plans reported that most of these new plans operated as lead systems.

Another difference between traditional and emerging systems is that development of measures used to be conducted exclusively by the HR department, with top-down approval by management. However, with a strategic perspective, employees are more likely to be involved in these decisions (in a bottom-up approach). Kahnweiler, Crane, and O'Neill (1994) reported in a survey of employer practices that approximately 50 percent of organizations now use employees to help develop performance measures.

Organizations have also shifted from static to dynamic or "nimble" pay systems (Ledford, 1995). That is, pay systems are redesigned frequently to match changes in business strategy. Responsiveness to changes in the market is seen as a source of competitive advantage (Crandall & Wallace, 1997; Kessler & Chakrabarti, 1996). However, decentralized systems can create inequity in pay across business units. This problem is likely intensified the greater the mobility of labor across business units.

Another factor that produces internal inequity in pay is when organizations decide at the strategic level to abandon internal equity for the sake of external equity. That is, strict market pricing replaces job evaluation, and resulting inequities are blamed on the market rather than the compensation system. As this brief discussion indicates, the logic behind the new pay systems differs from that of traditional pay systems. This logic has been translated into new forms of pay that we will now consider.

New Forms of Pay

General Issues

Before considering specific reward system innovations that can increase motivation, several general issues require comment. First, reward systems have multiple objectives, many of which are not directly related to motivation (Lawler, 1971, 1981, 1990; Lawler & Jenkins, 1992). For example, one objective of almost all reward systems is to attract and retain key personnel. Reward systems can also be used to help support business strategies, for example, by controlling compensation costs or by making pay more variable in cyclical businesses. Reward systems also help define organizational structure for employees, because the levels at which performance is measured and rewarded (individual, team, plant, division, business, or corporation) draw employee attention to those levels. Reward systems can also help foster a desired organizational culture (participative, innovative, paternalistic, conservative, and so on) by rewarding, punishing, or ignoring particular patterns of behavior.

Second, any of these reward system objectives may be in conflict with motivational objectives. For example, the need for cost control may limit the incentive value of a reward system. The need to attract adequate talent in a tight labor market may lead to the overpayment of base wages and a deemphasis on performance incentives that increase motivation. Different motivational objectives may be in conflict as well. For example, reward systems may motivate short-term performance at the expense of long-term performance.

Third, most modern reward systems are multilayered. Base pay (salary or fixed wage) is usually the largest component. Benefits, including retirement, health, insurance, and education benefits, are also substantial, often exceeding 40 percent of total compensation costs in the United States (Gerhart & Milkovich, 1992). Pay for performance may include separate incentives for multiple levels of performance, including individual, team, unit, division, and corporate performance. Finally, stock ownership plans or stock options are increasingly prominent rewards that promote broad-based employee ownership in the company. Thus important issues in reward system design are determining the relative mix of these different types of rewards for each population of employees and aligning the objectives of different components in a manner that supports business needs and informs rather than confuses employees.

An important concept in reward systems is line of sight. It refers to the degree to which an employee can see a clear connection between his or her behavior and a payout from an incentive system. Clear line of sight may involve a number of steps, including understanding how specific behaviors generate performance, how performance is measured in the incentive plan, and how the incentive plan provides different levels of reward for different levels of performance. This concept is clearly rooted in expectancy theories of motivation (Vroom, 1964) and helps explain why some reward systems have little direct motivational value while others have more powerful effects. For example, rewards for corporate performance (profit sharing or stock options, for example) may have a weak line of sight. Employees at the lowest levels of a large corporation may not believe they have the power to influence plan payouts because they do not see how they can affect corporate performance. By contrast, individual and small group incentives (for example, sales commissions) often have strong motivational effects.

With these concepts in mind, we will consider currently prominent innovations relevant to each component of a total reward system (base pay, benefits, pay for performance, and corporate ownership). We will focus first on describing each approach and then presenting a review of the limited research available for each approach.

Base Pay Options

Two major options in base pay design that are currently receiving widespread attention are broadbanding systems and skill-based pay systems. Broadbanding greatly simplifies job grading by revising the overall architecture of the pay system. Skill-based systems revise the basis for allocating pay within the overall architecture. Both systems are oriented more toward motivating employees to focus on long-term development, not necessarily on performance. Also, both systems promote greater flexibility in the use of human resources.

Broadbanding

Large organizations typically develop elaborate pay grade systems over time. Multiple pay grades permit firms to offer relatively frequent promotions to higher grades, to create pay distinctions that mirror the hierarchical and status distinctions in the organization, and to control salary progression within grades. Large companies often have dozens of pay grades between the lowest-paid employee and the top executives.

Broadbanding often radically reduces the number of grades in the organization (Abosch & Hand, 1994). Companies such as General Electric and Northern Telecom have recently combined grades to the point where as few as three to six remain in the entire corporation or a large business unit. As grades are combined, the spread between the bottom and top of the range increases from perhaps 35 to 50 percent to as much as 300 percent. In addition, firms using broadbanding usually eliminate traditional pay tools, such as point factor job evaluation and range controls. Some firms adopting broadbanding expect that most employees will remain within one band, such as an engineering band or middle manager band, during their entire career. For example, the Materials Group of Avery Dennison, a business with annual sales of nearly $1 billion, collapsed its complex grade structure into just three bands (one each for executives, lower and middle managers, and nonmanagers).

Broadbanding fits the strategy, structure, and culture of many firms. A company that has radically delayered in favor of flexible, lateral, team-oriented structures may find numerous grades to be anachronistic. Broadening bands can have a positive impact on motivation because it can give managers more flexibility in rewarding employee performance within a very broad band. It also encourages employees to focus on developing skills that make them more valuable, rather than chasing job evaluation points and grades. Broadbanding may reduce incidents in which employees are reluctant to take assignments that are not associated with opportunities for promotion to another pay grade. Companies adopting broadbanding often hope to reduce the time, effort, and energy currently needed to manage their complex pay grade systems.

Broadbanding may also create a variety of problems. For example, once more familiar methods of cost control have been abandoned, it may not be clear how pay costs will be controlled and pay equity will be maintained. Line managers typically assume a critical role in controlling compensation costs in broadbanding, and they may need to be evaluated partly on the basis of the effectiveness with which they perform this role. A well-developed performance management system is needed for managers to perform the cost containment role. Extensive communication is also needed in broadbanding to help employees understand how the new system works and how they can advance in it. Finally, escalating costs sometimes associated with broadbanding may lead organizations to create "control points," "pay zones," or "shadow ranges" within each broad band. In essence, these techniques simply create smaller bands within the larger bands to control costs. As a result, a large number of pay grades are re-created, though still under the guise of broadbanding. When this happens, it may appear to employees, and rightfully so, that little has changed other than the nomenclature.

The best research on broadbanding is a long-term evaluation of three pilot projects in the U.S. federal government (Schay, 1997). The study traced the effects of broadbanding experiments in three units covering thirteen thousand employees in professional, administrative, technical, and nonmanagement occupations. The units were two Navy research laboratories, the National Institute of Standards and Technology, and an Air Force logistics operation. The study found that wage costs increased somewhat because of the way the programs were managed but that the units also experienced a number of benefits. High performers were less likely to quit, and low performers were more likely to quit, than in control units; overall, pay attitudes were much more favorable in the pilot units; and organizational performance increased on several dimensions.

One benchmark survey of broadbanding practices has been conducted with about one hundred companies (Abosch & Hand, 1994). The number one reason for implementing broadbands was to "create more organizational flexibility." Less than 10 percent of the surveyed companies reported increased payroll costs associated with broadbanding, although 38 percent of the surveyed companies did not track changes in cost. Almost 77 percent of the survey respondents felt that their plan was "effective" or "fairly effective."

Companies that viewed their plan as effective, versus companies that viewed their plan as ineffective, spent more time on plan development, were in manufacturing, and had had experience with the plan for at least two years. These data offer some support for the concept of broadbanding, but they are limited by the self-report nature of the data collection process.

Pay for Skill, Knowledge, and Competency

The most common base pay system is job-based pay, which rewards employees for the job currently held. By contrast, skill-based pay (also termed pay for skills, knowledge-based pay, and competency-based pay) rewards employees for their repertoire of knowledge and skill (Lawler, 1990; Lawler & Ledford, 1985; Ledford, 1991). Systems that reward managers and professionals most often are called competency pay, while systems that reward lower-level employees are called skill-based pay or pay for knowledge plans. Typically, employees receive formal certification to show that they have obtained the skill before they receive additional pay. This differs from job-based pay, where the pay is attached to the job and employees receive immediate pay increases when they move to a new job even if they are not capable of performing it. In addition, skill-based pay systems usually deemphasize seniority and other factors unrelated to skill. This contrasts with the common use of maturity curves for engineers, which assume without proof that an employee becomes more valuable with greater experience.

Three types of skills are usually identified in skill-based pay systems:

- *Depth of skill* is increased knowledge of one technical specialty. Examples include the "technical ladder" for engineers, which provides opportunities for promotion based on expertise rather than hierarchical advancement, and apprenticeship systems for workers in the skilled trades.
- *Breadth of skill* is increased knowledge of a variety of tasks or jobs. For example, engineers might be rewarded for learning more than one discipline; factory workers may be rewarded for learning all jobs in their work team or factory.
- *Vertical skill* is self-management skill. For example, the Volvo Kalmar plant gave all team members a raise when they proved they could operate without a supervisor.

A skill-based pay plan can reward one, two, or all three of these types of increased skill. In the typical plan, manufacturing employees are rewarded for learning breadth skills so that they can participate in self-managing work teams.

The most common type of skill-based pay system is a base pay system, which is typically found in manufacturing plants and similar environments. These systems typically divide the work of the organization into skill "blocks" that each require perhaps four to twelve months to learn. Training requirements and certification standards are identified for each block. The design is often complex and careful, since employees receive permanent base pay rewards for increases in skill.

A new but increasingly important approach to skill-based pay uses bonuses instead of base wage increases to reward skill acquisition. This approach is appropriate in situations where the knowledge base is changing quickly or is difficult to specify. It makes sense in certain kinds of high-technology work, including the work of engineers and information systems professionals, for whom the knowledge base may become obsolete in as little as five years. It may not make sense to make permanent increases to salary for obtaining knowledge that will soon be out of date.

The bonus approach can also be combined with performance management systems. All employees can have learning objectives that are similar to performance objectives and can receive bonuses that vary in size, depending on the importance and difficulty of the learning objectives. This approach has the added motivational value of using specific, challenging goals as the basis for the reward. Organizations using this approach with managers and technical professionals include Avery Dennison, Rockwell, and the U.S. military.

Data from studies of Fortune 1000 companies indicate that almost two-thirds of U.S. companies now use some form of skill-based pay with at least some employees and that the percentage of firms using it has increased more than 50 percent since 1987 (Lawler, Mohrman, & Ledford, 1998). Most companies cover relatively few employees with these plans (typically 20 percent or less), but some prominent companies go much further. Procter & Gamble pays virtually all of its manufacturing workers on skill-based pay plans, and Polaroid pays all employees on a modified competency pay plan.

Large-scale surveys (Jenkins, Ledford, Gupta, & Doty, 1992) and case studies at General Mills (Ledford & Bergel, 1991), Honeywell (Ledford, Tyler, & Dixey, 1991), and Northern Telecom (Le Blanc, 1991) suggest that success rates for skill-based pay plans are relatively high. For example, a study of ninety-six skill-based pay plans (Jenkins et al., 1992) found that two-thirds of the survey respondents believed that skill-based pay plans in their organization resulted in improved productivity, quality, output, safety, attendance, and employee-management relations. Employees also tend to have favorable attitudes about skill and competency pay plans, in part because the plans reward the additional skills and knowledge employees develop (Heneman & Ledford, 1998).

One of the authors, Gerald E. Ledford Jr., has recently completed collection of extensive data about a mature competency pay system covering managers at a well-known food processing company. The system, now six years old, covers over one thousand managers at more than forty plants and distribution and sales centers throughout the United States. The system covers all managers from first-line supervisor up to the level of the plant management team.

The system was installed at a time of great change in the company. (Indeed, it was experiencing most of the changes in the nature of work noted earlier in this chapter.) Senior management approved the new pay system as a way to facilitate and support these changes. Senior management was redefining the role of the manager and eliminating levels of management, which reduced opportunities for hierarchical advancement. So the company collapsed a number of prior pay grades for managers on the system into one broad pay band that had a range spread of approximately 300 percent. The company did not use job descriptions for managers but used three generic titles within the broadband: "resource," "senior resource," and "site resource."

Managers were rewarded not for hierarchical advancement but for their progress in developing four competencies. It was possible to receive higher pay without receiving a higher job title, deliberately downplaying the hierarchy in the system and emphasizing that value to the company rather than job or job title drove pay increases. The pay system was based on four competencies that were derived from a management analysis of the company's strategic business direction. The competencies were leveraging technical and business systems, leading for results, building workforce effectiveness, and understanding and meeting customer needs. These competencies reflected the company's movement toward team-based systems that demanded more skill, higher motivation, and ongoing development among the workforce; the new definition of the role of the manager; and the company's quality initiative.

The research project involved an assessment of the plan based on surveys of almost seven hundred employees on the system, one survey per site completed by a senior manager, archival data (promotions and turnover), and performance rankings of twenty-one regions (each including one or more locations). The results suggested that there was a wide range of attitudes about the system and considerable variation in the level of implementation effectiveness across locations. Overall, on average, employees displayed mildly positive attitudes about the system.

The most interesting results concerned the relationship between performance and aggregated survey responses. The study measured performance at the individual level, the location level, and the region level. Individual performance was a self-rating that mirrored the company's performance appraisal rating. Location performance was a survey at the location-level survey. Region performance was based on the company's primary hard performance indicator, a composite performance score that combined indicators of productivity, cost, quality, and employee outcomes (primarily safety).

Predictor variables included a battery of indicators from the survey of managers on the competency pay system. The measures examined degree to which the system led to increased competency, its fit with business needs, its alignment with HR systems other than pay, administrative factors, and change management issues. These variables were summated to the site level for analyses with location as the performance measure and summated to the region level in analyses with the region performance indicator.

Correlational analyses indicated that there were essentially no significant or meaningful correlations between any of the predictors and individual-level performance but that there was a relatively strong relationship between a wide range of predictors and perceived location-level success and region-level performance. The lack of relationship to individual performance is surprising, given the large N (almost 700). The most interesting results for our purposes concerned the relationship between the predictors relevant to the changing nature of work and the hard measure of performance at the region level. Region performance was strongly and significantly correlated with the level of competency acquisition in the region (.66); the degree to which competencies fit a downsized, delayered management structure in the region (.53); the degree to which competencies helped create a lean management structure (.45); the degree to which competencies helped managers understand their new roles (.59); and the degree to which competencies led managers to take responsibility for their own development (.64). These results suggest that competency pay was effective because it was integrated with the new roles and structure of the business. Competency pay was implemented as a part of the business strategy rather than as a "stand-alone" compensation program.

Additional analyses offer support for the hypothesis that the effectiveness of the competency pay system and its fit with changes in the nature of work are causally related to performance in the expected direction. Controlling for salary, promotion, and both salary and promotion had essentially no impact on the correlations, so it does not appear that more favorable attitudes on the manager survey were the result of a higher average level of rewards at locations or regions. In addition, an analysis of the hard performance data over a three-year period suggested strong causal decay. That is, predictors were strongly related to outcomes in the year of the study and in the prior year but were not strongly related to performance two years earlier.

The results of this study are encouraging for several reasons. The study examines a mature system for managers and professionals. It provides some of the first good research evidence that a competency pay system is related to hard performance outcomes at the organization level. Finally, the study indicates that changes in the nature of work at the region level are significantly related to the effectiveness of the competency pay system and its impact on performance.

The best-designed study of skill-based pay to date was conducted by Murray and Gerhart (1998), who also found positive results for skill-based pay. In comparing a treatment plant with skill-based pay to a comparable comparison plant without skill-based pay, they reported greater productivity, lower labor costs, and improved quality in the treatment plant.

Organizations seem to accrue the benefits of such a plan only if it is designed to promote one or more of the following things:

- *Employee flexibility.* Skill-based pay may enhance cross-trained employees' ability to control and eliminate production or service delivery bottlenecks. It may also permit leaner staffing.
- *Support for high involvement.* Skill-based pay systems are used more often and are more effective in organizations with high levels of employee involvement. The pay system gives employees incentives to learn the technical and social skills they need to manage themselves effectively. This may bring advantages such as reduced need for management positions, more effective employee problem solving, and better cooperation across departments.
- *Acquisition of critical skills.* Certain types of employees may be attracted to join the organization and remain in it because of skill-based pay. This is one impetus for the extensive development of skill-based pay plans in information technology groups, for example.

Skill-based pay plans also typically run into problems even when they are successful (Ledford & Bergel, 1991). In some cases, these problems are so serious that the plans fail. The most serious concern to managers is the potential for higher costs. At the outset, higher costs are almost a certainty, due to the cost of wage incentives, increased training, and certification-related expenditures. The organization adopting skill-based pay must bet that these higher costs will be offset by benefits to the organization. Unless the benefits are realized, the plan will cost more than it is worth to the organization.

In addition, skill-based pay plans can be confusing because employees must understand the range of skill blocks for which they are eligible, the training and certification requirements for the blocks, the pay rates for each block, and so on. This means that skill-based pay systems require considerable communication to motivate the acquisition of knowledge and skills properly. Certification processes may be time-consuming, and employees may object to the certification criteria as unfair or inappropriate. If the skill-based pay system rewards employees for learning skills that they do not use, either because of limited work assignments or because skill blocks become obsolete as the technology changes, the plan will escalate wages for no benefit. Finally, not all employees have the ability or desire to learn new skills. If there are too many in the workforce who do not want skill-based pay, its chances of success are slim.

One common concern of managers is that employees will become disgruntled if they "top out" and cannot continually earn increases in a skill-based pay system. Topping out is probably not a serious problem, however, perhaps because employees realize that they are better off both financially and participatively under most skill-based pay systems than they would be in other systems.

Benefit Options

Because benefits are awarded on the basis of organizational membership or attainment of particular organizational levels, they probably have little impact on productivity. For example, many employees receive insurance and retirement benefits simply because they are employees. Moreover, most benefit plans are standardized for all employees and thus may not meet their specific needs at a certain point in time.

As the cost of benefits has escalated, many organizations have struggled with how to make them more variable and how to tie them more closely to employee behavior. Retirement benefits in particular are a large corporate expense that bears essentially no relationship to individual or company performance. For example, conventional pensions reward survival in the company over a long period of time, rather than performance. Perhaps the most interesting change in the benefits arena is variable funding of retirement plans based on corporate performance.

An example of a company that has adopted such an approach as part of a broader turnaround is Owens Corning (Capell, 1996). The Rewards and Resources program now applies to all salaried employees and is being negotiated into union contracts across the company. The company is reducing its match to a retirement savings plan and replacing it with a profit-sharing contribution of up to 4 percent of pay and an annual stock bonus worth up to 8 percent, each linked to corporate performance. Employees also are guaranteed yearly option grants of 4 percent of base pay.

More common is the attempt to tailor benefits to individual needs by means of "cafeteria-style" benefit plans. These plans allow employees to tailor their choices. For example, they may want to put less money into a retirement plan and more into tuition reimbursement benefits. These plans are used by about 70 percent of Fortune 1000 companies. The limited evidence suggests that allowing such choice may help reduce overall costs while increasing employee satisfaction (Barber, Dunham, & Formisano, 1992; Lawler, 1990).

Variable Pay

Paying for performance is a critical and complex issue. The starting point for variable pay needs to be an analysis of the business strategy, organizational structure, and organizational culture. This analysis will indicate the types of performance that the organization needs to reward (for example, cost, revenue, profit, customer service) and the level of analysis at which rewards should be located (team, business unit, or corporation).

Variable pay is the most common pay innovation that ties pay to performance at the team, business unit, or organizational level. There are many forms of variable pay, and variable pay plans have many names: gainsharing, profit sharing, team pay, and goal sharing are a few. Gainsharing is used by 45 percent of large U.S. firms, and profit sharing is used by 69 percent. The use of gainsharing has greatly increased over the past decade; only 26 percent of firms used gainsharing in 1987. The use of profit sharing has not increased much over the past decade (Lawler et al., 1998).

These plans have two common characteristics. First, they pay for performance through bonuses that are paid near the time that the performance occurs, and second, they pay for the performance of collectivities rather than individuals. Pay varies with performance, meaning that the organization pays out more when it can afford to and less when performance does not justify high payment. Some plans even go one step further and put pay "at risk." Under this approach, base pay is reduced to fund performance-based pay.

Successful variable pay plans seem to have two important characteristics: (1) a formula by which employees share monetarily in the performance gains of the organization and (2) structures and processes by which employees share in the creation of organizational performance gains. If the first element is not present, the plan will not motivate improved performance because there will be no line of sight—that is, no clear connection behavior performance and reward. The plan is simply a benefit that pays at some times and not at others. The second element is the means by which employees help create improved performance, generating a pool of money in which they share. Without it, employees will not be motivated because they will have no way to influence the size of their bonuses.

A case study highlights these two points. When Hughes Electronics won a contract to install a $1 billion air defense system for Saudi Arabia, it lived up to its reputation of providing great technology late and was in danger of losing a $50 million bonus for completing the project on time. The CEO of Hughes offered the nine hundred engineers involved in the project 40 percent of the $50 million bonus to split among themselves if the project was completed on time. They came from a year behind schedule to on-time installation, and each team member earned an average of $22,000. This bonus was motivating because it was high enough to be meaningful to all employees involved with it, because it was tied to a clear but challenging goal, and because the number of employees covered by it was small enough that project members could influence the payout.

Variable pay plans have a relatively high success rate. Reviews of the literature and large-scale studies suggest that variable pay plans result in increased organizational performance in most cases, perhaps two cases out of three (Bullock & Lawler, 1984; Bullock & Tubbs, 1987; Lawler, 1988; McAdams & Hawk, 1994; Mitchell, Lewin, & Lawler, 1990; Weitzman & Kruse, 1990; Welbourne, Balkin, & Gomez-Meija, 1995). Typical benefits reported for variable pay include increased productivity, better quality, lower costs, lower absenteeism and turnover, and more favorable employee attitudes. Unlike other innovative pay plans (such as broadbanding) that typically rely on self-report data, greater confidence can be placed in the results of these studies as they often use "hard" data.

For the plan to succeed in improving performance, it must change patterns of behavior that can in turn lead to increased performance. Increases in performance may result from increased employee suggestions for improvement; greater employee effort; better and more persistent problem solving; cooperation within and between groups in the organization, greater demands on management for improved performance, and better relations between management and employees.

Of course, there are also variable pay failures. Reasons for the failure of some variable pay plans are documented by McAdams and Hawk (1994). Plans may fail either because the formula is poorly designed or because the gain-producing structures are inadequate.

There are many potential problems with variable pay formulas. For example, with respect to design issues, the hurdle for achieving a payout may be too high, especially early in the life of the plan. Employees tend to give up on plans that do not pay out in the first year or two. Conversely, if the formula makes it is too easy to achieve a payout, the plan may fail because it does not cause employees to change their behavior. In addition, there may not be enough money available in the plan to motivate a change in behavior. Convention suggests that bonus opportunities must represent 5 to 10 percent of base pay to be motivating. The greater the amount of money available, the more motivating the plan; some plans make it possible for employees to earn 25 percent or more of base pay in bonuses, although a much lower amount is typical.

The formula may be designed to reward the wrong behaviors or may not cover all the relevant behaviors and metrics. For example, a formula that rewards increased labor productivity may lead employees not only to work harder but also to increase production of scrap and waste. Payouts may also be too infrequent. From a motivational point of view, frequent payouts are desirable, although this may not be practical for an organization's accounting system or performance cycles. Still other problems can be created by omitting key groups from the plan. For example, if the plan covers only direct labor employees, support employees such as maintenance workers and material handlers may resist changing their behavior in order to make it possible for others to earn a bonus. Finally, the formula can be too inflexible. Because the formula is tailored to a particular context, the formula needs to change as the business plan it is designed to support also evolves. This suggests the need for periodic changes to the variable pay plan, which can be difficult to negotiate or gain support for.

Beyond potential problems with formula design, the structures needed to support performance improvement may be absent or poorly implemented. Most variable plans require a participative system that generates and processes employee ideas for improvement. This may be a separate system of variable pay committees, or participation may be integrated into the role of existing work teams. Whatever the particular structure, unless employees have the opportunity to suggest improvements, they are left with the sole option of working harder to achieve a payout. Inadequate training and communication about the plan and organizational performance are other common sources of problems. Employees are not motivated by a plan unless they understand it and unless they know the direction of organizational performance and how it is changing.

These considerations suggest that another essential variable is trust. Employees must trust that the formula is fair, that they will receive a payout for their efforts, and that their ideas will lead to organizational changes. If trust is very low, adoption of variable pay should be reconsidered. Relatedly, management may be a barrier to success. Employees question why things have been done in certain ways in the past and challenge management to adopt changes faster. Some managers see this as a desirable aspect of variable pay, while others are threatened by such behavior.

The design of variable pay plan formulas is complex, and it has been the subject of numerous books, manuals, and training programs (see Belcher et al., 1998). We will highlight some of the most important issues.

There are several essential principles of variable pay design. First, such plans are usually designed to be self-funding, so that the money paid out in bonuses is derived from savings that the plan itself generates. Another principle is line of sight. There are many ways of increasing line of sight in variable pay plans and therefore increasing the motivational power of these plans. Simpler measures and formulas tend to produce greater line of sight; so do more frequent payouts. Paying out to smaller units (such as a teams) creates greater line of sight than paying out in a large plant or an

entire company. However, competition may also be heightened between groups by paying out to smaller groups. Support processes
can also be critical to creating line of sight. Considerable training
and information sharing must help employees understand a plan
that is not obvious to them.

Many different performance measures can be used as the basis
for a variable pay formula. These range from very concrete behavioral measures (accidents, absenteeism, safety inspection ratings)
to measures of unit performance (productivity, cost, quality, on-
time delivery, cycle time) to measures of financial performance (return on sales or investment, profit, economic value added). The
best measure for a given organization can be discovered only
through analysis of the business strategy, organizational structure,
and culture. The advantage of behavioral measures is that they
have strong line of sight and therefore greater motivational value.
For example, employees are motivated to reduce absenteeism because there is a clear connection between attendance and bonuses.

Financial performance metrics are more closely tied to the organization's ability to pay. If the organization is doing well, it can
afford to pay bonuses; if it is not doing well, no bonuses are paid
out. This often makes financially oriented plans attractive to managers. However, most employees often have modest control over financial performance. Whether the organization makes a high
profit or achieves a high rate of return depends on market conditions, competitor behavior, capital equipment purchases, and accounting decisions that employees cannot influence.

Nevertheless, there is a clear trend in the United States toward
using plans tied to the financial performance of the corporation.
The Big Three automakers all offer profit-sharing bonuses, which
have varied greatly with company performance in recent years. Before the Daimler-Chrysler merger, Chrysler workers earned $8,000
annually due to good performance, and General Motors workers
made $300 in bonuses for 1996. (Saturn workers, on a separate
plan that rewards quality and financial performance, received
$10,000 each.) Intel offered employees the equivalent of at least
one-third their annual salary as a bonus for good company performance in 1996. Levi Strauss is offering all employees an extra
year's pay as a bonus if the company achieves a cumulative cash
flow of $7.6 billion for the six-year period starting in 1996. Finally,

IBM paid bonuses averaging $4,979 for all employees worldwide based on 1996 performance.

In evaluating these plans, we must recognize that they have limited motivational value, lucrative as they are, because there is little line of sight between payouts and individual behavior. However, these plans have been linked to moderate productivity increases (Weitzman & Kruse, 1990) and may also have other advantages. They offer companies a way of paying employees well when they can afford to do so and help increase employee identification with the company and its success.

Unit performance metrics are in the middle on the continuum from line of sight to ability to pay. Employees can influence them more easily than financial performance measures, but not as easily as behavior measures. An organization that shows good performance on productivity tends to make a higher rate of return over the long run, but the relationship is not perfect. A plan based on unit performance or behavioral measures may pay out handsomely even when the total organization is losing money or may not pay out at all when the organization is making high profits. However, these metrics are the ones most often recommended in the gainsharing literature. Companies making heavy use of such metrics for unit-level gainsharing plans include TRW, Dana, Hughes, and Weyerhaeuser. All cover half or more of their workforce with gainsharing plans that use such metrics.

Many organizations attempt to realize the best of both worlds by combining different types of metrics in the same formula. For example, there may be a requirement that the organization is making a profit before it makes payouts on unit performance or behavioral measures. These and other options protect against payouts in bad times, but at the risk of making the plan more complex and difficult to understand. The plan may also inadvertently include so many safeguards that it cannot pay out.

Gainsharing formulas also highlight the design choice of whether to pay out when the organization does better than in the past (gainsharing when performance exceeds historical levels) or when the organization reaches targets that are defined by management (goal sharing). Gainsharing based on historical performance usually appears fair to employees. It also avoids employee fears of a "speed-up," a common problem in individual incentive plans such as piecework. From a motivational perspective, goal sharing is attractive because it takes advantage of the motivational power of specific, challenging goals. Goal sharing may also be the most practical approach in some situations. Historical data may be unavailable, as in a new plant, or may be irrelevant, as in the case of an organization that must perform at a much higher level than in the past to stay in business. Management-set targets are very flexible and can change annually to reflect new business directions and emphases.

Managers can determine the suitability of any particular formula only through an analysis of the needs of the organization. Different plans are appropriate to different settings. Also, we again emphasize that the support processes and structures are at least as important to success as the specifics of the formula itself.

Ownership Options

There are two primary ways in which companies offer opportunities for equity participation: employee stock ownership plans (ESOPs) and stock options. These plans have many of the same advantages and motivational problems as corporate profit sharing but are even more complex from the individual employee's standpoint. A wave of ESOP adoptions during the 1980s in the United States resulted from favorable tax legislation. Almost two-thirds of Fortune 1000 firms in the country have such plans, and one-third cover all employees with them (Lawler, Mohrman, & Ledford, 1998). Although it is possible to construct ESOP plans that have motivational value, especially in small companies, most are designed in ways that greatly mitigate motivational effects (Lawler & Jenkins, 1992). Most ESOP plans are part of the retirement system, meaning that any reward is very remote from the employee's point of view. In addition, employees typically are not allowed control of their shares until they retire, meaning that they cannot vote as a shareholder on corporate governance issues.

During the past few years, there has been an explosion in the use of broad-based stock options (Capell, 1996). These plans have become a standard part of pay packages in the high-technology sector, and high-tech firms often have serious recruitment and retention problems if they cannot offer stock options. The rewards for these plans can be spectacular in successful companies. Microsoft offers below-market base pay but stock options so lucrative that fully half of the workforce—and virtually all employees with more than five years' tenure—own over $1 million in company stock. PepsiCo was one of the first companies outside the high-technology sector to offer stock options to all employees, and options now cover millions of workers in the American economy in companies such as Monsanto, Starbucks, and Delta Air Lines. A recent survey indicates that the vast majority of Fortune 1000 firms use stock options, and 20 percent cover half or more of the workforce (Lawler et al., 1998).

Appealing as stock options and ESOP plans may be from the standpoint of employees who have been made wealthy by such plans, they have questionable motivational value. Few of Microsoft's twenty-eight thousand employees below the executive level can have a significant effect on the firm's stock performance. Not only is there low line of sight to company performance, there is no line of sight to the macroeconomic, international, financial, and market forces far beyond the company's boundaries that influence stock prices. In addition, employees often find the *meaning* of stock options very difficult to understand. An administrative employee at a leading biotechnology firm allowed $750,000 in stock options to expire because she did not understand how the plan worked. Once this happened, the company was legally powerless to correct the problem.

Privately held organizations, which do not have publicly traded stock, sometimes use "phantom stock." They issue internal stock to serve as a proxy for public stock. The phantom stock's value is based on the book value of the organization and is not the same as phantom stock for executives, defined as stock price appreciation plus dividends. By comparison, the value of publicly traded stock is its market. Although there have been no formal empirical studies of phantom stock plans, the theory of line of sight would suggest that phantom stock plans are more likely to be successful at motivating employee performance because book value reflects criteria (such as cost) more under the employees control than market value, which is at the mercy of market conditions as well as company performance. Major companies with phantom stock plans include Kinko's and Mary Kay (Tully, 1998).

The empirical evidence on employee stock ownership plans has been reviewed in two places. Conte and Kruse (1991) looked at the impact of ESOP plans on organizational effectiveness. The results suggest that ESOPs are not likely to have an impact on employee productivity. This result should not be surprising, given that the actual intent of most ESOP plans is to raise capital, not to raise labor productivity. The evidence on public stock ownership plans has been reviewed in meta-analysis by Ben-Ner and Jones (1995), who found that although ownership does affect productivity, it is dependent on the extent of participation in decision making that accompanies ownership.

Future Research

The new forms of pay reviewed here invite new advancements in compensation theory and research. Suggestions for future research follow and are summarized in Exhibit 6.1.

Changes in Pay Practices

Further theory development is crucial if we are to understand the new forms of pay. While categorization schemes such as the one shown in Exhibit 6.1 may be helpful from a heuristic perspective to show differences in pay system characteristics, theory development and application are needed to achieve an understanding of how these systems operate and the impact they have on individual and organizational outcomes.

Exhibit 6.1. Future Research Agenda.

Change at Work	Change in Pay Systems	Pay Outcomes
• Business strategy • Employment relationship • Organizational structure • Technology • Job design	• Broadbanding • Skill based • Benefits • Variable pay • Ownership	• Organizational effectiveness • Individual effectiveness • Employment • Fairness • Satisfaction

One approach to the study of the new pay is to look at the effects of the components of these systems in terms of main effects and interactions. To do so, careful construction of theory is needed to guide an examination of the synergistic effects between compensation components and changes in the nature of work (Delery & Doty, 1996; Gerhart, Trevor, & Graham, 1996). Thoughtful theoretical development is in direct contrast to a "shotgun empiricism" approach, wherein all available interactions are tested and then the significant interactions are given a post hoc explanation. Unfortunately, shotgun empiricism seems to dominate the current literature on "bundles" of human resource activities, including pay.

There is a growing theoretical base to draw on to guide compensation research in this era of new pay forms. New theory bases include organization justice (Welbourne et al., 1995), tournament theory (Becker & Huselid, 1992), agency theory (Conlon & Parks, 1990; Parks & Conlon, 1995), resource-based view of the firm (Barney & Wright, 1998), and population ecology (Welbourne & Andrews, 1996). As noted by Heneman (1992) and by Gerhart and Milkovich (1992), we are more likely to improve our knowledge of compensation systems if we adapt these theories to study compensation systems, rather than using compensation systems to study these theories. An excellent example here is Murray and Gerhart (1998), who used the job characteristics model and expectancy theory to study skill-based pay, rather than using skill-based pay to test expectancy theory and the job characteristics model.

Specific compensation problems need theoretical guidance to resolve them. For example, there are conflicting findings regarding the benefits and drawbacks of individual versus group rewards. Wageman (1995) reported in a study of intact work groups at Xerox that group performance was better when the pay plan was based on either group or individual performance rewards rather than a combination of group and individual rewards. Crown and Rosse (1995) found that for sports teams, a combination of group and individual performance goals resulted in better group performance than individual goals alone, but combined group and individual goals resulted in less effective group performance than group goals alone.

To resolve the conflicting findings regarding the utility of group and individual reward systems, theoretical concepts such as free riding and social loafing may need to be examined. Wagner (1995) found that social loafing and free riding were less likely in groups characterized by high collectivism, small group size, high accountability to the group, and low shared responsibility. Such groups may have less need for individual rewards to supplement group rewards.

Pay Outcomes

A common approach to studying pay outcomes is to use managerial or human resource ratings of pay plan and organizational effectiveness. For example, for a survey of over six hundred pay plans, the department variables used were human resource professionals' judgments regarding business performance, managerial perceptions, and employee perceptions (McAdams & Hawk, 1994). Though potentially suggestive of the likely outcomes associated with pay plans, these perceptual measures are clearly both deficient and potentially contaminated. They fail to tap actual business performance, employee perceptions, and managerial perceptions. Should these types of measures be abandoned? The answer is probably no because in some studies it is not possible to gather additional outcome measures, and these data do provide a start to our understanding of pay systems. Also, perceptual measures are sometimes correlated with more objective measures (Delaney & Huselid, 1996; Montemayor, 1996).

An obvious solution to the use of perceptual measures is to use operational (productivity) and financial (profit) outcome measures. Unfortunately, this obvious solution is not without limitations as well. Measures of this type are contaminated by many factors (technology, the business cycle) other than compensation. In addition, the reliability of productivity measures is only about .60, as shown by Heneman (1986) in a meta-analysis. A final problem is that these measures are sometimes available only at the corporate level, whereas pay plans often cover employees only at the business-unit level. As a result, the amount of variance explained using these measures may be very small and insignificant. More proximal operational measures are more likely to be affected by compensation systems, but they also suffer from measurement problems as well. For example, Cardy and Dobbins (1994) document the low reliability of customer service measures.

Given the problems associated with both subjective and objective measures, two steps seem appropriate. First, multiple measures of pay plan effectiveness should be used, since organizational effectiveness is rarely a unidimensional construct anyway (Whetten & Cameron, 1994). Second, when compensation theory is tested, corrections for attenuation in the dependent variable should be applied.

Along with the use of both subjective and objective measures, the use of new measures is to be recommended. Creative and important examples follow. Gerhart, Trevor, and Graham (1996) recommended that the financial risk involved with pay plans be studied, as well as the survival of pay plans. Reported reasons for pay plan termination include lack of performance against payout measures, management changes, change in market conditions, change in business strategy, lack of acceptance by employees and management, and cost of the plan (McAdams & Hawk, 1994). As noted earlier, a strategic view of human resources suggests that the relationship between human resource activities be linked with one another as well as with the business strategy.

Three studies serve as examples of the need to look at the effects of the compensation system on other human resource systems (such as staffing). First, Cable and Judge (1994) examined preferences for various pay systems in the job search decisions of college students. Organizations were perceived as more attractive places to work when flexible benefits, high proportions of base pay to variable pay, and individual rather than group rewards were offered. These effects were reported after controlling for pay level. The results suggest that the new pay programs reviewed in this chapter may not always be acceptable to college students. Le Blanc and Mulvey (1998) report similar pay preferences for a more general population. Second, Gerhart and Trevor (1996) examined layoffs as a function of the type of pay plan used. It was shown that organizations that value employment stability have a greater tendency to use variable pay.

Another set of dependent variables to be explored are process variables. Recent research by Snell and Youndt (1995) indicates that the control of processes is at least as important as the control of outcomes to the economic performance of the firm. Kessler and Chakrabarti (1996), for example, suggest that "innovation speed" is an important process variable needed for organizations to adapt to changing business environments. Reward systems are viewed as facilitating the speed at which products are developed. It is hypothesized that speed is likely to be changed by group reward systems that promote the exchange of information and ideas.

Changes in Work and Changes in Pay Practices

A question of strategic importance to compensation professionals is how compensation plans can be designed that help organizations adapt to changes in work and business environments. Concepts bandied about in discussing this issue include "fit," "flexibility," and "organizational learning." Two important articles provide some theoretical guidance in this area.

Wright and Snell (1998) argue that both fit and flexibility are required of human resource activities if they are to add value to the firm. *Fit* refers to the development of a formal organizational strategy and structure, with specification of the employee competencies to fulfill that strategy and structure. Pay systems can be used to motivate the acquisition and demonstration of competencies in alignment with the business strategy. *Flexibility* refers more to the development of individual competencies in the organization such that the organization can adapt to the changing business environment. If an organization has the needed competencies to adapt to the changing business environment, it is likely to gain advantage over organizations without such competencies. Competency- and skill-based pay systems, especially those that constantly update competency and skill blocks, are likely to develop human resources in the organization that can readily adapt to the changing business environment.

The need for flexibility points to the need for organizations to be able to learn in order to adapt to the business environment. Snell, Youndt, and Wright (1996) show how strategic human resource management activities can contribute to organizational learning. In brief, reward systems need to help develop or reinforce the three major components of organizational learning: creating knowledge, transferring knowledge, and institutionalizing knowledge. At the creation stage, competency-based pay could be used. At the transferring stage, team-based pay might be used to facilitate the sharing of learning. In the institutionalizing stage, employee ownership plans might be used to facilitate the retention of knowledge.

Changes in Pay Practices and Outcomes

There is a critical need for more and better studies that examine the impact of pay systems on individual and organizational outcomes. However, increasing the number of studies is problematic for a number of reasons. First, gaining access to data in organizations with new pay plans is difficult. Organizations usually only want to share successes (see Petty, Singleton, & Connell, 1992, for a notable exception), which poses a restriction-of-range problem. Moreover, the problem is exacerbated by the fact that organizations are unlikely to share the results of very successful plans because they are a potential source of competitive advantage to the organization (Cappelli & Crocker-Hefter, 1995). Even when organizations are willing to share, data collection may not be possible in some cases for university researchers. To protect human subjects, university review committees may, for example, preclude the researcher from matching up demographic and attitudinal data about the employee with pay and outcome measures. Even if permitted, it may be required to be on a voluntary basis, which creates a potential sampling bias.

A final problem has to do with the research design process. Providing meaningful findings is difficult without a control group or time-series data. For obvious reasons, it is often impossible to have a control group with pay interventions, and time-series data may take considerable time given the newness of these plans and their ongoing refinement, which may further confound the data.

Although these problems exist and are likely causes of the limited number of published studies on compensation relative to other industrial and organizational psychology topics, they are not insurmountable. Anonymity can be guaranteed in order to cushion the revelation of negative findings by organizations. If pay plans truly are a source of competitive advantage, organizations should not be able to obtain identical results simply by copying the pay practices of a competitor. A successful plan will fit the unique circumstances of each organization. University review committees can be shown that the benefits of the research outweigh the costs of losses of confidentiality. Steps can be taken to ensure that confidentiality is breached only by the researchers and not by others. Journal editors and reviewers can be sympathetic to internal validity threats and carefully trade off the need for well-designed research against the need for knowledge about new compensation plans. New outlets, such as the Scientist-Practitioner Forum at *Personnel Psychology,* may be more responsive to this trade-off than traditional I/O psychology outlets.

With regard to better research, three issues are salient. First, pay plans should not be treated as homogeneous constructs. For example, not all employee ownership plans are alike (Ben-Ner & Jones, 1995). These various components of pay plans need to be assessed in terms of their independent and combined effects. Ben-Ner and Jones point out, for example, that the separate and combined impact of financial participation and participation in decision making is not well understood in employee ownership plans.

Second, given the heterogeneity of pay plans under the same name, specific theories need to be developed for specific pay plans rather than grand theories that are applicable across all pay plans. This has been done for merit pay (Heneman, 1990), employee ownership (Pierce, Rubenfeld, & Morgan, 1991), and skill-based pay (Murray & Gerhart, 1998). Other forms of the new pay similarly need theoretical development.

Third, the cognitive revolution in psychology has provided great insight into performance appraisal, which is a closely allied subject of compensation systems. One would suspect that cognitive psychology would be useful in understanding compensation decision making. We should note two examples of inroads in this area. Henderson and Fredrickson (1996) found that executive compensation is in part a function of the cognitive demands placed on the executive by the organization. Bazerman, Lowenstein, and White (1992) report using a cognitive approach to explore the inconsistent manner in which interpersonal comparisons are made when making pay allocation decisions.

Conclusion

Organizations spend huge sums of money on compensation. It is not uncommon for labor costs to make up 70 percent or more of the total budget in service sector organizations. It is hardly surprising, then, that decision makers in organizations are carefully monitoring the utility of dollars spent on compensation to see to what extent compensation programs are contributing to organizational effectiveness. We are encouraged by the fact that organizations are experimenting with new forms of pay that may show a better return on investment than has been the case with traditional pay programs. The time is ripe for academics to capitalize on the attention executives are giving to pay systems by conducting meaningful theory-driven research in field settings.

Concurrently, theory is being developed in academic settings that is highly relevant to the study of these new pay systems. Newer theories come to us from business strategy, which focuses on human resource practices as a source of competitive advantage for organizations; from cognitive and social psychology, which offers important perspectives on decision making by individuals and teams; and from economics, which looks at the relationship between the owner (principal) and employee (agent) in compensation decision making.

Our hope is that the current opportunities in the field can be coupled with the advancement of theory in the academy. Sound practice and theory go hand in hand. We would like to see a new generation of compensation scholars address the effects of the changing nature of work on compensation. We now have a good start on developing a descriptive body of knowledge regarding these new pay practices. Professional associations, especially the American Compensation Association, and compensation consulting firms have led the way.

However, as was true for Opsahl and Dunnette (1966) as they reviewed research on traditional pay systems more than thirty years ago, we need more analytical work in compensation based on sound theory to show when and why innovative pay plans work. This next step should increase organizational effectiveness, because we will know not only that pay programs work but also, more important, *why* they work. Although we need to focus on the organizational outcomes associated with new pay plans, we must also devote attention to the study of the processes that lead to these outcomes.

References

Abosch, K. S., & Hand, J. S. (1994). *Broadbanding design, approaches, and practices.* Scottsdale, AZ: American Compensation Association.

American Compensation Association. (1996). *Raising the bar: Using competencies to enhance employee performance.* Scottsdale, AZ: Author.

Barber, A. E., Dunham, R. B., & Formisano, R. A. (1992). The impact of employee benefits on employee satisfaction: A field study. *Personnel Psychology, 45,* 55–75.

Barney, J. B., & Wright, P. M. (1998). On becoming a strategic partner: The role of human resources in gaining competitive advantage. *Human Resource Management, 37,* 31–46.

Bazerman, M. H., Lowenstein, G. F., & White, S. B. (1992). Reversals of preference in allocation decisions: Judging an alternative versus choosing among alternatives. *Administrative Science Quarterly, 37,* 220–240.

Becker, B. E., & Huselid, M. A. (1992). Direct estimates of SD_y and the implications for utility analysis. *Journal of Applied Psychology, 77,* 227–233.

Belcher, J. G., Jr., Butler, R. J., Cheatham, D. W., Goberville, G. J., Heneman, R. L., & Wilson, T. B. (1998). *How to design variable pay.* Scottsdale, AZ: American Compensation Association.

Ben-Ner, A., & Jones, D. C. (1995). Employee participation, ownership, and productivity: A theoretical framework. *Industrial Relations, 34,* 532–554.

Bridges, W. (1995). *Jobshift: How to prosper in a workplace without jobs.* Reading, MA: Addison-Wesley.

Bullock, R. J., & Lawler, E. E., III. (1984). Gainsharing: A few questions and fewer answers. *Human Resource Management, 23,* 23–40.

Bullock, R. J., & Tubbs, M. E. (1987). A case meta-analysis of gainsharing plans as organizational development interventions. *Journal of Applied Behavioral Science, 26,* 383–404.

Cable, D. M., & Judge, T. A. (1994). Pay preference and job search decisions: A person-organization fit perspective. *Personnel Psychology, 47,* 317–348.

Capell, K. (1996, July 22). Owens Corning plays share the wealth. *Business Week,* 82–83.

Cappelli, P., Bassi, L., Katz, H., Knoke, D., Osterman, P., & Useem, M. (1997). *Change at work.* New York: Oxford University Press.

Cappelli, P., & Crocker-Hefter, A. (1995). Distinctive human resources are firms' core competencies. *Organizational Dynamics, 24,* 7–22.

Cardy, R. L., & Dobbins, G. H. (1994). *Performance appraisal: Alternative perspectives.* Cincinnati, OH: South-Western.

Cohen, D., & Heneman, R. L. (1994). Ability and effort weights in pay level and pay increase decisions. *Journal of Business and Psychology, 8,* 327–343.

Conlon, E. J., & Parks, J. M. (1990). Effects of monitoring and tradition on compensation arrangements: An experiment with principal-agent dyads. *Academy of Management Journal, 43,* 603–622.

Conte, M. A., & Kruse, D. L. (1991). ESOPs and profit-sharing plans: Do they link employee pay to company performance? *Financial Management, 20,* 91–100.

Crandall, N. F., & Wallace, M. J., Jr. (1997). Inside the virtual workplace: Forging a new deal for work and rewards. *Compensation and Benefits Review, 29,* 27–36.

Crown, D. F., & Rosse, J. G. (1995). Yours, mine and ours: Facilitating group productivity through the integration of individual and group goals. *Organizational Behavior and Human Decision Processes, 64,* 138–150.

Delaney, J. T., & Huselid, M. A. (1996). The impact of human resource management practices on perceptions of organizational performance. *Academy of Management Journal, 39,* 949–969.

Delery, J. E., & Doty, D. H. (1996). Modes of theorizing in strategic human resource management: Tests of universalistic, contingency, and configurational performance predictions. *Academy of Management Journal, 39,* 802–835.

Finegold, D., Lawler, E. E., III, & Ledford, G. E., Jr. (1998). Competencies, capabilities, and strategic organizational design. In A. M. Mohrman Jr., J. R. Galbraith, & E. E. Lawler III (Eds.), *Tomorrow's organization: Crafting winning capabilities in a dynamic world.* San Francisco: Jossey-Bass.

Gerhart, B., & Milkovich, G. T. (1992). Employee compensation: Research and practice. In M. D. Dunnette & L. M. Hough (Eds.), *Handbook of industrial and organizational psychology* (2nd ed., Vol. 3, pp. 481–570). Palo Alto, CA: Consulting Psychologists Press.

Gerhart, B., & Trevor, C. O. (1996). Employment variability under different managerial compensation systems. *Academy of Management Journal, 39,* 1692–1712.

Gerhart, B., Trevor, C. O., & Graham, M. E. (1996). New directions in compensation research: Synergies, risk, and survival. *Research in Personnel and Human Resources Management, 14,* 143–203.

Gomez-Mejia, L. R., & Balkin, D. B. (1992). *Compensation, organizational strategy, and firm performance.* Cincinnati, OH: South-Western.

Gross, S. E. (1995). *Compensation for teams.* New York: AMACOM.

Hambrick, D. C., & Snow, C. C. (1989). Strategic reward systems. In C. C. Snow (Ed.), *Strategy, organization design, and human resource management* (pp. 333–367). Greenwich, CT: JAI Press.

Hedge, J. W., & Borman, W. C. (1995). Changing conceptions and practices in performance appraisal. In A. Howard (Ed.), *The changing network of work* (pp. 451–484). San Francisco: Jossey-Bass.

Henderson, A. D., & Fredrickson, J. W. (1996). Information-processing demands as a determinant of CEO compensation. *Academy of Management Journal, 39,* 575–606.

Heneman, H. G., III, Heneman, R. L., & Judge, T. (1997). *Staffing organizations* (2nd ed.). Burr Ridge, IL: Irwin.

Heneman, H. G., III, & Schwab, D. P. (1979). Work and rewards theory. In D. Yoder & H. G. Heneman Jr. (Eds.), *ASPA handbook of personnel and industrial relations* (pp. 6.1–6.22). Washington, DC: Bureau of National Affairs.

Heneman, H. G., III, & Schwab, D. P. (1985). Pay satisfaction: Its multidimensional nature and measurement. *International Journal of Psychology, 20,* 129–141.

Heneman, R. L. (1986). The relationship between supervisory ratings and results-oriented measures of performance: A meta-analysis. *Personnel Psychology, 39,* 811–826.

Heneman, R. L. (1990). Merit pay research. In G. R. Ferris & K. M. Rowland (Eds.), *Research in personnel and human resources management* (Vol. 8, pp. 203–263). Greenwich, CT: JAI Press.

Heneman, R. L. (in press). Merit pay. In C. H. Fay (Ed.), *The executive compensation handbook.* New York: Free Press.

Heneman, R. L., & Gresham, M. T. (1998). Linking appraisals to compensation and incentives. In J. W. Smither (Ed.), *Performance appraisal: State-of-the art methods for performance management* (pp. 496–536). San Francisco: Jossey-Bass.

Heneman, R. L., & Ledford, G. E., Jr. (1998). Competency pay for managers and professionals: Implications for teachers. *Journal for Personnel Evaluation in Education, 2,* 103–121.

Heneman, R. L., & von Hippel, C. (1996). The assessment of job performance: Focusing attention on context, process and group issues. In D. Lewin, D. J. B. Mitchell, & M. A. Zaidi (Eds.), *Handbook of human resource management* (pp. 587–617). Greenwich, CT: JAI Press.

Howard, A. (1995). A framework for work change. In A. Howard (Ed.), *The changing nature of work* (pp. 3–44). San Francisco: Jossey-Bass.

Ilgen, D. R., & Hollenbeck, J. R. (1991). The structure of work: Job design and roles. In M. D. Dunnette & L. M. Hough (Eds.), *Handbook of industrial and organizational psychology* (2nd ed., Vol. 2, pp. 165–208). Palo Alto, CA: Consulting Psychologists Press.

Jenkins, G. D., Jr., Ledford, G. E., Jr., Gupta, N., & Doty, D. H. (1992). *Skill-based pay: Practices, payoffs, pitfalls, and prescriptions.* Scottsdale, AZ: American Compensation Association.

Kahnweiler, W. M., Crane, D. P., & O'Neill, C. P. (1994, Spring). Employee involvement in design in and managing pay systems. *American Compensation Association Journal,* 68–81.

Kanfer, R., & Heggestad, E. D. (1997). Motivational traits and skills: A person-centered approach to work motivation. *Research in Organizational Behavior, 19,* 1–56.

Kessler, E. H., & Chakrabarti, A. K. (1996). Innovation speed: A conceptual model of context, antecedents, and outcomes. *Academy of Management Review, 21,* 1143–1191.

Lawler, E. E., III. (1971). Corporate profits and employee satisfaction: Must they be in conflict? *California Management Review, 14,* 46.

Lawler, E. E., III. (1981). *Pay and organizational development.* Reading, MA: Addison-Wesley.

Lawler, E. E., III. (1988). Pay for performance: Making it work. *Personnel, 65,* 22–27.

Lawler, E. E., III. (1990). *Strategic pay: Aligning organizational strategies and pay systems.* San Francisco: Jossey-Bass.

Lawler, E. E., III, & Cohen, S. G. (1992, Autumn). Designing pay systems for teams. *American Compensation Association Journal,* 6–18.

Lawler, E. E., III, & Jenkins, G. D., Jr. (1992). Strategic reward systems. In M. D. Dunnette & L. M. Hough (Eds.), *Handbook of industrial and organizational psychology* (2nd ed., Vol. 3, pp. 1009–1055). Palo Alto, CA: Consulting Psychologists Press.

Lawler, E. E., III, & Ledford, G. E., Jr. (1985). Skill-based pay: A concept that's catching on. *Personnel, 62,* 30–37.

Lawler, E. E., III, Mohrman, S. A., & Ledford, G. E., Jr. (1998). *Strategies for high-performance organizations.* San Francisco: Jossey-Bass.

Lazear, E. P. (1992). The job as a concept. In W. J. Bruns Jr. (Ed.), *Performance measurement, evaluation, and incentives* (pp. 183–215). Boston: Harvard Business School Press.

Le Blanc, P. V. (1991). Skill-based pay case number 2: Northern Telecom. *Compensation and Benefits Review, 23,* 39–56.

Le Blanc, P. V., & Mulvey, P. W. (1998). How American workers see the rewards of work. *Compensation and Benefits Review, 30,* 24–28.

Ledford, G. E., Jr. (1991). Three case studies on skill-based pay: An overview. *Compensation and Benefits Review, 23,* 11–23.

Ledford, G. E., Jr. (1995). Designing nimble reward systems. *Compensation and Benefits Review, 27,* 46–54.

Ledford, G. E., Jr., & Bergel, G. (1991). Skill-based pay case number 1: General Mills. *Compensation and Benefits Review, 23,* 24–38.

Ledford, G. E., Jr., Lawler, E. E., III, & Mohrman, S. A. (1995). Reward innovations in Fortune 1000 companies. *Compensation and Benefits Review, 27,* 76–80.

Ledford, G. E., Jr., Tyler, W. R., & Dixey, W. B. (1991). Skill-based pay case number 3: Honeywell ammunition assembly. *Compensation and Benefits Review, 23,* 57–77.

McAdams, J. L., & Hawk, E. J. (1994). *Organizational performance and rewards.* Scottsdale, AZ: American Compensation Association.

Miles, R. E., Snow, C. C., Mathews, J. A., Miles, G., & Coleman, H. J., Jr. (1997). Organizing in the knowledge age: Anticipating the cellular form. *Academy of Management Executive, 11,* 7–20.

Milkovich, G. T., & Newman, J. M. (1996). *Compensation* (5th ed.). Burr Ridge, IL: Irwin.

Mitchell, D. J. B., Lewin, D., & Lawler, E. E., III. (1990). Alternative pay systems, firm performance, and productivity. In A. S. Blinder (Ed.), *Paying for productivity: A look at the evidence* (pp. 15–94). Washington, DC: Brookings Institution.

Montemayor, E. F. (1994, Summer). A model for aligning teamwork and pay. *American Compensation Association Journal,* 18–25.

Montemayor, E. F. (1996). Congruence between pay policy and competitive strategy in high-performing firms. *Journal of Management, 22,* 889–908.

Murray, B. C., & Gerhart, B. (1998). An empirical analysis of a skill-based pay program and plant performance outcomes. *Academy of Management Journal, 41,* 68–78.

Naylor, J. C., Pritchard, R. D., & Ilgen, D. R. (1980). *A theory of behavior in organizations.* Orlando, FL: Academic Press.

O'Neal S. (1995, Autumn). Competencies and pay in the evolving and world of work. *American Compensation Association Journal,* 72–79.

Opsahl, R. L., & Dunnette, M. D. (1966). The role of financial compensation in industrial motivation. *Psychological Bulletin, 66,* 94–118.

Parks, J. M., & Conlon, E. J. (1995). Compensation contracts: Do agency theory assumptions predict negotiated agreements? *Academy of Management Journal, 38,* 821–838.

Patten, T. H., Jr. (1977). *Pay.* New York: Free Press.

Petty, M. M., Singleton, B., & Connell, D. W. (1992). An experimental evaluation of an incentive plan in the electric utility industry. *Journal of Applied Psychology, 77,* 427–436.

Pierce, J. L., Rubenfeld, S. A., & Morgan, S. (1991). Employee ownership: A conceptual model of process and effects. *Academy of Management Journal, 16,* 121–144.

Rousseau, D. M. (1997). Organizational behavior in the new organizational era. *Annual Review of Psychology, 48,* 515–546.

Saunier, A. M., & Hawk, E. J. (1994). Realizing the potential of teams through team-based rewards. *Compensation and Benefits Review* [Special issue], 24–33.

Schay, B. (1997). Paying for performance: Lessons learned in fifteen years of federal demonstration projects. In H. Risher & C. H. Fay (Eds.), *New strategies for public pay: Rethinking government compensation* (pp. 253–272). San Francisco: Jossey-Bass.

Schuster, J. R., & Zingheim, P. K. (1992). *The new pay.* San Francisco: New Lexington Press.

Shaw, D. G., & Schneier, C. E. (1995). Team measurement and rewards: How some companies are getting it right. *Human Resource Planning, 19,* 201–220.

Snell, S. A., & Dean, J. W., Jr. (1994). Strategic compensation for integrated manufacturing: The moderating effects of jobs and organizational inertia. *Academy of Management Journal, 37,* 1109–1140.

Snell, S. A., & Youndt, M. A. (1995). Human resource management and firm performance: Testing a contingency model of executive controls. *Journal of Management, 21,* 711–737.

Snell, S. A., Youndt, M. A., & Wright, P. M. (1996). Establishing a framework for research in strategic human resource management: Merging resource theory and organizational learning. In G. R. Ferris (Ed.), *Research in personnel and human resources management* (Vol. 14, pp. 61–90). Greenwich, CT: JAI Press.

Tsui, A. S., Pearce, J. L., Porter, L. W., & Tripoli, A. M. (1997). Alternative approaches to the employee-organization relationship: Does investment in employees pay off? *Academy of Management Journal, 40,* 1089–1121.

Tully, S. (1998, October 26). A better taskmaster than the market? *Fortune,* 277–286.

von Hippel, C., Mangum, S. L., Greenberger, D. B., Heneman, R. L., & Skoglind, J. D. (1997). Temporary employment: Can organizations and employees both win? *Academy of Management Executive, 11,* 92–103.

Vroom, V. H. (1964). *Work and motivation.* New York: Wiley.

Wageman, R. (1995). Interdependence and group effectiveness. *Administrative Science Quarterly, 40,* 145–180.

Wagner, J. A., III. (1995). Studies of individualism-collectivism: Effects on cooperation in groups. *Academy of Management Journal, 38,* 152–172.

Weitzman, M. L., & Kruse, D. L. (1990). Profit sharing and productivity. In A. S. Binder (Ed.), *Paying for productivity: A look at the evidence* (pp. 95–142). Washington, DC: Brookings Institution.

Welbourne, T. M., & Andrews, A. O. (1996). Predicting the performance of initial public offerings: Should human resource management be in the equation? *Academy of Management Journal, 39,* 891–919.

Welbourne, T. M., Balkin, D. B., & Gomez-Mejia, L. R. (1995). Gainsharing and mutual monitoring: A combined agency–organizational justice interpretation. *Academy of Management Journal, 38,* 881–899.

Whetten, D. A., & Cameron, K. S. (1994). Organizational effectiveness: Old models and new constructs. In J. Greenberg (Ed.), *Organizational behavior: The state of the science* (pp. 135–154). Mahwah, NJ: Erlbaum.

Wilson, T. B. (1995). *Innovative reward systems for the changing workplace.* New York: McGraw-Hill.

Wright, P. M., & Snell, S. A. (1998). Toward a unifying framework for exploring fit and flexibility in strategic human resource management. *Academy of Management Journal, 23,* 756–772.

CHAPTER 7

Bringing Organization and Labor Relationships into Psychological Research on Compensation

Peter D. Sherer

Robert Williams sold automobiles at Continental Nissan of Countryside, Illinois. Williams believed he worked for himself, not Continental Nissan, because he was paid on a commission basis for selling cars. The general manager for the dealership, Owen Brady, saw it differently. He believed that Williams worked for Continental Nissan as part of the sales team. Their different views of the relationship came to a head one snowy day. When Williams refused to stay after closing to help clear the lot for snow removal, Brady fired him. Williams went looking for work at another dealer. Brady regretted having to fire Williams, since turnover was high in the industry and customer retention required a committed workforce operating as a team to satisfy customers (Patterson, 1992).

How would psychological research on pay address the conflict between Robert Williams and Continental Nissan? Generally, it would rely on expectancy theory and call for linking rewards directly to sales, as is being done with the sales commission. Yet the commission seems to be part of the problem, not the answer to it.

Note: The author wishes to express his appreciation to Barry Gerhart and Sara Rynes for their many valuable comments. Their interest in strengthening the chapter and their patience in seeing it to completion were a source of inspiration.

As Eisenhardt (1989) and Anderson and Oliver (1987) argue, agency theory offers more options for addressing the conflict. It suggests that an organization and its labor can choose from two types of "contracts." Outcome-based contracts reward individuals on the basis of outputs (sales, for example). Behavior-based contracts reward individuals on the basis of inputs (such as effort). This typology can be used to suggest that Continental Nissan should move from an outcome-based contract to a more behavior-based one.

Missing from the agency theory notion of a contract, however, is a clear distinction between the form of control and the type of pay system that an organization uses. This chapter distinguishes between the two by showing that organizations have legal relationships with their labor. These organization and labor relationships (OLRs) involve different forms of organizational control and are distinct from the type of pay system (Sherer, 1996, 1998a). OLRs are based in the law of agency (whereby one party, a principal, has legal rights of control over another party, an agent, who works on the first party's behalf).

We are most familiar with one OLR—the *employment relationship*. In this OLR, an organization, as principal (the party that exercises control), has the legal right to exercise direct control or authority over individuals who act as the principal's agents (work on the principal's behalf). But this is not the only relationship an organization can have with its labor. Organizations as principals exercise partial control over agents in *contracting-in relationships*. Organizations also operate as both principals and agents when they exercise mutual control in *ownership relationships*.

This chapter explores how organizations combine the OLRs with behavior-based and outcome-based pay systems. It shows that there is considerable variety in the ways organizations combine the three OLRs with these two general types of pay systems. It shows too that different institutional arrangements with different meanings result from combining the same pay system with the different OLRs. Thus, for example, although both contracting-in and employment relationships make use of fixed or guaranteed payment, in the former case they are retainers and in the latter they are salaries.

The use of the various combinations is illustrated through a wide range of occupations, from sales forces to taxicab drivers to haircutters to lawyers to senior executives. These examples capture popular occupations with well-known institutional arrangements. They also capture less popular occupations with unique institutional arrangements that are important to address because they are increasingly being used in more popular occupations.

What is most striking given the variety is that organizations appear to use some combinations with greater frequency than they do others. Part of the reason has to do with legal regulations that compel organizations toward particular combinations and away from others. Another important reason, and the one that I focus on here, has to do with organizations using particular combinations to pursue such goals as getting the workforce to act as a team, be deployable, and be responsive to customers.

The goal of this chapter is thus to bring OLRs into psychological research on pay systems. Psychologists can play a major role in such research, for they have theoretical knowledge that is critical to understanding the effects of the various combinations of OLRs and pay systems on employee expectations, attitudes, and behaviors.

A Critique of Expectancy and Agency Theory

Expectancy theory was developed in the context of the employment relationship. Vroom (1964) stated in the introduction to *Work and Motivation:* "Our focus in this book will be on work roles in which the functions to be performed are specified by an employer who pays the role occupant a wage or salary for his services. This conforms to what Jacques (1961) has called employment work" (p. 6). Vroom and other early writers on expectancy theory came to an accumulated wisdom on what motivated individuals. They argued that individuals were motivated through (1) expectancy linkages between effort and performance, (2) instrumentality linkages between performance and rewards, and (3) the valence or utility of rewards.

Although the theory focused on the motivation of the individuals who did the work, it also addressed managers' concerns for maximizing motivation. It called for organizations to maximize motivation through pay systems that made rewards contingent on performance. Outcome-based pay systems like incentive pay or sales commissions were argued to create the strongest linkages because payment was based solely on units produced or sales made.

Even with sales forces where units of output can be measured, however, payment solely by outcomes is not that common in employment relationships (Anderson, 1985; Peterson, 1992). Rather, sales employees are typically paid a fixed salary or wage in addition to outcome-based rewards such as a commission.

Agency theory sheds light on why organizations rarely use payment systems based only on outcomes. Developed by economists, agency theory argues that those who exercise control as principals and those who act on behalf of them as agents often have a divergence of interest (Eisenhardt, 1989; Milgrom & Roberts, 1992; Pratt & Zeckhauser, 1985; Sappington, 1991). The principal wants the agent to work as hard as possible at the least cost, while the agent wants to work as little as possible at the highest wage. The divergence causes a problem when the principal does not have complete information on the agent. The theory argues that the lack of information creates an agency loss—the agent will not put forth a full effort.

Organizations seeking to maximize their profits remedy the agency loss in one of two ways. One option for an organization is to contract with an agent on outputs such as units produced or sales made. Outcome-based contracts involve a variable claim that places risks on individuals and for which the organization pays a risk premium (Anderson & Oliver, 1987; Eisenhardt, 1989; Oliver & Anderson, 1995). The risk aversion of individuals limits the extent to which organizations use outcome-based contracts.

The second option for an organization is to contract on the behavior of agents. In behavior-based contracts, an organization contracts with agents on the basis of inputs such as effort, attitude, or length of service. These agents typically receive the majority of their pay as a fixed salary or wage (Anderson & Oliver, 1987; Eisenhardt, 1989; Oliver & Anderson, 1995). Behavior-based contracts often impose costs on an organization because a manager may have to monitor inputs and because such contracts do not always provide strong linkages between performance and rewards.

Eisenhardt (1989) argues that contingencies drive the choice of which contract to use. Organizations use behavior-based contracts when it is difficult to measure outcomes. What are measured instead are an individual's inputs. Alternatively, organizations use outcome-based contracts when outcomes can be measured. It makes sense to use a variable claim like a sales commission when there is clear information about sales output.

The notions of behavior-based and outcome-based contracts capture important ways in which organizations manage their human resources. They do not, however, allow us to distinguish between the form of control and the type of pay system that an organization uses.

Seeing their distinctiveness is important for two reasons. First, although recent empirical work has shown that successful hybrids can be formed from behavior-based and outcome-based contracts (Gerhart, in press; Oliver & Anderson, 1995), there is not a clear understanding of which elements of the contracts go together. Seeing how the pay systems are distinct yet combine with the forms of control makes it clearer which elements of behavior- and outcome-based contracts are compatible and incompatible. Second, seeing the forms of control and types of pay system as distinct yet combinable encourages us to examine the combinations used most frequently by organizations and to explore what organizational concerns they meet.

Organization and Labor Relationships and Pay Systems

The law of agency is central to understanding how organizations exercise different forms of control through employment, contracting-in, and ownership relationships (Sherer, 1996, 1998a). Legally, agency represents a consensual relationship in which one party (the principal) has rights of control and the other party (the agent) acts on behalf of the principal (Sells, 1975; Steffen, 1977).

As summarized in Table 7.1, the status of an individual in one of the OLRs is determined by the nature of the agency and, correspondingly, by the form of control. It is important to note that whereas organizations make use of "hybrids" by bringing elements of one relationship into another, the law of agency is devised to determine an individual's status in one of the OLRs. Thus, for example, a contracted-in worker may take on some of the qualities of an employee. The law of agency, however, is used to determine that worker's primary status, be it a contracting-in relationship or an employment relationship.

**Table 7.1. Organization and Labor Relationships:
Nature of Agency and Form of Control.**

	Employment Relationships	Contracting-In Relationships	Ownership Relationships
Nature of Agency	Agent works fully on behalf of principal	Agent works partly on behalf of principal	Agent works on behalf of principal; agent is a principal
Form of Control	Direct	Partial	Mutual

In an employment relationship, the employee as agent works fully on behalf of the employer as principal. The employer has the legal right to exercise control over employees on what they do and how they accomplish work activities (Klein & Coffee, 1990; Morris, 1983; Sells, 1975; Steffen, 1977). These rights of direct control cover what and how activities are to be done, in what order, over what time frame, and at what level of effort and performance (Chamberlain, 1941; Simon, 1951). These rights of control mean that the employer has "authority" over employees. Even something so matter-of-fact as training implies, under the law, an employment relationship. That the employer is telling the employee how to do the work signals rights of control.

That individuals are "temporary" employees (in that they have a fixed or closed-ended term of employment) does not fundamentally alter the employment relationship. The temporary employee works fully on behalf of the organization for a fixed time and agrees to accept the direction of the organization for that time. Legally, what is determinative of the individual's status is whether the organization exercises direct control over the individual, not whether the arrangement is "permanent" or "temporary."

Institutional arrangements involving employment relationships have behavior-based pay systems, outcome-based pay systems, or hybrids. Employees can receive a salary or an hourly wage that does not vary as a function of performance or other factors. Alternatively, they can receive commission pay. With commissions, the Fair Labor Standards Act requires that most nonexempt employees be paid the federally mandated minimum wage if their commissions do not exceed that level. Finally, there are employment relationships that have both behavior- and outcome-based pay. Baseball players, for example, are employees who are paid salaries and often receive bonuses for meeting performance targets.

In contracting-in relationships, an agent works partly on behalf of an organization and the organization has partial control over the agent. The contracted-in individuals are quasi-agents under a principal's partial direction and are partly acting in the interest of the principal. They are subject to some control but have greater freedom than employees do.

Compared with employment relationships, contracting-in relationships have quite different legal implications. Because contracted-in workers are not working fully on behalf of organizations and under their direct control, organizations are less likely to assume liability for the actions of contracted-in workers than they are for the actions of employees. Since contracted-in workers are generally not covered under employment laws, organizations ordinarily do not, for example, have to provide workers' compensation or abide by the Fair Labor Standards Act when dealing with contracted-in workers. Because labor laws protecting employees' rights to join a union and engage in collective bargaining generally do not cover contracted-in workers, organizations are less vulnerable to unionization with contracted-in workers than they are with employees.

There is sometimes confusion about the status of temporary help. These workers are "rented out" by an agency and contracted in to an organization that needs "help." As help, these individuals work only partly on behalf of the organization that contracts them in and are subject only to partial control by it.[1]

Like employment relationships, the institutional arrangements for contracting-in relationships have behavior-based pay systems, outcome-based pay systems, or hybrids. In this case, behavior-based pay systems involve a fixed fee like a retainer that involves a set fee for a period of time. For example, outside lawyers that are contracted in as "of counsel" are commonly paid on retainer (Sherer, 1995).

Outcome-based pay systems involve variable claims in which payment is based on outputs or an operating lease under which an individual purchases goods for resale or rents space and keeps the revenues. For example, investment brokers, acting as lessees, rent space, secretarial services, and the like and keep all revenues from sales (Antilla, 1993).

Other contracting-in relationships have both behavior-based and outcome-based pay. A contracted-in worker might, for example, receive a larger portion of pay as a variable claim but be guaranteed a smaller fixed payment.

Ownership relationships involve owner-operators acting as both principals and agents. In their dual capacity, they both exercise control as principals and are subject to control as agents. Ownership in an organization implies partnership. Two or more individuals co-own an organization and are thus partners. Owners act as residual claimants, taking the remaining claims from revenues generated minus costs incurred. Owners share in not only the positive but also the negative profits of their organizations (Allen & Sherer, 1995).

Ownership relationships also have legal implications quite different from those of employment relationships. Partners are legally liable for their organizations' actions, whereas employees ordinarily are not. Partners are generally not covered under employment laws. Courts have held, for example, that partners are not employees and are therefore not protected under Title VII of the Civil Rights Act (Bureau of National Affairs, 1990).

Ostensibly, when partners act as residual claimants, their pay appears to be based on outcomes—most likely profits. However, profits still have to be divided, and an organization can choose to divide them on the basis of the individuals' behavior or outcomes.

Owners often decide to divide profits on behavior-based factors such as length of service. Such behavior-based pay is referred to as a "share" system because it calls for partners to have relatively equal shares of profits (for their tenure). Because all partners' shares of profits are lowered when any partner fails to carry his or her weight, share systems compel partners to monitor one another (Fama & Jensen, 1983).

Partners can, alternatively, decide to divide profits based on outputs, such as billings or revenues generated. Such an outcome-based pay system is popularly referred to as an "eat what you kill" pay system.

Furthermore, partners can decide to have pay based on both behavior and outcomes. For example, they might decide to share the larger portion of profits on the basis of an input like years of service and have a smaller portion of profits allocated by an outcome like revenues generated.

The foregoing discussion has established that each of the OLRs is separate yet can combine with the different pay systems. The actual variety will come to light by examining combinations used in different occupations.

OLR–Pay System Combinations in Different Occupations

The examples given here highlight some of the many occupations that use different combinations of OLRs and pay systems. The occupations include sales forces in corporations, haircutters in salons, drivers in taxicab organizations, lawyers in law firms, and senior-level executives in large corporations. Some of the occupations, such as sales, were selected because they are quite popular. Others are less popular but were selected because their institutional arrangements are increasingly being used in other, more popular occupations. For example, leasing arrangements, like those found for some time among taxi drivers (Sherer, Rogovsky, & Wright, 1998), are now being used by investment brokers (Antilla, 1993).

Sales Forces

Sales forces for organizations are typically either in employment or contracting-in relationships. Organizations most often use employees, "going direct," to sell their products or services (Anderson, 1985). Sales employees are typically paid a fixed wage or salary plus a bonus of approximately 10 to 20 percent of their total pay for achieving outcomes (Anderson, 1985; Peterson, 1992).

Organizations contract in sales forces by using manufacturer representatives who are not employees of the organizations (Anderson, 1985). Instead, the representatives operate as independent sales agents. They work solely on a commission basis and often sell several different companies' products or services. They incur expenses in selling products, such as travel costs (Anderson, 1985), which they, not the contracting organization, are responsible for paying.

Organizations also contract in through direct sales representatives, such as those at Mary Kay Cosmetics (Kotter, 1980; Sherer et al., 1998). Mary Kay sales representatives purchase their products and keep the revenues from sales. They incur expenses from setting up social events where they provide food and beverages and samples of cosmetics. Their compensation is equal to the selling price for the product minus the purchase price and other incurred costs.

Haircutters

Haircutters are typically employees paid an hourly wage, a commission on their total number of cuts, or both. When they are contracted in, they typically rent space in an establishment (Sherer, 1998b). This institutional arrangement is referred to as a salon rental. Although salon renters may view themselves as individual proprietors, they have to abide by certain organizational rules. Instances also arise in which a group of haircutters, usually well-established ones, get together and act as a partnership. As owner-operators, they jointly own and manage the organization, although they still have to abide by its rules. They may agree to share profits, revenues, or only costs.

Taxicab Drivers

Employees make up only a minority of the drivers in taxicab organizations (Sherer et al., 1998). Although employee-drivers are sometimes paid an hourly wage, they more typically receive a fare-based commission. A taxicab organization has the legal right to tell employee drivers what to do and how to do it.

Most drivers in organizations today, however, are contracted in under leasing arrangements. A driver leases a cab from a cab company for a fee (Gilbert & Samuels, 1982). The leasing fee is often paid daily or weekly but can be monthly or extended even further in time. The lessor exercises control with lessees on such matters as who gets to drive and on which days and times but does not have as much control with lessees as with employees.

Owners constitute another minority of drivers in taxicab organizations. Owner-drivers pool their resources by sharing such costs as cab maintenance, dispatcher service, and advertising (Russell, 1985, 1991). An owner-driver receives profits based on the revenues he or she generates. Owner-drivers are subject to the organization's control on such matters as use of dispatcher calls and cab maintenance and typically exercise rights of voice and vote on governance matters and expenditure of organizational funds.

Lawyers

Partners in law firms have profit- and loss-sharing rights, decision and control rights, and contributions in and control over capital funds (Hillman, 1990). These rights and contributions are typically weighted heavily toward behavior-based pay but can also be based on direct contributions to profits (Gilson & Mnookin, 1985, 1989).

Employees, referred to as associates, are hired on a fixed-term basis, receive a fixed or guaranteed salary and typically get a year-end bonus. They are trained, supervised, and evaluated by partners (Sherer, 1995). They are typically on a career track that involves going up to partner or out of the firm, known as the up-or-out system (Sherer & Lee, 1998). Firms also contract in lawyers, referred to as "of counsel." The American Bar Association requires that they have a long-term relationship with a law firm (Wagner, 1986). They can be paid on a case-by-case basis or placed on retainer.

Senior Executives

Most often senior executives are employees, receiving a salary plus a bonus, with separation of ownership from control (Berle & Means, 1932). In recent years, the distinction between ownership and control has begun to blur (Useem & Gottlieb, 1992), and it has become much more popular for senior executives to have equity in their firms. Legally, however, in most cases, even senior executives with equity are employees. Their primary role still is to take direction from a board and stockholders.

In recent years, executives have also been contracted in (Hogg, 1989). They are often referred to as "rented" or "portable" executives. Although they are usually paid a fixed fee, they may also be rewarded on the basis of a firm's financial outcomes.

These examples point to the variety in occupations with respect to the different combinations of OLRs and pay systems. Next we examine modal combinations.

Modal Combinations of the OLRs and Pay Systems

As the discussion so far suggests, each OLR has the potential to combine with behavior-based and outcome-based pay systems. Given this potential variety, the question arises as to what are the most frequent or modal combinations across industries.

Many employment relationships, even for sales forces, have the majority of pay as a fixed claim, like an hourly wage or salary. What an employer is paying for is the legal right to exercise direct control over employees (Sherer et al., 1998), which is how employers get employees to do their jobs. An added part of pay can come at risk, as outcome-based pay. This portion is not so much to get employees to do their job as it is to motivate them to do it better.

Contracted-in workers are typically paid either on units produced or sales generated or else are treated as lessees. Their outcome-based pay is viewed as a form of "market control" that acts as a substitute for the greater managerial control an organization has with employees (Anderson & Oliver, 1987). An organization is limited in its use of behavior-based pay with contracted-in workers because it legally has less direct control over them and thus has less influence on their inputs.

Owners share or pool resources. As Gilson and Mnookin (1985) argue, individual owners pool together through partnership to diversify their risk. A partner has to be concerned that other partners are maintaining high standards of performance, for they share in profits, losses, and reputation. As Fama and Jensen (1983) argue, mutual monitoring or collegiality is critical to maintaining high standards of performance in professional partnerships.

These arguments lead to three propositions on the frequencies of particular combinations of the OLRs and pay systems:

Proposition 1a: Employment relationships are most frequently weighted toward behavior-based pay systems but often include significant yet smaller components of outcome-based pay.

Proposition 1b: Contracting-in relationships are most frequently weighted heavily toward outcome-based pay systems.

Proposition 1c: Ownership relationships are most frequently weighted heavily toward behavior-based pay systems.

These propositions serve as a first step in determining the frequencies for particular combinations of OLRs and pay systems. Now let us examine explanations for the frequency with which these particular combinations occur.

Linking Teamwork, Deployment, and Customer Responsiveness to Combinations of the OLRs and Pay Systems

Increasingly, organizations have had to rethink what their efforts should be maximized toward. A key part of the shift in thinking has to do with organizations now being more in the business of providing services, regardless of whether they are service or manufacturing organizations (Handy, 1990; Johnston, 1987; Quinn, 1992). Also, related to the change has been the "consumer revolution" (Heskett, Jones, Loveman, Sasser, & Schlesinger, 1994), which has led organizations to be much more concerned with being responsive to customers. Another key part of the shift has to do with the increasing need by organizations to be able to respond to turbulence and changes in their environment (Kotter, 1996; Tushman & O'Reilly, 1997).

The implications of the shift are addressed by examining three key concerns of organizations: getting individuals to work as a team, being able to deploy a workforce across tasks and locations, and having a workforce that is responsive to customers. Although these are not exhaustive of the concerns organizations face today, they are critical ones, and they affect organizations' choices in terms of which combinations of OLRs and pay systems to use.

Teamwork

Organizations use teamwork to perform activities that are harder for individuals to accomplish by themselves. Alchian and Demsetz

(1972) address what teamwork is with a very simple yet compelling example:

> Two men jointly lift cargo into tracks. Solely by observing the total weight loaded per day, it is impossible to determine each person's marginal productivity. With team production it is difficult, solely by observing total output, to define or determine *each* individual's contribution to this output of the cooperating inputs. The output is yielded by a team, by definition, and it is not a *sum* of separable outputs of each of its members. Team production of Z involves at least two inputs, X_i and X_j. . . . The production function is *not* separable into two functions, each only involving only inputs X_i or only inputs X_j. Consequently, there is no sum of Z of two separable functions to treat as the Z of the team production function. . . . There exist production techniques in which the Z obtained is greater than if X_i and X_j had produced separable Z. (p 779)

As Katzenbach and Smith (1994) argue, teamwork is a key element of many successful organizations. This argument calls for seeing which combinations of OLRs and pay systems are most effective at producing teamwork.

The starting point for the discussion is Williamson's argument on how employment relationships and pay systems affect cooperation in a workforce. Williamson (1980) argues that employment, particularly hourly-based, ensures employee cooperation. Hourly employment allows for an employer to exercise his or her legal rights of control over employees. The employer can require employees to cooperate and work as a team as a condition of continuing employment. To the extent that incentives are used, Pfeffer (1994) cautions that they should not cause great dispersion among employees.

Williamson's argument can be extended to ownership relationships with behavior-based pay systems. Such systems promote cooperation in a workforce because partners share in the residual claims. A partner's pay is affected by what other partners achieve. Partners will cooperate with one another to ensure that others are pulling their weight. The sharing of profits associated with behavior-based pay thus encourages collegiality among partners (Allen & Sherer, 1995; Brill, 1990; Fama & Jensen, 1983; Sherer, 1995, 1998a).

Ownership may provide little in the way of teamwork when partners have outcome-based pay. Partners have less incentive to cooperate on revenues and may be vulnerable to internal competition (Sherer et al., 1998). For example, when an organization has a large market share, the chief competitors are inside the organization. The situation is ripe for internal rivalry as partners compete among themselves, exploiting internal resources at others' expense.

Contracting-in relationships with outcome-based pay systems are typically not used to promote cooperation among a workforce. Contracted-in workers on variable pay are generally not used in teams. They may, in fact, be used to create competition with an existing workforce of employees (Pearce, 1993; Pfeffer & Baron, 1988).

These arguments lead to three propositions:

Proposition 2a: Employment relationships with behavior-based pay and some outcome-based pay promote teamwork.

Proposition 2b: Ownership relationships heavily weighted toward behavior-based pay strongly promote teamwork.

Proposition 2c: Contracting-in relationships heavily weighted toward outcome-based pay do not promote teamwork. They may be used to create competition with employees.

Deployment

Organizations have to deploy their workforces in response to environmental contingencies. These contingencies range from the snow that fell on Continental Nissan's lot to the dramatic changes in consumer markets that many organizations now confront.

Organizations often seek the commitment or dedication of the workforce as a means to ensure its ready deployment (Pfeffer, 1994; Simon, 1951). The commitment of the workforce is argued to give organizations the needed internal flexibility to make adjustments and shifts in response to changes in their environments (Kochan & Osterman, 1994; Pfeffer, 1994).

With change occurring at a more rapid rate in many industries, however, organizations are being pushed continually to find ways to redeploy their workforces (Miles, 1989; Sherer, 1996, 1998a; Ulrich,

1997). The increasing rate of change has meant that some organizations have sought to gain capabilities for deployment in other ways than through the commitment of the workforce. Instead, they have sought to bring in free-agent employees or to contract in with individuals who already have the skills and knowledge to do the work (Sherer, 1996, 1998a).

The starting point for theoretical arguments concerning the deployment of a workforce is Herbert Simon's classic article on the employment relationship. Simon (1951) argued that in an employment relationship, an employee explicitly or implicitly agrees to perform any number of activities (x_i) within a zone of acceptance (X). An incomplete contract of sorts is formed in which an employer has latitude within specified parameters to direct employees.

The agreement is valuable to an organization. It gains the ability to deploy its employees without having to negotiate every time it wants them to do something (Williamson, 1975). The organization gains "internal liquidity" by having an inventory of employees that are committed and can be deployed in different ways depending on contingencies (Sherer et al., 1998).

Ownership relationships with behavior-based pay offer organizations even greater possibilities for deploying their workforces. Being a partner typically requires more commitment to an organization than is true for employees (Allen & Sherer, 1995; Sherer, 1998a). An owner invests in his or her organization and has more difficulty leaving it. This commitment can be leveraged by an organization to gain greater capability for deploying its workforce.

Contracting-in relationships with outcome-based pay have less potential for deploying a workforce through commitment. They succeed at deployment where employment and ownership relationships are weaker. They offer organizations greater access to human capital from outside the organization, assuming that appropriate candidates are available. Instead of having an inventory of employees, an organization goes to the external labor market and acquires labor when it needs it, and it just as readily discharges that labor when it no longer needs it.

Consider two contracting-in relationships. One, a contingent contract, involves an organization making an agreement in which pay is contingent on future conditions that are specified in advance (Williamson, 1975). For example, a cab driver might contract with a taxicab organization for all fares going to a particular destination. The contract would be contingent in that the cab driver's getting the job is contingent on location. A second, a sequential spot contract, involves an organization creating a new contract each time a situation arises (Williamson, 1975). For example, a cab driver who had a sequential spot contract with a taxicab organization would work out an agreement with the organization every time a fare came through the dispatcher.

Both contingent and sequential spot contracts allow organizations to avoid labor inventories. There is no excess labor. Organizations hire and pay individuals only when there is something specific for them to do. Organizations terminate those individuals when they no longer need them.

These arguments lead to three further propositions:

Proposition 3a: Employment relationships with behavior-based pay and some outcome-based pay allow an organization to gain the commitment to deploy its employees.

Proposition 3b: Ownership relationships heavily weighted toward behavior-based pay allow an organization to achieve high levels of commitment needed to deploy its owners fully.

Proposition 3c: Contracting-in relationships heavily weighted toward outcome-based pay are generally not used by organizations to gain the commitment needed to deploy contracted-in labor. Instead, they are used to gain a capability for deployment or external flexibility through ease of hiring and firing.

Customer Responsiveness

Organizations are increasingly focused on responding to customers. Heskett et al. (1994) argue that customer focus changes the way organizations view both customers and their workforce: "Top level executives of outstanding service organizations spend little time setting profit goals or focusing on market share, the management mantra of the 1970s and 1980s. Instead, they understand that in the new economics of service, front line workers and customers need to be the center of management concern" (p. 164).

Several authors (Heskett et al., 1994; Quinn, 1992) suggest that customer responsiveness requires a focus on gaining customer loyalty or retention. Heskett et al. (1994) argue, "The lifetime value of a customer can be astronomical, especially when referrals are added to the economics of customer retention and repeat purchases of related products. For example, the lifetime revenue stream from a loyal pizza eater can be $8,000.00, a Cadillac owner $320,000.00, and a corporate purchaser of commercial aircraft literally billions of dollars" (p. 164). Quinn (1992) similarly states in favor of retained customers: "The typical cost of bringing in a new customer is five to ten times as high as retaining an existing customer" (p. 169). Quinn concludes that "a company's loyal customer base . . . is often its most valuable single asset" (p. 245).

Williamson's work (1975, 1985) on the specificity of assets has been used to suggest when customers will be loyal (Anderson, 1985). Asset specificity has to do with the firm-specific nature of skills and knowledge. At times, skills and knowledge are not specific to an organization and are valued at multiple organizations. At other times, they are specific to a firm and have their greatest value there. When products or services are more specific to an organization, a sales force or other group with a customer interface is needed that has knowledge specific to those products and services.

The implication is that not just any salesperson will do. The salesperson must have firm-specific knowledge about the products and services and tie it to the specific needs of the customer. Specific knowledge about an organization's products and services ordinarily requires being with that organization for an extended period of time. The customer develops a loyalty because he or she has to go to that salesperson and organization to get a highly informed level of service. Depth of knowledge about customers requires getting to know those customers' needs and preferences over an extended period of time.

Although the emphasis in the literature has been on long-term relationships with customers, some organizations may be most concerned with short-term customer responsiveness. Organizations that focus more on short-term customer responsiveness may operate in markets where meeting customers' immediate needs is the most critical concern. In those markets, short-term customer responsiveness leads to increased revenues and greater customer satisfaction. It may also have positive implications for customer retention.

Combinations of OLRs and pay systems affect customer responsiveness differentially. Ownership relationships with behavior-based pay systems have considerable potential for long-term customer responsiveness. Partners have positive and negative residual claims in their organizations, and their pay grows with their tenure. Share systems involving lockstep seniority pay promote customer loyalty by matching long-term partners with long-term customers (Gilson & Mnookin, 1989; Sherer, 1995). Thus, for example, law firms that provide general counsel for long-term clients often lock in partners through seniority-based profit sharing.

Employment relationships with behavior-based pay and some outcome-based pay are also used to gain customer loyalty. A highly committed workforce comes from stable pay, which is derived from stable employment and pay that has a significant portion of a fixed or guaranteed claim (Kochan & Osterman, 1994; Pfeffer, 1994). It is combined with some outcome-based pay to motivate better customer service.

Contracting-in relationships with outcome-based pay systems are not as effective at gaining customer loyalty. When individuals contracted in get no base pay or start in the red, they may not have the financial resources or patience to develop long-term relationships. What they are good at is generating short-term customer responsiveness. For example, lessee cab drivers are best at getting cab fares based on spot market or on-demand transactions (Sherer et al., 1998). Given that the cab drivers start in the red, they are quite "hungry" and willing to work hard and provide short-run customer responsiveness.

These arguments lead to three more propositions:

Proposition 4a: Ownership relationships weighted heavily toward behavior-based pay have the greatest potential for developing the long-term relationships among owners that are critical to customer loyalty.

Proposition 4b: Employment relationships with behavior-based pay and some outcome-based pay can lead employees to seek out long-term relationships and customer loyalty.

Proposition 4c: Contracting-in relationships weighted heavily toward outcome-based pay are used by organizations to maximize short-term customer responsiveness.

The foregoing propositions are addressed next by looking to the empirical literature. It indicates not only what we know about the propositions but also what we need to know.

What the Literature Says

Several studies offer evidence on when organizations use different combinations of the OLRs and pay systems to achieve teamwork, deployment of the workforce, or customer responsiveness. These studies provide an important foundation for future study. Their results are combined and summarized in Table 7.2.

Employment Versus Contracting-In Relationships

Four studies have examined when organizations use employment versus contracting-in relationships with different pay systems. In two of the four studies (Davis-Blake & Uzzi, 1993; Pearce, 1993), the choice by an organization to contract in occurred when there was already an existing workforce of employees. Those studies address the effects of an organization adding to its workforce through contracting in (rather than addressing the choice of using employment versus contracting-in relationships). The result of adding a contracted-in workforce to an existing employee base can be rivalry or demoralization (Cook & Campbell, 1979).

Anderson (1985) compared the use of direct sales forces in employment relationships with manufacturer representatives in contracting-in relationships. Her sample was composed of thirteen electrical component manufacturers covering 159 U.S. sales districts. Her findings indicated organizations "went direct" when selling products that required a great deal of specific knowledge and nonselling activity. The specificity of the products required a committed workforce that had firm-specific knowledge about products and would be responsive to clients even when their efforts did not lead directly to sales.

Although Anderson did not collect data on the exact type of the pay system for the employee sales force, she stated that most direct sales forces receive salaries plus bonuses amounting to 15 to 20 percent of their base pay. It would be useful, however, to assess the actual range of the fixed and variable payments for sales forces.

Table 7.2. Summary of Results.

	Employment Relationships	Contracting-In Relationships	Ownership Relationships
Favoring Teamwork	Behavior-based (hourly or salary) pay system; some hybrid pay systems		Possible effect for sharing pay systems
Favoring Long-Term Deployment Through Commitment	Hourly and salaried employment; some hybrid pay systems		Possible effect for share pay systems
Favoring Short-Term Deployment Through External Flexibility		Independent contractors and lessees	
Favoring Long-Term Customer Responsiveness	Salaried employment; some hybrid pay systems		Possible effect for share pay systems
Favoring Short-Term Customer Responsiveness	Outcome-based pay; some hybrid pay systems	Lessees	

Researchers could use that information to assess what happens to short- and long-term customer responsiveness and other outcomes as the percentage of variable or fixed pay increases.

Davis-Blake and Uzzi (1993) examined why organizations contract in with independent contractors when they already have an existing workforce of employees. The sample was based on over two thousand organizations surveyed by the U.S. Department of Labor. They found that organizations used independent contractors to gain the flexibility needed to augment or reduce their workforce rapidly. Davis-Blake and Uzzi did not examine whether and to what extent existing employees had variable pay. It would be valuable, however, to determine whether organizations that use varying degrees of variable pay with employees have the same need for flexibility (Gerhart, in press). Presumably, an organization that used employees with more outcome-based pay would have less need for the flexibility provided by independent contractors.

Pearce (1993) examined the use by a large aerospace company of engineers or engineering technicians that were contracted in to work alongside existing employees. Pearce did not find that employees were more cooperative or committed. She did find, however, that supervisors deployed employees over contracted-in workers on activities that required a team effort.

Pearce also found that adding contracted-in workers led existing employees to be less trusting of the organization. The finding shows the demoralizing effects of adding contracted-in workers to an existing workforce of employees and may help, at least in part, to explain why Pearce did not find higher commitment and cooperation among employees compared with those contracted in.

Sherer et al. (1998) examined taxicab organizations use of employee drivers versus those contracted in as lessees. They found that hourly employees, but not commission employees, were used to provide services such as picking up a client's children from school or taking a company's visitor to the airport. They argued that hourly employees allow organizations to deploy a workforce to accomplish activities that involve uncertainty and where a buffer or inventory of labor is useful. In contrast, lessees were used to gain passengers on demand through a short-term customer focus. The motivation of lessees to generate revenues came from their starting the day with a deficit and their keeping all the revenues from rides.

Although Sherer et al. argued that most leasing arrangements involved the lessee's paying in advance for the cab, it would be useful to determine the behavioral impact of having lessees pay the lease fee after they earned revenues. They would still get to keep the revenues they made from passenger fees, but they would not start in the red. The issue is whether having less immediate pressure from being in debt would lead them to be more responsive to customers over a longer time horizon.

Comparisons of Employment Relationships

Studies of employment relationships have examined the impact on employees of behavior-based pay versus output-based pay.[2] The results of these studies are often used to infer differences between employment and contracting-in relationships, since the latter typically have a great deal of outcome-based pay. However, this comparison may not hold, because individuals contracted in legally have a level of independence that employees do not have. Therefore, caution needs to be exercised in extrapolating from findings on employment relationships to contracting-in relationships.

Cravens, Ingram, La Forge, and Young (1993) compared the attitudes of employee sales forces whose pay was primarily behavior-based but was weighted more or less to outcome-based pay. With a sample of 144 diverse sales organizations, they found that (1) employment involving payment based more on outcomes was positively associated with having an intense and immediate customer focus and (2) employment involving payment based more on behaviors was positively associated with a team orientation.

Craven and colleagues' findings raise the question of whether there are simple trade-offs in using outcome versus behavior-based pay systems or whether elements of these pay systems can be combined. That is, can organizations develop hybrid pay systems that combine the intense and immediate customer focus of outcome-based pay with the team orientation associated with behavior-based pay?

Oliver and Anderson (1995) tested whether a hybrid of an outcome-plus-behavior-based pay system was more effective with sales forces than pure outcome- or behavior-based pay systems. Their sample was composed of sales employees from a large number of sales organizations in the electronic components industry. They defined a behavior-based pay system as one in which sales employees were paid fixed salaries with merit increases based on subjective performance evaluations. They defined an outcome-based pay system as one in which pay was based strictly on sales. Their hybrid involved a majority of pay as a fixed claim, but not so much as in the behavior-based pay system. They found that sales forces with hybrid pay systems were most committed to their organizations, best at accepting direction, most willing to work as sales teams, and most knowledgeable about their products.

These findings suggest benefits from combining behavior- and outcome-based pay systems in employment relationships. There remain questions, however, about which elements of the pay systems go together, which create conflicts, and what role managers have in making the two types of pay systems operate without redundancy, conflict, and excess costs.

Tsui, Pearce, Porter, and Tripoli (1997) examined the use by organizations of pay and other HR practices that focused on transactional (short-term exchange) or unbalanced forms of employment versus mutual investment (long-term and equally beneficial exchange) forms of employment. Their sample was composed of permanent employees at ten companies in five industries: computer manufacturing, electronics and semiconductors, telecommunications, food and groceries, and apparel. Survey results suggested that forms of employment involving mutual investment, as opposed to transactional or unbalanced forms of employment, led to greater dependability, commitment, and trust in coworkers.

Tsui et al. concentrated on employees, but it would have been useful to examine workers in contracting-in relationships as well. These workers' exchanges with organizations are often distinctly more transactional than those of employees. Given the frequency of such institutional arrangements, the question arises as to whether there might be different expectations and outcomes among contracted workers than among regular employees subject to a transactional exchange. One possibility is that contracted-in workers expect a transactional exchange and that using other forms of exchange with them would not affect them or perhaps even affect them negatively. The alternative possibility is that any deviation from a transactional exchange to a mutual investment exchange would have more of a positive effect on contracted-in workers than employees for they would see it as more of a gift (Ackerloff, 1984).

Comparisons of Ownership Relationships

In light of the paucity of research comparing payment systems in ownership relationships, we have one study to guide future research. Samuelson and Jaffe (1990) examined the effects on profits of behavior-based pay involving share systems (such as seniority-based pay) versus outcome-based pay (such as revenues generated), using data from 219 law partnerships. They found that firms with share systems had higher profits, on average. They argued that in more profitable firms, share systems both lead to and reinforce partners pulling their weight. They suggest that in less profitable firms, there are often concerns that partners are loafing. They note that in a number of cases, less profitable firms switched from behavior-based to outcome-based pay. Consistent with their observations, Brill (1990) argued that firms often switch to "eat what you kill" pay systems when partners no longer pull their weight under share systems.

Samuelson and Jaffe (1990) provide important findings on profitability. To add to their findings, it would be valuable to have studies that determine more precisely how behavior-based pay systems contribute to profits (through partners working as a team, being more deployable, being responsive to customers, and so on).

Limitations of the Research

Although the studies generally support the propositions and raise important questions, their limitations need to be addressed. What is most striking is that the studies typically did not identify either the OLR or the pay system. Interpreting the findings, therefore, required various assumptions about the nature of the OLR and the pay system.

Conclusion

Not surprisingly, we know the most about employment relationships. Combined with pay systems weighted toward behavior plus some, but not a great deal, of outcome-based pay, they appear to provide organizations with employees that have a team orientation, can be readily deployed, and are responsive to customers over a longer- and shorter-term horizon. Employment relationships combined with the different pay systems provide organizations with many options and considerable adaptability (Wernerfelt, 1997).

An important issue that psychologists could address is the extent to which these objectives would continue to be met as an organization moved further toward outcome-based pay. As the case of Robert Williams, the car salesman, suggests, it is likely that employees will resort to reactance (noncompliance with direction and control) beyond a certain level of outcome-based pay (Brehm, 1966). Employees are asked to take risks with such outcome-based pay, but control still resides with the employer. Since individuals who take significant risks generally want to have control over decisions that affect them, employees may not perceive that they have the freedom to act in ways that allow them necessary control. They might therefore react by not complying with the wishes of the organization.

We know little about the value of contracting-in relationships with different pay systems. Combining them with outcome-based pay appears to give organizations greater capabilities for augmenting or reducing their workforces and for generating an intense short-term customer focus. There is little evidence, however, that they can be used to promote teamwork or to develop a team orientation in a workforce. To the contrary, they appear to promote competition with an existing workforce (Pearce, 1993). The growth in the popularity of contracting-in relationships with outcome-based pay suggests that organizations are responding to competition by increasing flexibility in staffing, reducing the costs associated with employment laws, promoting workforce competition, and fostering a strong short-term customer focus.

The growing popularity of these contracting-in relationships calls for research that examines their impact on individuals. Various theoretical arguments suggest that organizations with contracting-in relationships and outcome-based pay will disproportionately attract and "sort in" individuals who prefer risk and also that individuals who learn how to deal with risk will be the ones that remain (Bloom & Milkovich, 1996; Lazear, 1992; Milgrom & Roberts, 1992). Psychologists can add considerable value in determining whether individuals actually do "sort in" to organizations based on their risk preferences and why certain individuals learn how to deal better with risk.

There is also the question of whether expectations are similar for contracted-in labor and for employees. Tsui and colleagues' study (1997) suggests that employees are most satisfied and committed when they have long-term exchanges with organizations that are mutually beneficial. However, many contracted-in workers, such as those in the computer industry, are not in such exchanges by choice. The question is whether contracted-in workers define "mutually beneficial" in different ways than employees do. Is their idea of mutual benefit an exchange that is transactional but still a fair deal? And would they see a long-term exchange as an impediment to their mobility and growth rather than as a benefit?

We know little about the value of different pay systems in ownership relationships. Although there is evidence that owners have higher profits in more behavior-based pay systems, we do not know how that occurs. A plausible explanation is that partnerships with behavior-based pay are especially effective at fostering a strong form of teamwork and commitment—collegiality. An important way to address this point would be to explore whether such ownership has social facilitation effects (Allport, 1920): Can and do partners spur each other on to perform better through collegiality?

Finally, return to the case of Robert Williams and Continental Nissan. What is now clear is that Williams is an employee whose pay is outcome-based (although legally he must be paid the minimum wage if his commission does not exceed that amount). The tension in the relationship occurs because Williams bears the responsibility for his actions, but he is not free to act as he sees fit. Williams reacts by not complying with the wishes of the organization.

What options could there have been for Williams and Continental Nissan? One would have been for Continental Nissan to have switched to an employment relationship weighted heavily or entirely toward behavior-based pay—an approach that is being promoted by automobile dealers in recent years.

Another option would have been for Continental Nissan to switch to a contracted-in sales force operating as lessees. They might have been charged a monthly rental fee for space and also pay a monthly fee for administrative services and maintenance. Given that lessees would start the month in the red, they would be quite hungry to make sales. Although they would ensure an intense and short-term customer focus, they would not meet the organization's additional concerns for teamwork, long-term responsiveness, and deployment through commitment.

Another option would have been for Continental Nissan to have the sales force join in the ownership of the organization. As owners, members of the sales force would have to buy their way into the organization, and in return, they would have rights to exercise control and shares of the profits. The question for the automobile dealer would be whether this option would be going too far in its efforts to solve its conflict with the sales force and in meeting its concerns. The question for the sales staff would be whether they would want to invest their financial and emotional capital in the dealership, as well as whether they could get the financial capital to make such an investment.

This chapter has taken the position that OLRs and pay systems are separate but combine in particular modal ways to drive key organizational concerns. Psychologists interested in pay systems can make significant contributions to advancing this literature. Psychological theories can provide us with an understanding of how OLRs and pay systems influence expectations, attitudes, and behaviors. The conflict between Robert Williams and Continental Nissan attests to the need for the research and its potential benefits.

Notes

1. Legally, what is confusing about the status of temporary help workers is that although they are not typically employees of the hiring organization, they may be employees of the temporary help agency.
2. Eisenhardt (1988) conducted an important study in which she examined whether retail stores used outcome- versus behavior-based pay with their sales employees. The study was a test of agency and institutional theory and only indirectly touches on the propositions posed in this chapter.

References

Ackerlof, G. (1984). Gift exchange and efficiency wages: Four views. *American Economic Review, 74,* 79–83.

Alchian, A. A., & Demsetz, H. (1972). Production, information costs, and economic organization. *American Economic Review, 62,* 777–795.

Allen, F., & Sherer, P. D. (1995). The design and redesign of organizational form. In B. Kogut & E. Bowman (Eds.), *Redesigning the firm* (pp. 183–196). New York: Oxford University Press.

Allport, F. H. (1920). The influence of group upon association and thought. *Journal of Experimental Psychology, 3,* 159–182.

Anderson, E. (1985). The salesperson as outside agent or employee: A transaction cost analysis. *Marketing Science, 4,* 234–254.

Anderson, E., & Oliver, R. L. (1987). Perspectives on behavior-based contracts versus outcome-based salesforce control systems. *Journal of Marketing, 51*(4), 76–88.

Antilla, S. (1993, January 17). The latest free agents: Brokers. *New York Times,* sec. 3, p. 15.

Berle, A. A., & Means, G. C. (1932). *The modern corporation and private property*. Orlando, FL: Harcourt Brace.

Bloom, M. C., & Milkovich, G. T. (1996). Issues in managerial compensation research. In C. L. Cooper & D. M. Rousseau (Eds.), *Trends in organizational behavior* (Vol. 3, pp. 23–47). New York: Wiley.

Brehm, J. W. (1966). *A theory of psychological reactance*. Orlando, FL: Academic Press.

Brill, S. (1990, March). The changing meaning of partnership. *American Lawyer* [Suppl.].

Bureau of National Affairs. (1990, December 6). U.S. Court of Appeals: Ann B. Hopkins v. Price Waterhouse. *Daily Labor Report*, pp. F1–F10.

Chamberlain, N. W. (1941). *The union challenge to management control*. New York: HarperCollins.

Cook, T. D., & Campbell, D. T. (1979). *Quasi-experimentation: Design and analysis issues for field settings*. Skokie, IL: Rand McNally.

Cravens, D. W., Ingram, T. N., La Forge, R. W., & Young, C. E. (1993). Behavior-based and outcome-based salesforce control systems. *Journal of Marketing, 57*(4), 47–59.

Davis-Blake, A., & Uzzi, B. (1993). Determinants of employment externalization: A study of temporary workers and independent contractors. *Administrative Science Quarterly, 38,* 195–223.

Eisenhardt, K. M. (1988). Agency and institutional explanations of compensation in retail sales. *Academy of Management Journal, 31,* 488–511.

Eisenhardt, K. M. (1989). Agency theory: An assessment and review. *Academy of Management Review, 14,* 57–74.

Fama, E., & Jensen, M. (1983). Agency problems and residual claims. *Journal of Law and Economics, 26,* 327–349.

Gerhart, B. (in press). Balancing results and behaviors in pay-for-performance plans. In C. H. Fay (Ed.), *The executive compensation handbook*. New York: Free Press.

Gilbert, G., & Samuels, R. E. (1982). *The taxicab*. Chapel Hill: University of North Carolina Press.

Gilson, R. J., & Mnookin, R. H. (1985). Sharing among the human capitalists: An inquiry into the corporate law firm and how partners split profits. *Stanford Law Review, 37,* 313–392.

Gilson, R. J., & Mnookin, R. H. (1989). Coming of age in a corporate law firm: The economics of associate career patterns. *Stanford Law Review, 41,* 567–595.

Handy, C. (1990). *The age of unreason*. Boston, MA: Harvard Business School Press.

Heskett, J. L., Jones, T. O., Loveman, G., Sasser, W. E., & Schlesinger, L. A. (1994). Putting the service-profit chain to work. *Harvard Business Review, 72*(2), 164–174.

Hillman, R. (1990). *Law firm breakups*. New York: Little, Brown.

Hogg, C. (1989, October). Executive for hire. *Director,* 134–138.

Jacques, E. (1961). *Equitable payment*. New York: Wiley.

Johnston, W. H. (1987). *Workforce 2000: Work and workers in the year 2000*. Indianapolis, IN: Hudson Institute.

Katzenbach, J. R., & Smith, D. K. (1994). *The wisdom of teams: Creating the high-performance organization*. New York: HarperCollins.

Klein, W., & Coffee, J. C. (1990). *Business organization and finance: Legal and economic principles* (4th ed.). Westbury, NY: Foundation Press.

Kochan, T. A., & Osterman, P. (1994). *The mutual gains enterprise*. Boston: Harvard Business School Press.

Kotter, J. P. (1980). *Mary Kay Cosmetics Inc*. Boston: Harvard Business School Case Service.

Kotter, J. P. (1996). *Leading change*. Boston: Harvard Business School Press.

Lazear, E. (1992). The new economics of personnel. In D. Lewin, O. S. Mitchell, & P. D. Sherer (Eds.), *Research frontiers in industrial relations/human resources* (pp. 341–380). Madison, WI: Industrial Relations Research Association.

Miles, R. E. (1989). Adapting to technology and competition: A new industrial relations system for the 21st century. *California Management Review, 31*(2), 9–28.

Milgrom, P., & Roberts, J. (1992). *Economics, organization, and management*. Upper Saddle River, NJ: Prentice Hall.

Morris, C. J. (1983). *The developing labor law* (2nd ed.). Washington, DC: Bureau of National Affairs.

Oliver, R. L., & Anderson, E. (1995). Behavior- and outcome-based sales control systems: Evidence and consequences of pure-form and hybrid governance. *Journal of Personal Selling and Sales Management, 15*(4), 1–15.

Patterson, G. (1992, March 12). Tough business: A car salesman finds it's hard for him to get a good deal. *Wall Street Journal,* pp. A1, A12.

Pearce, J. L. (1993). Toward an organizational behavior of contract laborers: Their psychological involvement and effects on employee co-workers. *Academy of Management Journal, 36,* 1082–1096.

Peterson, T. (1992). Payment systems and the structure of inequality: Conceptual issues and an analysis of salespersons in department stores. *American Journal of Sociology, 98,* 67–104.

Pfeffer, J. (1994). *Competitive advantage through people*. Boston: Harvard Business School Press.

Pfeffer, J., & Baron, J. N. (1988). Taking the workers back out: Recent trends in the structuring of employment. In B. M. Staw & L. L. Cummings (Eds.), *Research in organizational behavior* (Vol. 10, pp. 257–303). Greenwich, CT: JAI Press.

Pratt, J. W., & Zeckhauser, R. J. (1985). Principals and agents: An overview. In J. W. Pratt & R. J. Zeckhauser (Eds.), *Principals and agents: The structure of business* (pp. 1–35). Boston: Harvard Business School Press.

Quinn, J. B. (1992). *Intelligent enterprise.* New York: Free Press.

Russell, R. (1985). Employment, ownership, and internal governance. *Journal of Economic Behavior and Organization, 6,* 217–241.

Russell, R. (1991). Sharing ownership in the services. In R. Russell & V. Rus (Eds.), *International handbook of participation in organizations* (Vol. 2, pp. 45–66). New York: Oxford University Press.

Samuelson, S. S., & Jaffe, L. L. (1990). A statistical analysis of law firm profitability. *Boston University Law Review, 70,* 185–211.

Sappington, D. E. M. (1991). Incentives in principal-agent relationships. *Journal of Economic Perspectives, 5*(2), 45–66.

Sells, W. E. (1975). *Agency.* Westbury, NY: Foundation Press.

Sherer, P. D. (1995). Leveraging human assets in law firms: Human capital structures and organizational capabilities. *Industrial and Labor Relations Review, 48,* 671–691.

Sherer, P. D. (1996). Toward an understanding of the variety in work arrangements: The organization and labor relationships framework. In C. L. Cooper & D. M. Rousseau (Eds.), *Trends in organizational behavior* (Vol. 3, pp. 99–122). New York: Wiley.

Sherer, P. D. (1998a). *The competitive implications of the multiple fits of human resource systems and firm capabilities: The organization and labor relationship framework.* Unpublished manuscript, Lundquist College of Business, University of Oregon.

Sherer, P. D. (1998b). *How do haircutters cut it with their organizations?* Unpublished manuscript, Lundquist College of Business, University of Oregon.

Sherer, P. D., & K. Lee. (1998). *Innovation and imitation of nonstandard human resource practices in law firm offices: The interaction of competitive and institutional forces.* Unpublished manuscript, Lundquist College of Business, University of Oregon.

Sherer, P. D., Rogovsky, N., & Wright, N. (1998). What drives employment relationships in taxicab organizations? *Organization Science, 9,* 34–48.

Simon, H. (1951). A formal theory of the employment relationship. *Econometrica, 19,* 293–305.

Steffen, R. T. (1977). *Agency partnership.* St Paul, MN: West.

Tsui, A. S., Pearce, J. L., Porter, L. W., & Tripoli, A. M. (1997). Alternative approaches to the employee-organization relationship: Does investment in employees pay off? *Academy of Management Journal, 40,* 1089–1121.

Tushman, M. L., & O'Reilly, C. A. (1997). *Winning through innovation.* Boston: Harvard Business School Press.

Ulrich, D. (1997). *Human resource champions*. Boston: Harvard Business School Press.

Useem, M., & Gottlieb, M. M. (1992). Corporate restructuring, ownership-disciplined alignment, and the reorganization of management. *Human Resource Management, 29,* 285–306.

Vroom, V. H. (1964). *Work and motivation*. New York: Wiley.

Wagner, D. (1986, July). Variations on the "of counsel" theme. *California Lawyer,* 59–64.

Wernerfelt, B. (1997). On the nature and scope of the firm: An adjustment-cost theory. *Journal of Business, 70,* 489–514.

Williamson, O. (1975). *Markets and hierarchies*. New York: Free Press.

Williamson, O. (1980). The organization of work: A comparative institutional assessment. *Journal of Economic Behavior and Organization, 1,* 5–38.

Williamson, O. (1985). *The economic institutions of capitalism*. New York: Free Press.

CHAPTER 8

Psychological Contract Issues in Compensation

Denise M. Rousseau
Violet T. Ho

Poor Trust is dead.
Bad pay killed him.
Old English Proverb

Compensation is a defining feature of employment. "Employee compensation" includes direct and indirect payments to employees such as wages, bonuses, stock, and benefits (Gerhart & Milkovich, 1992).[1] Compensation is fundamental to the value and meaning that workers, employers, and third parties (from laymen to jurists) ascribe to the employment relationship. Historically, compensation has signaled much about the nature of a specific employment agreement. In the Bible, for example, a compensation practice was used to symbolize a religious doctrine (the same eternal benefits for all the faithful, in the parable of the vineyard owner who hired laborers throughout the day for the same wages; Matthew 19).[2] In modern times, the AFL-CIO maintains a Web site that allows a firm's workers to check on their CEO's compensation package. Our

Note: Paul Goodman contributed helpful comments in the preparation of this manuscript, as did editors Sara Rynes, Barry Gerhart, and Neil Schmitt. We wish to express our appreciation also to Carole McCoy for word processing and Catherine Senderling for editing early drafts of this chapter.

273

thesis is that compensation practices play a fundamental and distinctive role in the formation, fulfillment, and violation of psychological contracts in employment.

The psychological contract refers to individual beliefs, shaped by the organization, regarding the terms of a reciprocal exchange agreement binding both the individual and the organization (Rousseau, 1989, 1995). Both employees and employers (including managers and executives) have psychological contracts based on their perceptions of mutual obligations (pay for performance, for example). Compensation practices contribute significantly to these beliefs (Bloom & Milkovich, 1996; Gerhart & Milkovich, 1992).

Compensation can be broadly conceptualized as a "bundle" of valued returns offered in exchange for an array of employee contributions (Bloom & Milkovich, 1996). In this view, the bundle of returns is an interrelated collection of reparations, benefits, and other inducements, shifting our focus from discrete one-for-one exchanges (for example, pay for hours worked) to bundles whose meaning arises from the interrelations among the whole (for example, a high-involvement career with sustained levels of pay, job security, and internal advancement in exchange for hard work, loyalty, and continuous learning). This broader meaning comprises the way in which parties interpret the exchange agreement, including not only its specific terms but also what it signals about the quality of relationship between employee and employer.

Compensation practices are a central feature of the HR strategy of a firm, constituting a major component of the administrative and managerial arrangements firms employ in directing workforce efforts toward implementing business strategy (see Figure 8.1). By their effects on worker skills and motivation, HR practices, from recruiting through termination, provide critical resources to the firm supporting or constraining its strategy implementation. In particular, HR practices influence business strategy implementation through their effects on the psychological contracts individuals form with their employers and the motivation levels that result. In one sense, compensation practices are but one of many mechanisms through which the psychological contracts of employment can be created, fulfilled, changed, or violated. However, compensation is probably among the most salient HR practices from the perspective of workers (whose jobs are often their sole source of income), employers (often focused on reducing labor costs), and society (whose laws and culture have direct effects on the forms compensation takes).

Compensation is typically one of the earliest terms of employment to emerge during the hiring process, signaling much about the employment relationship's present nature and future potential (Bloom & Milkovich, 1996). Often changes in employment relations in contemporary organizations are readily observable in effects on compensation practices. Contemporary firms increasingly view employee compensation as a variable rather than fixed cost while reallocating risk from their owners or stockholders to their employees. These actions signal fundamental changes in the psychological contracts of workers and employers.

This chapter describes how psychological contract theory contributes to our understanding of compensation practices. It identifies key features of the psychology of compensation from a psychological contract perspective. The chapter is divided into four parts. The first examines how the *cognitive processes* that are related to psychological contracts and resource exchange theory shape individual responses to compensation practices. The second focuses on the link between *compensation attributes* and psychological contracts. The third outlines the *basic types of psychological contracts* and the *compensation practices* that characterize them, discussing this framework's implications for contract formation and change. Throughout,

Figure 8.1. Compensation Practices with a Strategic Framework.

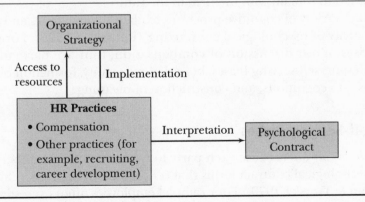

we identify propositions to guide research on compensation from a psychological contracts perspective, and so the fourth part suggests further *research implications.*

Psychological Contract Theory

By definition, the psychological contract is subjective, reflecting an individual's beliefs regarding an exchange agreement binding that individual and another party. Because the psychological contract is subjective, each party might believe that mutual agreement exists regarding commitments each has made to the other. However, there need not necessarily be mutuality or complete agreement in fact for a psychological contract to exist.[3] Although mutual agreement is likely to promote more positive outcomes for both employee and employer, there is evidence that organizations can function despite varying degrees of disagreement between the two regarding the terms of the exchange relationship (Guzzo, Noonan, & Elron, 1994; Rousseau, 1995). For instance, employees and employers can have divergent understandings of what the promise of "training" means (Nordhaug, 1989): an employer might offer potential employees a benefit such as training as an incentive to join, while some employees might view attendance at a training program as a contribution they are making on their employer's behalf, and others see being asked to participate in training as a sign of the firm's commitment to retain them. Similarly, an employee might view tuition reimbursement as compensation for work done today, while an employer might believe that workers who accept the offer have committed to remain with the firm in the future.

A variety of cognitive processes explain the dynamics and subjectivity of psychological contracting (Rousseau, 1995). For purposes of our discussion of compensation, four are particularly relevant: self-serving biases, bounded rationality, formation of status quo cognitions, and construction of meaning.

Self-Serving Biases

Self-serving biases cause each party to focus on and remember the psychological contract terms that reflect its own interests (Kahneman & Tversky, 1979). For example, employees often overestimate how much they contribute to health care benefits and underestimate contributions made by their employers, a tendency that has led an increasing number of firms to list contributions on employee pay stubs. The classic problems associated with piece-rate compensation systems are another example of divergent perspectives due to self-oriented biases. A common practice is to base the payment rate on an estimate of what a typical worker should produce (the basis for setting a piece rate). However, when a worker earns more than a certain amount, management often cuts the payment rate on the assumption that the price is set too high. Cutting the piece rate does not disturb the employer, which believes it is proper to correct a mistake. The production worker believes differently, however: he or she has been cheated of honest earnings (Lincoln, 1951). The divergent vantage points of manager and worker—and the different kinds of information available to them in the first place—promote self-oriented biases, causing them to recall and weigh information about the compensation system differently. Consequently, trust between worker and manager becomes a central issue in the implementation of successful piece-rate systems (Lincoln, 1951).

Bounded Rationality

Bounded rationality (March & Simon, 1958) also plays a role in generating nonmutuality. Most psychological contracts are incomplete at the time they are created. Parties to an employment agreement cannot convey all the details of employment conditions at the time of hire due to cognitive limits, as well as the confounding effects of uncertainty over future circumstances that will affect employment. Moreover, both employee and employer might hold unstated assumptions (for example, that pay levels stay the same or go up but never down). Thus psychological contracts are prone to incompleteness, and each party attends to facts, retains information, and assumes conditions somewhat differently.

Human cognitive limits make compensation a particularly salient aspect of the employment relationship: persons can with computational ease compare their pay or benefits to another's or to what was promised. Such comparisons are more difficult to make concerning more qualitative or intrinsic terms of employment such as "interesting work" or "stimulating colleagues." Compensation practices are thus readily available signals to workers regarding the terms and nature of the employer-employee exchange.

Information conveyed by compensation practices can be either explicit or implicit (see Table 8.1). Explicit information indicates the payoffs or utilities explicitly associated with employee behavior, including performance contingencies such as commissions, profit sharing, and equity positions. Contingent rewards focus employee attention on behaviors that the firm values, such as meeting a sales quota. Implicit information conveys more indirect signals regarding the nature and quality of the employment relationship. These signals must be interpreted to derive their meaning. For example, small start-up businesses that explore offering 401(k) plans for employees may seek not only to reward retention (an explicit message) but also to signal the founding entrepreneurs' intention to reward loyalty (Tibbets & Donovan, 1989). Benefits have a particular signaling value, as suggested by research findings that offering benefits contributes to perceptions of high organizational support, which is itself in turn strongly related to employee commitment to the firm (Eisenberger, Hutchinson, Huntington, & Sowa, 1986). Both explicit and implicit cues associated with compensation can be provided by a variety of message senders in a given firm, from immediate supervisors to human resource representatives and the CEO.

Table 8.1. Compensation as a Source of Explicit and Implicit Information.

Explicit Cues: Utilities

Performance contingencies

Estimate of employee market value

Focus of attention on desired behavior or results

Implicit Cues: Signals

Quality of employment relationship

Firm's interest in retaining the individual

Value of future employment with the firm

Despite a potential array of explicit and implicit cues, the joint effect of cognitive limits and self-serving biases can cause employee and employer exchanges to diverge. Each party is more likely to perceive itself to have fulfilled its obligations and less likely to perceive that the other party has done so in return. Thus where compensation is contingent on employee performance, it is likely that employees will believe they have provided contributions that warrant contingent pay while believing that the employer has reciprocated their contribution to a somewhat lower degree. Similarly, it is likely that employers (such as supervisors) will underestimate employee contributions and overestimate the inducements they have provided in return. Indeed, Robinson, Kraatz, and Rousseau (1994) found evidence of this pattern among employees for a variety of employer and employee obligations, including pay and performance. Moreover, since self-serving biases and bounded rationality are generalizable characteristics of human cognition, similar patterns are expected among employers and their agents (for example, supervisors and human resource managers).

On the basis of these dynamics, we propose the following:

Proposition 1a: An individual's beliefs regarding how well he or she has fulfilled obligations to an employer will tend to be greater than his or her beliefs regarding how well the employer has fulfilled its reciprocal obligations.

Proposition 1b: The employer's beliefs regarding how well he or she has fulfilled his or her obligations to an employee will tend to be greater than his or her beliefs regarding how well the employee has fulfilled his or her reciprocal obligations.

In contingent compensation agreements, the net impact of cognitive biases are for workers to believe they have met the standards employers have set to access contingent pay, regardless of their true performance against the standard. We expect that this bias will be more evident when the standards set for accessing contingent pay are ambiguous. Such a prediction is consistent with equity theory (see Adams, 1965) as well as economic modeling of the effects that increased firm size and complexity have on the perceived accuracy of subjective evaluations of contributions. In the latter case, increases in size are predicted to be associated with a greater use of explicitly specified performance criteria (Baker, Gibbons & Murphy, 1993). Greater use of objective performance criteria in large firms is also attributed to escalating costs of monitoring behaviors as size increases.[4]

Cognitive Status Quo

The formation of a *cognitive status quo* is a third process essential to understanding the psychological contract. Once a set of promises is exchanged, the psychological contract contains initial conditions regarding the employment relationship, on which individuals rely. In essence, the parties to a psychological contract will act on promises regarding the future that were made by another in the past.

The initial experiences employees have with a firm, including the hiring process, orientation, and other early socialization activities, tend to have powerful and sustained effects on their subsequent beliefs regarding both the firm's culture (Gundry & Rousseau, 1994) and the mutual obligations between themselves and their employer (Rousseau, 1995). There is ample evidence that people maintain the beliefs they have come to rely on over time as a basis for interpretation and action (Ross, Lepper, & Hubbard, 1975; Tesser, 1978). Initial conditions have a sustained effect on psychological contracts. Information regarding the nature of the employment relationship that individuals gather in the early phases of organizational socialization typically creates a stable belief system, or "mental model," that resists revision. Over time, the psychological contract is subject to automatic information processing that allows individuals to interpret subsequent events in the context of a preexisting mental model. Thus it is common for employees in the same firm, some hired in 1980 and the others hired fifteen years later, to have distinctly different psychological contracts, each reflecting the era in which the individuals were hired. Human resource practices prevalent at the time of hire create a status quo against which individuals evaluate subsequent experiences.

Proposition 2: Initial conditions of employment affect the terms of the psychological contract over prolonged periods of time.

Individuals tend to experience psychological contract terms as beneficial, reflecting the attractive conditions of employment that they accepted voluntarily. Changes—that is to say, departures from the status quo—are typically seen as negative (Kahneman & Tversky, 1979). The old adage "nothing hurts worse than the loss of money" is consistent with a psychological tendency to resist changes in psychological contract terms that are perceived as losses.[5]

A second consequence of this status quo orientation is that psychological contract terms can be differentiated into *core* and *peripheral* terms (Rousseau, 1995). Core terms reflect beliefs that are a well-established part of the status quo of a particular employment arrangement, and these terms are expected to be sustained for the duration of the relationship. When a firm has a long, successful history of paying a profit-sharing bonus, employees are likely to react negatively when the bonus is cut due to declining profits (a scenario that has led more than a few firms to borrow money to pay bonuses during unprofitable years). Core terms can arise from the history of specific employment practices, such as promotion from within. This history can be tied to broader societal or institutional characteristics of employment (for example, Social Security benefits, job property rights) or assumptions that are taken for granted (for example, that one's employment is with a specific firm that will not be sold to another). Peripheral terms are conditions expected to change during the duration of employment (for example, who one's coworkers are or a special onetime incentive offered to attract workers to accept a new assignment). Whereas core terms are often taken for granted, shifts in peripheral terms are not only more acceptable but also can be used by employers to reward individual performance or organizational productivity without threatening the status quo. Bonuses regularly added to the weekly paycheck become part of the status quo, taken for granted when given and creating a perception of loss when taken away. Conversely, separating the paycheck from a bonus check can signal the conditional nature of the latter. Labeling a benefit "special" makes its fluctuation or loss easier to bear (Rousseau, 1995).

Proposition 3: Changes in core psychological contract terms are associated with greater perceptions of loss than changes in peripheral psychological contract terms.

Interestingly, the tendency of compensation systems to form part of the core of an employee's psychological contract may help explain a phenomenon first reported by Frederick Herzberg. He and his colleagues found that pay was virtually always a "dissatisfier"; that is, workers whom they interviewed described it as a source of dissatisfaction rather than satisfaction in their day-to-day work experiences, in contrast to other more intrinsic characteristics of work (Herzberg, Mausner, Peterson, & Capuell, 1957). Four decades later, looking at this finding through the lens of psychological contract theory, we can say that the traditional compensation systems Herzberg's subjects typically experienced incorporated pay into the core terms of the employment contract. Compensation at that time consisted predominantly of benefits coupled with pay, with individual performance leading to little variation in the latter. Under such conditions, pay was salient primarily when it was lower than what workers believed it would be (Adams, 1965). The concept of pay as a dissatisfier reflects its traditional role as a condition of the core psychological contract.

That employees base their interpretation of the employment relationship on the status quo is particularly evident in terms of wages and benefits. Labor economics refers to the phenomenon of "sticky wages" (Okun, 1981), whereby wages paid by a given employer tend to remain the same or go up but seldom go down even in response to market downturns (however, see Klaas & Ullman, 1995, for recent evidence of some erosion of this pattern). Typically, employees lack the ready access to capital markets that a firm's stockholders or owners have and face great difficulty responding to wage decline given a fixed base of expenses. Thus employers are under great pressure to offer stable, if not accelerating, wages.

The distinction between core and peripheral contract components is likely to play a role in those enduring sets of expected benefits that have come to be known as "entitlements." Despite the common attribution that it is workers who believe themselves to be entitled to a benefit, entitlement works both ways. Employers can believe themselves entitled as well. We suggest that the most common form of employer entitlement is the belief that workers "owe" them continued hard work. Pritchard, Jones, Roth, Stuebing, and Ekeberg (1988) found that managerial decision makers at the firm discontinued a goal-setting and feedback program that included increased incentives, despite dramatic productivity gains. The managers who terminated the new incentive system believed that "personnel should not get something for doing what they were already supposed to do" (p. 354). In effect, these managers believed they were entitled to worker efforts and should not need to reward them specifically. In another study, this time of managers whose employees had been fired and then rehired by an outsourcing firm, Ho and Ang (1998) found that managers who continued to supervise the same workers had greater expectations of hard work and high performance from their former employees than they did of agency employees whom they had not managed previously. Managers who continued to treat their former workers as if they were employees could be construed to have a sense of entitlement to those workers' efforts at prefiring levels. From a psychological contract perspective, entitlement means a belief in one's right to conditions of employment that the entitled party believes he or she earned.

Creating Meaning

Creating meaning is the fourth cognitive process that is relevant to compensation. Human beings seek meaning, a "cognitive organization" of their experiences. This cognitive organization commonly takes the form of belief systems (and their more complex variant, schemata) that promote understanding, predictability, and efficiency in information processing (Welch Larson, 1994). The elements perceived to be part of the compensation bundle shape the meanings that individuals ascribe to the exchange. For instance, if employees perceive they are being offered a supportive environment in which to work, they are more likely to interpret their job as reflecting a personal relationship with the employer (Foa & Foa, 1974; Rousseau, 1998). In contrast, if compensation is limited to an exchange of "a fair day's work for a fair day's pay," employment is likely to be viewed as a limited economic transaction.

A conceptually rich framework for understanding how individuals derive meaning from exchanges is Foa and Foa's resource theory (see Figure 8.2). The six types of resources Foa and Foa (1974) describe are as follows:

Money—currency or tokens that have a standard unit of exchange (such as pay, tuition, or benefits)

Goods—tangible products, objects, or materials (as in the case of factories in Ukraine that pay workers in the form of goods they can sell locally for cash or barter)

Services—activities that affect the body or belongings of a person (for example, an exercise room at work)

Information—advice, facts, opinions, instruments, or enlightenment (excludes information that conveys status such as positive feedback, but includes training and skill development)

Status—evaluative judgments that convey prestige, regard, esteem, or respect or confirm self-worth (such as titles or awards)

Love—expressions of positive feelings of regard, affection, camaraderie, and togetherness (as when executives refer to the workplace as a family, as in the "Disney family")

Foa and Foa (1974) characterized the cognitive structure of resources in terms of two qualities: particularistic versus universalistic and concrete versus symbolic. The particularism continuum reflects whether the value of a given resource is influenced by the particular persons involved in the exchange or whether that value is constant regardless of the participants. The source of a particularistic resource affects its meaning and acceptability to the person who receives it (for example, employees do not accept

Figure 8.2. Foa and Foa's Resource Exchange Framework.

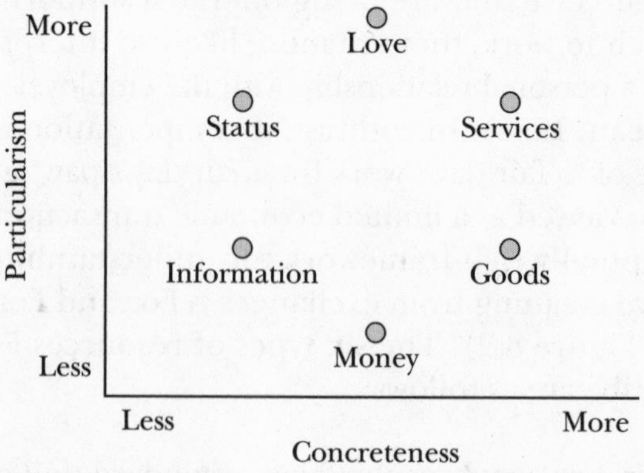

Source: Foa (1971), fig. 1, p. 347.

a change in supervisor with indifference). Particularistic resources can be provided (and accepted) only when certain kinds of relationships exist between the parties—for example, trust must be present for these resources to be accepted. In contrast, universalistic resources can be exchanged in almost any type of relationship (between a firm and a temporary worker or among total strangers, for example).

The concreteness continuum reflects the way in which a specific resource is generally expressed. Thus while status typically is expressed symbolically in gestures and words, goods are concrete and can be handed from one person to another. Information also tends to be symbolic (organization-related facts conveyed orally or in writing by managers). In contrast, love and money can be conveyed in both concrete and symbolic terms. Love may be reflected in both words of support and offers of time off when employees must deal with personal problems. Money can be conveyed in the form of actual payments as well as anticipated future earnings. Foa and Foa (1974) observed in a variety of experiments a preference for repayment in kind and through resources that are near each other on the particularism and concreteness scales (as represented in Figure 8.2; for example, exchanging love for service would be preferred over exchanging love for money, which translated into organizational terms would mean that an employer who sponsored an employee through an assistance program during a stressful time in his personal life would be more inclined to accept greater loyalty in return than try to seek reimbursement for program expenses).

Two basic assumptions of economic models of compensation are that workers' wages reflect their marginal productivity and that differences in compensation reflect differences in productivity from one worker to the next (see Rosen, 1982). Frank (1984) provides evidence that these assumptions are often untrue: the most productive members in a firm often are paid substantially less than their marginal product, and the least productive members may be paid substantially more. Yet there is abundant evidence that people do care about their incomes relative to others' (Adams, 1965). Frank argues that nonpecuniary elements of compensation such as titles (that is, status) are devices for rewarding higher producers without generating excessively adverse reactions from lower-paid employees.

Employment relationships worldwide have long mixed particularistic, nonmonetary and universalistic, economic elements. In particular, "employers of choice"—those that attract and retain a highly competent and motivated workforce—typically provide not only wages at or above market level but also information and services (skills, training, career development) and, indeed, love (employee support, concern for employee and family well-being), as Pfeffer (1998) describes in *The Human Equation,* subtitled *Building Profits by Putting People First.*[6]

Because the nature of an employment relationship puts constraints on the exchange of particularistic resources, employers are able to give a broad array of resources only when their employees are willing to accept them. A firm in which workers do not trust management would, in effect, be unable to effectively bestow symbolic awards such as "employee of the month" (Rousseau, 1998). Economic rewards such as money would be more readily accepted by this firm's employees.

Proposition 4a: Exchange of particularistic resources increases with the duration of employment.

Proposition 4b: Exchange of symbolic resources increases with the duration of the employment.

Proposition 5a: Employment arrangements of limited duration are characterized by exchange of universalistic resources. Employment arrangements of longer duration are characterized by exchange of both particularistic and universalistic resources.

Proposition 5b: Employment arrangements of limited duration are characterized by exchange of concrete resources. Employment arrangements of longer duration are characterized by exchange of both concrete and symbolic resources.

Based on the elements that comprise them and the meanings created by their combinations, psychological contracts take a variety of forms (reviewed in greater detail later in the chapter). To a great extent, the mix of resources involved in an exchange gives rise to the meaning workers and employers attach to a particular employment arrangement. Employees in employment arrangements with limited duration, receiving universalistic (that is, monetary) resources almost exclusively, are likely to interpret their relationship with their employer differently than workers who have long-standing ties and receive particularistic resources. Thus the psychological contract is expected to differ as function of the resources accessed.

In summary, the cognitive processes underlying the formation of psychological contracts in employment influence the dynamics of compensation systems. Subjective and divergent understandings of a compensation system can characterize how employee and employer interpret its nature and implementation. From a psychological contract perspective, initial compensation arrangements at the time of hire can have sustained influence over employee reactions to subsequent compensation changes. Reactions to changes in compensation are also influenced by whether the features changed were understood to be part of the core or peripheral features of the psychological contract. Last, the interrelations among the elements included in the compensation package shape the meaning employees and employers give to the employment relationship. When the compensation package is wholly monetary, a highly transactional employment arrangement is likely. In contrast, where the compensation package combines monetary and nonmonetary exchanges, participants are likely to construct the employment arrangement as relational. Building on these concepts, we next address the psychological contract–related features of specific compensation practices and the compatibility of specific psychological contracts for the HR strategies these compensation systems are designed to implement.

Psychological Contract Features in Pay Systems

Although most workers have probably found themselves at a relative disadvantage vis-à-vis employers in recent years, there appears to be a subset of individuals whose market power has dramatically increased. These tend to be high-performing individuals in occupations where individual performance is highly variable and clearly observable, skills are widely transferrable, and there are very large rewards for being the best performer, as opposed to a second-best or an average performer (see Frank & Cook, 1995). The combined impact of these two trends (decreased market power for most employees, increased power for a few others) has created work environments that are not only more transitory or transactional but also often more clearly segmented in terms of earnings and benefits levels, job security, and bonus opportunities. For example, benefitless, part-time contract workers increasingly work alongside long-term, full-time employees with benefits; professional and less skilled workers are paid from compressed pay structures while executive compensation soars; and highly paid parent-country expatriates work alongside host-country nationals paid far less. These trends suggest that for the foreseeable future, firms will be under considerable pressure to create a sense of fairness and equity among workers with contrasting employment arrangements and highly divergent compensation packages.[7]

We shall review a variety of forms of compensation from a psychological contract perspective. As outlined in Table 8.2, six attributes are particularly relevant to the psychological contracts to which these forms of compensation give rise: core versus peripheral, variable versus fixed, short-term versus long-term, idiosyncratic versus mass, monetizable versus nonmonetizable, and individual versus organizational.

Core Versus Peripheral

This attribute relates to whether the compensation practice tends to be a basic and relatively enduring feature of the employment relationship (core) or an ancillary or add-on (peripheral) feature. Some core compensation practices can be deeply rooted in the organizational culture. In a steel mill decades ago, men who worked on Saturday received part of their overtime compensation in cash. When a new manager took over, he tried to reduce the large quantity of cash on hand and pay the men entirely by check. An uproar ensued, and the Saturday crew demanded return to cash payments. As it turns out, the Saturday payment was known as "beer money," which could be quickly spent at the local pub. As the chastised manager said years later, "The wife cashed the paycheck, but the husband kept the cash he got on Saturday, and 'what mama didn't know, mama didn't know.'" Enduring compensation practices become an indelible part of the organization's culture.

The cultural underpinnings of compensation practices are often most evident in how overtime is viewed. The concept of overtime pay (often legally enforced) emerged both as an incentive to get people to work more than a normal workweek and as a penalty for an employer's failure to schedule work appropriately (Gerhart & Milkovich, 1992). However, overtime pay can become part of the status quo if workers are required routinely to work extra hours, as is common in industrial firms. Overtime pay in the steel industry is a striking example of the intertwining of culture and psychological contracts in compensation. The steel and coal industries were traditionally closely tied by production relationship and geographical proximity. Coal mines were traditionally closed on Sunday. When steel industry unions were organized at the beginning of the twentieth century, they followed the Sunday closing system. As union leader John L. Sullivan proclaimed, "Steel doesn't work on Sunday." This practice meant shutting down steel mill furnaces on Saturday and firing them up again Monday morning (not an issue in coal mines, where continuous-process technologies did not exist). In steel, the workweek became a five-and-three-quarter-day week with overtime paid for three-quarters of a day on Saturday. However, from a continuous-processing perspective, shutting down the mill was highly inefficient and created a management-led move to run the mill continuously seven days a week. The major source of resistance was not to running the plant without a break but to the loss of overtime. The bargaining agreement, which led to seven-day continuous operation, involved adding overtime pay into base salary, paying the men five-and-a-quarter time for working five days.

Recalling our earlier argument that changes in core terms in the psychological contract will engender greater perceived losses than changes in peripheral terms, we expect that compensation system changes that leave the core intact while changing peripheral features of compensation will be more readily accepted. Moreover, as predicted by expectancy theory, changes in pay systems are expected to be more readily accepted when employees expect their net outcome will be either no loss or a gain (a prediction related to Proposition 3 as well).

Proposition 6: Changes in core psychological contract terms are associated with greater negative reactions than changes in peripheral psychological contract terms.

Table 8.2. Types of Compensation and Psychological Contracts.

Compensation	Typical Attributes/Features					
	Core/Peripheral[a]	Fixed/Variable[b]	Long-Term/Short-Term[c]	Idiosyncratic/Mass[d]	Monetizable/Nonmonetizable[e]	Individual/Organizational[f]
Salary (membership, skills, seniority)	C	F	S	I/M	M	I
Commission	C	V	S	M	M	I
Bonus						
Fixed formulas	C	F	S	M	M	O
Performance bonus	C	V	S	M	M	I
Recruiting bonus	C	V	S	M	M	I
Incentive plan, short term						
Financial: money, trips, merchandise, personal recognition	P	V	S	M	N	I
Nonfinancial: recognition, status, group belonging (psychic income)			S	M	N	I
Special awards and distinct symbols of recognition at company events	P	V	S	M	N	I
Status and publicity of worker's contributions and skill	P	V	S	M	N	I
Incentive plan, middle term						
Profit sharing	C	V	L	I/M	M	O

Incentive plan, long term						
Stock option plan	C	V	L	M	N	I/O
Benefits						
Life, accident, dental or medical insurance	C	F	L	M	N	I/O
Education assistance	C	F	L	M	N	I/O
Pension plans	C	F	L	M	M	O
Retirement plans	C	F	L	M	N	I/O
Car club or association memberships	C	F	L	I	M	I
Moving expenses	C/P	F/V	L	I/M	M	I/O
Salary continuation program	P	F	L	M	M	I/O
Group medical coverage	C	F	L	M	M	I/O
Long-term disability coverage	C	F	L	M	M	I/O
Child-care assistance or on-site day-care facilities	P	F	L	M/I	M	I/O
Employee assistance programs for personal problems	P	F	L	M	N/M	I/O
Equity						
Employee stock ownership plan (ESOP)	C	V	L	M	M	O
Current stock	C	V	S	I	M	O

Table 8.2. Types of Compensation and Psychological Contracts, Cont'd.

Compensation		Typical Attributes/Features				
	Core/Peripheral[a]	Fixed/Variable[b]	Long-Term/Short-Term[c]	Idiosyncratic/Mass[d]	Monetizable/Nonmonetizable[e]	Individual/Organizational[f]
Deferred stock	C	V	L	I	M	O
Restricted stock (like "golden handcuffs")	C	V	L	I	M	O
Phantom options or stocks	C	V	L	I	M	O
Stock appreciation rights (SARs)	C	V	L	I	M	O
Incentive stock options (ISO; vesting schedule)	C	V	L	I	M	O
Nonqualified stock options (NSO; vesting schedule)	C	V	L	I	M	O
Stock purchase plan	C	V	L	M	M	O
Guaranteed continuous employment plan	C	F	L	M	N/M	I/O

[a] C = *Core:* stipulated in an initial or ongoing employment agreement; P = *Peripheral:* not explicitly stipulated in the agreement.

[b] F = *Fixed:* amount or value is preset; V = *Variable:* amount or value is contingent on some criterion (such as profitability of the organization).

[c] L = *Long-term:* to promote retention of employees; S = *Short-term:* to reward short-term performance.

[d] I = *Idiosyncratic:* applicable only to specific individuals (such as executives) and negotiated individually; M = *Mass:* applicable to broad classes, groups, or categories of employees.

[e] M = *Monetizable:* monetary value of the compensation item can be determined; N = *Nonmonetizable:* monetary value of the compensation item cannot be determined.

[f] I = *Individual-level reward:* compensation is based on individual characteristic (such as individual performance). O = *Organizational-level rewards:* compensation is based on overall organizational characteristics (such as organizational performance).

Variable Versus Fixed

This attribute concerns whether the amount of compensation received is contingent on organizational or individual performance. Under fixed conditions, pay levels are preset, and employees have little risk in contrast to the remuneration of firm owners or stockholders. Under variable conditions, pay is contingent on performance criteria, and employees and owners share the risk to a greater degree. Assumptions regarding risk are fundamental to the employment relationship, particularly in terms of prespecified duties, responsibilities, and the results for which employees are responsible. Introduction of new or significantly greater risks after hire threatens the status quo. Thus successful introduction of risk sharing is likely to include an implementation process that provides support to increase employee skills and help employees become psychologically ready to perform successfully under conditions of risk. Though moderated by employee risk tolerance and the upside potential of risk taking, any transition to pay at risk is also likely to be smoother when a substantial proportion of base pay remains fixed. A related factor in performance-contingent pay is the nature of the performance evaluation process, particularly its perceived fairness.

Proposition 7: Employee responses to a shift from fixed to variable pay systems will be (a) negatively related to the proportion of pay at risk, (b) positively related to implementation processes that increase skills and psychological readiness to perform successfully under conditions of risk, (c) positively related to the degree of individual impact on the performance target, and (d) positively related to employee perceptions of the fairness of the performance evaluation process.

There has been a veritable explosion of variable-pay plans. In 1995, only 14 percent of U.S. companies put employee pay at risk, but another 6 percent were installing such systems, with an additional 26 percent giving the matter serious consideration (Wysocki, 1995). One important feature of variable pay from a psychological contract perspective is that it can be either core or peripheral, depending on how it is introduced and particularly on whether variable pay was an initial condition of employment. Different effects can be expected from the introduction of variable pay for new hires as opposed to workers already on the job (Rousseau, 1995).

Short-Term Versus Long-Term

This attribute reflects whether compensation is accessed in the present or near term as opposed to the long term. Short-term compensation rewards short-term contributions to the firm (recent attendance, current performance, and the like). Long-term compensation means that employees access rewards by contributing to the firm's long-term success, an incentive that rewards efforts targeted to firm growth as well as employee retention. Variable-pay schemes differ considerably in how they weigh short-term performance or long-term contributions to the firm. Because there is a tendency for short term objectives to be more salient than long-term goals (Beinhocker, 1991), a clear understanding of priorities is needed for long-term objectives to be reinforced through compensation. Sources of information regarding the employee contributions that will be rewarded include feedback from first-line supervisors, demands from customers, presentations by top management, and formal human resource practices such as merit pay systems. These sources have been characterized as psychological contract makers (Rousseau, 1995): employees rely on information from various sources to interpret their roles in the employment relationship. Mixed messages from different contract makers can complicate interpretation, and inconsistency across contract makers can undermine credibility. Pritchard (1990) developed the PROMES system, which is based on consensus among different constituents, to make the performance terms to which employees are obligated more consistent and better understood over the long term. Effective specification of long-term performance contingencies may require more consistency among contract makers than short-term contingencies. Employees can easily observe in the short term whether promises made to them regarding pay for short-term performance are true. Greater trust in both managerial intentions and competency is required to make long-term incentive systems effective motivators (Nystrom, 1990).

Proposition 8: Successful implementation of changes in long-term performance contingencies requires greater agreement among contract makers than changes in short-term contingencies do.

Proposition 9: Successful implementation of changes in long-term performance contingencies requires greater employee trust of the employer than changes in short-term contingencies do.

Idiosyncratic Versus Mass

This attribute concerns whether a compensation arrangement is likely to be unique to a particular employee, in contrast to a mass arrangement that all employees, or all employees in a given position or job grade, might access. Idiosyncratic arrangements are negotiated individually and can reflect the unique contributions of a given individual or role or a reward system that is highly particularistic or political. In contrast, mass compensation arrangements apply to a broad class of employees and tend to signal and reinforce a common identity or sense of "we" (Gaertner, Dovidio, & Bachman, 1996; Rousseau, 1998). Firms that make an effort to reduce compensation differences across employee levels, roles, and functions signal a cultural message of unity (Ben and Jerry's is an example; another is low ratios among executives, managers, and employees in Japanese firms; Ouchi, 1981). The lower the disparity in compensation among organizational members, the more likely it is that individuals will be party to similar psychological contracts—what Nicholson and Johns (1985) and Rousseau and McLean-Parks (1993) referred to as a shared, "normative contract."

Proposition 10: In contrast to idiosyncratic compensation practices, mass compensation practices increase the degree of agreement among the psychological contracts of individual employees.

Firms that employ mass compensation practices signal the value they place on firmwide equality rather than individual market value or marginal productivity. These arrangements can have advantages in creating a cohesive bond between members, regardless of rank and function. Thus at PeopleExpress, a 1980s start-up airline, all employees received low base salaries and an equity stake, reinforcing their need to collaborate regardless of their roles, which were relatively undifferentiated—even pilots loaded bags on board—creating a joint interest in making the airline successful. Mass compensation systems are most effective where organizational norms exist supporting high performance. Absent such norms, the disadvantages of mass compensation systems arise from indifference to high or low performers. In the case of wage policies implemented by the Chinese government beginning in the 1980s, state-owned enterprises introduced a bonus system to reward high-performing workers and managers. However, firms tended to divide the bonuses equally among individuals and to pay more than the actual level of productivity gained (Takahara, 1992; Walder, 1987). Despite evidence that Chinese firms support the idea of idiosyncratic rewards for individuals (based on their friendship relations; Xin & Pearce, 1996), formal compensation has tended to be relatively undifferentiated. However, mass compensation systems can be effective in creating a sense of unity or identification among a firm's workers.

Monetizable Versus Nonmonetizable

This reflects whether a monetary value can be objectively established for the reward or benefit. Monetizable compensation is readily compared to the external market. Nonmonetizable compensation can indicate the absence of an external market infrastructure (for example, agricultural cooperatives in Russia sometimes pay their workers in food). In market-oriented societies, compensation that takes the form of nonmonetizable rewards is associated with relational rather than transactional employment arrangements. Thus employers who throw Christmas parties, sponsor summer camps, or (as in the case of the U.S. manufacturer Fel-Pro and other "employers of choice") offer a plethora of benefits from legal services to Thanksgiving turkeys signal a broad employment relationship, in contrast to employers who compensate solely on a cash basis.

Proposition 11: In market economies, a greater proportion of nonmonetizable compensation signals a psychological contract that is relational. Conversely, a lower proportion of nonmonetizable compensation signals a psychological contract that is transactional.

Individual Versus Organizational

If compensation is contingent on performance, is it linked to individual or organizational outcomes? The critical issue with regard to tying compensation to firm performance is the degree of interdependence among the individuals who contribute to overall performance. When people are highly interdependent, incentives for group performance are more appropriate than incentives for individual contribution (Gerhart & Milkovich, 1992). Moreover, from a psychological contract perspective, the sharing of a common incentive system tied to firmwide performance affects the meaning of the exchange relationship. This meaning includes the belief that employment is a relationship as well as an economic transaction, which can reinforce the collective identity of individuals within the firm (as in the case of Southwest Airlines, where office workers and mailroom clerks who have little impact on the timeliness of airplane arrivals may experience psychic benefits greater than the $47 they receive each month for participating in a collective bonus system tied to on-time performance).[8]

Proposition 12: Compensation that is contingent on firm performance will promote higher organizational identification than a compensation system based on individual performance.

Proposition 13: Compensation that is contingent on firm performance will promote employees' beliefs in a relational contract with their employer.

In summary, characteristics of compensation systems affect the nature and terms of psychological contracts in employment. Moreover, how changes in compensation practices are interpreted by employees is influenced by their psychological contracts. Great diversity exists in contemporary employment arrangements. Next we provide a framework for thinking about the kinds of psychological contracts associated with different pay systems.

Types of Psychological Contracts and Compensation Practices

Psychological contracts have been characterized in terms of the intersection of two major dimensions in employment: time span or duration (whether short-term or open-ended) and explicit performance contingencies (the extent to which rewards are explicitly tied to levels of individual contribution to the firm). Time span reflects the stability of the employment relationship and the degree of employee and employer investment in the relationship. Explicit performance contingencies reflect the degree to which individuals access rewards, including continued employment, based on performance. Together these dimensions form a two-by-two framework differentiating types of psychological contracts (see Table 8.3).

Transactional contracts are of limited duration with well-specified performance terms (for example, retail clerks hired during peak shopping season). These contracts are characterized by low ambiguity, easy exit and high turnover, and low member commit-

Table 8.3. Psychological Contract Types and Compensation.

| | **Performance Contingencies** | |
	Specified	**Not Specified**
Short-Term	Transactional	Transitional
	Example: sales	Example: during restructuring
	Pay based on short-term job performance or results	Pay not linked to performance or membership, often an erosion of initial pay levels
	• Commission	• Fixed or declining wages
	• Pay for hours worked	• Eroding benefits
	• Market-based wages	• Incentives to quit
	• Limited benefits	(severance)
	• Incentives to stay (bonuses)	
Long-Term	Balanced	Relational
	Example: high-involvement team	Example: traditional business
	Pay based on contribution	Pay based on membership, length of service
	• Pay for skills	• Salary largely reflects internal market factors
	• Blend of internal and external market considerations	• Annual bonus loosely tied to performance
	• Short-term and long-term incentives	• Nonpecuniary rewards
	• Nonpecuniary rewards	• Substantial benefits
	• Individual- and organizational-level performance	
	• Flexible benefits	

(Duration is the left-side label spanning Short-Term and Long-Term rows.)

ment and identification with the firm. Compensation in transactional contracts is highly monetized and dominated by market factors; individual pay is based on the market value of the skills presented at entry, typically weighted by the number of hours worked. Often pay is at least partly tied directly to results (sales or completed projects, for example). Benefits tend to be limited or, in the case of independent contractors and part-time workers with transactional contracts, nonexistent. Competitive advantage from transactional contracts derives from the flexibility employers obtain in the face of turbulent and unpredictable environments. Such contracts are not particularly effective in sustaining a competitive edge through service or innovation because of their more narrow, short-term focus.

Because high turnover is characteristic of transactional employment conditions, employers often provide financial incentives to induce employees to stay. An example is the hypercompetitive Singapore labor market, where workers are paid a thirteenth-month bonus (one month's extra salary if they remain with an employer for a year). Similarly, expatriates who work in Hong Kong universities can receive as much as an additional year's pay if they stay for three years (significantly, this is sometimes presented as a "keep back," whereby the employer promises a certain annual salary but keeps a percentage of it to be paid only if the employee completes three years of service).

The shift toward more transactional employment for many individuals has been widely documented (see, for example, Kanter, 1989). This change has affected compensation practices in a variety of ways. For example, employers have sought various means of reducing the amount of fixed pay (through one-time bonuses rather than merit increases, a higher number of contract employees, or longer work hours for current employees in lieu of hiring new workers, to cite just a few). At the same time, these employers may increase the amount of nonrecurring income that can be earned for high performance in a particular time period.

Relational contracts feature open-ended membership and incomplete or ambiguous performance contingencies. In some relational employment arrangements, workers with long-standing ties to a firm participate in the exchange of a broad spectrum of resources, from skill development to information sharing and support.

These contracts are characterized by high member commitment, high firm investment in employees, integration and identification between firm and employees, and stability. Compensation packages for relational contract parties include base pay typically tied to factors such as seniority and rank. Compensation systems based on seniority are consistent with internal labor markets that reward individuals for firm loyalty. Seniority-based compensation practices affirm that employee-employer arrangements reflect an underlying relationship involving economic and socioemotional concerns (Rousseau, 1989). If a merit system exists in a relational firm, salary is shaped by individual contributions; however, evidence suggests that such systems are more often espoused than actually implemented (Belliveau, 1998). Annual bonuses can exist but may be loosely tied to performance.

Monetary and nonmonetary benefits tend to foster worker attachment to the firm. From an employee perspective, benefits accessed through the firm signal the quality of the employment relationship and its stability (Eisenberger et al., 1986; University of Chicago, 1993), with employers' providing generous benefits being regarded as more relational (Rousseau, 1990).

Although the form of relational contract promising "lifetime employment" has been declared dead by many (see Hall, 1996; Hirsch, 1987), relational contracts continue to be created and maintained worldwide, largely in response to the combination of the firm's need for a stable, reliable labor force and the impact of governmental policies promoting stable employment (Rousseau & Schalk, 2000). Moreover, Pfeffer (1994, 1998) has amassed a substantial number of examples of highly profitable firms that maintain relational contracts with employees.

An emphasis on the relational aspects of employment, including noncash compensation and benefits, may be particularly important in developing countries, where firms often need to make up for the lack of resource access in the broader society. For example, in Kazakhstan, a former republic of the Soviet Union, the general absence of governmental supports means that employers seeking to obtain reliable and qualified workers need to attend to the broader issues of employee welfare, from housing and meals (revamping the state farm) to entertainment (subsidizing the local soccer team; as in the case of Hurricane Hydrocarbons Ltd., a Canadian-based firm; Pope, 1997). It can also mean repaying salaries and pension obligations owed by previous owners, to establish trust.

Transitions in the economy of China demonstrate similar pressures on employers as well as employees. State-owned enterprises in China pay employees relatively low wages and, accordingly, demand low levels of contribution. Employees participate in the state-administered benefits system, which provides housing, child education, medical care, and other family supports. However, workers who leave the state system to work at a multinational firm effectively become nonpersons, unable to access benefits through the state. Multinational employers typically offer a package of financial support that allows the person to rent or buy an apartment, pay for medical care, and educate children. Many non-Chinese firms have had difficulty recognizing the level of support they must provide to offset their employees' lack of state-provided benefits.[9] It is likely that changing practices in the global labor force (for example, shifts from job security to career security) will pressure society's welfare component, necessitating either changes in public policy (such as portable pensions and health care) or changes in the benefits employers provide.[10]

Balanced contracts include open-ended employment with well-specified performance contingencies that are subject to change over time. The balanced contract blends transactional and relational contract terms in varying degrees. It is characterized by high member commitment, integration and identification, ongoing development of employee skills, mutual support, and dynamic performance conditions (such as high-performance teams).

Compensation for employees with a balanced psychological contract is often a mix of base pay with a skill component and incentives based on short-term and, in some cases, longer-term performance. The conditions of a balanced contract may create an internal market in which skill development forms a basis for career advantage within the firm (and often outside the firm as well; Arthur & Rousseau, 1996). Outside hires, which may include top management team members, are often paid a premium compared to internal successors due to the distinctive skills they offer and incentives needed to attract them away from other employers (Harris & Helfat, 1997). In balanced arrangements, career security (sometimes labeled "employability"; Arthur & Rousseau, 1996) replaces job security and exclusive reliance on the internal labor market.

Though researchers use the transactional versus relational distinction to characterize a panoply of relationships, from supplier-customer relations (Lusch & Brown, 1996) to employment (Rousseau, 1990), there is evidence that employment relationships are increasingly hybrids mixing transactional and relational patterns. The rise of this mixed psychological contract form stems from its emphasis on flexible stability, promoting high performance through innovation and flexibility while supporting employee retention and career development inside and outside the firm (Pfeffer, 1998).

Compensation system changes in a firm shifting from a relational to a balanced contract are exemplified in the following case: A jet parts factory plagued with quality and labor problems created a team of twenty-two production and administrative employees to design a new pay and job classification system that focused on linking pay with learning new techniques. Where employees had been rewarded previously for seniority, the pay structure featured three concentric rings representing rising levels of skill. The inner circle represented the basic requirements for holding a job. To reach the next ring, workers would have to manage the flow of parts through their machining cells. To reach the highest-paid circle, workers were required to lead projects that cut costs or improved quality (White, 1996). In this setting, the transition from old system to new provided for income stability (protecting the status quo) while giving raises only for increased skill levels. Although some workers complained about the extra training required for a raise, employees had a two-year period to take advantage of training opportunities. As the jet factory's compensation system demonstrates, it is possible to make multiple levels of contribution and investment part of the psychological contract's core.

Flexible benefits are another frequent characteristic of balanced contracts. Kirchmeyer's research on employee preferences regarding child care arrangements (1995) suggests that although employees value help with nonwork issues, they also prefer to choose how that support is deployed (for example, most prefer to have employers subsidize off-site day care rather than provide on-site facilities). The movement toward flexible, menu-like benefit packages is an attempt to manage the costs of benefits while allowing individuals to access resources that can serve their idiosyncratic needs.

Transitional arrangements essentially represent a breakdown of the employment contract during organizational restructuring or downsizing, through the erosion of previous commitments. In times of drastic change, firms may cease to make (credible) commitments regarding future employment and provide few, if any, explicit performance demands or contingent incentives. Transitional compensation systems are often highly ambiguous, reflecting internal firm turmoil. Commonly, the focus of employees and the firm is on the nature of buyout packages and related severance issues. Firms in transition are characterized by fixed or declining wages and benefits, severance packages giving employees incentives to quit, and incentives to retain employees deemed indispensable to the organization (retention bonuses for staying with the firm for a specified length of time, for example).

This discussion of the link between compensation practices and psychological contract forms is not intended to downplay the role of individual differences in the emergence of psychological contracts. Different forms of psychological contracts characterize employees with distinct career motives (Rousseau, 1990) and different levels of trust and commitment to the firm (Robinson & Rousseau, 1994; Rousseau & Tijoriwala, 1999). Compensation practices give potential employees information about the firm that is recruiting them, giving them at least one reason to join the firm or seek employment elsewhere.

However, changes in the competitive environment of firms are likely to be a major source of changes in psychological contracts. New forms of employment, including "boundaryless careers" (Arthur & Rousseau, 1996), the use of contractors or part-timers, and network employment (Snow, Miles, & Coleman, 1992) cause an increase in the incidence of both transactional and balanced psychological contracts, in conjunction with increased performance pressures on workers. In highly competitive labor markets such as information technology (Ang & Slaughter, 1998), worker mobility leads to a high incidence of transactional terms in employee psychological contracts. Moreover, the trend for a firm to compensate workers differently as a function of their employment status (for example, contractors versus full-time employees) increases the level of segmentation in employment contracts and introduces new challenges to the creation and maintenance of equity in the workplace.

Implications for Future Research

The various propositions presented in this chapter constitute a rudimentary research agenda, bringing psychological contract theory to bear on our understanding of compensation. Prior research in compensation has typically focused on compensation as a broad generic category, as in labor economics, or has limited its focus to pay (cash-based compensation), as in the case of pay satisfaction research. A richer and more realistic understanding of compensation can be obtained by examining the elements of the compensation "bundle" (Bloom & Milkovich, 1996)—and a psychological contract perspective appreciates that the bundle as a whole conveys meanings to employees and that each element of that compensation bundle (from discrete incentives to benefits) can be interpreted differently by individual employees and between employee and employer.

The theory of psychological contracts also permits more systematic study of compensation system change. Psychological contracts, once formed, constitute a cognitive status quo and are relatively enduring. Changes in compensation practices can take on different meanings to employees hired at different periods of time or with different organizational histories. Psychological contract theory predicts a variety of strategies that can lead to more effectively implemented change in compensation practices, particularly surrounding the distinction between core and peripheral terms of the psychological contract.

The meaning of compensation systems is far broader than mere economic terms, signaling much about the nature of the employment relationship and the attachment between worker and firm. The role that national culture plays in shaping the meanings ascribed to elements of the compensation system will be an important organizational research topic as firms become increasing global in their scope, reflected in the management prescription to "think globally and pay locally" (Thompson & Richter, 1998, p. 29). International firms seeking to alter compensation practices for strategic purposes (for example, to create a more internally consistent global firm) are likely to find that the psychological contract, like the people who are party to it, is often more local than global (Rousseau & Schalk, 2000).

Conclusion

This chapter has presented a psychological contract perspective on employment compensation. Compensation systems are major features of the human resource practices firms employ in implementing their business strategy. Compensation plays two important roles in implementing business strategy. The first is to signal to employees the contributions (for example, short-term results versus long-term investments) that the firm values through incentives and pay-for-performance contingencies. The second role is to promote a particular form of employment relationship based on what the compensation system signals, in conjunction with other human resource practices, regarding the attachment between workers and the firm. Through these two roles, compensation practices constitute important information employees rely on in interpreting the psychological contract with the employer.

By viewing compensation as an interrelated bundle of resources that are exchanged for worker contributions, building on the work of Gerhart and Milkovich (1992) and Bloom and Milkovich (1996), we have explored the cognitions and meanings associated with compensation. Changes in compensation systems can signal fundamental shifts in the employment relationship and are likely to be interpreted in light of the preexisting psychological contract between employee and firm. Significantly, as market economies emerge worldwide, shifts in the nature of employment compensation (replacing state social supports with private sector activities) create fundamental changes in the nature of firms and employment. A broad view of the nature of compensation (see Bloom & Milkovich, 1996) is necessary for a thorough understanding of psychological contracts in a time of worldwide change.

Notes

1. *Compensation* has slightly different meanings in different languages and cultures, ranging from "reward" to "making equal" to "replacement of a loss" or "making up for an imbalance" (Bloom and Milkovich, 1996). Note also that work that is uncompensated, which

may take forms as diverse as volunteerism, slavery, and child rearing, is not considered employment.

2. The essential point is summarized in the quote "Many of the last shall be first, and many of the first shall be last."

3. The classic example of apparent mutuality without mutuality in fact is two students who agree to meet the next day at the library to study together. They each agree to meet at 8 o'clock, but the night owl believes this means 8 P.M., whereas the early riser interprets the commitment to mean 8 A.M. Each has a belief in the mutuality of their agreement, but there is no mutuality in fact.

4. Note that objective standards are not always seen as fairer. Employees can feel unfairly treated if performance on objective measures (such as sales growth) is influenced by factors beyond their control. However, it is often easier to remedy unfairness in objective measures, by creating offsets (for example, corrections for market changes) and use of multiple indicators, than it is to correct the perceived biases associated with subjectivity. Reducing the adverse effects of subjectivity often means improving the level of trust and quality of communication between workers and raters of their performance.

5. We are not arguing that psychological contract terms never change. Indeed, their change can take many forms, particularly following interventions to alter the nature of the employment relationship (such as restructurings or redesigning the firm's HR strategy). Firms can "change the deal while keeping the people" (Rousseau, 1996). However, successful change efforts are based on strategies influencing the cognitive processes described here (Rousseau, 1995). Moreover, a successful change is often predicated on shifting employees' focus from losses to gains. Thus shifting from fixed to more variable pay systems may be viewed as beneficial when employee skills are increased to help them access higher returns under the variable pay system.

6. An interesting (mis)application of the concept of monetary rewards is found in a recent *Wall Street Journal* op-ed piece: "Noncash benefits corrupt the employer-employee relationship . . . when 40 percent of total compensation is in the form of benefits, it is difficult for employees to put a true market value on their compensation package or to walk away from a job they don't like. From management's point of view, it is difficult to have true pay-for-performance when employees see 40 percent of their compensation as an 'entitlement'" (Cantoni, 1997). From the writer's point of view, the only viable incentive system is wholly cash-based. Cantoni ignores the symbolic value (which may lead to lower labor costs on the whole) of a host of other resources available through employment.

7. Where workers have a choice regarding alternative arrangements, they are more likely to access preferred arrangements that meet their personal needs. Perceived fairness and equity are predicted to be higher under conditions of choice.
8. Normative contracts—psychological contracts that are common across groups of workers—may be more likely to form around such bonus systems because pay is observable and the performance to which it is attached is highly public.
9. For many married couples in today's China, the ideal combination is to have one spouse work for the government and the other for a multinational to obtain both benefits and a high salary.
10. Providing employee benefits is an increasingly contentious issue, at least in developed nations. Social critics have referred to organizational performance of social activities (such as caring for an individual in sickness or old age) as the demise of the civil society (Perrow, 1996) and the rise of the "market mentality" (Polyani, 1957).

References

Adams, J. S. (1965). Inequity in social exchange. In L. Berkowitz (Ed.), *Advances in experimental social psychology* (Vol. 2, pp. 267–299). Orlando, FL: Academic Press.

Ang, S., & Slaughter, S. (1998). Effects of information systems employment outsourcing: Multiple informants' perspectives. *Proceedings of the Hawaiian International Conference on Systems Sciences,* pp. 112–120.

Arthur, M. B., & Rousseau, D. M. (1996). *The boundaryless career: A new organizational principle for a new organizational era.* New York: Oxford University Press.

Baker, G., Gibbons, R., & Murphy, K. J. (1993). *Subjective performance measures in optimal incentive contracts.* Unpublished manuscript.

Beinhocker, E. D. (1991). *GTE Corporation: Long-term incentive plan* (Case No. 9–191–005). Cambridge, MA: Harvard Business School.

Belliveau, M. (1998). *Merit-based compensation?* Unpublished manuscript, Fuqua School of Business, Duke University, Durham, NC.

Bloom, M. C., & Milkovich, G. T. (1996). Issues in management compensation research. In C.L. Cooper & D. M. Rousseau (Eds.), *Trends in organizational behavior* (Vol. 3, pp. 23–47). New York: Wiley.

Cantoni, C. J. (1997, August 18). The case against employee benefits. *Wall Street Journal.*

Eisenberger, R., Huntington, R., Hutchinson, S., & Sowa, D. (1986). Perceived organizational support. *Journal of Applied Psychology, 71,* 500–507.

Foa, U. G. (1971). Interpersonal and economic resources. *Science, 171,* 345–351.

Foa, U. G., & Foa, E. B. (1974). *Societal structures of the mind.* Springfield, IL: Thomas.

Frank, R. H. (1984). Are workers paid their marginal products? *American Economic Review, 74,* 549–571.

Frank, R. H., & Cook, P. J. (1995). *Winner take all.* New York: Penguin.

Gaertner, S. L., Dovidio, J. F., & Bachman, B. A. (1996). Revisiting the contact hypothesis: The induction of common group identity. *International Journal of International Relations, 20,* 271–290.

Gerhart, B., & Milkovich, G. T. (1992). Employee compensation: Research and theory. In M. D. Dunnette & L. M. Hough (Eds), *Handbook of industrial and organizational psychology* (2nd ed., Vol. 3, pp. 481–569). Palo Alto, CA: Consulting Psychologists Press.

Gundry, L. R., & Rousseau, D. M. (1994). Communicating culture to newcomers. *Human Relations, 47,* 1068–1088.

Guzzo, R. A., Noonan, K. A., & Elron, E. (1994). Expatriate managers and the psychological contract. *Journal of Applied Psychology, 79,* 617–626.

Hall, D. T. (1996). Protean careers of the 21st century. *Academy of Management Executive, 10*(4), 8–16.

Harris, D., & Helfat, C. (1997). Specificity of CEO human capital and compensation. *Strategic Management Journal, 18,* 895–920.

Herzberg, F., Mausner, B., Peterson, R. O., & Capuell, D. F. (1957). *Job attitudes: Review of research and opinion.* Pittsburgh, PA: Psychological Services of Pittsburgh.

Hirsch, P. M. (1987). *Pack your own parachute.* Reading, MA: Addison-Wesley.

Ho, V. T., & Ang, S. (1998, August). *When employees become contract labor: Persistent expectations of the principal in an outsourcing context.* Paper presented at the annual meeting of the Academy of Management, San Diego, CA.

Kahneman, D., & Tversky, A. (1979). Prospect theory: An analysis of decision under risk. *Econometrica, 47,* 263–291.

Kanter, R. M. (1989). *When giants learn to dance.* New York: Simon & Schuster.

Kirchmeyer, C. (1995). Managing the work-nonwork boundary: An assessment of organizational responses. *Human Relations, 48,* 515–536.

Klaas, B. S., & Ullman, J. C. (1995). Sticky wages revisited: Organizational responses to a declining market-clearing wage. *Academy of Management Review, 20,* 281–310.

Lincoln, J. (1951). *Incentive management.* Cleveland: Lincoln Electric Co.

Lusch, R. F., & Brown, J. R. (1996). Interdependency, contracting, and relational behavior in marketing channels. *Journal of Marketing, 60,* 19–38.

March, J. G., & Simon, H. A. (1958). *Organizations.* New York: McGraw-Hill.

Nicholson, N., & Johns, G. (1985). The absence culture and the psychological contract: Who's in control of absence? *Academy of Management Review, 10,* 397–407.

Nordhaug, O. (1989). Reward functions of personnel training. *Human Relations, 42,* 373–388.

Nystrom, P. C. (1990). Vertical exchanges and organizational commitments of American business managers. *Group and Organization Studies, 15,* 296–312.

Okun, A. (1981). *Prices and quantities: A macroeconomic analysis.* Washington, DC: Brookings Institution.

Ouchi, W. (1981). *Theory Z: How American business can meet the Japanese challenge.* Reading MA: Addison-Wesley.

Perrow, C. (1996). The bounded career and the demise of civil society. In M. B. Arthur & D. M. Rousseau (Eds.), *The boundaryless career: A new employment principle for a new organizational era* (pp. 297–314). New York: Oxford University Press.

Pfeffer, J. (1994). *Competitive advantage through people: Unleashing the power of the workforce.* Boston: Harvard Business School Press.

Pfeffer, J. (1998). *The human equation: Building profits by putting people first.* Boston: Harvard Business School Press.

Polyani, K. (1957). *The great transformation.* Boston: Beacon Press.

Pope, H. (1997, November 18). Extra baggage: To get Kazakhstani oil, small firm takes on soccer team, camels. *Wall Street Journal,* p. A6.

Pritchard, R. D. (1990). *Measuring and improving organizational productivity.* New York: Praeger.

Pritchard, R. D., Jones, S. D., Roth, P. L., Stuebing, K. K., & Ekeberg, S. E. (1988). Effects of group feedback, goal setting, and incentives on organizational productivity. *Journal of Applied Psychology, 73,* 337–358.

Robinson, S. L., Kraatz, M. S., & Rousseau, D. M. (1994). Changing obligations and the psychological contract: A longitudinal study. *Academy of Management Journal, 37,* 137–152.

Robinson, S. L., & Rousseau, D. M. (1994). Violating the psychological contract: Not the exception but the norm. *Journal of Organizational Behavior, 15,* 245–259.

Rosen, S. (1982). Authority, control, and distribution of earnings. *Bell Journal of Economics, 13,* 311–323.

Ross, L., Lepper, M. R., & Hubbard, M. (1975). Perseverance in self-perception and social perception: Biased attribution processes in the debriefing paradigm. *Journal of Personality and Social Psychology, 32,* 880–892.

Rousseau, D. M. (1989). Psychological and implied contracts in organizations. *Employee Rights and Responsibilities Journal, 2,* 121–139.

Rousseau, D. M. (1990). New hire perceptions of their own and their employer's obligations: A study of psychological contracts. *Journal of Organizational Behavior, 11,* 389–400.

Rousseau, D. M. (1995). *Psychological contracts in organizations: Understanding written and unwritten agreements.* Thousand Oaks, CA: Sage.

Rousseau, D. M. (1996). Changing the deal while keeping the people. *Academy of Management Executive, 10,* 50–61.

Rousseau, D. M. (1997). Organizational behavior in the new organizational era. *Annual Review of Psychology, 48,* 515–546.

Rousseau, D. M. (1998). Why workers still identify with their organizations. *Journal of Organizational Behavior, 19,* 217–233.

Rousseau, D. M., & McLean-Parks, J. M. (1993). The contracts of individuals and organizations. In L. L. Cummings & B. M Staw (Eds.), *Research in organizational behavior* (Vol. 15, pp. 1–43). Greenwich, CT: JAI Press.

Rousseau, D. M., & Schalk, R. (2000). *Psychological contracts in employment.* Thousand Oaks, CA: Sage.

Rousseau, D. M., & Tijoriwala, S. A. (1999). What's a good reason to change? Motivated reasoning and social accounts in organizational change. *Journal of Applied Psychology, 84,* 514–528.

Snow, C. C., Miles, R. E., & Coleman, H. J. (1992). Managing 21st-century network organizations. *Organizational Dynamics, 21,* 5–21.

Takahara, A. (1992). *The politics of wage policy in post-revolutionary China.* Houndmills, England: Macmillan.

Tesser, A. (1978). Self-generated attitude change. In L. Berkowitz (Ed.), *Advances in experimental social psychology* (Vol. 11, pp. 289–338). Orlando, FL: Academic Press.

Thompson, M. A., & Richter, A. S. (1998, Summer). Using cultural principles to resolve the paradox of international remuneration. *American Compensation Association Journal,* 28–37.

Tibbets, J. S., & Donovan, E. T. (Jan/Feb 1989). Compensation and benefits for start-up companies. *Harvard Business Review,* pp. 140–144.

University of Chicago. (1993). *Added benefits: The link between family responsive policies and job performance.* Chicago: Author.

Walder, A. G. (1987, March). Wage reform and the web of factory interests. *China Quarterly,* pp. 22–41.

Welch Larson, D. (1994). The rate of belief systems and schemas in foreign policy decision making. *Political Psychology, 15,* 17–32.

White, J. B. (1996, December 26). Dodging doom: How a creaky factory got off the hit list, won respect at last. *Wall Street Journal,* pp. A1–A2.

Wysocki, B. (1995, December 14). Unstable pay becomes ever more common. *Wall Street Journal,* p. A1.

Xin, K. R., & Pearce, J. L. (1996). Guanxi: Connections as substitute for formal institutional support. *Academy of Management Journal, 39,* 1641–1658.

CHAPTER 9

Rethinking Compensation Risk

Robert M. Wiseman
Luis R. Gomez-Mejia
Mel Fugate

The risk construct is central to the study of compensation and has been growing in importance during the past two decades as a greater proportion of pay received by workers comes in variable form through such programs as gainsharing, key contributor bonuses, on-spot awards, team bonuses, and profit sharing (Barkema & Gomez-Mejia, 1998; Martocchio, 1998). Increasingly, employment insecurity and compensation risk go hand in hand. This is because employees who lag behind on the performance criteria set in many of these plans are implicitly at greater risk of termination. This usually means the loss of all income from the employer. The old days when employees received a fixed salary pegged to a job title, determined through a job evaluation procedure, and with considerable employment security, are gone in most major corporations facing fierce domestic and global competition. Similarly, in the executive ranks, although total pay received has increased considerably since the mid-1980s, at least half of it on average now comes in the form of variable compensation paid through a myriad of bonus programs and stock-based plans (Gomez-Mejia & Wiseman, 1997). Boards of directors have also become far more vigilant in replacing CEOs when performance targets are not met ("Executive Compensation Scoreboard," 1998).

Surprisingly, most of the practitioner and scholarly literature on compensation does not devote much effort to understanding how pay at risk affects employee behavior or decisions. However, there is a parallel literature on risk that is almost totally ignored by compensation scholars and that can shed light on these issues. This chapter attempts to enhance our understanding of the causes and consequences of compensation risk by learning from the broader literature on risk across a variety of fields.

Agency Theory and Compensation Risk

The best-developed conceptual treatment of risk in compensation comes from agency theory, although as argued later, agency notions of risk still remain oversimplified and underdefined. Though most of the agency research concerns top executives, the essential logic of agency theory has also been used in other contexts such as gain-sharing (Welbourne & Gomez-Mejia, 1995), faculty pay (Gomez-Mejia & Balkin, 1992), and sales (Eisenhardt, 1988). To simplify our discussion, we will focus on top executives, first describing agency views on risk and then showing how the risk literature should be incorporated into the study of compensation.

Agency theory is concerned with situations where principals (such as shareholders) hire agents (individuals who perform services on the principals' behalf). The typical agency model assumes that agents are risk-averse, that agents have self-interests, and that those interests may differ from the interests of the principal. This gives rise to an agency problem because the agent is tempted to take advantage of the principal. This is referred to as *moral hazard.* Since the agent is assumed to have interests that differ from the interests of the principal, the principal may not know if the agent has acted consistently with the principal's interests in mind. This is particularly true when tasks are nonprogrammable, information asymmetries are great, and it is costly or difficult for monitors to observe actual agent behavior (as in the case of top executives).

To reduce moral hazard, the principal transfers risk to the agents by linking the agents' pay (in the form of, say, bonuses) to outcomes (such as profits) that are important to the principal. This arrangement, designed to create a common fate between agent and principal through risk sharing, is formally referred to as *in-*

centive alignment in agency theory. A paradox in agency theory, however, is that the principal cannot transfer too much risk to the agent (who is assumed to be risk-averse) because the agent would then make overly conservative decisions that might hurt the principal. For instance, an executive's job security and pay are not protected by diversification in the same way as most stockholders' portfolios are. To maintain their standard of living, executives cannot usually absorb the loss of earnings to the extent that stockholders can afford fluctuations in income. Management's only method of spreading its own personal risk is through diversifying various projects or business units within the firm or through acquisitions, even though these decisions may lead to lower returns to shareholders. That is, incentive alignment may both overcome individual risk aversion (by creating a common fate between principal and agent) and make it worse (by shifting too much risk to the agent).

This basic argument about the influence of compensation design on agent behavior demonstrates the critical importance of risk to compensation design. Yet definitions of key concepts of risk in compensation, such as "risk bearing" and "risk preferences," are surprisingly few. For example, despite the central role of risk bearing in their study of executive compensation, Beatty and Zajac (1994) provide no explicit definition of the term. Indeed, our own search through organizational studies of compensation produced almost no explicit definitions of risk bearing beyond implicit assumptions that variability of compensation (compensation risk) provides a reasonable proxy for agent risk (see David, Kochhar, & Levitas, 1998; Gray & Cannella, 1997).

Following our discussion of agency theory, we see two primary roles for risk in compensation design. First, agents and principals each bear some risk in the agency relation. Principals bear investment risk (the risk associated with their capital investment), while agents bear employment risk (the risk associated with employment). If agents are successful at allocating the principals' capital among various strategic options (adding capacity, developing new products, and so on), principals receive the residual wealth generated from those allocations. Principals incur *investment risk* from the possibility that their investment will be lost (due to insolvency) or when returns on their investment fail to compensate for this risk. Principals may reduce this risk by diversifying wealth through a portfolio of investments (Sharpe, 1964). This risk reduction technique allows principals to be risk-neutral in their preferences for any one investment.

Agent risk bearing also reflects threats to personal wealth. This has generally included employment risk and compensation risk. *Employment risk* represents the possibility that one's employment will be terminated either due to unsatisfactory performance or insolvency of the business. Traditionally, *compensation risk* is viewed as the potential variability of future compensation and is generally measured as the proportion of variable pay or performance-contingent pay within the total compensation scheme (see, for example, David et al., 1998; Finkelstein & Boyd, 1998; Sanders & Carpenter, 1998). Unlike the principals' investment risk, an agent's employment and compensation risks are not diversifiable. This leads many to assume that agents are generally risk-averse in their decisions on behalf of the firm.

Differences in the source and degree of risk borne by each party has led to considerable interest in issues of risk sharing between principals and agents and the effects of risk bearing on agent risk preferences. Differences in their respective abilities to diversify risk results in differences in risk bearing that are argued to affect differentially their respective risk preferences (which are key to residual creation). Differences in risk preferences resulting from differences in risk bearing have led to considerable importance being placed on the sharing of risk between agents and principals. Primarily, this attention has concerned how much risk principals should transfer to agents in order to align the agent's risk preferences with those of the principal (Beatty & Zajac, 1994; Coffee, 1988).

Our major criticisms of this argument are that little attention has been given to whether agents (or principals for that matter) perceive the risk they purportedly bear and whether risk preferences are as static and uniform as generally assumed. Although most scholars have relied on objective measures of variability (such as pay mix) to capture agent risk bearing, it is not at all clear that agents themselves equate this variability with personal risk bearing. If, as we suspect, they do not, we must reconsider models of compensation where risk bearing plays a critical role in determining agent risk preferences. Specifically, we must revise our conceptualization and measurement of compensation risk to reflect agent perceptions of risk bearing. The best place to begin looking for guidance in this effort is the literature on risk perception. Further-more, examining risk bearing through the lens of risk perception should also help us improve our understanding of risk shifting and risk sharing in compensation design since these concepts are sub-sumed within risk bearing. Ultimately, this examination helps us understand more clearly how the allocation of risk through com-pensation design influences agent behavior.

Recent research into choice behavior under uncertainty ques-tions the descriptive validity of agency theory's assumption con-cerning risk. For example, some research into decision making indicates that risk preferences vary with other factors such as cur-rent wealth, goal attainment, and prospects for changes to wealth (Currim & Sarin, 1989; Kahneman & Tversky, 1979; Lattimore, Baker, & Witte, 1992; Loehman, 1998; Smidts, 1997; Tversky & Fox, 1995; Weber & Milliman, 1997; Wu & Gonzalez, 1996). This re-search has suggested entirely different risk preference functions from those generally underlying models of compensation. These new risk preference functions allow for observed inconsistencies in preference ordering across decision contexts, as well as for observed *risk seeking* (accepting options where the risk is not fully compen-sated). Indeed, Wiseman and Gomez-Mejia (1997) have argued that relaxing restrictive notions of agent risk preferences and replacing assumptions of a risk-averse utility function with an asymmetric pref-erence function, suggested by Kahneman and Tversky (1979), pro-duces quite different predictions regarding the influence of compensation design on executive choice behavior (see also Wise-man & Gomez-Mejia, 1998).

Providing a clearer understanding of just what risk is, how it is perceived, and how to capture agent risk preferences can only lead to improved predictions regarding compensation. We next focus on what is meant by risk. The final portion of the chapter reviews research and theory regarding subjective aspects of risk, including risk perceptions and risk preferences. Each discussion suggests im-plications for research and theorizing in compensation design.

What Is Risk?

As noted, the concepts of risk preferences and risk bearing are cru-cial elements in compensation design. Key to analyzing these ele-ments is an understanding of what is meant by the core concept "risk." Defining risk, however, is not a trivial task, for there are a variety of conceptualizations and numerous measures contending for acceptance (for example, Brehmer, 1987; Hale, 1987; Vlek & Stallen, 1981). Various reviews of risk have appeared over the years in management (Baird & Thomas, 1990), marketing (Aaker & Jacobson, 1990), psychology (Brehmer, 1987; Fischhoff, 1992; Vlek & Stallen, 1981), and economics (Heijdra, 1988; Machina, 1987). An examination of these reviews finds both convergence and divergence in how to think about and measure risk.

The concept of risk is traceable back to Pascal, who developed the notion of probability to resolve problems involving gambles, and was later expanded on by Bernoulli (Bernstein, 1996). It is on this legacy that our present-day ideas of risk are based. Specifically, development of probability theory turned an ambiguous unknowable future determined solely by fate into a knowable but "risky" future resting on probabilistic predictions about potential outcomes. This was done by allowing for reliable predictions about gambling outcomes (and later generalized to all future events) based on prior experience with those outcomes. More significant, probability theory created confidence in these predictions in that it allowed for *ex ante* estimates of the degree of reliability in these predictions. Risk was therefore distinguished from *ambiguity*,[1] in which probabilities are unknown (Ellsberg, 1961; Johnson, Hershey, Meszaros, & Kunreuther, 1993; Tversky & Fox, 1995), by the use of probabilities derived from frequencies of historical events to predict future occurrences of those events. Our modern views of risk appear firmly rooted in probability theory, and hence our measures of risk have generally rested on examinations of choices between gambles exhibiting specific probability distributions (Luce & Raiffa, 1957; Tversky & Fox, 1995; Yates & Stone, 1992).

Since that early definition of risk, a substantial amount of scholarship has considered the meaning and measurement of risk. For example, Vlek and Stallen (1981) identified at least six definitions of risk in the literature (see also Hale, 1987):

- The probability of loss
- The size of the possible loss
- The function (normally the product) of probability and size of loss

- The variance of the probability distribution of all possible consequences of a course of action
- The semivariance of the distribution of all negative consequences (losses) only, with respect to some adopted reference value
- A weighted linear combination of the variance of and the expected value of the distribution of all possible consequences

In our view, these definitions contain three basic elements (variously measured) that appear either alone or in combination: total variability across all outcomes (gain or loss), probability of loss, and magnitude of loss. Since probability of loss (semivariance) represents a subset of total variability (variance), definitions of risk generally choose one or the other of these in defining and measuring risk, depending on whether they assume decision makers consider overall uncertainty or only downside outcomes when gauging the risk of a decision (Markowitz, 1952).

The closest parallel in the compensation literature to the six elements of risk may be found in Tosi and Gomez-Mejia (1989), who identify three dimensions of pay risk:

- *Variability.* The degree of risk is lower when the pay package is designed so that a substantial portion of income is received on a stable, relatively fixed, predictable basis over time with minimum variance.
- *Downside risk.* The amount of risk is lower when the pay package has a downside hedge against poor performance. For example, there may be a minor or no penalty contingent on lower values of the performance indicators (for example, return on equity). This means that although an individual's pay may go up considerably when performance improves, it is unlikely to go down if performance declines.
- *Uncertainty.* Uncertainty (and therefore risk) in pay increases as the number of unforeseen and uncontrollable events affecting the payoff criteria increase.

Although all definitions of risk recognize the role of loss, a debate has arisen about the measurement of risk. This debate concerns the use of variance measures reflecting overall uncertainty versus measures that capture only downside potential. For example, building on the capital asset pricing model (CAPM) (Sharpe, 1964; Lintner, 1965), finance scholars continue to decompose the total variance in firm returns into two types of risk known as "systematic" (market) and "unsystematic" (business) risk (Libby & Fishburn, 1977). The importance of this debate extends beyond simple measurement issues to the underlying assumptions about agent risk preferences that are at the heart of agency-based models of compensation. Put another way, the debate can be characterized as a concern for parsimony against a concern for external validity. Thus while most economists and compensation researchers continue to use parsimonious measures rooted in overall variance, psychologists and a growing number of organizational scholars favor downside measures on the basis of external validity.

Use of variance measures of risk can be traced to Markowitz (1952), who replaced semivariance with total variance in a model of expected utility due to the mathematical intractability of using semivariance. Thus although Markowitz (1987) recognized that decision makers may be more concerned with potential loss than with uncertainty, parsimony led him to use total variance. The use of variance to represent risk has persisted, leading some scholars to equate variability or uncertainty with risk. This misperception of risk is demonstrated by the use of compensation variability when measuring compensation risk (Gray & Cannella, 1997).

This confusion may be an unfortunate inheritance of Pascal's early work. As noted, Pascal developed his notion of risk from studying gambling, where the risk of a gamble was related to the dispersion of possible outcomes. Though it would seem that gambles and risky decisions are both choices involving uncertainty and loss, research by Shapira (1995) finds that managers see clear differences between the two. In Shapira's study of managerial risk taking, managers reported that due to skill and the presence of control over consequences, risky decisions differ from gambling, where consequences are determined purely by probability.

Challenging the risk-as-variance view are scholars in management and psychology who have noted that decision makers are generally more sensitive to potential loss than to uncertainty when considering the riskiness of a decision (Duncan, 1972; Slovic, 1962; Slovic, Fischhoff, & Lichtenstein, 1980, 1985, 1986; Vlek & Stallen,

1981). That is, decision makers are more concerned with the probability of loss than they are with the entire dispersion of losses and gains (Fishburn, 1982, 1984; Sarin, 1987). Indeed, many do not consider variability in outcomes at all relevant to determinations of decision risk (Baird & Thomas, 1990; Fishburn, 1984; Mac-Crimmon & Wehrung, 1986; March & Shapira, 1987; Sarasvathy, Simon, & Lave, 1998; Shapira, 1995).

Others criticize variance measures on conceptual grounds for including positive payoffs (gains), which, they contend, may not reflect decision makers' concerns about risk. For example, Yates and Stone (1992) argue that operationalizing risk as total variance leads to a positive skew or bias in the actual representation of risk. This bias arises when the measure includes alternatives that are expected to yield positive results and actually do. At the extreme, this would include scenarios where decision makers choose among only "winning" or beneficial alternatives. Clearly, in such cases, the potential for net losses is neither expected nor realized, regardless of the choice made. The argument questions whether choices involving only gains are truly viewed as "risky" by decision makers.[2] For example, using the three dimensions of compensation risk advanced by Tosi and Gomez-Mejia (1989), if there is only a potential for gains but no pay penalty contingent on lower values of the performance indicators, pay may not be seen as risky by decision makers.

Although some research streams continue to use variance in measures of risk, most definitions now conceptualize risk as hazard or loss (Fishburn, 1982, 1984; Sarin, 1987; Weber & Milliman, 1997). One advantage of this view is that it corresponds more closely to common conceptualizations of risk (one dictionary definition is "the chance of injury, damage, or loss; a hazard"), as well as empirical evidence about how decision makers actually perceive risk (Fishburn, 1984; Shapira, 1995). For compensation research, this suggests that measures of compensation risk and risk bearing should focus on potential losses of wealth (that is, the probability and magnitude of loss) rather than simple variability in compensation.

Indeed, the growing support for viewing risk as loss raises important questions about the external and descriptive validity of risk measures in compensation research that attempt to capture variability in compensation (for example, the proportion of bonuses and long-term income in the pay mix). Although widely used, these measures may be capturing a form of uncertainty that is of less concern to executives than measures focusing on potential losses of wealth.[3] If the widespread use of certain measures can affect how we conceive of risk, one wonders how compensation theory has been driven by objective measures of risk having questionable external validity. In other words, have we let convenient measures of risk lead our theory development? If so, might this not account for some problems in settling issues about the effects of compensation design on executive behavior?

This question leads us to suggest that future compensation research examine how executives view compensation, particularly the variability of their compensation, where variability occurs among generally positive outcomes. For example, if we view risk as loss, it would seem that whether some portions of compensation are viewed as a reward or an entitlement would have very different effects on risk bearing. We'll say more on this later when we discuss the concepts of utility and value that we believe lie at the heart of understanding risk.

Subjective Risk

The foregoing discussion took a primarily objective view of risk, in which risk is the consequence of the choice characteristics the decision maker faces, such as probability and magnitude of loss. Here we take a subjective view by examining risk perception and risk preferences.

Considering that most of the early research on compensation came from psychology rather than economics, it is surprising how little attention has been paid to the subjective assessment of pay risk. For instance, equity and expectancy models (which represent traditional underpinnings of compensation as an academic subfield) regard subjectivity as a critical factor in determining how each employee reacts to the pay system. Equity theory argues that employee behaviors such as effort and turnover depend on perceived fairness of the pay system, with employees subjectively exchanging a set of inputs or contributions (education, experience, long-term commitment, and so on) for a set of outcomes (pay, promotion, prestige, and the like). Yet perceptions of pay risk are largely ignored in both the conceptual and empirical compensation literature.

As noted earlier, a key debate in compensation scholarship regards the possible effects of certain compensation designs on agent risk bearing (Beatty & Zajac, 1994). Underlying this debate is an implied assumption that the objective risk characteristics of compensation design are perceived by the agent and therefore lead to agent risk bearing. Challenging this assumption is the considerable weight of empirical evidence that finds consistent and systematic differences between subjectively determined risk and objectively derived measures of risk, which appear to arise from judgmental biases in the subjective assessment of risk (Slovic, 1987; Slovic, Fischhoff, & Lichtenstein, 1982). In short, *risk perception* concerns subjective assessments of the riskiness of an alternative. Clearly, understanding risk perception should be useful to an analytical treatment of compensation risk bearing.

Risk Perception

One could argue that people do not actually perceive risks directly but instead experience "feelings" of risk based on individual assessments that combine intuitive estimates and those generated by objective means. For example, Brehmer (1987, p. 26) asserts that "it makes little or no sense to ask whether risk is correctly perceived"; rather, we should only be concerned with the comparison of the intuitive and objective estimates. This suggests that a decision maker's consideration of risk is colored by individual (that is, subjective) assessments of the decision context in addition to whatever objective information may be available.

Studies of risk perception have identified a variety of factors that appear to influence individual perceptions of riskiness. These factors include acuteness (immediacy of hazard), volition (does the potential victim have a choice?), locus of control (who controls the potential for hazard?), beneficiary (is the potential victim also the potential beneficiary of the risk?), and plausibility (how complex are the events leading to hazard?) (see Hale, 1987).

Holtgrave and Weber (1993), in particular, postulate a model of perceived risk that is a linear function of five dimensions: probability of loss, probability of gain or benefit, probability of status quo, expected value of the loss, and expected value of the gain or benefit. Some dimensions exhibit a positive influence on risk (value and probability of loss), while others exhibit a negative influence on risk assessment (probability of gain and status quo).

Although some evidence supports this model (Keller, Sarin, & Weber, 1986; Yates & Stone, 1992), other evidence finds that only two dimensions, probability and magnitude of loss, explain most of the variance in subjective estimates of risk. These two dimensions correspond roughly to research by Slovic, Fischhoff, and Lichtenstein (1984, 1986), who find that subjective risk tends to reflect two dimensions: *dread,* or degree of consequences of the event, and *observability,* or degree to which the risk is known (see also Palmer, 1996). Thus risk perception would seem to rest primarily on the estimates of the size and probability of loss rather than on some general uncertainty about possible outcomes. However, the accuracy of these estimates has been called into question.

Considerable empirical evidence supports the existence of differences between subjective assessments of risk and objective characteristics of decisions and their outcomes (Slovic, 1987), which may account for observed suboptimal choices in studies of decision making (Neumann & Politser, 1992). In particular, subjective estimates of the likelihood of probabilistic events consistently deviate from objectively derived probabilities (Brehmer, 1987; Slovic et al., 1984; Tversky & Fox, 1995), and these differences cannot be explained by differences in experience with the events (Brehmer, 1987). In general, differences between subjective and objective risk measures appear to arise from a variety of judgmental biases, including availability bias (Bach, 1973; Fischhoff, Slovic, & Lichtenstein, 1978; Lichtenstein, Slovic, Fischhoff, Layman, & Coombs, 1978; Tversky & Kahneman, 1973, 1974), overconfidence (Fischhoff, Slovic, & Lichtenstein, 1977; Fischhoff, Slovic, Lichtenstein, Read, & Coombs, 1978), anchoring (Fischhoff & MacGregor, 1980; Poulton, 1968; Tversky & Kahneman, 1974), framing effects (Bottom, 1990; Schurr, 1987; Tversky & Kahneman, 1981; Weber & Bottom, 1989; Weber & Milliman, 1997), and escalation of commitment (Tosi, Katz, & Gomez-Mejia, 1997).

For compensation research, formal acknowledgment of judgmental biases in models of compensation risk is largely unexplored. For example, it is not at all clear that simply because more variable pay is added to a compensation design, agents perceive greater risk to future wealth. Further, few studies actively distinguish between *layering*, or adding new variable pay to an existing compensation scheme, and *restructuring* compensation, whereby variable pay replaces some portion of base pay in an existing scheme. How agents perceive and respond to these two different changes in compensation design would seem key to predicting agent responses to compensation redesign.

Beyond the judgmental biases that can affect subjective estimates of objective probability, decision makers appear to exhibit preference behaviors that indicate that they subjectively weight known objective probabilities. That is, even when objective probabilities are known, decision makers differentially weight these probabilities such that low probabilities are consistently overweighted and relatively higher probabilities are generally underweighted (Kahneman & Tversky, 1979; Lattimore et al., 1992; Tversky & Fox, 1995). This *over-under weighting bias* extends Allais's paradox (Allais, 1979), which holds that certain outcomes (where the probability is 100 percent) are overvalued in relation to less certain outcomes (where probability is less than 100 percent). Further, incorporating this bias into expected utility models of risk preferences appears to improve the descriptive power of models of decision-maker utility (Camerer & Ho, 1994; Currim & Sarin, 1989; Lattimore et al., 1992; Loehman, 1998; Neumann & Politser, 1992; Wu & Gonzalez, 1996).

This relatively unexplored area in compensation promises to hold significant implications for compensation design. Clearly, different forms of compensation have different probabilities of award. Base pay or salary would seem to have a relatively high probability, possibly approaching certainty in the mind of the agent, whereas some forms of variable pay clearly have a lower probability of award. Given an over-under weighting bias, we must ask how decision makers view different forms of compensation.[4] To our knowledge, little research has examined how this particular bias might affect preferences for (and ultimately treatment of) various forms of compensation (one exception is Strahilevitz, 1992). One path for future research, therefore, examines how different forms of compensation are treated and perceived.

Risk Perception and Its Implication for Compensation

Whether we view risk broadly as uncertainty or narrowly as potential for loss can have very important implications for how we conceive of and design compensation. For example, viewing risk as variability in outcomes leads us to measure agent risk bearing through the degree of volatility in the overall compensation design. Thus adding variable pay awards with no downside loss potential (a common practice in industry) is assumed to increase agent risk bearing since it increases the variability of compensation over time. However, it isn't clear that uncertainty in positive payoffs is truly relevant to agent perceptions of risk.

In the work of Sitkin and Pablo (1992), risk perceptions are a combination of labeling of risky situations, estimating the probability and controllability of the inherent risks, and confidence in those estimates. This definition is a synthesis of earlier work and would seem to reflect the implied nature of risk bearing found in most compensation models. That is, risk bearing reflects the degree of uncertainty regarding agent wealth.

It seems trivial to suggest that agents must perceive risk to be affected by it, yet the literature on risk bearing appears to ignore this important element. Instead it views risk bearing as a function of the contract and assumes that agents universally perceive and react to the uncertainty created in the contract. If agent perceptions of risk depart from implicit assumptions of what risk represents to agents and how it is created, alternative predictions about how compensation design influences risk bearing are possible. Clearly, if perceived risk departs systematically from objective measures of risk, models of compensation that rest on objective measures of risk must be revisited to determine how judgmental biases in agent risk assessment may affect predictions of how compensation design may influence agent risk preferences and behavior. For example, Weber and Milliman (1997) find evidence that changes in perceptions of riskiness precipitate changes in risk propensity (risk-taking behavior) without affecting more stable risk attitudes (risk preferences). Whether changes in perception account for variance in risk choices or whether risk preferences themselves are affected will be addressed shortly. For now, it seems clear that a better understanding of risk perception, and of subjective risk assessment in particular, is necessary to improve predictions of how compensation influences agent risk bearing and risk taking. Exploring perceptions of compensation and, in particular, compensation risk is an important underexamined area of research.

Risk Preferences

A second concept of interest to compensation scholars is *risk preference*. Risk preferences refer to individual inclinations for or against risk. As noted earlier, agency-based compensation research has built on neoclassical assumptions that individuals are inherently risk-averse. This has led compensation scholars to assume that agents are risk-averse but principals are risk-neutral due to diversification. This risk differential between principal and agent has led to a considerable amount of research focusing on how to align agent risk preferences with those of the principal (Coffee, 1988).

In contrast, developments in behavioral economics have challenged this simplistic view of risk preferences by finding that in practice, decision makers exhibit a variety of risk preferences, including risk seeking and risk neutrality (Asch & Quandt, 1988; Lattimore et al., 1992; Smidts, 1997). Further, observed risk preferences are not necessarily consistent across choice contexts (Fagley & Miller, 1990; Highhouse & Paese, 1996; Lattimore et al., 1992; Mowen & Mowen, 1986; Smidts, 1997), due to a variety of factors, including judgmental biases and framing effects (Lopes, 1987; Tversky & Kahneman, 1981). These findings suggest that models of compensation that assume that agents are universally risk-averse may lack descriptive validity and, ultimately, prescriptive power. More important, replacing the theoretical risk-averse utility function of agency-based compensation models with a more complex empirically derived preference function can significantly alter predictions about compensation design (see Wiseman & Gomez-Mejia, 1998).

Risk preferences can mean different things to different fields. Owing to their separate traditions, economists and psychologists use the phrase somewhat differently. Psychologists, for example, view risk preferences as a character trait of being attracted to or repelled by risk. Sitkin and Pablo (1992), for example, distinguish risk preferences from *risk propensity*, which they describe as the likelihood of taking or not taking objectively defined risks in a given

choice situation. *Risk preferences,* in contrast, reflect a more enduring personality trait. Thus psychologists see an individual's propensity to take risks as the product of an enduring personality trait,
personal experience with risky choices, and perceptions of situational variables.

Whether or not risk preferences reflect an inherent personality trait is a matter of some debate (see Bromiley & Curley, 1992)
and one that goes beyond the boundaries we have set for this review. Suffice it to say, however, that few studies have examined the
role of specific personality traits on the efficacy of compensation
design (exceptions include Stewart, 1996, and Miceli, Jung, Near,
& Greenberger, 1991). For example, one of the authors recently
conducted an extensive research of the compensation literature to
find measures of individual risk propensity or risk preferences and
came out almost empty-handed. The only relevant measure found
was a "willingness to take risks" scale, based on original research of
Slovic (1972), and later adaptations by Gupta and Govindarajan
(1984) and Gomez-Mejia and Balkin (1989). The latter study
found some evidence suggesting that risk propensity does matter:
employees with a low willingness to take risks are more likely to experience withdrawal cognition if they work for a firm that relies on
variable compensation. More recently, Cable and Judge (1994)
used an adapted version of the Slovic measure to examine the influence of risk aversion (among other traits) on preference for
contingent versus fixed pay. Consistent with previous findings, they
found that risk aversion correlated positively with a preference for
fixed pay.

The focus on how risk preference translates into preferences
for certain pay designs still leaves open the question of how risk
preference interacts with pay design to influence agent behavior.
Assuming that individuals vary in their risk propensity, we wonder
if compensation design (and indeed internal corporate governance in general) doesn't interact with these individual differences
to affect behavior and firm-level outcomes. For example, what happens to executive behavior and firm performance if incentives for
taking risks are provided to individuals inclined toward risk taking?
Would they take on too much risk? Would risk-averse agents facing
strong incentive pay become more or less risk-averse? Exploring

this interaction between compensation design and individual risk characteristics remains another area where behavioral scholars can make a significant contribution to compensation research.

Expected Utility and Risk Preference

Economists view risk preference as an attitude toward risk that is both endogenously determined by one's utility function and exogenously influenced by wealth considerations (in the context of executive compensation, these considerations are embedded in the principal-agent contract). Building on the expected utility framework, economists traditionally model risk preferences through a probability indifference curve $u(x)$, or utility curve, where the curvature of the function represents the risk preference of the individual (von Neumann & Morgenstern, 1947).[5] In this tradition, individuals' choices reflect the shape of their utility function. The shape of this function invokes specific preference labels of "risk-averse" (concave), "risk-neutral" (linear), or "risk-seeking" (convex). The curve itself is measured by means of lotteries[6] that do not refer to the intensity of satisfaction associated with the choice (Fishburn, 1989). Thus changes in choices of risk are modeled as changes in the utility function hypothesized to underlie the choices.

Weber and Milliman (1997) challenge the use of expected utility to model risk preferences because the expected utility model combines two factors, each of which can account for the observed curvature of the utility function: marginal value of wealth and attitude toward risk. They note that Bernoulli (1738/1954) argued for diminishing sensitivity to wealth (resulting in a concave relation between objective value and marginal value; see Figure 9.1a), and he combined this with an assumption that individuals exhibit a neutral (that is, linear) attitude toward risk (see Figure 9.1b) to explain the observed incidence of risk aversion (that is, the concave relation between value and utility; see Figure 9.1c). Conversely, von Neumann and Morgenstern (1947) assumed that individuals have a constant marginal value for wealth (a linear relation between objective value and marginal value; see Figure 9.1a) and a negative attitude toward risk (a concave relation between marginal value and utility; see Figure 9.1b) in arguing for an identical concave utility function (see Figure 9.1c).

Figure 9.1. Expected Utility Model of Risk Preference.

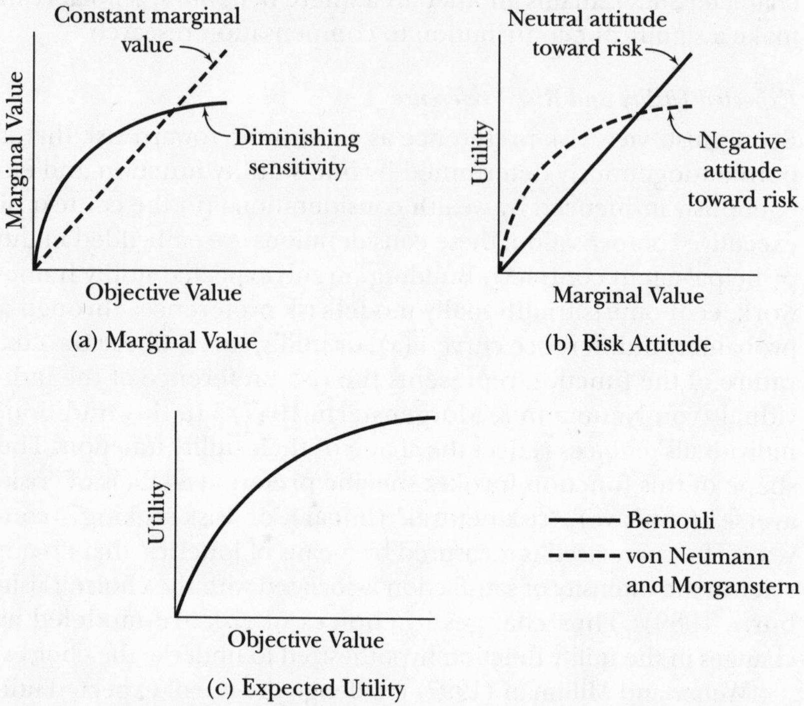

(a) Marginal Value

(b) Risk Attitude

(c) Expected Utility

——— Bernouli

- - - - von Neumann and Morganstern

Source: Reprinted by permission, E. U. Weber and R. A. Milliman, "Perceived risk attitudes: Relating risk perception to risky choice." *Management Science,* Vol. 43, p. 127. Copyright 1997, the Institute for Operations Research and the Management Sciences (INFORMS), 901 Elkridge Landing Road, Suite 400, Linthicum, Maryland 21090–2909 USA.

In this sense, traditional utility models of risk preferences are underspecified, in that it is not clear whether the preference is due to diminishing sensitivity to value or to a negative attitude toward risk. Knowing the underlying cause of risk preferences would seem especially important to designers of compensation schemes, for a given compensation scheme would produce very different results across the two factors.

An extension of the traditional expected value model that attempts to resolve this underspecification problem is the *risk-return trade-off* or *risk value* model currently used in finance as a basis for the CAPM (Bell, 1995; Sarin & Weber, 1993). Here risk preferences are captured through a risk-return framework where (1) expected value is measured separately from risk through "relative risk attitude" (Dyer & Sarin, 1982; Sarin & Weber, 1993), (2) greater value and lower risk are assumed to be more desirable, and (3) an individual's preference for risk is assumed to determine his or her risk-value trade-off (Weber & Milliman, 1997).

Essentially, this framework gives explicit attention to the valuation function of Bernoulli so that one's risk attitude can be determined separately. Risk preference is thus viewed as the effect of diminishing marginal value $v(x)$ plus one's risk attitude. The utility function then becomes a transformation of the strength of preference function: $u(x) = f(v(x))$ and the curvature of $u(x)$ that has traditionally been used to reflect risk attitude. This model gives explicit attention to the functional relationship between $v(x)$ and $u(x)$ (Bell, 1981; Bell & Raiffa, 1982; Sinn, 1985; Smidts, 1997).

Although the risk-return trade-off model distinguishes between utility valuation and risk attitude, it continues to rely on the expected utility framework (see Bell, 1995; Jia & Dyer, 1996), which has been challenged as descriptively inadequate (Fishburn, 1988; Kahneman & Tversky, 1979; Luce, 1992; Shoemaker, 1982). Specifically, this model views risk as a necessary evil that must be weighed against returns in making choices. Hence it is implicitly assumed that risk aversion is an intrinsic behavior common to most decision makers (Arrow, 1965; Shoemaker, 1982).

For example, Bell (1995) characterizes risk aversion as a sense that more risk is worse, thus suggesting that risk is undesirable. In support, he finds that risk aversion is a decreasing function of wealth. This mirrors the view expressed in his earlier work, which asserts that people have a "preference for less uncertainty in a gamble for any given expected value" (Bell, 1988, p. 1416).

However, as will be noted, considerable evidence supports a contrary view that decision makers at least occasionally exhibit risk-loving or risk-seeking behavior (Lattimore et al., 1992; Loehman, 1998; Mowen & Mowen, 1986). Although "risk loving" (Asch & Quandt, 1988) can be incorporated into risk-return models by recognizing a utility of risk (such as thrill seeking), the research on choice behavior suggests that the real explanation for observed risk-seeking choices lies elsewhere.

Further, risk-return models continue to view risk as uncertainty. Building on Markowitz (1952, 1987), these models continue to rely on variance measures of the probability distribution of outcomes to represent risk (Ruefli, La Cugna, & Collins, 1996). By focusing on uncertainty without regard to whether outcomes represent gains or losses, the models continue to lack external validity, since they contradict empirical evidence indicating that decision makers are more concerned with threats to wealth (losses) than to overall uncertainty regarding future wealth (possible gains and losses). Thus models that continue to equate risk preferences with preferences for or against uncertainty will fail to reflect actual choice behavior.

In sum, neither the traditional expected utility model nor the risk-return trade-off model of risk preference completely describes observed choice behavior (Luce, 1988). It is not surprising, therefore, that agency-based models of compensation that rely on them have failed to produce clear and unambiguous predictions of executive behavior.

Behavioral Economics and Risk Preferences

Challenging the expected utility notions of choice behavior under risk is a newly developing field called *economic psychology* or *behavioral economics* (Hey, 1988; Lea, Webley, & Young, 1992; Lewis, 1988). Behavioral economics builds on the rigid analytical-theoretical traditions of economics while using the empirical traditions of psychology to develop more descriptively accurate models of economic behavior (Hey, 1988; Lewis, 1988). In this tradition, Tversky and Kahneman (1991) developed a comprehensive prospect theory model of risk preferences. Their model consists of three elements: a value function $v(x)$ corresponding to a utility function, a decision-weighting function p corresponding to probability estimates of outcomes, and an editing rule. The resulting preference function for the value of option x becomes $v(x)(p)$.

The value function $v(x)$ exhibits three characteristics: it defines values relative to a reference point of wealth, it assumes that gains and losses to wealth diminish in value, and the value of losses is greater than equivalent gains. The characteristics of this function that distinguish it from traditional utility functions are, first, that actual levels of wealth do not matter. This implies that the reference point instantaneously adjusts with the acquisition of wealth.

This is known as *instant endowment* (Thaler, 1980). Second, decision makers are assumed to be *loss-averse* in that they are more sensitive to losses than to gains. Finally, the diminishing sensitivity to value suggests that individuals are more sensitive to adjustments of wealth near the reference point.

The resulting preference function differs from normal expected utility models in that it displays an S shape (see Figure 9.2) with concavity in the area of gains and convexity in the area of losses around a central reference point of current wealth (Kahneman & Tversky, 1979). Further, the function is also steeper in the realm of losses than in the realm of gains to reflect the overvaluation of losses relative to gains. Finally, the location of the reference point distinguishing gains from losses adjusts with wealth, experience, and possibly aspirations (Lant, 1992). This functional form (see Figure 9.2) challenges the normative view of risk preferences as decreasingly risk-averse with wealth (Bell, 1995). Indeed, direct comparisons between the predictive accuracy of prospect theory and various expected utility models finds strong support for prospect theory in both laboratory (Tversky & Kahneman, 1985) and field studies (Currim & Sarin, 1989; Loehman, 1998).

The second element, known as the decision-weighting function *p*, replaces the probability estimates of subjective expected utility (Savage, 1954). Building on the certainty effect of Allais (1979), Tversky and colleagues (Kahneman & Tversky, 1979; Tversky & Fox, 1995; Tversky & Wakker, 1995) developed a model of probability that recognizes the overweighting of certainty relative to less

Figure 9.2. Valuation Function.

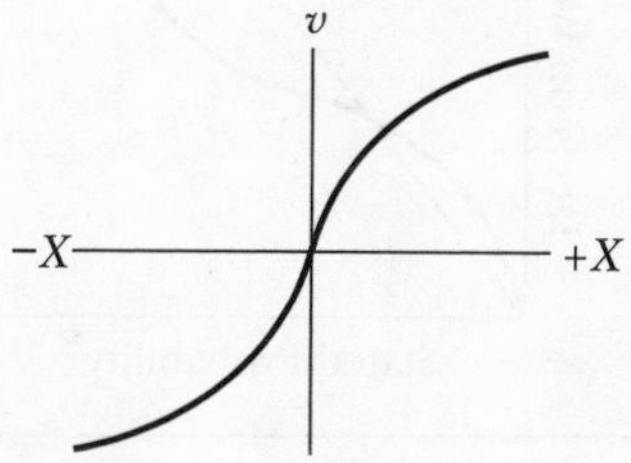

Source: Kahneman and Tversky (1979). © Econometric Society. Used with permission.

than certain probabilities. That is, they found that individuals preferred certainty over slightly less certain payoffs of otherwise equal value but were indifferent between two equivalent gambles with a similar difference between their respective probabilities.

Typically, the weighting function (see Figure 9.3) found in studies of risk choice exhibits steep concavity near zero probability and steep convexity near certainty (Lattimore et al., 1992; Tverksy & Fox, 1995; Wu & Gonzalez, 1996). This form has been formally developed to show how it contributes toward explaining risk preferences (Tversky & Wakker, 1995) and in particular how it explains observed violations of expected utility predictions regarding choice behavior (Currim & Sarin, 1989; Heijdra, 1988; Luce, 1990, 1992; Wakker & Tversky, 1993).

Finally, the "editing rule" or framing effect (Tversky & Kahneman, 1981) describes how decision makers edit choices down to a simple choice between options framed as either gains or losses. Further, depending on the frame of reference as either gain or loss, decision makers have demonstrated inconsistent preferences across equivalent choice situations. That is, decision makers exhibit risk aversion when facing a choice between options framed as gains but exhibit risk seeking when facing a choice between identical options framed as losses (Fagley & Miller, 1990; Frisch, 1993; Highhouse & Paese, 1996; Kahneman & Tversky, 1979; Mowen & Mowen, 1986).

Figure 9.3. Decision-Weighting Function.

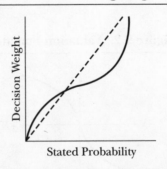

Stated Probability

Source: Tversky and Fox, 1995. © 1995 by the American Psychological Association. Reprinted with permission.

The importance of this model of risk preference can be seen when modeling choice behavior under uncertainty. Specifically, several studies have found that decision makers appear to accept greater uncertainty in order to avoid loss, which contradicts traditional assumptions of risk aversion whereby decision makers are assumed to accept lower returns in order to avoid uncertainty. In a classic study conducted by Kahneman and Tversky (1979) and repeated in various forms and settings (see Highhouse & Paese, 1996; Mowen & Mowen, 1986), individuals were given the choice between two options:

If you take option A, you will make $200.

If you take option B, you have a 1 in 3 chance of getting $600 and a 2 in 3 chance of getting nothing.

Most people prefer the certain $200 over the chance of getting $600 even though, in economic terms, the two options have an equivalent value $(1/3 \times \$600 + 2/3 \times \$0 = \$200)$. In contrast, when this same problem is framed in terms of losses, research finds that individuals prefer option B over option A; for example:

If you take option A, you will lose $200.

If you take option B, you will have a 1 in 3 chance of losing $600 and a 2 in 3 chance of not losing anything.

As with the previous choice, the economic value of each option is the same (–$200). However, when framed in the negative (in terms of loss), individuals generally prefer option B over option A because it provides an opportunity to avoid the loss altogether. This concept is commonly referred to as *loss aversion* and is distinguished form risk aversion, whereby people are thought to prefer options with lower uncertainty when the outcomes of each option are economically equivalent. Risk-averse people should prefer option A in both cases because the options have the same economic value but option A is less uncertain (less risky). If this finding extends to compensation, important implications arise.

Implications from Behavioral Models of Risk Preference for Compensation

Although considerable research supports the preference function (and resulting choice behavior) we have identified, there is still some question about both the external validity of these findings (Heijdra, 1988) and the application of this research to the study of compensation. For example, a key element of prospect theory concerns the distinction between loss and gain. This raises questions about what constitutes loss in the context of compensation design.

Because sanctions are an infrequent element of compensation, one must ask where loss occurs. That is, we must ask whether loss occurs solely in terms of opportunity costs or whether actual wealth, real or perceived, is at stake as well. Our distinction between opportunity costs and perceived wealth is itself open to question since in our view, perceived wealth represents anticipated wealth for which the property rights have yet to be transferred to the agent. Thus before we can fully incorporate behavioral views of risk preferences into models of compensation, we must ask several questions about how loss and future wealth are perceived. In short, what constitutes loss in compensation? Further, how does compensation differ from the context normally used in modeling loss-averse risk preferences?

One approach to dealing with this question recognizes a distinction between context and framing. In this view, compensation is recognized in a gain context because accumulated wealth from past compensation is not threatened in the same manner that investors' wealth is at risk from firm failure. That is, money that has already been earned (and presumably spent or saved) is under no perceptible threat should the employee lose his or her job or should the employer fail. Thus choices affecting future compensation would appear to occur within the realm of gains such that choices occur between various nonnegative outcomes (including zero) differing in risk and return potential.[7]

However, a gain context can also be framed as loss, depending on how problems are phrased (Highhouse & Paese, 1996). That is, we can frame pay around either the minimum (such as base salary) or the maximum (bonus and salary) possible outcomes. For example, pay outcomes can be viewed in relation to minimum pay, as in thinking, "Under this alternative, I am likely to earn 20 percent bonus beyond base," or in relation to maximum pay potential: "Under this alternative, I am likely to lose 20 percent of the bonus award." The former view frames pay as gain while the latter frames it as loss, depending on whether the reference point is associated with base pay or total compensation. Thus the framing effect corresponds to shifts in the location of one's reference point for judging outcomes and appears related to an anchoring bias. That is, depending on the location of one's reference point, various outcomes may appear as potential losses or gains and ultimately color one's judgment of potential risk. Although this framing effect has been demonstrated in several settings, it has not received much attention in compensation research.

One exception is the behavioral agency model of compensation developed by Wiseman and Gomez-Mejia (1997). Their model extends reference-dependent framing to compensation and results in several predictions about the effects of stock options on executive behavior that challenge current beliefs about the nature and role of this form of compensation. Their argument is that executives count relatively certain forms of future income, such as base salary, in their calculations of personal wealth. Thus base salary may be analogous to an annuity that pays a fixed amount (which may grow with inflation) on into retirement. Anything that threatens this future income stream is considered a threat of loss.

By contrast, forms of future income that are highly uncertain, such as stock options and highly variable cash bonuses, are probably not counted. Therefore, actions that result in receiving this type of compensation are not viewed as "risky." This is not to say that risk for the executive does not arise but rather that risk occurs as threats to employment arising from the uncertainty surrounding the pursuit of variable compensation. If to gain variable pay, the executive must pursue projects that have both large upside and downside potential (the project may fail and create losses for the firm), and if project failure increases employment risk, executives will incur risk from the *pursuit but not the existence* of variable pay. Since the costs of failed risk attempts are more observable than the opportunity costs from risk aversion, agents are clearly better off being more risk-averse.

This distinction between the roles that variable pay may play in agent risk has not been acknowledged or explored in compensation research. One implication from acknowledging this distinction is that if executives count future employment and thus future salary and possibly even future earning potential in their calculations of personal wealth, they must either have that pay secured through things like golden parachutes or be compensated for any risk to these forms of pay that result from pursuing other, variable pay awards.[8]

One way of compensating for the risk to counted wealth is to offer huge returns on variable pay awards if the pursuit of those awards pays off. Therefore, by extension, we should stop worrying about whether executives are getting too much pay in the form of stock options or bonus awards and should instead be increasing this portion of the compensation package. If the objective of compensation is to motivate executives to take risks on behalf of shareholders, the payoffs from successful investments must compensate for the risk to the executives' perceived personal wealth. This means that the payoffs must be large enough to induce an executive to risk losing all future income the executive has already counted as personal wealth (and may even have spent on a home and other long-lived assets).

Thus it is in the shareholders' interests to pay large variable pay awards to executives if they want those executives to pursue risky projects that could produce large returns. Although this prediction doesn't appear markedly different from extant arguments about executive risk bearing, Wiseman and Gomez-Mejia (1997) demonstrate that due to over-under weighting bias and reference point framing effects, the amount of variable pay necessary to compensate for perceived risk to future income is much larger than that required by traditional models of compensation.

An interesting extension of this argument concerns the effect of annual stock option awards. Using the same logic as before, executives probably count the current value of stock options held as part of wealth. That is, some discounted value of options (defined as the difference between current stock price and exercise price) previously granted but not yet exercised are also included in perceived current wealth. Actions that threaten this value by lowering stock prices in the future when the executive wishes to exercise those options will be avoided in order to protect this portion of perceived wealth. Indeed, it is likely that as the current value of held stock options rises, executives will increasingly prefer strategies that minimize stock price fluctuations over strategies that may promise higher stock prices but also increase stock price volatility. The conclusion from these arguments is that variable pay awards, such as stock options, must increase exponentially with each succeeding award if they are to compensate for threats to current and perceived pay and thus continue to induce the type of risk-taking behavior shareholders desire.

An important implication from this prescription is the potentially harmful effects it may have on lower-level employees. One outcome of paying large amounts of variable pay to top executives is that executives will raise the overall risk exposure of the firm. Increasing the firm's risk exposure translates into greater threats to organizational survival, which would have disproportionate consequences for lower-level employees. For example, if executive risk taking increases the probabilities of downside risk for the organization, this could lead to an increased risk of downsizing. Because lower-level employees bear the brunt of downsizing initiatives, it is likely that increased risk taking by senior executives increases the risk bearing of lower-level employees. This begs the question of whether, in addition to providing higher incentives for executives to entertain more risk, firms should also compensate lower-level employees for the increased risk they may bear from this increased risk taking.

For compensation research, a variety of questions arise from recognizing the framing effects from a reference-dependent view of compensation. First, we should examine how compensation is viewed by agents. This means asking how various forms of compensation are counted in calculations of personal wealth. Do people establish implicit property rights to some forms of future income? If so, how is future income discounted, if at all? If, as we have suggested previously, risk concerns threats to what we value, then determining what is counted in perceived wealth and how it is valued would seem an important first step in reexamining our models of compensation. Simply assuming that all forms of compensation are valued equally after controlling for variability denies recent behavioral discoveries about individual risk preferences.

Further, we need to look at how the framing of compensation outcomes may influence their pursuit. This means looking at factors influencing the location of the reference point used in distinguishing between gain and loss outcomes in compensation. Is this reference point determined solely within the compensation design itself, or are other factors such as peer income or prior personal income also important? Further, if decision makers are truly more loss-averse than risk-averse, sanctions and downside outcomes take on an even more important role in compensation design than previously thought.

Clearly, there are numerous questions for compensation raised by acknowledging new assumptions about agent risk perception and preferences. It is hoped that incorporating the more descriptively accurate models of risk preferences suggested by behavioral economics research into models of compensation will result in a better understanding of compensation and ultimately improved predictions for compensation design.

Conclusion

Developing better insights on the causes and consequences of pay risk represents a major opportunity for compensation scholars. Although agency-based models have proved useful in the examination and understanding of compensation, developments in other fields challenge the simplistic assumptions about risk that underlie the agency-based approach. Indeed, we believe that it is precisely this underdevelopment of the concept of risk in compensation that has lead to ongoing and apparently irreconcilable debates over the influence of incentive alignment on agent behavior and risk bearing. It is our belief that by appealing to the new behavioral views of risk, risk perception, and risk preferences that have arisen in other fields, we can move beyond the endless debates that have hindered the advancement of research and theory in the study of compensation.

Notes

1. Although some commentators use the term *uncertainty* to refer to actions where the probabilities of consequences are unknown (see, for example, Luce & Raiffa, 1957), we prefer to define *uncertainty* as "variability or volatility in outcomes."

2. A counterargument is that opportunity costs could create a risk of "loss" in choices involving only potential gains.
3. We say "attempted" because some research suggests that actual variance in compensation as a measure of risk provides better results than measures of pay mix in models of compensation (Miller & Gomez-Mejia, 1999).
4. Some research has suggested that windfall gains are treated differently from anticipated income (Arkes, Joyner, & Stone, 1994; Henderson & Peterson, 1992; O'Curry & Lovallo, 1992; Rucker, 1984; Shefrin & Thaler, 1988). However, this research has not been convincingly extended to understand how different forms of compensation may be treated.
5. Taking a decidedly Bayesian approach, Savage (1954) proposed an extension of this framework that incorporates subjective probability estimates into a model of expected utility. *Subjective expected utility* recognizes that choices under uncertainty reflect not only maximization of utility but also incomplete information about the likelihood of events.
6. A commonly used measure is the Pratt-Arrow measure of risk attitude, $-u'(x)/u''(x)$, where u'' and u' denote the first and second derivatives of the utility function u, respectively (Arrow, 1971; Pratt, 1964).
7. Possible exceptions arise when sanctions are imposed on employees, stakeholders threaten individuals in the firm with lawsuits (as when shareholders launch litigation against senior executives), or retroactive wage and benefit concessions are possible.
8. This view parallels the *permanent income hypothesis* (PIH) (Friedman, 1957), where consumption is considered a function of expectations for future income (Lucas, 1976), which is viewed as an annuity of current financial and human wealth. In practice, however, the PIH is modeled as a martingale function of current income (Deaton, 1992). In our view, defining income is problematic because financial wealth in hand (current salary and earning assets) is not distinguished from financial wealth that is promised but not yet delivered (bonus and stock option income). It is the degree to which delivery of anticipated wealth is perceived to be at risk that we feel distinguishes between wealth that is counted and wealth that is not counted in calculations of personal wealth.

References

Aaker, D., & Jacobson, R. (1990). The risk of marketing: The roles of systematic, uncontrollable and controllable unsystematic, and downside risk. In R.A. Bettis & H. Thomas (Eds.), *Risk, strategy, and management* (pp. 137–160). Greenwich, CT: JAI Press.

Allais, M. (1979). The foundations of a positive theory of choice involving risk and a criticism of the postulates and axioms of the American School. In M. Allais & O. Hagen (Eds.), *Expected utility hypotheses and the Allais paradox*. Dordrecht, Netherlands: Reidel.

Arkes, H. R., Joyner, C. A., & Stone, E. (1994). The psychology of windfall gains. *Organizational Behavior and Human Decision Processes, 59*, 331–347.

Arrow, K. (1965). *Aspects of the theory of risk bearing*. Helsinki, Finland: Yrjo Jahssonin Saatio.

Arrow, K. (1971). *Essays in the theory of risk bearing*. Chicago: Markham.

Asch, P., & Quandt, R. (1988). Betting bias in exotic bets. *Economics Letters, 28*, 215–219.

Bach, R. (1973). Nothing by chance. *American Way, 6*, 32–38.

Baird, I., & Thomas, H. (1990). What is risk anyway? Using and measuring risk in strategic management. In R.A. Bettis & H. Thomas (Eds.), *Risk, strategy, and management* (pp. 21–52). Greenwich, CT: JAI Press.

Barkema, H. G., & Gomez-Mejia, L. R. (1998). Managerial compensation and firm performance: A general research framework. *Academy of Management Journal, 41*, 135–145.

Beatty, R. P., & Zajac, E. J. (1994). Managerial incentives, monitoring, and risk bearing: A study of executive compensation, ownership, and board structure in initial public offerings. *Administrative Science Quarterly, 39*, 313–335.

Bell, D. E. (1981). Components of risk aversion. In J. P. Brans (Ed.), *Operational research* (pp. 371–378). Amsterdam: North-Holland.

Bell, D. E. (1988). One-switch utility functions and a measure of risk. *Management Science, 34*, 1416–1424.

Bell, D. E. (1995). Risk, return, and utility. *Management Science, 41*, 23–30.

Bell, D. E., & Raiffa, H. (1982). Marginal value and intrinsic risk aversion. In H. Kunreuther (Ed.), *Risk: A seminar series* (pp. 325–349). Laxenburg, Austria: International Institute for Applied Systems Analysis.

Bernoulli, D. (1954). Specimen theoriae novae de mensura sortis. *Econometrica, 22*, 23–36. (Original work published 1738)

Bernstein, P. L. (1996). *Against the gods: The remarkable story of risk*. New York: Wiley.

Bottom, W. K. (1990). Adaptive reference points in integrative bargaining. In K. Borcherding, O. I. Larichev, & D. M. Messick (Eds.), *Contemporary issues in decision making* (pp. 472–502). Amsterdam: Elsevier.

Brehmer, B. (1987). The psychology of risk. In W. T. Singleton & J. Hovden (Eds.), *Risk and decisions* (pp. 25–39). New York: Wiley.

Bromiley, P., & Curley, S. P. (1992). Individual differences in risk taking. In J. F. Yates (Ed.), *Risk-taking behavior* (pp. 87–132). New York: Wiley.

Cable, D. M., & Judge, T. A. (1994). Pay preferences and job search decisions: A person-organization fit perspective. *Personnel Psychology, 47,* 317–348.

Camerer, C., & Ho, T. (1994). Violations of the betweenness axiom and nonlinearity in probability. *Journal of Risk and Uncertainty, 8,* 167–196.

Coffee, J. C. (1988). Shareholder versus managers: The strain in the corporate web. In J. C. Coffee, L. Lowenstein, & S. Rose-Acherman (Eds.), *Knights, raiders, targets* (pp. 40–62). New York: Oxford University Press.

Currim, I., & Sarin, R. K. (1989). Prospect versus utility. *Management Science, 35,* 22–41.

David, P., Kochhar, R., & Levitas, E. (1998). The effect of institutional investors on the level and mix of CEO compensation. *Academy of Management Journal, 41,* 200–208.

Deaton, A. (1992). *Understanding consumption.* Oxford, England: Clarendon Press.

Duncan, R. B. (1972). Characteristics of organizational environments and perceived environmental uncertainty. *Administrative Science Quarterly, 17,* 313–327.

Dyer, J., & Sarin, R. K. (1982). Relative risk aversion. *Management Science, 28,* 8.

Eisenhardt, K. M. (1988). Agency and institutional explanations of compensation in retail sales. *Academy of Management Journal, 31,* 488–511.

Ellsberg, D. (1961). Risk, ambiguity, and the savage axioms. *Quarterly Journal of Economics, 75,* 643–669.

Executive compensation scoreboard. (1998, April 20). *Business Week,* 64–90.

Fagley, N., & Miller, P. (1990). The effect of framing on choice: Interactions with risk-taking propensity, cognitive style, and sex. *Personality and Social Psychology, 16,* 496–510.

Finkelstein, S., & Boyd, B. K. (1998). How much does the CEO matter? The role of managerial discretion in the setting of CEO compensation. *Academy of Management Journal, 41,* 179–199.

Fischhoff, B. (1992). Risk taking: A developmental perspective. In J. F. Yates (Ed.), *Risk-taking behavior* (pp. 133–162). New York: Wiley.

Fischhoff, B., & MacGregor, D. (1980). Judged lethality (Decision Research Report No. 80–4). Eugene, OR: Decision Research.

Fischhoff, B., Slovic, P., & Lichtenstein, S. (1977). Knowing with certainty: The appropriateness of extreme confidence. *Journal of Experimental Psychology: Human Perception and Performance, 3,* 552–564.

Fischhoff, B., Slovic, P., & Lichtenstein, S. (1978). Fault trees: Sensitivity of estimated failure probabilities to problem representation. *Journal of Experimental Psychology: Human Perception and Performance, 4,* 330–334.

Fischhoff, B., Slovic, P., Lichtenstein, S., Read, S., & Coombs B. (1978). How safe is safe enough? A psychometric study of attitudes toward technological risks and benefits. *Policy Sciences, 9,* 127–152.

Fishburn, P. (1982). Foundations of risk measurement: Effects of gains on risk. *Journal of Mathematical Psychology, 25,* 226–242.

Fishburn, P. (1984). Foundations of risk measurement: Risk as probable loss. *Management Science, 30,* 396–406.

Fishburn, P. (1988). *Nonlinear preference and utility theory.* Baltimore: Johns Hopkins University Press.

Fishburn, P. (1989). Retrospective on the utility theory of von Neumann and Morgenstern. *Journal of Risk and Uncertainty, 2,* 127–158.

Friedman, M. (1957). *A theory of the consumption function.* Princeton, NJ: Princeton University Press.

Frisch, D. (1993). Reasons for framing effects. *Organizational Behavior and Human Decision Processes, 54,* 399–429.

Gomez-Mejia, L. R., & Balkin, D. (1989). Effectiveness of individual and aggregate compensation strategies. *Industrial Relations, 28,* 431–445.

Gomez-Mejia, L. R., & Balkin, D. (1992). *Compensation, organizational strategy, and firm performance.* Cincinnati, OH: South-Western.

Gomez-Mejia, L. R., & Wiseman, R. M. (1997). Reframing executive compensation: An assessment and outlook. *Journal of Management, 23,* 291–374.

Gray, S., & Cannella, A. (1997). The role of risk in executive compensation. *Journal of Management, 23,* 517–540.

Gupta, A. K., & Govindarajan, V. (1984). Business unit strategy, management characteristics, and business unit effectiveness at strategy implementation. *Academy of Management Journal, 27,* 25–41.

Hale, A. R. (1987). Subjective risk. In W. T. Singleton & J. Hovden (Eds.), *Risk and decisions* (pp. 67–89). New York: Wiley.

Heijdra, B. (1988). Neoclassical economics and the psychology of risk and uncertainty. In P. Earl (Ed.), *Psychological economics: Developments, tensions, and prospects* (pp. 67–84). Boston: Kluwer.

Henderson, P. W., & Peterson, R. A. (1992). Mental accounting and categorization. *Organizational Behavior and Human Decision Processes, 51,* 92–117.

Hey, J. D. (1988). Prospects for mathematical psychological economics. In P. Earl (Ed.), *Psychological economics* (pp. 85–99). Boston: Kluwer.

Highhouse, S., & Paese, P. (1996). Contrast effects on strategic-issue framing. *Organizational Behavior and Human Decision Processes, 65,* 95–105.

Holtgrave, D., & Weber, E. (1993). Dimensions of risk perception for financial and health risks. *Risk Analysis, 13,* 553–558.

Jia, J., & Dyer, J. (1996). A standard measure of risk and risk-value models. *Management Science, 42,* 1691–1705.

Johnson, E. J., Hershey, J., Meszaros, J., & Kunreuther, H. (1993). Framing, probability distortions, and insurance decisions. *Journal of Risk and Uncertainty, 7,* 35–51.

Kahneman, D., & Tversky, A. (1979). Prospect theory: An analysis of decision under risk. *Econometrica, 47,* 263–291.

Keller, L., Sarin, R. K., & Weber, M. (1986). Empirical investigation of some properties of the perceived riskiness of gambles. *Organizational Behavior and Human Decision Process, 38,* 114–130.

Lant, T. (1992). Aspiration level adaptation: An empirical exploration. *Management Science, 38,* 623–644.

Lattimore, P., Baker, J., & Witte, A. (1992). The influence of probability on risky choice: A parametric examination. *Journal of Economic Behavior and Organization, 17,* 377–400.

Lea, S. E., Webley, P., & Young, B. M. (1992). Economic psychology: A new sense of direction. In S. E. Lea, P. Webley, & B. M. Young (Eds.), *New directions in economic psychology* (pp. 1–12). Brookfield, VT: Elger.

Lewis, A. (1988). Some methods in psychological economics. In P. Earl (Ed.), *Psychological economics* (pp.189–210). Boston: Kluwer.

Libby, R., & Fishburn, P. (1977). Behavioral models of risk taking in business decision: A survey and evaluation. *Journal of Accounting Research, 15,* 272–292.

Lichtenstein, S., Slovic, P., Fischhoff, B., Layman, M., & Coombs, B. (1978). Judged frequency of lethal events. *Journal of Experimental Psychology: Human Learning and Memory, 4,* 551–578.

Lintner, J., Jr. (1965). The valuation of risk assets and the selection of risk investment in stock portfolios and capital budgets. *Review of Economics and Statistics, 47,* 13–37.

Loehman, E. (1998). Testing risk aversion and nonexpected utility theories. *Journal of Economic Behavior and Organization, 33,* 285–302.

Lopes, L. (1987). Between hope and fear: The psychology of risk. *Advances in Experimental Social Psychology, 29,* 255–295.

Lucas, R. E. (1976). Economic policy evaluation: A critique. In K. Brunner & A. Meltzer (Eds.), *The Phillips curve and labor markets* (Carnegie-Rochester Conference Series on Public Policy, Vol. 1, pp. 19–46). Amsterdam: North-Holland.

Luce, R. D. (1988). Rank-dependent, subjective expected utility representations. *Journal of Risk and Uncertainty, 1,* 305–322.

Luce, R. D. (1990). Rational versus plausible accounting equivalences in preference judgments. *Psychological Science, 1,* 225–234.

Luce, R. D. (1992). Where does subjective expected utility fail descriptively? *Journal of Risk and Uncertainty, 5,* 5–27.

Luce, R. D., & Raiffa, H. (1957). *Games and decisions.* New York: Wiley.

MacCrimmon, K., & Wehrung, D. (1986). *Taking risks: The management of uncertainty*. New York: Free Press.

Machina, M. J. (1987). Choice under uncertainty: Problems solved and unsolved. *Economic Perspectives, 1,* 121–154.

March, J., & Shapira, Z. (1987). Managerial perspectives on risk and risk taking. *Management Science, 33,* 1404–1418.

Markowitz, H. (1952). The utility of wealth. *Journal of Political Economy, 60,* 151–158.

Markowitz, H. (1987). *Mean-variance analysis in portfolio choice and capital markets.* New York: Blackwell.

Martocchio, J. (1998). *Strategic compensation.* Upper Saddle River, NJ: Prentice Hall.

Miceli, M. P., Jung, I., Near, J. P., & Greenberger, D. B. (1991). Predictors and outcomes of reactions to pay-for-performance. *Journal of Applied Psychology, 76,* 508–522.

Miller, J., & Gomez-Mejia, L. R. (1999). *Balancing compensation risk and context: Risk-sharing, discretion, and executive pay.* Working paper, University of Wisconsin–Milwaukee.

Mowen, M., & Mowen, J. (1986). An empirical examination of the biasing effects of framing on business decisions. *Decision Sciences, 17,* 596–602.

Neumann, P., & Politser, P. (1992). Risk and optimality. In J. F. Yates (Ed.), *Risk-taking behavior* (pp. 27–47). New York: Wiley.

O'Curry, S., & Lovallo, D. (1992). *Preference reversals with lottery and income.* Working paper, University of California, Berkeley.

Palmer, C. G. S. (1996). Risk perception: An empirical study of the relationship between worldview and the risk construct. *Risk Analysis, 16,* 717–723.

Poulton, E. C. (1968). The new psychophysics: Six models for magnitude estimation. *Psychological Bulletin, 69,* 1–19.

Pratt, J. W. (1964). Risk aversion in the small and the large. *Econometrica, 32,* 122–136.

Rucker, M. H. (1984). Allocation of windfall income: A case study of a retroactive pay increase to university employees. *Journal of Consumer Affairs, 18,* 101–118.

Ruefli, T. W., La Cugna, J. R., & Collins, J. M. (1996). *Risk measures in strategic management research: Auld lang syne?* Working paper, University of Texas–Austin.

Sanders, W. G., & Carpenter, M. A. (1998). Internationalization and firm governance: The roles of CEO compensation, top team composition, and board structure. *Academy of Management Journal, 41,* 158–178.

Sarasvathy, D. K., Simon, H. A., & Lave, L. (1998). Perceiving and managing business risks: Differences between entrepreneurs and bankers. *Journal of Economic Behavior and Organization, 33,* 207–225.

Sarin, R. K. (1987). Some extensions of Luce's measures of risk. *Theory and Decision, 22,* 125–141.

Sarin, R. K., & Weber, M. (1993). Risk-value models. *European Journal of Operational Research, 70,* 135–149.

Savage, L. (1954). *The foundations of statistics.* New York: Wiley.

Schurr, P. (1987). Effects of gain and loss decision frames on risky purchase negotiations. *Journal of Applied Psychology, 72,* 351–358.

Shapira, Z. (1995). *Risk taking: A managerial perspective.* New York: Russell Sage Foundation.

Sharpe, W. F. (1964). Capital asset prices: A theory of market equilibrium under conditions of risk. *Journal of Finance, 19,* 425–442.

Shefrin, H. M., & Thaler, R. H. (1988). The behavioral life-cycle hypothesis. *Economic Inquiry, 26,* 609–643.

Shoemaker, P. (1982). The expected utility model: Its variants, purposes, evidence, and limitations. *Journal of Economic Literature, 20,* 529–563.

Sinn, H. (1985). Psychophysical laws in risk theory. *Journal of Economic Psychology, 6,* 185–206.

Sitkin, S., & Pablo, A. (1992). Reconceptualizing the determinants of risk behavior. *Academy of Management Review, 17,* 9–38.

Slovic, P. (1962). Convergent validation of risk-taking measures. *Journal of Abnormal and Social Psychology, 65,* 68–71.

Slovic, P. (1972). Information processing, situation specificity, and the generality of risk-taking behavior. *Journal of Personality and Social Psychology, 22,* 128–134.

Slovic, P. (1987). Perception of risk. *Science, 236,* 280–285.

Slovic, P., Fischhoff, B., & Lichtenstein, S. (1980). Facts versus fears: Understanding perceived risk. In D. Kahneman, P. Slovic, & A. Tversky (Eds.), *Judgment under uncertainty: Heuristics and biases* (pp. 463–489). Cambridge, England: Cambridge University Press.

Slovic, P., Fischhoff, B., & Lichtenstein, S. (1982). Response mode, framing, and information processing effects in risk assessment. In R. Hogarth (Ed.), *New directions for methodology of social and behavioral science: Question framing and response consistency.* San Francisco: Jossey-Bass.

Slovic, P., Fischhoff, B., & Lichtenstein, S. (1984). Behavioral decision theory perspectives on risk and safety. *Acta Psycologica, 56,* 183–203.

Slovic, P., Fischhoff, B., & Lichtenstein, S. (1985). Characterizing perceived risk. In R. Kates, C. Hohenemser, & J. Kasperson (Eds.), *Perilous progress: Managing the hazards of technology* (pp. 91–125). Boulder, CO: Westview Press.

Slovic, P., Fischhoff, B., & Lichtenstein, S. (1986). The psychometric study of risk perception. In V. T. Covello, J. Menkes, & J. Mumpower (Eds.), *Risk evaluation and management* (pp. 544–574). New York: Plenum.

Smidts, A. (1997). The relationship between risk attitude and strength of preference: A test of intrinsic risk attitude. *Management Science, 43,* 357–370.

Stewart, G. L. (1996). Reward structure as a moderator of the relationship between extraversion and sales performance. *Journal of Applied Psychology, 81,* 619–627.

Strahilevitz, M. A. (1992). *Applications of prospect theory to the design of salesforce compensation plans.* Working paper, Center for Research in Management, University of California, Berkeley.

Thaler, R. (1980). Toward a positive theory of consumer choice. *Journal of Economic Behavior and Organization, 1,* 39–60.

Tosi, H. L., & Gomez-Mejia, L. R. (1989). The decoupling of CEO pay and performance: An agency theory perspective. *Administrative Science Quarterly, 34,* 169–189.

Tosi, H. L., Katz, J., & Gomez-Mejia, L. R. (1997). Disaggregating the agency contract: The effects of monitoring, incentive alignment, and term in office on agent decision making. *Academy of Management Journal, 40,* 584–602.

Tversky, A., & Fox, C. (1995). Weighting risk and uncertainty. *Psychological Review, 102,* 269–283.

Tversky, A., & Kahneman, D. (1973). Availability: A heuristic for judging frequency and probability. *Cognitive Psychology, 5,* 207–252.

Tversky, A., & Kahneman, D. (1974). Judgment under uncertainty: Heurisitcs and biases. *Science, 185,* 1124–1131.

Tversky, A., & Kahneman, D. (1981). The framing of decisions and the rationality of choice. *Science, 211,* 453–458.

Tversky, A., & Kahneman, D. (1991). Loss aversion in riskless choice: A reference dependent model. *Quarterly Journal of Economics, 197,* 1039–1061.

Tversky, A., & Wakker, P. (1995). Risk attitudes and decision weights. *Econometrica, 63*(6), 1255–1280.

Vlek, C., & Stallen, J. P. (1981). Judging risks and benefits in the small and in the large. *Organizational Behavior and Human Performance, 28,* 235–271.

von Neumann, J., & Morgenstern, O. (1947). *Theory of games and economic behavior* (2nd ed.). Princeton, NJ: Princeton University Press.

Wakker, P., & Tversky, A. (1993). An axiomatization of cumulative prospect theory. *Journal of Risk and Uncertainty, 7,* 147–176.

Weber, E., & Bottom, W. (1989). Axiomatic measures of perceived risk: Some tests and extensions. *Journal of Behavioral Decision Making, 2,* 113–131.

Weber, E., & Milliman, R. (1997). Perceived risk attitudes: Relating risk perception to risky choice. *Management Science, 43,* 123–144.

Welbourne, T., & Gomez-Mejia, L. R. (1995). Gainsharing: A critical review and a future research agenda. *Journal of Management, 21,* 559–609.

Wiseman, R. M., & Gomez-Mejia, L. R. (1997, August). *Reconsidering executive compensation from a behavioral perspective.* Paper presented at the annual meeting of the Academy of Management, Boston.

Wiseman, R. M., & Gomez-Mejia, L. R. (1998). A behavioral agency model of managerial risk taking. *Academy of Management Review, 25,* 133–152.

Wu, G., & Gonzalez, R. (1996). Curvature of the probability weighting function. *Management Science, 42,* 1676–1690.

Yates, J. F., & Stone, E. (1992). The risk construct. In J. F. Yates (Ed.), *Risk-taking behavior* (pp. 1–25). New York: Wiley.

PART 3

Conclusion

CHAPTER 10

Bringing Compensation into I/O Psychology (and Vice Versa)

Sara L. Rynes
Barry Gerhart

The primary objective of this volume has been to increase I/O psychologists' interest in studying compensation. We are hardly the first to fix on this objective; prominent psychologists have been attempting to generate interest in compensation for more than thirty-five years.

For example, in 1963, Haire, Ghiselli, and Porter expressed surprise that there was so little psychological research on pay, since "the basic assumption—that [pay] motivates people to work—is a psychological one" and since "the details of wage and salary systems—for example, decisions about the size of increments—demand further assumptions about the way people see pay and its structure" (p. 3).

In 1966, Opsahl and Dunnette remarked that although money was generally agreed to be the major mechanism for influencing behavior at work, less research and theory had been pursued in compensation than in almost any other field related to management. They argued that this lack of research contributed to practitioner use of faddish compensation systems with little empirical support (for a more recent version of this theme, see Abrahamson, 1996) and offered a menu of future research suggestions to move the field forward. (Nevertheless, the first volume of the

Handbook of Industrial and Organizational Psychology, which was edited by Dunnette 1976 ten years later, did not include a chapter on compensation.)

In 1971, Ed Lawler published a very important book that, among other things, reviewed the history of psychological research on pay. Lawler continued to argue that the topic was understudied and attempted to generate increased interest in compensation research by highlighting a number of characteristics that make pay an attractive subject of investigation for psychologists. First, Lawler argued that because labor costs accounted for 50 to 75 percent of many organizations' total expenditures, it was a topic of considerable interest to employers as well as employees. He agreed with Opsahl and Dunnette that the paucity of pay research left employers to fend for themselves in designing pay systems and argued that employers would be greatly interested in the results of compensation research.

Second, Lawler (1971) argued that pay had a number of attributes (central importance to employers and employees, ability to satisfy multiple needs, and standardized measurement and easy comparability, among others) that made it an excellent vehicle for studying broader questions of human behavior and organizational life: "It is impossible to state a valid theory of how people react to pay without contributing to the understanding of many basic psychological influences on behavior. . . . Work on the psychological issues involved in pay can make important contributions to fundamental research and thinking in such areas as motivation, attitudes, and social comparison theory" (p. 2).

Third, Lawler argued that despite many claims to the contrary, there was clear and compelling evidence (even in 1971) that pay was an important motivator of employee attraction, retention, and performance. He spent much of his first chapter showing how past theories and management philosophies that had been used to deemphasize the importance of pay as a motivator (for example, the human relations movement, Maslow's hierarchy of needs) had been largely discredited by empirical evidence. As just one example, he noted that during the human relations movement, although a great deal of evidence already showed that pay was an important motivator of performance, "it was systematically ignored or distorted" (p. 8). He found it particularly ironic that the Western Electric studies, which are generally thought of as the "birth-place" of the human relations movement, had actually shown that pay is a motivator of performance. In summary, Lawler argued that existing evidence in 1971 overwhelmingly suggested that pay was a major determinant—in many cases, the most important deter-minant—of workers' attitudes, behaviors, and performance. As the chapters in this volume demonstrate, this conclusion has been even more firmly substantiated in the intervening years. And yet the study of pay has been languishing in I/O psychology (May, 1996; Shippmann & Hartmann, 1995), even as it has been ex-panding in other disciplines such as economics, finance, and stra-tegic management (see, for example, Barkema & Gomez-Mejia, 1998; Gerhart, Trevor, & Graham, 1996).

In the interest of motivating psychologists to pay greater at-tention to this issue in future, we will put it bluntly: one cannot be a true expert on employee attitudes, behaviors, motivation, or per-formance unless one has a firm understanding of the role of com-pensation in influencing these outcomes. The remainder of this chapter is divided into two sections. In the first (and in Table 10.1), we summarize what is currently known with respect to the issues addressed by each of the preceding chapters, as well as what re-mains to be discovered via future research. In the second section, we synthesize common themes that emerge from the chapters and make broad recommendations for future compensation research.

Chapter Summaries

In Chapter One, Sara Rynes and Joyce Bono show that recent psy-chological pay determination research has focused more than any other topic on whether pay-setting processes are biased with respect to employee demographics (particularly gender and race). These questions stem from I/O's long-standing interest in questions of eq-uity and justice, as well as from attempts to determine the likely con-sequences of legislative initiatives such as the Civil Rights Act, the Equal Pay Act, or various state comparable worth statutes. In gen-eral, a review of this literature found little evidence of pay discrimi-nation when the question was studied via experimental research designs. However, limitations of existing experimental research make this conclusion somewhat tentative. Conversely, studies that have

Table 10.1. Summary of Volume Chapters.

Chapter	Topic	Findings and Conclusions	Suggestions for Future Research
1: Rynes & Bono	Psychological pay determination research, 1986–1998	Individual pay is influenced by factors other than individual performance Decision makers show individual differences in pay decisions Field surveys of actual pay suggest racial and gender-based pay discrimination; experiments suggest little or no discrimination	Examine more strategic (as opposed to routine administrative) pay decisions Conduct more field research Obtain access to executive decision makers Study organizational start-ups and changes in strategy Examine leaders' mental models of pay Place pay determination research in an environmental and social context
2: Barber & Bretz	Effects of pay on employee attraction and retention	Apparent importance of pay depends on method used to investigate it There is more evidence of gender differences in pay expectations than in pay importance Pay importance declines with increasing age and work experience Organization-level research shows negative relationships between pay level and turnover and between benefits and turnover	Examine individual differences (particularly ability, personality, performance, and values) and differences in person-organization fit in relationships between pay, performance, and turnover Study "push" effects of pay, pay variability, and changes in pay systems on employee turnover Evaluate effects of amount of pay information (ambiguity, secrecy) on attraction and turnover Increase understanding of choice of pay referents and standards for pay evaluation Examine possible spillover of initial pay outcomes and pay negotiations on subsequent employee commitment and turnover

3: Heneman & Judge	Affective employee reactions to pay and pay administration	There are distinct dimensions of pay satisfaction for pay level, raises, and benefits Pay level is a weak but consistent predictor of pay satisfaction Pay administration and process factors contribute importantly to pay satisfaction Pay dissatisfaction has multiple negative cognitive and behavioral outcomes Distributive justice appears to be more important than procedural justice in explaining pay satisfaction; however, procedural justice appears to be very important where adverse pay decisions (such as pay cuts or freezes) are necessary Some of the recent changes in compensation (such as team-based and variable pay) are likely to be unattractive to many U.S. workers	Research how recent changes in administrative pay practices have affected employee attitudes Expand the use of qualitative measurement procedures and intensive case studies Examine reactions to changes in pay procedures, rather than reactions to static practices Study pay satisfaction-outcome linkages at the organizational level of analysis Further explicate the relationships between procedural and distributive justice and pay satisfaction Examination of effects of pay systems or pay "bundles" on employee attitudes Conduct cross-cultural research on determinants, dimensionality, and outcomes of pay attitudes
4: Bartol & Locke	Incentives and motivation	Theories of incentives and motivation are more complementary than conflicting Different theories tend to address different aspects of the pay-performance relationship Moving from general theoretical principles to effective pay implementation is very complex Context is likely to matter in terms of the effectiveness of pay plan features	Separating the effects of pay plan characteristics per se from communication, implementation, and informational effects Trade-offs and issues involved in behavior-based versus outcome-based pay Appropriate level of aggregation for rewards and incentives Impact of strategic pay decisions on pay-performance perceptions

Table 10.1. Summary of Volume Chapters, Cont'd.

Chapter	Topic	Findings and Conclusions	Suggestions for Future Research
			Choice of pay comparisons or reference groups
			Appropriate degrees of pay variability and risk; introduction and implementation of pay-at-risk programs
			Relationships between pay and other work outcomes
5: Gerhart	Pay strategy and firm performance	Organizations exhibit stable differences in pay strategies	Vertical, horizontal, and internal alignment of pay strategies and their relationship with firm performance
		Managers have varying amounts of discretion in determining pay strategy	Development of improved measures of corporate performance, business strategy, and pay strategy
		Differences in pay strategy—especially how pay is delivered—have an effect on firm performance	Improved ability to discern causality and intervening variables in pay strategy–firm performance relationships
		Organizational performance appears to be positively associated with the proportion of employees receiving variable compensation	Pay strategies in global contexts and under varying economic conditions
		There is evidence for best practices with respect to proportion of employees on variable pay	Top management decision processes in the determination of pay strategy
		There is also some evidence that pay strategy fit (with business strategy, amount of business risk, and so on) is important	Strategy-performance relationships for employee groups other than top managers

| 6: Heneman, Ledford, & Gresham | Changes in pay systems | Changes in pay programs have been dramatic: increases in broadbanding, skill-based pay, variable pay, unit-based pay, ownership pay (stock and options), cafeteria benefits, and profit-based funding of retirement pay

Most existing research on innovative pay suggests positive outcomes; however, improvements are needed in research designs and measures

Conducting field research on changes in pay practices presents multiple challenges | Develop more complex theories to study new forms of compensation

Examine main effects and interactions between changes in work, changes in pay systems, and pay outcomes

Do more research on combinations of individual, team, and higher-unit performance-based pay

Make greater use of objective outcomes, as well as a greater range of outcome variables

Examine compensation systems in conjunction with other HR systems

Incorporate developments from cognitive psychology into pay research |
| 7: Sherer | Organization-labor relationships (OLRs) and compensation systems | It is useful to distinguish OLRs from compensation systems

Compensation systems may operate differently under different organizational control systems

Agency theory is potentially more useful than expectancy theory for understanding the limitations of outcome-based pay systems

Generally speaking, fixed pay "buys" an employer flexibility with respect to its labor force

Too much outcome-based pay may lead to problems with respect to teamwork, flexibility, and customer responsiveness

There has been an increase in nonemployment OLRs, such as contracting in and ownership | More research on compensation practices in contracting-in and ownership OLRs

More research that "unbundles" pay from other HR practices

More research that examines what happens as behavior-based pay is increasingly pushed toward outcome-based pay

More research on how employees and employers come to define or "understand" the nature of the employment relationship |

Table 10.1. Summary of Volume Chapters, Cont'd.

Chapter	Topic	Findings and Conclusions	Suggestions for Future Research
8: Rousseau & Ho	Psychological contract issues in compensation	Compensation and benefits are major aspects of the psychological contract (PC) between employers and employees	Broaden the conception of compensation to include compensation "bundles" (pay, benefits, training opportunities) and symbolic as well as concrete aspects of reward systems
		Characteristics of PCs (core versus peripheral, particularistic versus universal) are useful for predicting employee responses to compensations changes	Use the theory of PCs to guide more systematic study of compensation system changes
		In the United States, the trend has been toward transactional or balanced (mixed transactional-relational) contracts	Examine the role that national culture plays in shaping the meaning ascribed to compensation elements
		The meaning of pay systems extends far beyond economic factors in signaling the relationship between worker and firm	
9: Wiseman, Gomez-Mejia, & Fugate	Compensation risk	Conventional measures of risk (such as overall pay variability) do not correspond to subjective perceptions of risk (which center primarily on losses)	Construct validity assessments of such constructs as risk, risk bearing, and risk preference
		There are different implications for compensation if loss aversion more accurately describes reactions to risk than risk aversion	Do additional research on how executives and employees actually perceive risk, relative to objective probabilities of loss or gain
		Behavioral models of risk (such as prospect theory) better account for observed risk-taking behaviors than expected utility or risk-return trade-off models	Conduct more research on how the framing of compensation outcomes influences pursuit of those outcomes
			Research individual differences in risk perception and risk propensity
		Behavioral models of risk suggest that incentives for risk-taking behavior must be considerably higher than suggested by other models if executives are to overcome their risk aversion	Look into the effects of increased executive incentives for risk-taking on lower-level employees

attempted to infer discrimination on the basis of field data have uniformly found at least some gender or racial differences in pay that cannot be explained by differences in other factors such as education or experience. However, in field studies of observed compensation outcomes, pay differentials can never be directly attributed to discrimination, since they might always be due to other unmeasured productivity-related characteristics of employees or employers.

Apart from the rather steady interest in potential pay discrimination, most other pay determination research has been idiosyncratic, often consisting of only a single study per topic (for example, whether there are work group effects on individual pay raise decisions, whether managers attend to prosocial behaviors in valuing employee output, or how compensation administrators decide which firms to survey for job evaluation purposes). Overall, Rynes and Bono conclude that I/O research on pay decision making "has not kept pace with changes in real-world pay systems, with developments in other disciplines, or with the concerns of practitioners." With respect to the divergence between practice and research, they found few studies examining decisions that have led to a number of prominent real-world phenomena, such as the increasing variation in corporate pay strategies, in individual- and job-based pay differentials, and in alternative pay forms. Similarly, with respect to developments in other disciplines, psychologists have been slow to incorporate theories (for example, tournament, agency, and social networking theories) that appear to provide at least partial explanations for observed changes in compensation outcomes. Finally, there have been few attempts to address the many questions posed by practitioners about the effects of team versus individual incentives or indirect pay and benefits on employee attitudes and behaviors.

However, looking at the situation from a more positive perspective, each gap in the literature presents a potentially important opportunity for psychologists to contribute to future compensation theory and practice. For example, future pay determination researchers can increase their influence by broadening their focus beyond pay discrimination (which often involves subconscious decision processes) to incorporate a wider variety of deliberate strategic decisions about pay (for instance, how much egalitarianism, individualism, or risk to incorporate into pay systems). In addressing such questions, it will be important to examine not only what decisions managers make but also why they make them. By uncovering the mental models or implicit theories of individual decision makers, it may be possible to develop a relatively parsimonious taxonomy of pay philosophies, followed by examination of the individual and organizational differences that tend to be associated with each philosophy.

In Chapter Two, Alison Barber and Bob Bretz examine prior research on the relationships between pay and employee participation behaviors, particularly job choice and turnover. They find that pay is an important factor in both job choice and turnover decisions, although the precise extent of its importance appears to depend on a wide variety of factors (including methodology) that are at present only partially understood.

Barber and Bretz suggest three general areas in which psychologists might play an important role in elaborating pay-participation relationships. First, consistent with the growing literature on person-organization fit, they recommend additional investigation of individual differences in reactions to pay. In particular, they suggest looking at the role that individual differences such as cognitive ability, personality, expectations, and values play in decisions to join and leave organizations. Second, Barber and Bretz argue that psychologists are particularly well suited to study how individuals process and evaluate information about pay in decisions about job choice and job leaving. In particular, they recommend additional research on how applicants and employees respond to differing amounts and types of pay information, since information is a factor that organizations have at least partly under their control. This suggestion also fits well with the virtual explosion of salary information on the Internet, a development that is widely believed to have increased the bargaining power of individuals relative to organizations (Lublin, 1998), even if the evidence is purely anecdotal to date. Finally, drawing on the notion of psychological contracts, Barber and Bretz suggest that researchers look for possible spillover between the role of pay in applicant attraction and subsequent effects on employee reactions and behaviors (for example, whether characteristics of initial salary negotiations influence subsequent attitudes and negotiating behaviors). This is an interesting idea that becomes increasingly important as interorganizational mobility increases at all job levels.

In Chapter Three, Herb Heneman and Tim Judge provide a comprehensive assessment of how our understanding of pay attitudes has progressed over the past fifteen years. For example, they demonstrate that we now have a better understanding of the multiple dimensions of pay satisfaction and their specific antecedents; accumulating evidence of the negative consequences of pay dissatisfaction; a growing body of evidence regarding the relationships between procedural justice, distributive justice, and pay satisfaction; and accumulating evidence regarding both general pay preferences (for individualistic pay increases, fixed pay, flexible benefits, and so on) and sources of individual differences in preferences.

In addition, Heneman and Judge examine the interrelationships between the pay satisfaction and pay justice literatures and suggest the need for future research that will produce greater construct clarity both within and between these largely independent literatures. By exploring alternative possible nomological networks and raising the possibility of construct equivalence across these separate domains, they provide a model and discussion that might well be emulated in the broader satisfaction and justice literatures.

Although Heneman and Judge laud the accomplishments of recent pay attitudes research, they also outline a number of shortcomings. In particular, they are concerned with the lack of research relating to the many changes that have occurred in actual pay practices: "Organizations' pay practices have changed dramatically and forcefully, and our research has simply ignored or glossed over the changes. . . . When viewed against this [changed] backdrop, our pay satisfaction research seems meager, misguided, and myopic."

Not surprisingly, then, many of Heneman and Judge's recommendations for future research involve examining employee reactions to new compensation practices such as broadbanding, pay-at-risk, team-based pay, pay for knowledge or skill, and stock options and ownership. Another need is to study relationships between pay, attitudes, and behaviors at multiple levels of analysis. Heneman and Judge also call for examination of the impact of pay on attitudes and behaviors in international contexts, in light of clear cultural differences in attitudes, values, and expectations concerning pay across national boundaries (Hofstede, 1997; Ronen, 1994; see also Chapter Eight). Finally, like other authors in this volume, they note that increasing disparities in pay outcomes merit fresh examination of pay equity concerns, particularly studies that shed light on how individuals choose pay referents in this new and highly differentiated pay environment.

In Chapter Four, Kay Bartol and Ed Locke summarize a wide variety of motivational theories from psychology and economics and synthesize their insights into broad principles for the design of pay systems. For the most part, they emphasize similarities rather than differences across theories because, with the possible exception of Deci and Ryan's theory of intrinsic motivation, Bartol and Locke see more consistencies than inconsistencies with respect to what alternative theories suggest about human behavior. Where they do observe differences, most relate to the particular aspects of motivation that each theory seeks to explain (for example, prospect theory emphasizes employee reactions to risk, while agency theory focuses on potential conflicts of interest between owners and employees).

However, Bartol and Locke also caution that there is considerable difficulty in moving from these general theoretical prescriptions to practical guidelines for implementation. This difficulty arises from a variety of sources. For example, the theories themselves are rather general, people have differing values and beliefs about what is "satisfying, motivating, or fair," and contextual factors such as corporate culture and other human resource practices are likely to interact with pay in producing ultimate effects on motivation. Furthermore, where discrepancies do arise between theory and empirical evidence, it is difficult to disentangle whether the source is poor theory, flawed implementation, or both.

Given the complexity of the topic and the number of unanswered questions in this area, Bartol and Locke provide a long list of questions worthy of empirical investigation and theoretical refinement. Across the fifteen suggested categories, however, a smaller number of broad themes seem to emerge.

For example, a number of the topics (including pay communications, pay as a lead or lag system, and pay as information about what is valued) have in common a concern with distinguishing pay processes from pay outcomes in determining how individuals respond to alternative pay systems. Another concern is with examining the possibility of integration or synergy among various theories or objectives (for example, between intrinsic motivation, standard-of-living, and recognition objectives; between strategic pay considerations and pay-for-performance relationships; between pay as a motivator, a satisfier, and a determinant of attraction and retention). Yet another concern has to do with trade-offs: between behavior- and outcome-based pay, between pay and other motivators, between broad business strategies and individual motivation, and between variable and fixed pay components. Anyone seeking to develop a compensation research agenda will find plenty of inspiration in this chapter.

With Chapter Five, Barry Gerhart moves us from the more conventional compensation topics covered in Part One (relationships between pay and employee attraction, retention, satisfaction and performance) to some relatively new areas of practical interest and research covered in Part Two (for example, pay strategy, changes in pay systems, psychological contracts, and pay at risk). He begins Part Two with an examination of compensation strategy and firm performance.

In contrast to some of the topics reviewed in earlier chapters, Gerhart suggests that research on pay strategy has been relatively programmatic and that a considerable amount has been learned over the past decade. Gerhart takes as his point of departure the first major review of the pay strategy literature (Milkovich, 1988), summarizing what was known at that point and what has been learned since then.

At the time of Milkovich's review, there was only limited evidence that organizations differed significantly in terms of pay strategy, managerial discretion in choosing pay strategies, and relationships between choice of pay strategy and organizational performance. In contrast to this earlier state of affairs, Gerhart concludes that there is now considerable evidence of managerial discretion in pay policymaking and practices across organizations. In addition, a credible body of evidence has accumulated suggesting that differences in pay strategies can be associated with fairly sizable differences in organizational performance.

What is still debated, however, is whether there are "best practices" in terms of pay strategy or whether the effectiveness of particular practices depends on their alignment with other factors such as business and human resource strategies. At present, some evidence supports each perspective. For example, seven of eight reviewed studies showed positive main effects of pay-for-performance plans on firm performance. In contrast, a series of studies by Balkin and Gomez-Mejia (1987, 1990) as well as two more recent studies (Bloom & Milkovich, 1998; Rajagopalan, 1996) showed differential effectiveness of pay strategies in conjunction with different business strategies or differing degrees of business risk.

Gerhart argues that before we can draw firm conclusions in this regard, it may be necessary to improve the measures and methods employed in this type of research. For example, there are important construct validity issues with respect to all three major constructs associated with this research—business strategy, pay strategy, and firm performance. In addition, insufficient attention has been paid to interrater reliability in assessing business and pay strategies, as well as to the possibility of reverse or simultaneous causation.

In Chapter Six, Rob Heneman, Gerry Ledford, and Maria Gresham examine how changes in the nature of work (improved information systems, organizational delayering, job broadening, team-based production, and the like) have brought about changes in the way employees are compensated. The authors compile a broad base of case studies and survey research to demonstrate that substantial changes have occurred in real-world compensation practices.

Overall, the authors' survey of the research literature suggests that most new pay developments (with the exception of ESOPs, which are generally adopted for reasons other than employee motivation) appear to produce mostly positive results. For example, most studies of broadbanding report improved managerial flexibility and improved retention of high-performing individuals, without undue increases in costs. Similarly, studies of skill-based pay report mostly positive outcomes, including greater productivity, lower labor costs, and improved quality. Finally, predominantly positive findings have been reported for gainsharing as well, with the authors estimating that two-thirds of such plans survive and produce improved performance.

At the same time, Heneman and colleagues caution that there are a number of problems with this literature that may make results appear more positive than they actually are. For example, many studies have used subjective rather than objective measures of pay characteristics and organizational performance, with the informant often being someone who is responsible for the pay program. In addition, measures of pay plan characteristics have generally not been collected prior to measures of organizational or unit performance, raising the possibility of reverse causality (for example, successful organizational performance may lead to positive perceptions of pay programs). Finally, there is a concern that unsuccessful pay innovations may be underreported in the research literature, resulting in a positive bias among published results.

Given these research characteristics, Heneman and colleagues call for many of the same improvements in research as Gerhart did in Chapter Five. For example, the authors of both chapters emphasize the need for improved measurement of pay practices, pay strategy, and organizational or unit performance. Similarly, all emphasize the need for causally appropriate research designs and for illuminating the process "black box" between changes in pay and changes in performance. Finally, all emphasize the need for more careful attention to separating main effects from interactions, using a combination of improved theory, measurement, and analysis.

Chapter Six concludes on a very positive note with respect to pay practices and the opportunities they present for conducting important research: "We are encouraged by the fact that organizations are experimenting with new forms of pay that may show a better return on investment. . . . The time is ripe for academics to capitalize on the attention executives are giving to pay systems by conducting meaningful theory-driven research in field settings."

In Chapter Seven, Peter Sherer examines the effects of behavior- and outcome-based pay under different legal relationships between employers and employees (organization-labor relationships, or OLRs). Drawing on data from a wide variety of occupations (such as law, sales, haircutting, investment banking, and taxi driving), he explores the consequences of behavior-based versus outcome-based pay for such outcomes as teamwork, flexibility, and customer responsiveness under different OLR arrangements.

To date, the vast majority of research on pay systems has been conducted in a single type of OLR, the traditional employment relationship. Employment relationships involve organizations, as principals, that have a legal right to exercise direct control over individuals (employees) who act as their agents. However, two other forms of OLR—contracting in and ownership—have been increasing in recent years. In contracting in, organizations as principals exercise only partial control over agents, who instead tend to be subjected to a much higher degree of market (rather than organizational) control. In ownership relationships (such as law partnerships), organizations operate as both principals and agents in exercising mutual control.

Generally speaking, different pay systems tend to be associated with different OLRs. For example, workers who are contracted in typically have much higher proportions of outcome-based pay than workers in the other two OLRs. This in turn has implications for the amount of teamwork, behavioral flexibility, and customer responsiveness that an organization can expect from its workers.

Because contracting-in and ownership OLRs (as well as hybrids between these two control systems and conventional employment) have been growing in market importance, Sherer argues for their incorporation into psychological research on pay practices and outcomes. Perhaps the most important question for future research concerns the shape of the pay-performance relationship under differing degrees of outcome-based pay within each of the three OLRs. Like most of the other authors in this volume, Sherer suggests that attention be focused not only on ultimate financial outcomes but also on mediating processes and intermediate outcomes such as teamwork, workforce deployability, organizational culture, and customer satisfaction.

Sherer also shares other authors' concerns about the importance of distinguishing the effects of pay systems from those of other HR systems and from interactions with different forms of OLRs as well. This will be an important part of any research program that seeks to determine the extent to which certain pay practices are in fact best practices, as opposed to practices that work better in some contexts than others. In some of his earlier work, for example, Sherer found that the highest-performing organizations in a given industry were ones that developed employment systems that ran counter to normative or expected practices for their type (Sherer, 1995).

Whereas Sherer focuses on the legal rights and responsibilities associated with various OLRs, in Chapter Eight, Denise Rousseau and Violet Ho focus on the psychological expectations and entitlements associated with alternative compensation arrangements. They begin by illuminating the cognitive processes that can cause various parties (owners, managers, and workers) to come to differing views of their rights and obligations in the employment exchange. These include the widespread existence of self-serving cognitive biases in information processing, anchoring on the status quo despite changed conditions, and attaching different types of meaning to a given aspect of compensation (for example, employees may see tuition reimbursement as a reward for past performance, while managers see it as a way of obligating future employee loyalty and commitment).

Rousseau and Ho show how these cognitive processing biases, combined with a multitude of changes in the economic environment, have increased the difficulty of creating employment relationships that are likely to be regarded as equitable by employees. For example, employees hired at different times and under differing economic conditions are likely to anchor on substantially different psychological contracts, making it difficult to design an overall system that meets all employees' expectations. Similar complications are likely to arise as firms move into other parts of the world and attempt to implement their unique cultures in highly variant local environments.

In the third part of their chapter, Rousseau and Ho outline the basic types of psychological contracts (transactional, relational, balanced, and transitional) and the forms of compensation that tend to be associated with each. Their typology shows strong similarities to Sherer's categorization of OLRs in Chapter Seven: Rousseau and Ho's "transactional" psychological contract is similar to Sherer's "contracting-in" OLR, the "relational" psychological contract is similar to Sherer's "employment" OLR, and the "balanced" relationship is similar to Sherer's "ownership" and hybrid OLRs. Also like Sherer, Rousseau and Ho argue that economic pressures are making it more and more difficult for employers to maintain purely relational contracts (at least in the United States) and that other forms of employment exchange are gaining in usage.

An interesting feature of Rousseau and Ho's chapter is its focus on likely differences in expectations and meanings of the employment relationship in different national contexts. For example, they indicate that U.S. employers are likely to be rather surprised by the broad array of benefits and other relational forms of compensation expected by employees in more collectivist countries such as

China or Kazakhstan (see also Hofstede, 1997). In addition, since psychological contracts tend to be interpreted largely according to local norms, employers will find it challenging to develop strategic employment systems that produce an internally consistent global firm as well as satisfied and productive employees at each location.

In Chapter Nine, Bob Wiseman, Luis Gomez-Mejia, and Mel Fugate examine the likely effects of variable compensation on agent (in this case, executive and managerial) behaviors. They begin by noting that different literatures have developed different definitions and measures of such constructs as risk, risk bearing, and risk preference. They then argue that conventional conceptualizations of risk (as potential variability in future compensation), as well as conventional measures of risk (as proportions of bonuses and long-term income in the pay mix), do not accurately describe how managers actually perceive risk or how they make real decisions in risky choice situations.

More generally, Wiseman and colleagues suggest that conventional measures of risk, as well as traditional assumptions of agency theory about risk, are both conceptually and empirically flawed. Rather, they argue that behavioral models of risk (Kahneman & Tversky, 1979; Tversky & Kahneman, 1991)—which assume that individuals are primarily loss-averse rather than risk-averse—are better at explaining decision makers' actual choices in risky situations.

In addition, they argue that the main risk of loss to executives from pursuing risky actions comes from risk to their future employment status, with all of its attendant future benefits (salary, bonus, stock options, and so on). Given the large amount of potential loss from being fired for pursing risky actions that fail, the authors argue that the only way to counter executives' risk aversion is to offer "huge returns on variable pay awards if the pursuit of those awards pays off." They go on to say that "by extension, we should stop worrying about whether executives are getting too much pay in the form of stock options or bonus awards and should instead be increasing this portion of the compensation package."

Wiseman and colleagues see a bright future for psychologists in contributing to knowledge about the impact of risky pay on managers and employees. The ability to assess subjective perceptions of risk is one of psychology's competitive advantages, relative to other disciplines. Therefore, the authors encourage psychologists to conduct research that will increase our understanding of how executives perceive various aspects of compensation in terms of risk (for example, as potential gains versus potential losses), as well as how those perceptions influence subsequent behaviors.

Future Research

The authors of the other chapters in this book have offered suggestions for future research with respect to their particular topics, as summarized in Table 10.1. We will now attempt to summarize research needs in terms of broad categories that cut across several or all of the individual chapters.

Field Research

One priority mentioned by several authors concerns the need for more field research: "We must enter the field, rather than merely survey it, if we are fully to understand and appreciate its content and changes" (Chapter Three). Although some topics in compensation are appropriate for experimental study (for example, whether certain factors influence pay when everything else is held constant), other issues are clearly best studied in the field.

On the pay decision-making side, one of the most important of these concerns the extent to which particular issues (such as pay equity, employee retention, and cost control) are even on the "radar screens" of individuals who make actual pay decisions. For example, in the lab, we can "force" experimental subjects to attend to cross-occupational equity issues by constructing decision scenarios that compare, say, executive and nonexecutive pay policies or outcomes. In this way, we can discover how individuals are likely to respond in the field if confronted with a similar situation in real life. However, in most real organizations, executive compensation decisions are completely separated from pay decisions for other employees. Thus it is entirely possible that cross-hierarchical equity issues are rarely even considered in field settings.

A second reason to conduct at least some decision-making research in the field is to ensure that we are studying the decision processes of people who actually make such decisions. In the case of compensation decision making, there are strong institutional and contextual factors that tend to shape how various parties frame the relevant issues (see Crystal, 1991; Livernash, 1980; Slichter, Livernash, & Healy, 1960; Treiman & Hartmann, 1981; Zajac & Westphal, 1995). Consequently, even though lab and field studies often produce similar results in many areas (Locke, 1986), we must be very careful about generalizing from student subjects to decision makers in the area of pay setting.

Similar arguments can be made on the pay outcomes side, where laboratory research is often considerably different from field contexts with respect to potentially important boundary conditions. This point is most clearly seen with respect to the extensive literature on the motivational effects of intrinsic versus extrinsic rewards, where laboratory subjects, tasks, reward size, study duration, and measurement of "motivation" have often differed considerably from those same variables in the typical work environment.

Although extensive critiques exist of the studies designed by the "pro-intrinsics" camp (see Chapter Four), it is less well known that most of the experimental rebuttals have also been far removed from adult employment contexts (for example, subjects have often been elementary schoolchildren, and the extrinsic rewards have been candy, praise, or very small amounts of money; see Eisenberger & Cameron, 1996). In addition, extreme experimental task artificiality is easy to spot in other areas of compensation research as well (see Singh, 1995).

In recommending more field research on compensation, we are mindful that such research is likely to prove challenging because of the sensitivity and importance of compensation issues in real employment situations. However, like the authors of Chapter Six, we believe that the challenges are not insurmountable (for examples, see Brown & Huber, 1992; Greenberg, 1990; Petty, Singleton, & Connell, 1992).

To increase the amount of compensation field research, psychological researchers might pursue partnerships with consulting firms that analyze attitudinal, process, and performance data (such as the Gallup Organization or Bain and Company; Buckingham & Coffman, 1999; Reichheld, 1996) or with benchmarking organizations like the Mayflower Group that compare themselves on such (generally proprietary) characteristics. Relatedly, we might follow the model of the Labor and Human Resources Center at Ohio

State University, which has partnered with the American Compensation Association to produce a database including more than eight hundred incentive plans. Alternatively, we might align ourselves with scholars from finance or business strategy as a way of integrating the knowledge (and organizational access) of those disciplines with that of psychology. Finally, psychologists might work more assertively to disseminate the results of compensation studies that begin as consulting projects (see Rynes, McNatt, & Bretz, 1999).

Longitudinal Research and Studies of Change

Another theme running through many of the chapters in this volume is the need to produce more studies of change in compensation practices (for good examples of change-based studies, see Barber, Dunham, & Formisano, 1992; Brown & Huber, 1992; Greenberg, 1990; Murray & Gerhart, 1998; Petty et al., 1992; Wagner, Rubin, & Callahan, 1988). On the pay decision-making side, studies of change can help illuminate the conditions under which decision makers shift from automatic to conscious decision processing with respect to pay (as when considering new pay-for-performance or stock option plans). Moreover, change studies can reveal the factors that determine whether such decisions, once actively considered, are actually adopted. For example, Collins, Hatcher, & Ross (1993) found that among all the employers that expressed preliminary interest in implementing gainsharing systems, only those that already had compatible organizational cultures and employee participation structures were likely actually to adopt such systems.

On the outcomes side, studies of change can reveal whether different methods of implementation produce differential success rates (see Greenberg, 1990), whether some objectives are achieved at the expense of others (for example, higher productivity but lower satisfaction), or whether some outcomes are more important than others in determining a new pay system's fate. For example, a variety of studies (including Gerhart et al., 1996; Petty et al., 1992; Pritchard, Jones, Roth, Stuebing, & Ekeberg, 1988) have shown that incentive systems are sometimes discontinued for "political" reasons despite general increases in both productivity and employee satisfaction.

Studies of change are also necessary to determine how changes in pay policies affect the mix of employees who are attracted to and remain with the organization. For example, Harrison, Virick, and William (1996) found that maximally contingent pay systems disproportionately weeded out low performers, and Cable and Judge (1994) found that team-based pay systems disproportionately discouraged individualistic job seekers. More recently, Lazear (1999) found that approximately half the performance improvements from a new incentive system were due to existing employees working smarter or harder, while the remaining half were due to attracting and retaining more able or more motivated employees.

Improved Measurement

Several chapter authors also make pleas for improved measurement in future compensation research. One obvious problem concerns the relatively large number of studies, particularly in the pay strategy area, that suffer from common method and common source biases. Specifically, in many pay strategy studies, measures of both pay policies and outcomes are provided by the same person—often the person who is also responsible for their administration and success—at a single point in time (see Chapters Five and Six). All else being equal, use of the same person (especially an interested party) to provide both independent and dependent variable information is likely to lead to systematic biases that produce inflated estimates of relationships relative to true effect sizes.

Another difficulty with the use of single raters is that interrater reliabilities may be very low with respect to reports of a particular employer's HR practices and strategies (Gerhart, Wright, McMahan, & Snell, 1998). In fact, Gerhart and colleagues suggest that when both raters and items are recognized as sources of measurement error, the reliability of single rater self-reports may be less than .20. In contrast to the systematic bias noted earlier, these types of random errors may cause true relationships to be underestimated or undetected.

The foregoing concerns suggest that any research regarding pay policies or practices should be based on multiple assessments of those policies. Perhaps the most promising strategy for building such databases will be to partner with consulting organizations that gather perceptual data from entire workforces. In addition, we suggest that perceptions of pay practices be supplemented with objective coding of formal pay policies. By collecting formal measures of pay policies, subjective employee assessments of pay practices, and multiple measures of unit performance, researchers can begin to untangle the separate effects of policy and implementation on different dependent variables (see also Chapter Four).

Finally, the authors of Chapters Five and Six call for additional validation work on important constructs such as pay strategy, business strategy, human resource strategy, and organizational performance. Relatedly, they suggest that pay strategy be decoupled from other aspects of HR strategy (such as selection and employee development) to facilitate distinctions between best practices or most generalizable aspects of pay policy and aspects that interact with or depend on business strategy (vertical fit), other HR practices (horizontal fit), or other environmental or contextual features.

Programmatic Research and Cumulation of Findings

In several areas examined in this volume, the authors noted that much of the existing research has been idiosyncratic, with few central questions guiding what is studied (see Chapters One and Two, for example). Other authors noted that there are a number of important issues that have produced discrepant findings across studies, such as questions about optimal combinations of individual versus team-based incentives (Wageman, 1995), about optimal pay differentials between highest- and lowest-paid workers (Becker & Huselid, 1992; Bloom, 1999; Cowherd & Levine, 1992), and about main versus configural effects of pay on organizational outcomes (see Chapter Five).

Cumulative knowledge about compensation can be aided first of all by encouraging more programmatic research. Two good models for programmatic research are Locke and Latham's work on goal setting, pay, and performance (1984) and Balkin and Gomez-Mejia's work on the relationships between pay strategy, business strategy, and organizational performance (1987, 1990). Both these research streams have been guided by theory— in the first case, goal-setting theory, and in the second, contingency theory.

Although we, like several other chapter authors, would like to encourage the development of more programmatic research streams, we do not wish to discourage more idiosyncratic types of research studies, particularly if they can help answer important practical questions. Still, one of the benefits of programmatic research is that it is more likely to lead to the ability to cumulate results through techniques such as meta-analysis, which can then help separate generalizable effects from those that are more contingent on context.

Levels of Analysis

To date, few studies have examined pay-outcome relationships at multiple levels of analysis. The most notable exception is Markham (1988), who used within- and between-subjects analysis to show that pay-for-performance relationships that looked weak at the individual level of analysis ($r = .19$) were considerably stronger at the group level ($r = .45$). These results are intriguing, particularly in conjunction with Heneman and Cohen's finding (1988) that some of the variance in the salary increases of manufacturing employees can be explained as a function of their supervisor's own salary increase—a finding that would be consistent with higher salary increase budgets for some units than others. As Markham argued, to the extent that rewards for performance are differentially distributed above the "individual within group" level, conventional pay studies have probably underestimated the true size of performance-pay relationships (see also Ostroff, 1992).

A second issue related to levels of analysis concerns a curious feature of the pay strategy literature. In this literature, organizational financial performance has almost always been analyzed as a function of the compensation system for top executives, particularly the CEO. This design feature has the misleading effect of appearing to attribute all variations in organizational performance to the incentive systems (and presumed consequent actions) of a very small number of individuals at the top. Although this is done primarily because data on executive compensation are more readily available than lower-level pay data, it may have the unintended side effect of creating the impression that people at lower levels of the organization make little contribution to organizational performance. If so, the way in which we have studied pay strategy may be an unwitting contributor to a sense that executives and professionals are the only keys to organizational success and that lower-level employees are largely interchangeable parts (see, for example, Stewart, 1997, ch. 6).

Finally, it should be noted that several strategic issues in pay are fundamentally cross-level issues. For example, there is currently a debate about the optimal level of pay differentials across hierarchical levels, with some organizations (Lincoln Electric, Ben & Jerry's, Southwest Airlines) explicitly minimizing differences in pay across levels and other organizations accentuating them (as in law or consulting partnerships based on "up or out" models).

Alternatively, there are questions about whether the most important cross-level equity issues concern the size of differential outcomes or whether the main issue is one of procedural justice (whether all employees are rewarded according to roughly the same rules). For example, Microsoft employees may not begrudge Bill Gates his billions because their pay also increases (though to a far lesser extent) with increases in Microsoft's stock. In contrast, General Motors employees might well have been incensed at Roger Smith's far smaller levels of executive compensation in the late 1980s, given that he was receiving large pay increases at the same time production workers were enduring massive layoffs and wage pressures.

The authors of Chapter Six define strategic pay as pay practices that are "focused on organizational outcomes." This definition would seem to incorporate incentive systems for lower-level employees (such as gain sharing and stock ownership) under the umbrella of "strategic" pay. Accordingly, we encourage "pay strategy" researchers to extend their examinations of pay practices to include ever-lower levels of the organization. At the same time, we urge those who study organization-based pay programs at subexecutive levels to position their research more boldly as "strategic."

Multiple Measures

Wherever possible, we encourage researchers to incorporate multiple measures of inputs, processes, and outcomes. Although at first blush it might seem that we need to know only whether various pay practices are positively correlated with performance, a closer examination shows that it is also important to know how, why, and how consistently such relationships are produced, as well as whether they are achieved at the expense of other desirable outcomes (such as cost control).

Some well-designed studies from the recent literature reveal the value of multiple measures for illuminating pay processes and ruling out alternative interpretations of results. For example, in an excellent study of the implementation of a new incentive plan, Petty et al. (1992) collected twelve measures of performance in both experimental and control divisions of the same electrical utility. A year after the plan's introduction, eleven of the twelve measures revealed performance improvements in the experimental unit (including reduced unit costs, net savings relative to budget, and five productivity measures). Nevertheless, the incentive was discontinued due to friction between the union and management, "even though the majority of all participants (i.e., management and union) would like to continue working under an organizational incentive plan" (p. 432).

Similar results were presented by Pritchard et al. (1988), who found that a combination of goal setting, performance feedback, and an incentive plan (with paid time off as the incentive) had very large effects on group productivity, as well as improved work attitudes in some areas. Nevertheless, the program was discontinued in one of the two units because a new manager did not want to use the incentive system. Without multiple measures of pay inputs and outcomes, a reader would always be left to wonder whether these two plan discontinuations were due to dysfunctional outcomes that went unmeasured and therefore undetected. However, because of careful measurement, political aspects come to the fore as forces that must be reckoned with in pay plan implementation.

Another benefit of multiple measures is that they can illustrate the potential win-win aspects of pay innovations and thereby increase practitioner willingness to experiment with new practices (see also Chapter Six). For example, in another exemplary study, Wagner et al. (1988) showed that after the introduction of a group incentive system, productivity continued to increase for more than nine years without corresponding increases in labor costs or employee grievances. Similarly, Murray and Gerhart (1998) were able to show that the introduction of a skill-based pay plan produced not only higher productivity, improved product quality, and higher pay for workers but also lower unit labor costs.

Without multiple measures, readers will never know whether plans are discontinued (or continued) for productivity reasons or political ones, or whether productivity is improving due to "working smarter" or "hiring smarter workers." Multiple measures can also be valuable in determining the boundary conditions for successful program implementation. Focusing increased attention on potential boundary conditions in compensation is highly recommended, particularly as both environmental conditions and resultant pay practices become more variable.

Contextual Factors

Although there is clear evidence that some pay practices are generally beneficial for organizational performance (for example, linking employee pay to organizational performance), most compensation experts believe that the extent to which pay programs succeed in practice depends on their appropriateness to the context in which they are implemented (see Chapter Four). For example, Slichter et al. (1960) emphasized the importance of broader employee-union-management relationships for the success of incentive systems, Lawler (1971) emphasized the role of management style, and recent research has emphasized the importance of broader business and HR strategies (see Chapter Five). Although the list of potentially important contextual variables is nearly endless, we highlight a few that we believe will become increasingly important in future years.

One such variable is organizational culture. As organizations increasingly differentiate themselves in terms of business strategy (extent of globalization, customer focus, cost control, research and development, use of technology, and so on), they also develop highly diverse corporate cultures (for examples, see Freiberg & Freiberg, 1996; Rosenbluth & Peters, 1992; Schultz & Yang, 1997; Strasser & Becklund, 1991; Stross, 1996). Although it is likely that different compensation systems produce varying levels of success in different organizational cultures, the possibility has gone largely uninvestigated to date. Perhaps the greatest challenge in this area will be trying to reduce the complexities of organizational culture to a manageable yet meaningful set of smaller dimensions so that knowledge can be cumulated.

It will also be important to assess the influence of national cultures on the effectiveness of alternative compensation systems. The global expansion of corporations and the increasing international mobility of workers mean that workers with very different cultural assumptions and reinforcement histories are increasingly working side by side in organizations, sometimes under very different pay schemes. The affective and behavioral implications of such close interactions between individuals with different cultural backgrounds, reinforcement histories, and current compensation levels have barely been examined.

Recent developments in cross-cultural I/O psychology would appear to offer some exciting prospects for future research on the design and likely effectiveness of international compensation schemes. In particular, Hofstede (1997), Ronen (1994), and others have developed relatively parsimonious typologies of national cultural differences that would appear to have direct relevance to the likely effectiveness of alternative compensation systems. The underlying dimensions of these typologies are, for Hofstede, individualism versus collectivism, femininity versus masculinity, power distance, uncertainty avoidance, and, with the incorporation of more recent data from Asia, time horizon. For Ronen, they are individualism versus collectivism and materialism versus humanism. Other potentially important cultural differences across countries are differences in work centrality, organizational attachment, and the extent to which recognition and affiliation act as motivators in particular cultures (Redding, Norman, & Schlander, 1994; Triandis, 1994).

Other contextual factors of likely importance are the state of the labor market and the general economy. For example, changes in levels and types of unemployment affect the relative bargaining power of workers and employers and may also affect employee attitudes toward pay risk. Similarly, a buoyant economy may improve employee attitudes toward organizationally based pay for performance as well as toward variable pay.

A final development that seems likely to have considerable impact on employee reactions to pay is the increasing variability in pay outcomes both within and across occupations (Bok, 1993; Frank & Cook, 1995; Galbraith, 1998). Increasing pay differentiation—in both pay level and pay form—suggests that it will be increasingly important to take account of the influence of pay variability on employee attitudes and behaviors (see also Rynes, Schwab, & Heneman, 1983).

At present, this issue can be illustrated most clearly with respect to the relationship between pay and employee participation behaviors (such as attraction and retention). Some observers have argued that as pay variability increases, individuals' job choices are influenced not only by average earnings potential but also by the highest possible earnings (Bok, 1993; Frank & Cook, 1995). This notion has received considerable support in the popular business press as an explanation of shifts in graduating students' job choices over time. For holders of an M.B.A., for example, shifts have been occurring from manufacturing to service industries such as investment banking and consulting, and more recently from investment banking and consulting toward venture capitalism, Web commerce, and entrepreneurship (Morris, 1999; Munk, 1998; Taylor, 1998). On the turnover side, opportunities to make very large amounts of money very early in one's career have been cited as the reason that many college graduates leave blue-chip corporations shortly after joining them (Labich, 1995; Munk, 1998).

Together these developments suggest that in times of increasing pay differentiation, employee and applicant decisions are likely to take place within a broader framework that includes simultaneous consideration of the individual's desired occupation, industry, firm life cycle, and career earnings profile. So far this broader environment has gone largely unexamined in the pay-participation literature, but it definitely merits future consideration in job choice and turnover research. More generally, pay variability in both level and form merits greater attention as a dependent variable, as well as a contextual or interactive one.

Conclusion

As Gerhart and Milkovich (1992) noted in the *Handbook of Industrial and Organizational Psychology*, compensation is at the core of the employment relationship. And yet, as this volume has made clear, there are many gaps in our research knowledge. For example, additional research is needed to determine the optimal mix of individual, team, and organization-level incentives; optimal levels of pay risk in different situations; the precise nature of the relationships between compensation strategy, other human resource strategies, and broader business strategies—along with a host of other issues.

Although more compensation research is clearly needed, a great deal of knowledge has already accumulated in certain areas, particularly with respect to the effects of monetary incentives on employee performance. And yet, as we have shown, some of this research is rather persistently ignored or misinterpreted. For example, despite copious evidence to the contrary, some widely read authors continue to claim that pay is not an effective motivator (see, for example, Kohn, 1993) and that it has detrimental effects on intrinsic interest or creativity (see Deci & Flaste, 1995). As demonstrated by Lawler (1971), the tendency to discredit the positive effects of financial incentives on employee performance (and often satisfaction as well) goes back at least a century, to the advent of scientific management.

Given the centrality of compensation to the employment relationship, it is essential that psychologists become more aware of what is and is not known about compensation. We hope that this volume will contribute significantly toward building that awareness.

References

Abrahamson, E. (1996). Management fashion. *Academy of Management Review, 21,* 254–285.

Balkin, D. B., & Gomez-Mejia, L. R. (1987). Toward a contingency theory of compensation strategy. *Strategic Management Journal, 8,* 169–182.

Balkin, D. B., & Gomez-Mejia, L. R. (1990). Matching compensation and organizational strategies. *Strategic Management Journal, 11,* 153–169.

Barber, A. E., Dunham, R. B., & Formisano, R. A. (1992). The impact of flexible benefits on employee satisfaction: A field study. *Personnel Psychology, 45,* 55–74.

Barkema, H. G., & Gomez-Mejia, L. R. (1998). Managerial compensation and firm performance: A general research framework. *Academy of Management Journal, 41,* 135–145.

Becker, B. E., & Huselid, M. A. (1992). The incentive effects of tournament compensation systems. *Administrative Science Quarterly, 37,* 336–350.

Bloom, M. (1999). The performance effects of pay dispersion on individuals and organizations. *Academy of Management Journal, 42,* 25–40.

Bloom, M., & Milkovich, G. T. (1998). Relationships among risk, incentive pay, and organizational performance. *Academy of Management Journal, 41*, 283–297.

Bok, D. (1993). *The cost of talent: How executives and professionals are paid and how it affects America.* New York: Free Press.

Brown, K. A., & Huber, V. L. (1992). Lowering floors and raising ceilings: A longitudinal assessment of the effects of an earnings-at-risk plan on pay satisfaction. *Personnel Psychology, 45*, 279–311.

Buckingham, M., & Coffman, C. (1999). *First, break all the rules.* New York: Simon & Schuster.

Cable, D. M., & Judge, T. A. (1994). Pay preferences and job search decisions: A person-organization fit perspective. *Personnel Psychology, 47*, 317–348.

Collins, D., Hatcher, L. & Ross, T. L. (1993). The decision to implement gainsharing: The role of work climate, expected outcomes, and union status. *Personnel Psychology, 46*, 77–104.

Cowherd, D. M., & Levine, D. I. (1992). Product quality and pay equity between lower-level employees and top management: An investigation of distributive justice theory. *Administrative Science Quarterly, 37*, 302–320.

Crystal, G. S. (1991). *In search of excess: The overcompensation of American executives.* New York: Norton.

Deci, E. L., & Flaste, R. (1995). *Why we do what we do: The dynamics of personal autonomy.* New York: Plenum.

Dunnette, M. D. (1976). *Handbook of industrial and organizational psychology.* Skokie, IL: Rand McNally.

Eisenberger, R., & Cameron, J. (1996). Detrimental effects of reward: Reality or myth? *American Psychologist, 51*, 1153–1166.

Frank, R. H., & Cook, P. J. (1995). *The winner-take-all society.* New York: Free Press.

Freiberg, K., & Freiberg, J. (1996). *Nuts! Southwest Airlines' crazy recipe for business and personal success.* New York: Broadway Books.

Galbraith, J. K. (1998). *Created unequal: The crisis in American pay.* New York: Free Press.

Gerhart, B., & Milkovich, G. T. (1992). Employee compensation: Research and practice. In M. D. Dunnette & L. M. Hough (Eds.), *Handbook of industrial and organizational psychology* (2nd ed., Vol. 3, pp. 481–569). Palo Alto, CA: Consulting Psychologists Press.

Gerhart, B., Trevor, C., & Graham, M. (1996). New directions in employee compensation research. In G. R. Ferris (Ed.), *Research in personnel and human resources management* (Vol. 14, pp. 143–203). Greenwich, CT: JAI Press.

Gerhart, B., Wright, P., McMahan, G., & Snell, S. (1998, August). *Measurement error in research on human resource decisions and firm performance: How much error is there, and how does it influence effect size estimates?* Paper presented at the 58th annual meeting of the Academy of Management, San Diego, CA.

Greenberg, J. (1990). Employee theft as a reaction to underpayment inequity: The hidden costs of pay cuts. *Journal of Applied Psychology, 75,* 561–568.

Haire, M., Ghiselli, E. E., & Porter, L. W. (1963). Psychological research on pay: An overview. *Industrial Relations, 3,* 3–8.

Harrison, D. A., Virick, M., & William, S. (1996). Working without a net: Time, performance, and turnover under maximally contingent rewards. *Journal of Applied Psychology, 81,* 331–345.

Heneman, R. L., & Cohen, D. J. (1988). Supervisory and employee characteristics as correlates of employee salary increases. *Personnel Psychology, 41,* 345–359.

Hofstede, G. (1997). *Cultures and organizations: Software of the mind.* New York: McGraw-Hill.

Kahneman, D., & Tversky, A. (1979). Prospect theory: An analysis of decision under risk. *Econometrica, 47,* 263–291.

Kohn, A. (1993). Why incentive plans cannot work. *Harvard Business Review, 71*(5), 54–63.

Labich, K. (1995, February 20). Kissing off corporate America. *Fortune, 131,* pp. 44–55.

Lawler, E. E., III. (1971). *Pay and organizational effectiveness: A psychological view.* New York: McGraw-Hill.

Lazear, E. P. (1999). Personnel economics: Past lessons and future directions. *Journal of Labor Economics, 17,* 199–236.

Livernash, E. R. (Ed.). (1980). *Comparable worth: Issues and alternatives.* Washington, DC: Equal Employment Advisory Council.

Locke, E. A. (1986). *Generalizing from laboratory to field settings: Research findings from industrial-organizational psychology, organizational behavior, and human resource management.* San Francisco: New Lexington Press.

Locke, E. A., & Latham, G. P. (1984). *Goal setting: A motivational technique that works!* Upper Saddle River, NJ: Prentice Hall.

Lublin, J. S. (1998, September 22). Web transforms art of negotiating raises. *Wall Street Journal,* p. B-1.

Markham, S. E. (1988). Pay-for-performance dilemma revisited: Empirical example of the importance of group effects. *Journal of Applied Psychology, 73,* 172–180.

May, K. E. (1996). Work in the 21st century: Implications for compensation. *Industrial Psychologist, 34,* 73–77.

Milkovich, G. T. (1988). A strategic perspective on compensation management. *Research in Personnel and Human Resources Management, 6,* 263–288.

Morris, B. (1999, August 2). MBAs get .com fever. *Fortune,* pp. 60–71.

Munk, N. (1998, March 16). The new organization man. *Fortune,* pp. 62–74.

Murray, B. C., & Gerhart, B. (1998). An empirical analysis of a skill-based pay program and plant performance outcomes. *Academy of Management Journal, 41,* 68–78.

Opsahl, R. L., & Dunnette, M. D. (1966). The role of financial compensation in industrial motivation. *Psychological Bulletin, 66,* 95–116.

Ostroff, C. (1992). The relationship between satisfaction, attitudes, and performance: An organization-level analysis. *Journal of Applied Psychology, 77,* 963–974.

Petty, M. M., Singleton, B., & Connell, D. W. (1992). An experimental evaluation of an organizational incentive plan in the electric utility industry. *Journal of Applied Psychology, 77,* 427–436.

Pritchard, R. D., Jones, S. D., Roth, P. L., Stuebing, K. K., & Ekeberg, S. E. (1988). Effects of group feedback, goal setting, and incentives on organizational productivity. *Journal of Applied Psychology, 75,* 386–393.

Rajagopalan, N. (1996). Strategic orientations, incentive plan adoptions, and firm performance: Evidence from electric utility firms. *Strategic Management Journal, 18,* 761–785.

Redding, S. G., Norman, A., & Schlander, A. (1994). The nature of individual attachment to the organization: A review of East Asian variations. In H. C. Triandis, M. D. Dunnette, & L. M. Hough (Eds.), *Handbook of industrial and organizational psychology* (2nd ed., Vol. 4, pp. 647–688). Palo Alto, CA: Consulting Psychologists Press.

Reichheld, F. F. (1996). *The loyalty effect.* Boston: Harvard Business School Press.

Ronen, S. (1994). An underlying structure of motivational need taxonomies: A cross-cultural confirmation. In H. C. Triandis, M. D. Dunnette, & L. M. Hough (Eds.), *Handbook of industrial and organizational psychology* (2nd ed., Vol. 4, pp. 241–270). Palo Alto: Consulting Psychologists Press.

Rosenbluth, H. F., & Peters, D. M. (1992). *The customer comes second.* New York: Quill/Morrow.

Rynes, S. L., McNatt, D. B., & Bretz, R. D., Jr. (1999). Academic research inside organizations: Inputs, processes, and outcomes. *Personnel Psychology, 52,* 869–898.

Rynes, S. L., Schwab, D. P., & Heneman, H. G., III. (1983). The role of pay and market pay variability in job application decisions. *Organizational Behavior and Human Performance, 31,* 353–364.

Schultz, H., & Yang, D. J. (1997). *Pour your heart into it: How Starbucks built a company one cup at a time.* New York: Hyperion.

Sherer, P. D. (1995). Leveraging human assets in law firms: Human capital structures and organizational capabilities. *Industrial and Labor Relations Review, 48,* 671–691.

Shippmann, J. S., & Hartmann, S. (1995). SIOP customer survey results: II. *Industrial-Organizational Psychologist, 33*(2), 37–42.

Singh, R. (1995). "Fair" allocations of pay and workload: Tests of a subtractive model with nonlinear judgment function. *Organizational Behavior and Human Decision Processes, 62,* 70–78.

Slichter, S. H., Livernash, E. R., & Healy, D. (1960). *The impact of collective bargaining on management.* Washington, DC: Brookings Institution.

Stewart, T. A. (1997). *Intellectual capital.* New York: Currency/Doubleday.

Strasser, J. B., & Becklund, L. (1991). *Swoosh: The story of Nike and the men who played there.* Orlando, FL: Harcourt Brace.

Stross, R. E. (1996). *The Microsoft way.* Reading, MA: Addison-Wesley.

Taylor, A. (1998, April 13). Consultants have a big people problem. *Fortune,* pp. 162–165.

Treiman, D. J., & Hartmann, H. I. (Eds.). (1981). *Women, work, and wages: Equal pay for jobs of equal value.* Washington, DC: National Academy Press.

Triandis, H. C. (1994). Cross-cultural industrial and organizational psychology. In H. C. Triandis, M. D. Dunnette, & L. M. Hough (Eds.), *Handbook of industrial and organizational psychology* (2nd ed., Vol. 4, pp. 103–172). Palo Alto, CA: Consulting Psychologists Press.

Tversky, A., & Kahneman, D. (1991). Loss aversion in riskless choice: A reference-dependent model. *Quarterly Journal of Economics, 197,* 1039–1061.

Wageman, R. (1995). Interdependence and group effectiveness. *Administrative Science Quarterly, 40,* 145–180.

Wagner, J. A., Rubin, P. A., & Callahan, T. J. (1988). Incentive payment and nonmanagerial productivity: An interrupted time-series analysis of magnitude and trend. *Organizational Behavior and Human Decision Processes, 42,* 47–74.

Zajac, E. J., & Westphal, J. D. (1995). Accounting for the explanations of CEO compensation: substance and symbolism. *Administrative Science Quarterly, 40,* 283–308.

Name Index

Subject Index